The Gospel According to Mark
Meaning and Message

OPENING THE SCRIPTURES

The Gospel According to Mark
Meaning and Message

George Martin

LOYOLAPRESS.

CHICAGO

LOYOLAPRESS.

3441 N. ASHLAND AVENUE
CHICAGO, ILLINOIS 60657
(800) 621-1008
WWW.LOYOLABOOKS.ORG

Nihil Obstat
Reverend James P. McIlhone, Ph.D.
Censor Deputatus
April 6, 2005

Imprimatur
Reverend George J. Rassas
Vicar General
Archdiocese of Chicago
April 12, 2005

The *Nihil Obstat* and *Imprimatur* are official declarations that a book is free of doctrinal and moral error. No implication is contained therein that those who have granted the *Nihil Obstat* and *Imprimatur* agree with the content, opinions, or statements expressed. Nor do they assume any legal responsibility associated with publication.

Royalties from the sale of this book go to the Catholic Near East Welfare Association to assist the Church in the Holy Land.

Scripture excerpts are taken from the *New American Bible with Revised New Testament and Psalms* Copyright © 1991, 1986, 1970 Confraternity of Christian Doctrine, Washington, DC. Used with permission. All Rights Reserved. No part of the *New American Bible* may be reproduced in any form without permission in writing from the copyright owner.

Translations of material from Josephus (page 144), *Psalms of Solomon* (page 207), Tacitus (page 347), and Pliny (page 413) are by Kevin Perrotta.

Cover images: detail and full version of a styled cross with Jesus Christ and the Four Evangelists; detail shows the Lion of St. Mark. Both images are © Elio Ciol/Corbis.

Cover design by Adam Moroschan
Interior design by Adam Moroschan and Megan Duffy Rostan

Library of Congress Cataloging-in-Publication Data
Martin, George, 1939–
  The Gospel according to Mark : meaning and message / George Martin.
    p. cm.— (Opening the scriptures)
  Includes bibliographical references and index.
  ISBN 0-8294-1970-5
  1. Bible. N.T. Mark—Commentaries. 2. Bible. N.T. Mark—Textbooks.
I. Title. II. Series.
BS2585.53M37 2005
226.3'077—dc22

                                                          2004026617

Printed in the United States of America
05 06 07 08 09 10 Versa 10 9 8 7 6 5 4 3 2 1

To my parents,
Arthur T. and Evelyn A. Martin,
in gratitude and admiration

CONTENTS

PREFACE

The two disciples who walked with the risen Jesus on the road to Emmaus exclaimed afterward, "Were not our hearts burning [within us] while he spoke to us on the way and opened the scriptures to us?" (Luke 24:32).

We too would like the Scriptures opened to us so that we could understand their meaning, their significance, their message. No book can duplicate what Jesus did for the two disciples on the road to Emmaus or replace the guidance of the Holy Spirit. But a book can explore what meaning the words of Scripture had for their first readers and what message an inspired author conveys by his words. The aim of this book is to help women and men of the twenty-first century understand words that were written in the first century so that we can grasp their significance for us as followers of the risen Jesus.

While this book has some features of a commentary, it is not a scholarly commentary. Many issues and questions that are of legitimate interest to scholars are passed over. The focus of this book is on what Mark's words meant when he wrote them, with an eye toward their meaning for readers today. This book is intended for men and women who want to read and understand Mark's Gospel as Scripture, as God's word conveyed in human words.

Reading a Gospel as Scripture is like having a conversation. Conversing requires listening. Good listening means paying close attention to what another person is saying; it can also mean noting what is implied and what may be left unsaid. This book will closely examine the text of Mark's Gospel, sometimes commenting on the meaning of the words the author uses, sometimes drawing out an implication, occasionally noting what is left unsaid.

A good conversation presumes the two parties share some common background. For example, a conversation about American politics requires that those conversing have a shared knowledge of the American system of government and American political parties. Similarly, understanding the Gospel of Mark requires some knowledge of Jewish life and thinking in Palestine in the first third of the first century. What Jesus did and said must be understood in light of the context in which Jesus lived. This book will try to fill in some of that background, as far as we can reconstruct it today, to help make sense of the teachings and actions of Jesus.

Another factor that makes good conversations possible is the two parties' knowledge of each another. Often our conversations revolve around interests and concerns that arise from our experiences and personal situations. We converse quite easily with old friends who know us and our concerns. What was Mark's situation, and what were his concerns? This book adopts the ancient tradition that Mark's Gospel was written in Rome during or after Nero's persecution of Christians, which began in AD 64. I will occasionally suggest what significance Mark's words might have had in this context. A short essay at the end of this book addresses the writing of Mark's Gospel. Rather than say more in this preface about the Gospel of Mark, we will let its character and purpose unfold as it is read.

Sometimes a conversation will include an account of something that has happened; for example, a man might have told his granddaughter about his taking part in the Normandy landing during the Second World War and about the welcome he received in a French village afterward. Any narrative invites the listener to enter into the world of the story, which in this example would entail imagining what it must have been like to scale a cliff under gunfire and see the joy on the faces of the French villagers, even if the listener has never visited Normandy or the village. Mark's Gospel is a narrative of what Jesus did and taught. As a narrative, it invites us to enter into the world of Jesus, to put ourselves on the scene. This book reads Mark's Gospel as a coherent narrative and sometimes suggests what might have been going on for a scene to play out as it does.

This book focuses on the Gospel that is "According to Mark," the title it bears in the oldest manuscripts. It does not try to compare or synthesize what Mark wrote with the other Gospels. It is difficult to carry on four conversations at once; it is easier to pay attention to one person at a time. After paying close attention to the Gospel according to Mark, we can later compare what Mark wrote with what Matthew, Luke, and John wrote. For each passage of Mark, this book indicates where similar material may be found in the other Gospels.

This book deals with the text of Mark's Gospel as it has come down to us in the Bible. It does not go into matters like the sources Mark may have drawn on, nor does it raise questions like "Did this really happen exactly as Mark presents it?" While such considerations can have validity, it is the Gospel of Mark as we have it that is inspired Scripture for us. This book presents what I hope is a responsible interpretation of the Gospel of Mark, laying out the meaning I find in Mark's words. I make no claim that my interpretation is the only possible reading of Mark: there are riches of meaning in a Gospel that no single exposition can capture.

A few words about the format of this book:

Mark wrote his work as a continuous account, without chapter breaks. For practical reasons I divide the Gospel into sections, but the divisions are not Mark's and have no absolute importance. The traditional chapter and verse numbers are printed at the top of each page to assist readers in locating passages. Some sections of Scripture are introduced by a few sentences of "orientation" that give the context of the reading. A list of parallel passages in the other Gospels and of related Old Testament and New Testament passages are provided for each section of Scripture. The exposition follows, with the words of Scripture set in boldfaced type.

Interspersed throughout the book are some blocks of information about the social, economic, political, and religious background of Mark's Gospel; some discuss scriptural terms of special interest. I also offer my comments at a few points. An index at the end of the book lists the page where each background entry and comment is located.

Also interspersed throughout the text are questions "for reflection." They indicate possible ways that a reader might ponder and apply the text. Using these reflection questions is entirely optional; their inclusion reflects my view that reading a Gospel as Scripture is like having a conversation. Careful listening to the words of Scripture is only half of the conversation; the other half is our response. This book cannot supply your side of the conversation with the Gospel of Mark; you must do that yourself. This book can lay out Mark's side of the conversation as I understand it and raise issues for you to reflect on and respond to. The most important issues, invitations, questions, and challenges will be those that the Gospel itself puts to you.

The Gospel of John calls for the reader's response when it says that it was "written that you may [come to] believe that Jesus is the Messiah, the Son of God, and that through this belief you may have life in his name" (John 20:31). This, essentially, is Mark's intention also.

I considered calling this book *Listening to the Gospel according to Mark*. Mark's original audience did not usually read his Gospel but listened to it being read aloud at a gathering of Christians, perhaps for the Eucharist. Many in Mark's first audience were illiterate; few were wealthy enough to afford their own copy of a Gospel.

We too listen to the Gospel of Mark being read aloud in the context of worship. In the Catholic liturgy, after a passage from Mark is read the reader proclaims, "The Gospel of the Lord." The reader does not say, "The Gospel of Mark." Even though we are listening to words written by Mark, our real conversation partner is the Lord Jesus. We listen to Jesus teaching, even if it is Mark who gives expression to Jesus' words. It is Jesus who invites our response, even if it is Mark who conveys Jesus' invitation.

One response to reading a Gospel is prayer. There is a long tradition in the Church of "sacred reading" (*lectio divina* in Latin). This type of reading involves paying careful attention to a passage of Scripture, verse by verse and word by word, and pausing for reflection and prayer. My fondest hope is that this book will prove useful as an aid to sacred reading. I suggest that those who wish to use this volume for prayerful reading return to the words of Scripture after having read the exposition, offer a brief prayer asking for the guidance of the Holy Spirit, and enter into conversation with the one who speaks to them through the Gospel of Mark.

ACKNOWLEDGMENTS

I drew on the knowledge and insights of many biblical scholars in writing this exposition of Mark's Gospel. Footnotes acknowledging my debts to them would have complicated a book intended to be as simple as possible, but my debts are real nonetheless. Some of the commentaries and studies I consulted are listed in the bibliography at the end of this book. My indebtedness to these scholars does not, of course, imply their endorsement of my interpretation of Mark.

I am also indebted to many individuals for their help and encouragement. John Boucher and Stephen Peterson suggested that I undertake an exposition of the Gospels. Kevin and Louise Perrotta and Bert Ghezzi evaluated my first attempts. Stephen J. Binz, Peter S. Williamson, and Marsha Daigle-Williamson critiqued portions of the first draft. Mary Martin and Susan Manney read and commented on the entire first draft. I am grateful to all of them. I am also grateful to Loyola Press and its publisher, George Lane, SJ, for taking on this project and to Jim Manney, editorial director, for shepherding it with patience and enthusiasm. Kevin Perrotta translated some background material and painstakingly edited the entire manuscript for content; any misstatements that remain are at my insistence. Heidi Hill edited it for clarity and style; I am indebted to her for her diligence. Megan Duffy Rostan and Adam Moroschan wrestled with the complexities of the layout and triumphed—thank you! Above all, I am grateful to my wife, Mary, for gracefully accepting that my idea of a Florida retirement is spending my time studying and writing about Scripture.

A NOTE ON THE TEXT

Format

Each page contains the text of the Gospel of Mark (printed in boldfaced type) accompanied by a verse-by-verse exposition.

Everything else, printed in smaller or different type, is auxiliary material and consists of the following:

- *Orientations* to certain passages in Mark's Gospel, when such introductions might be helpful

- After the text of each passage of Mark, *Gospel parallels* indicating where similar material may be found in the other Gospels, along with Old Testament (*OT*) and New Testament (*NT*) references to material that bears on the passage from Mark

- *Old Testament quotations,* when reading them in conjunction with a passage of Mark might throw light on the passage

- Questions for the reader's *reflection*

- *Background* information pertaining to the world of Jesus or that of Mark's audience

- A few *comments* that explore implications of Mark's Gospel

An index to *background* material and *comments* may be found at the end of this book.

Abbreviations Used for Books of the Bible

Acts	Acts	2 Kings	2 Kings
Amos	Amos	Lam	Lamentations
Baruch	Baruch	Lev	Leviticus
1 Chron	1 Chronicles	Luke	Luke
2 Chron	2 Chronicles	1 Macc	1 Maccabees
Col	Colossians	2 Macc	2 Maccabees
1 Cor	1 Corinthians	Mal	Malachi
2 Cor	2 Corinthians	Mark	Mark
Dan	Daniel	Matt	Matthew
Deut	Deuteronomy	Micah	Micah
Eccl	Ecclesiastes	Nahum	Nahum
Eph	Ephesians	Neh	Nehemiah
Esther	Esther	Num	Numbers
Exod	Exodus	Obad	Obadiah
Ezek	Ezekiel	1 Pet	1 Peter
Ezra	Ezra	2 Pet	2 Peter
Gal	Galatians	Phlm	Philemon
Gen	Genesis	Phil	Philippians
Hab	Habakkuk	Prov	Proverbs
Hag	Haggai	Psalm(s)	Psalms
Heb	Hebrews	Rev	Revelation
Hosea	Hosea	Rom	Romans
Isaiah	Isaiah	Ruth	Ruth
James	James	1 Sam	1 Samuel
Jer	Jeremiah	2 Sam	2 Samuel
Job	Job	Sirach	Sirach
Joel	Joel	Song	Song of Songs
John	John	1 Thess	1 Thessalonians
1 John	1 John	2 Thess	2 Thessalonians
2 John	2 John	1 Tim	1 Timothy
3 John	3 John	2 Tim	2 Timothy
Jonah	Jonah	Titus	Titus
Joshua	Joshua	Tobit	Tobit
Jude	Jude	Wisd	Wisdom
Judg	Judges	Zech	Zechariah
Judith	Judith	Zeph	Zephaniah
1 Kings	1 Kings		

Scripture citations that do not include the name of a biblical book are to the Gospel of Mark (for example, the citation 8:34 would be to chapter 8, verse 34 of Mark's Gospel).

Scripture citations follow the chapter and verse numbering used by the New American Bible. Other translations sometimes employ slightly different numbering (for example, in Malachi and some of the psalms).

The New American Bible requires preservation of certain of its conventions, including its paragraph breaks and square brackets around words not found in all ancient manuscripts. When poetry is set here as prose, the New American Bible requires that slashes be used to indicate line breaks.

The Catholic Church and most Orthodox Churches accept as canonical Scripture the books of Baruch, Judith, 1 and 2 Maccabees, Sirach (Ecclesiasticus), Tobit, and Wisdom (Wisdom of Solomon), along with some additional material in the books of Daniel and Esther. Protestant Churches do not accept these writings as part of the biblical canon, but some Protestant Bibles include them in a section labeled Apocryphal Works.

The Gospel According to Mark

Meaning and Message

CHAPTER 1

ORIENTATION: *Mark announces that we are at "the beginning" of the good news of Jesus Christ, but his Gospel starts near the end of Jesus' life: the events recounted in the Gospel of Mark could fit within the span of a year. Rather than describing Jesus' earlier life, Mark introduces us to John the Baptist.*

The Beginning

¹ The beginning of the gospel of Jesus Christ [the Son of God].
² As it is written in Isaiah the prophet:

"Behold, I am sending my messenger ahead of you;
he will prepare your way.
³ A voice of one crying out in the desert:
'Prepare the way of the Lord,
make straight his paths.'"

⁴ John [the] Baptist appeared in the desert proclaiming a baptism of repentance for the forgiveness of sins. ⁵ People of the whole Judean countryside and all the inhabitants of Jerusalem were going out to him and were being baptized by him in the Jordan River as they acknowledged their sins. ⁶ John was clothed in camel's hair, with a leather belt around his waist. He fed on locusts and wild honey. ⁷ And this is what he proclaimed: "One mightier than I is coming after me. I am not worthy to stoop and loosen the thongs of his sandals. ⁸ I have baptized you with water; he will baptize you with the holy Spirit."

Gospel parallels: Matt 3:1–12; 11:10; Luke 3:1–18; 7:27; John 1:23–28
OT: Exod 23:20; Isaiah 40:3–5; Ezek 36:25–27; Joel 3:1–5; Mal 3:1–2, 23
NT: Acts 1:5; 11:16; 13:24–25

1 **The beginning of the gospel of Jesus Christ [the Son of God].** Mark tells us that what he has written is the **gospel,** using a Greek word that means good news. God was doing something very new and very good for us through **Jesus Christ.** Good news is such a fitting description of

3

Mark's message that his book will come to be called "good news"—a Gospel. Mark's opening words are an invitation to us to read what he writes as the best possible news we will ever hear.

Mark starts at **the beginning** of the gospel of Jesus Christ. If verse 1 is intended to be the title for the whole book, then Mark is telling us that he is presenting only the beginning of the good news of Jesus, good news that continues in the Church and in our lives. We are, as it were, unfinished pages of the gospel story.

If verse 1 is connected just with the following verses, then it means that the good news about Jesus Christ begins with the ministry of John the Baptist. Each of the four Gospel writers picked a different point to begin his account of Jesus; Mark was part of a tradition that began the good news with Jesus' encounter with John (see Acts 1:21–22; 10:36–38).

Mark is writing the good news about **Jesus Christ [the Son of God].** We will need to read Mark's entire Gospel in order to fully grasp his proclamation of Jesus as the Christ and Son of God. **Jesus** is an Aramaic form of the name Joshua, the name of Moses' right-hand man. Jesus was a popular name among Jews in the first century. Mark calls Jesus **Christ,** which comes from the Greek word that means anointed; its Hebrew counterpart gives us the word *messiah.* To name Jesus as the Christ is to proclaim him the Messiah, the agent sent by God to establish God's reign.

Aramaic: See What languages did Jesus speak? page 124

Messiah, Christ: See page 204

BACKGROUND: GOSPEL The English word *gospel* comes from the Anglo-Saxon word *godspel,* which means good news. Good news is in turn a literal translation of the Greek word *euangelion* used by Mark; *euangelion* gives us such English words as *evangelist.* Mark did not invent the word *euangelion:* it is found in ancient Greek literature as a term for a message of victory or any other message that brings joy. The Greek translation of Isaiah uses forms of this word: "Go up onto a high mountain, / Zion, herald of glad tidings; / Cry out at the top of your voice, / Jerusalem, herald of good news!" (Isaiah 40:9). Paul, whose letters predate Mark's Gospel, was the first New Testament author to use the word *euangelion* as an expression for the message of Christ: "Our *gospel* did not come to you in word alone, but also in power and in the holy Spirit" (1 Thess 1:5; emphasis added).

Mark says that Jesus is also **the Son of God** (some ancient manuscripts of Mark omit these words in the first verse, which is why the New American Bible prints them in brackets). To call Jesus **the Son of God** goes beyond simply identifying him as the Messiah: as the Son, Jesus has a very special relationship with God. It took the Church several centuries of reflection to clarify what it means that Jesus is uniquely the Son of God.

Son of God: See page 64

Mark's Gospel begins with a proclamation of who Jesus is. Part of the drama of Mark's Gospel lies in how Jesus is perceived by his contemporaries. Will they be able to recognize him as the Messiah sent by God; indeed, as God's Son?

For reflection: Will I accept what Mark has to say about Jesus, even if it means modifying my image of Jesus? Will I welcome the Jesus proclaimed by Mark as good news for me?

2 **As it is written:** just as John the Baptist will provide the context for the beginning of Jesus' ministry, so the Old Testament sets the stage for John. By beginning his Gospel with what is written in Scripture, Mark indicates that John the Baptist and Jesus were in continuity with, and a fulfillment of, what had gone before. **Written in Isaiah the prophet:** since the words that follow are not limited to Isaiah, Mark may be using Isaiah as a representative of all Old Testament prophets.

Behold, I am sending my messenger ahead of you; / he will prepare your way. Mark's Scripture quotation begins with a line from the prophet Malachi, which in turn is an echo of Exodus. In Exodus, God tells his people, after their escape from Egypt, that he is sending an angel (the Hebrew word for angel also means messenger) before them to guard them on the way. Centuries later, God spoke through Malachi to say that he was sending a messenger to prepare the way for God's coming to his people on a "day of the Lord" (Mal 3:1, 23). Mark presents John the Baptist as God's messenger, sent in preparation for what God is about to do. In Malachi the messenger is sent to prepare the way for God; in Mark the messenger prepares **your way,** referring to Jesus' way. This indicates that Jesus has come as God's agent to carry out God's work.

Angels: See page 321

See, I am sending an angel before you, to guard you on the way and bring you to the place I have prepared.

Exod 23:20

Lo, I am sending my messenger to prepare the way before me.

Mal 3:1

3 **A voice of one crying out in the desert: / "Prepare the way of the Lord, / make straight his paths."** These are Isaiah's words, but with adjustments. In Mark's citation of the prophecy, **in the desert** is the setting for the voice crying out, not (as in the Hebrew text of Isaiah) what the voice cries out. Mark thus applies Isaiah's prophecy to John the Baptist, who is crying out in the desert.

A voice cries out:
In the desert prepare the way of the LORD!
Make straight in the wasteland a highway for our God!
Every valley shall be filled in,
every mountain and hill shall be made low;
The rugged land shall be made a plain,
the rough country, a broad valley.
Then the glory of the LORD shall be revealed,
and all mankind shall see it together,
for the mouth of the LORD has spoken.

Isaiah 40:3–5

Prepare the way of the Lord, / make straight his paths. Isaiah announces that Israel's exile in Babylon is nearing its end and calls for a straight and level highway through the wilderness separating Babylon and Jerusalem so that God's people can travel home. God himself will lead their triumphal procession back to Jerusalem. In Isaiah, preparing **the way of the Lord** means preparing for the coming of God. In Mark's use of Isaiah's prophecy, **the Lord** refers to Jesus: God will be coming to his people in the person of Jesus. John the Baptist's role is to prepare people for Jesus.

Lord: See page 332

4 **John [the] Baptist appeared in the desert.** Mark tells us nothing about John's background or life up to then; his significance for Mark lies solely in what he does once he comes on the scene. John comes **proclaiming a baptism of repentance for the forgiveness of sins.** While Jews practiced ritual washings (Lev 15; 16:4, 24), John's baptism is distinctive. Unlike ritual washings, it is a onetime event, not repeated; it is administered by John, not done to oneself. It is so distinctive that it gives John his nickname: the Baptist. The word **baptism** did not previously have special religious significance. The word *baptize* was an ordinary Greek word that meant to dip, immerse, or wash. The essential feature of what John does is the washing away of dirt from the body as a symbol for the washing away of sins. It is not magic; it is **a baptism of repentance,** a ritual that expresses the repentance of those John washes.

The Greek word for **repentance** that is used here means a changing of one's mind. It also means a feeling of remorse, an undergoing of conversion, or a changing of one's behavior. We often focus on the aspects of remorse and behavioral change when we think of repentance. Sometimes what is needed is a change of thinking and fundamental outlook if our remorse and changed behavior are to have lasting results.

Repentance: See page 17

John's baptism is **for the forgiveness of sins:** the Greek could convey "for the purpose of the forgiveness of sins." It is not clear at this point in Mark's Gospel whether the sins of those who repent are forgiven through John's baptism or whether his ritual prepares them for forgiveness yet to come. We can note that Jews sought forgiveness of sins through sacrificial offerings in the Temple, in accordance with the prescriptions of the Old Testament. John is doing something new in proclaiming an alternative manner of seeking forgiveness of sins.

BACKGROUND: BAPTISM The Greek word *baptize* means to dip, plunge, immerse, drench, soak, or wash. Mark uses a variant of this word to describe the washing of dishes (Mark 7:4). There is some indication that John's baptism involved fully immersing a person in water: John 3:23 suggests that John needed ample water, and Mark 1:10 speaks of Jesus "coming up out of the water" after being baptized. In Christian practice, baptism took on special meaning as a sign of God's accomplishing far more than bodily washing.

---

5 **People of the whole Judean countryside and all the inhabitants of Jerusalem were going out to him and were being baptized by him in the Jordan River as they acknowledged their sins.** John the Baptist attracted quite a following. Most who came to him apparently did not remain indefinitely with him but after being baptized returned to their homes and jobs. Some did stay with John as his disciples (see 2:18; 6:29). John baptized those who **acknowledged their sins.** Admitting one's sins is the first step toward receiving forgiveness, and it is often the most difficult step. Some of us would rather tell ourselves that something we do is not really a sin than face the fact that it is sinful and that we need to change our behavior and seek forgiveness.

For reflection: What sins am I reluctant to acknowledge?

6 **John was clothed in camel's hair, with a leather belt around his waist. He fed on locusts and wild honey.** There is a similarity between the garb of John the Baptist and that of the prophet Elijah (2 Kings 1:8), and the question of John's relationship to Elijah will come up later (9:11–13). However, John's attire and diet may have simply reflected the dress and makeshift diet of those who lived in the wilderness. The region in which John preached was hot and desolate, and those who sojourned there had a harsh life. In centuries after John, men and women (the "Desert Fathers") would go into the wilderness and embrace its harsh solitude as an opportunity to live for God alone.

7 **And this is what he proclaimed: "One mightier than I is coming after me."** Mark has portrayed John the Baptist as a messenger (verse 2) who proclaims a baptism of repentance (verse 4), but verse 7 is the first time we hear directly from John. His message concerns another person who will appear on the scene, a person who is mightier than he. Given Mark's introductory statement (1:1), we immediately identify this mightier one as Jesus. However, it is not clear that John is able to make this identification. John knows that one mightier is coming, and he knows what this mightier one will do (verse 8), but nothing in Mark's Gospel establishes that John recognizes Jesus as the mightier one.

I am not worthy to stoop and loosen the thongs of his sandals. Even if John does not know who will come after him, he knows where he stands in relation to the coming one. Removing another's sandals was humbling work, requiring one to kneel before another. Later Jewish writings speak of removing another's sandals as a service so demeaning that it cannot be required of Jewish slaves.

For reflection: If a person as great as John had such reverence toward the one who came after him, what should my attitude be toward Jesus?

8 **I have baptized you with water; he will baptize you with the holy Spirit.** John's lowly status in relation to the coming one is reflected in what each of them is able to accomplish. John baptizes with **water** as a symbol for the washing away of sins. The one coming after John will **baptize you with the holy Spirit.** Just as John washes people in water, the one coming after John will wash them with the Holy Spirit. Many Jews lived in the hope that God would

---

COMMENT: TO READ MARK We will be most sensitive to the message Mark wishes to proclaim in his Gospel if we read it as a Gospel in itself. We bring a great deal of knowledge to our reading of Mark, including what the Gospel of John tells us about John the Baptist. In the fourth Gospel, the Baptist recognizes and proclaims Jesus as the one who comes after him (John 1:26-34). In arriving at a final assessment of John the Baptist, we need to take into account all that is said about him in all four Gospels. But reading Mark's Gospel for the message it proclaims is a different matter. To do so we need to pay attention to what Mark says—and doesn't say—and not automatically import information into Mark's Gospel from the other Gospels.

There is a second, related requirement. In reading Mark's Gospel we need to distinguish between what we know because Mark tells us and what the characters in Mark's Gospel know or do not know. Mark has told us that John the Baptist is the one sent to prepare the way for Jesus (1:1-3). But John the Baptist has not read Mark's Gospel and might not know what we know. Mark has told us from the very beginning that Jesus is the Christ (1:1), but those Jesus meets in the course of his ministry will be slow to recognize who Jesus is.

If John did not recognize Jesus, what does that tell us about the Baptist's call? Perhaps it tells us that God asked John to play a particular role but did not inform him of the full implications of his role. Something similar may well be true for many of us. We have been given certain responsibilities by God, perhaps even a clearly defined mission in life. But we may be in the dark about the ultimate outcome of our actions. We know what to do but not what it will accomplish in God's perspective.

---

one day pour out his Spirit and wash his people of their sins (Isaiah 43:25; 44:3; Ezek 36:25–27; Joel 3:1–5). John announces that this will be accomplished by the one who is coming after him: **he will baptize you with the holy Spirit.**

The Spirit: See page 12

> *I will sprinkle clean water upon you to cleanse you from all your impurities, and from all your idols I will cleanse you. I will give you a new heart and place a new spirit within you, taking from your bodies your stony hearts and giving you natural hearts. I will put my spirit within you.*
>
> Ezek 36:25–27

We can now understand John's baptism as a preparatory rite, a symbolic washing away of sins after repentance in anticipation of the actual cleansing that would be done by the Holy Spirit. Only God can forgive sins: our repentance prepares us to receive God's forgiveness, but repentance in itself does not wipe the slate clean or purify our hearts. That God must do. The one coming after John would be the agent sent to release an outpouring of God's purifying and life-giving Spirit. Something radically new was about to happen.

> *For reflection: What John's baptism foreshadowed is available to me. Am I willing to take the plunge and allow myself to be completely drenched in the Holy Spirit?*

The Baptism of Jesus

⁹ It happened in those days that Jesus came from Nazareth of Galilee and was baptized in the Jordan by John. ¹⁰ On coming up out of the water he saw the heavens being torn open and the Spirit, like a dove, descending upon him. ¹¹ And a voice came from the heavens, "You are my beloved Son; with you I am well pleased."

Gospel parallels: Matt 3:13–17; Luke 3:21–22; John 1:32–34

OT: Psalm 2; Isaiah 42:1–9

NT: Mark 9:7

9   **It happened in those days that Jesus came from Nazareth of Galilee and was baptized in the Jordan by John.** Jesus' first appearance in the Gospel of Mark is abrupt: Mark tells his readers nothing about Jesus' earlier life, save that he came from Nazareth. Mark does not pin down the date or even the year when Jesus came to John, nor does he tell us Jesus' age: Mark simply says **it happened in those days,** when John was baptizing. Jesus **came from Nazareth of Galilee** to John. Nazareth was an insignificant farming village of several hundred people that is not mentioned in the Old Testament. Perhaps that is why Mark has to tell his readers that it lay in **Galilee,** a region in the northern part of Palestine. (Palestine was the Roman name of the area that included Galilee, Samaria, and Judea.)

Nazareth: See page 127
Galilee: See page 30

Jesus **came** to John **and was baptized in the Jordan by John.** People accepted John's baptism as a symbolic washing away of their sins. Does this mean that Jesus considered himself a sinner and sought out John as a path to forgiveness? Mark offers no explanation. Perhaps the conclusion we should draw is that Jesus completely identified with our sinful humanity, even to the extent of submitting to a baptism of repentance. (Elsewhere the New Testament insists that Jesus was without sin: 2 Cor 5:21; Heb 4:15; 1 Pet 2:22.)

10 **On coming up out of the water he saw the heavens being torn open and the Spirit, like a dove, descending upon him.** It is Jesus who sees the heavens open and the Spirit descend; the implication is that no one else (not even John) sees what Jesus sees. We as readers of Mark are let in on something that those around Jesus apparently do not know. Jesus sees **the Spirit, like a dove, descending upon him.** Jesus will be able to baptize with the Spirit (1:8) because Jesus bears the Spirit. The Spirit appearing **like a dove** is unique to the baptism of Jesus; nowhere else in Scripture is the Holy Spirit represented as a dove.

11 **And a voice came from the heavens, "You are my beloved Son; with you I am well pleased."** The heavenly voice tells Jesus, **You are**

my beloved Son, but Mark gives no indication that the voice is audible to others. Again, we as readers are being given information that those around Jesus will be slow to perceive. Mark began his Gospel by proclaiming Jesus to be the Messiah and Son of God (1:1); now God himself proclaims, **You are my beloved Son.** Jesus is God's **beloved** Son: the relationship between God as Father and Jesus as **Son** is one of love. The Greek word for beloved can convey the notion of *only beloved:* Jesus is God's only Son. There is a unique relation between Jesus and the God of Israel, for Jesus is able to call upon God as his Father (14:36). God tells Jesus, **With you I am well pleased.** God is pleased with Jesus and delights in him even before Jesus begins his public ministry: God's love for Jesus is not something that Jesus has to earn.

Son of God: See page 64

Those of Mark's first readers who were familiar with the Old Testament might have detected some echoes of it in his Gospel. **You are my beloved Son** is an echo of Psalm 2:7, in which God tells an Israelite king as he takes the throne, "You are my son." In verse 8 of this psalm,

---

BACKGROUND: THE SPIRIT The opening verses of the Old Testament speak of a "mighty wind" (Gen 1:2) that sweeps over the waters as God begins his work of creation. The phrase translated "mighty wind" might also be translated "Spirit of God," for the Hebrew word *ruah* means wind, breath, or spirit; the Hebrew word taken here to mean mighty is also the word for God. It is the breath of God breathed into humans that gives life (Gen 2:7). When the Old Testament speaks of the Spirit of God, it generally refers to God's influence or power at work, as in, for example, the inspiration of prophets (Isaiah 61:1). The Spirit of God is not yet thought of as a person in the Old Testament. The New Testament bears witness to a deeper experience and understanding of the Spirit. Paul speaks of the Spirit many times in his letters but writes more about what the Spirit does than who the Spirit is. In the Gospel of John, Jesus speaks of the Spirit as the Paraclete, or Advocate, who will carry on his work (John 14:16–17, 26; 15:26; 16:7–11). The Gospel of Matthew ends with Jesus' instruction that baptism be done "in the name of the Father, and of the Son, and of the holy Spirit" (Matt 28:19). The Council of Constantinople in AD 381 proclaimed the Spirit to be "the holy, the lordly and life-giving one, proceeding forth from the Father, co-worshipped and co-glorified with Father and Son, the one who spoke through the prophets."

God tells him that authority to rule the earth is his for the asking, and verse 2 speaks of the king as God's "anointed" (*messiah* in Hebrew and *Christ* in Greek) who faces opposition. **With you I am well pleased** is a faint echo of a prophecy of Isaiah, in which God proclaims, "Here is my servant whom I uphold, / my chosen one with whom I am pleased" (Isaiah 42:1).

> *I will proclaim the decree of the* LORD,
> *who said to me, "You are my son;*
> *today I am your father.*
> *Only ask it of me,*
> *and I will make your inheritance the nations,*
> *your possession the ends of the earth."*
>
> Psalm 2:7–8

> *Here is my servant whom I uphold,*
> *my chosen one with whom I am pleased,*
> *Upon whom I have put my spirit;*
> *he shall bring forth justice to the nations.*
>
> Isaiah 42:1

Jesus is both one with sinful men and women (as signified by his accepting John's baptism) and the unique Son of God. How can this be? Jesus will ask his followers, "Who do you say that I am?" (8:29). Mark's Gospel confronts his readers with this question from its opening pages.

For reflection: Who do I say that Jesus is?

Jesus Confronts Satan
¹² At once the Spirit drove him out into the desert, ¹³ and he remained in the desert for forty days, tempted by Satan. He was among wild beasts, and the angels ministered to him.
Gospel parallels: Matt 4:1–11; Luke 4:1–13
OT: Lev 16:10; 1 Kings 19:3–8
NT: Matt 12:43; Mark 3:22–30; Luke 11:24

12 We might have expected Jesus to linger at the Jordan, basking in the glow of the Spirit and relishing his Father's comforting words. But **at once the Spirit drove him out into the desert:** *now* is the moment for Jesus to begin his work as the beloved Son. The Spirit **drove** (a forceful word) Jesus into the desert: there is nothing vague or uncertain about Jesus being led by the Spirit. The Spirit drives Jesus **out into the desert.** Jesus was baptized in a desolate area of the Jordan River (1:4), but he now apparently goes into the Judean wilderness between Jerusalem and the Dead Sea, a barren wasteland of limestone hills and deep ravines.

For reflection: How have I experienced the Spirit's leadings and promptings?

13 **And he remained in the desert for forty days, tempted by Satan.** The **forty days** perhaps recalls the forty years the Israelites spent in the desert but more closely echoes Elijah's forty-day trek through the desert (1 Kings 19:3–8). The reason the Spirit leads Jesus into the desert is apparently so that he can be **tempted by Satan.** The name **Satan** means adversary; the Gospels portray Satan as having authority over evil spirits. The desert was considered the abode of evil spirits (Lev 16:10; Isaiah 34:14; see also Matt 12:43; Luke 11:24); Jesus confronts Satan on his own ground.

Satan: See page 71

What does it mean that Jesus was **tempted** by Satan? We naturally think of the three temptations we find in Matthew's and Luke's accounts (Matt 4:1–11; Luke 4:1–13), but Mark does not mention them. Mark's message may be different from Matthew's and Luke's. The Greek word for temptation also means trial, tribulation, or test. In Mark's account, *tempted* seems to mean tested, as in a test of strength. Jesus' forty days in the desert were the first phase of his struggle with Satan, his battle against the forces of evil. The Spirit drove Jesus into the abode of evil to begin the showdown.

He was among wild beasts. The obvious connotation is that Jesus is in a desolate area full of dangerous animals. Mark's first readers may also have been reminded of wild beasts in Roman arenas where Christians were being tested by the forces of evil and martyred. They may have taken the mention of wild beasts as a message that they were not being asked to suffer anything that Jesus had not faced.

And the angels ministered to him. We may think of the angels' ministry in terms of spiritual consolation, but one meaning of the Greek word for minister is to wait on table. Mark may mean that angels brought food to Jesus, as an angel earlier brought food to Elijah for his forty-day journey through the desert (1 Kings 19:3–8). Mark does not tell us that Jesus fasted or became hungry during his time in the desert—another hint that Mark might have viewed Jesus' time in the desert not as a period of preparation but as part of what he had come to do.

Mark's emphasis is on the Spirit driving Jesus into the realm of Satan to confront Satan. The battle will not end in the desert: it will continue until the cross. Jesus will replace Satan's reign with the reign of God, which is the subject of Jesus' preaching in the verses that immediately follow. The Spirit has come upon Jesus (1:10); the kingdom of God is at hand (1:15).

Angels: See page 321

For reflection: How have I had to do battle with evil? What meaning do I find in Mark's account of Jesus' time in the desert?

ORIENTATION: *The scene shifts from the Judean wilderness to Galilee as Jesus begins his public ministry. Save for Jesus' final days in Jerusalem, most of the action in Mark's Gospel takes place in or around Galilee.*

Jesus Announces That the Kingdom of God Is at Hand

¹⁴ After John had been arrested, Jesus came to Galilee proclaiming the gospel of God: ¹⁵ "This is the time of fulfillment. The kingdom of God is at hand. Repent, and believe in the gospel."

Gospel parallels: Matt 4:12–17; Luke 4:14; John 4:1–3
OT: Isaiah 52:7; 61:1–2

14 Jesus began proclaiming the kingdom of God **after John had been arrested.** John's mission was over: he had announced that one would

come after him (1:7), and now the torch had been passed. John had been **arrested:** the Greek literally reads that he had been "handed over"; Mark will use the same word for Jesus being betrayed and handed over to death (14:10–11, 41; 15:15) and for Jesus' followers being handed over to persecutors (13:9–12). The shadow of the cross stretches back to John and forward to all followers of Jesus. Jesus went from Nazareth in Galilee to the lower Jordan, where John was baptizing (1:9), and now Jesus has returned **to Galilee.**

Galilee: See page 30

Jesus comes to Galilee **proclaiming the gospel of God.** Since the word *gospel* means good news, **the gospel of God** means good news that comes from God or good news about God. Isaiah spoke of a Spirit-anointed messenger sent by God bearing good news (Isaiah 61:1–2). Those of Mark's readers who were familiar with Isaiah's prophecies would have made a connection with Jesus, upon whom the Spirit had descended (1:10). Some whom Jesus encounters will think of him as a prophet (8:27–28), as God's messenger, and Jesus is that even though he is more than that.

Gospel: See page 4

> The spirit of the Lord GOD is upon me,
>> because the LORD has anointed me;
> He has sent me to bring glad tidings to the lowly,
>> to heal the brokenhearted.

Isaiah 61:1

15 The good news from God that Jesus proclaims is that **this is the time of fulfillment. The kingdom of God is at hand.** These words summarize Jesus' central message. Jesus announces that now, as he speaks, the decisive moment has arrived: **this is the time of fulfillment.** It is the time decided upon by God to bring his plan of salvation to fulfillment. All of God's dealings with his people have led up to this crucial moment. God is acting to shatter the powers of evil and to establish his dominion over his people and all peoples: **the kingdom of God is at hand.** God is acting through Jesus to establish his reign, but the accent in Jesus' initial proclamation is on what God is doing rather than on what Jesus is doing

as God's agent. Jesus announces that the time for the establishment of God's long-awaited reign **is at hand.** "At hand" can mean that God's reign has arrived or is near.

Kingdom of God: See page 96

Since God's reign is at hand, Jesus calls upon his listeners to respond: **Repent, and believe in the gospel.** Jesus' call to **repent** is not only a call for a change of life but also a call for a change of thinking, a call for his listeners to accept his message that the kingdom of God is at hand. Accepting Jesus' message is not the same as accepting a meteorologist's report of rain when one can look out the window and see it pouring. Now, as during the life of Jesus, God's reign is not so fully established that it is self-evident to all impartial observers. The signs marking the presence of God's reign can be discerned only through faith; hence Jesus' call to **believe in the gospel,** to believe the good news he proclaims.

For reflection: How would I have responded to Jesus' message about God's reign if I had been in his original audience? How do I respond today to the message of Jesus?

Jesus Calls His First Disciples
¹⁶ As he passed by the Sea of Galilee, he saw Simon and his brother Andrew casting their nets into the sea; they were fishermen. ¹⁷ Jesus said to them, "Come after me, and I will make you

---

BACKGROUND: REPENTANCE In the Old Testament, the Hebrew verb used for repent means to turn back or return: "Return, O Israel, to the Lord, your God" (Hosea 14:2). The New Testament expresses repentance differently: the Greek word translated repentance literally means a change of mind. A change of mind means recognizing that one's views are wrong or inadequate. If wrong views lead to wrong actions, then a change of mind should result in a change of behavior. Summing all this up is the notion of conversion, a profound reorientation of oneself. When John the Baptist and Jesus called for repentance, they were calling for an acceptance of the messages they proclaimed and for life changes on the basis of their messages. Repentance is not simply a matter of feeling sorry but also of adopting new attitudes and a new behavior.

---

fishers of men." **¹⁸ Then they abandoned their nets and followed him. ¹⁹ He walked along a little farther and saw James, the son of Zebedee, and his brother John. They too were in a boat mending their nets. ²⁰ Then he called them. So they left their father Zebedee in the boat along with the hired men and followed him.**

Gospel parallels: Matt 4:18–22; Luke 5:1–11

NT: John 1:35–42

16 Mark tells us that after announcing that God's reign had arrived, Jesus immediately began to gather disciples to himself. This is striking, and a sign that the reign of God is first of all found in those gathered with Jesus. **As he passed by the Sea of Galilee, he saw Simon and his brother Andrew casting their nets into the sea; they were fishermen.** Jesus encountered his followers as they were going about their everyday lives. Jesus **saw** Simon and Andrew, and he saw as well who they could become. Jesus is likewise present in our everyday lives, seeing us and who we can become. **Simon** will later be named Peter (3:16). The phrase **casting their nets into the sea** indicates that they are using small circular casting nets, thrown by hand from a boat or while wading.

Sea of Galilee: See page 100

17 **Jesus said to them, "Come after me."** Jesus takes the initiative; Simon and Andrew do not volunteer to become Jesus' followers. Jesus asks them to do more than become his students; he asks them to come after him, to follow him, to be with him, to share his life, and to pattern their lives on his life. Being a disciple of Jesus means entering into a personal relationship with him and thereby entering God's reign.

Disciple: See page 20

For reflection: How has Jesus taken the initiative with me? How did I first hear his call? What is my relationship with Jesus?

Come after me, and I will make you fishers of men. Those who follow Jesus are to share his mission as well as his life. Simon and Andrew have been gathering fish into nets; in the future they will gather men and women into God's reign. **I will make you fishers of men:** Jesus takes responsibility for his followers becoming what he calls them to be, even though their response is a necessary ingredient. Sharing Jesus' mission requires growth, as does sharing his life.

For reflection: How has Jesus transformed my life? How have I grown in discipleship and service?

18 **Then they abandoned their nets and followed him.** Simon and Andrew's response to Jesus is immediate and (for the moment) complete. Was this their very first encounter with Jesus, or had Jesus gradually prepared them for their moment of call? Mark does not describe any earlier contact between the brothers and Jesus, nor does he rule it out. Mark's focus is on the two most essential elements of discipleship: Jesus' call and the response of the one being called. How long we have known about Jesus or flirted with commitment to him is secondary to the response we finally make to his call.

19 **He walked along a little farther and saw James, the son of Zebedee, and his brother John. They too were in a boat mending their nets.** Fishermen used dragnets deployed from boats as well as casting nets; sometimes two boats deployed a net between them. The proximity of the

---

BACKGROUND: FISHING The Sea of Galilee was ringed with villages with harbors and has been commercially fished from ancient until modern times. Commercial fishing activities, rather than sportfishing, are reflected in the Gospels. There were about twenty species of fish in the Sea of Galilee, and three made up the bulk of commercial catches: the sardine, the carp, and the musht (*Tilapia galilea*). Musht feed on plankton and must be caught with nets, not with hooks and bait. Musht weigh up to three pounds and swim in schools; the great nettings of fish reported in the Gospels were probably catches of musht. Fishermen used various forms of nets, including nets that could be cast and nets that were deployed from boats. Remains of a first-century fishing boat were discovered in 1986 buried in the mud near the shore of the Sea of Galilee at Gennesaret (an area Jesus visited: Matt 14:34; Mark 6:53). This boat, 26½ feet long, 7½ feet wide, and 4½ feet high, was apparently typical of the fishing boats mentioned in the Gospels. It had a rounded stern and may have had decks fore and aft. It would have had a small square sail and a crew of four rowers and a rudderman. It could have carried an additional ten to twelve passengers when it was not transporting nets and fish.

---

boat of Simon and Andrew and that of James and John might suggest that they fished cooperatively.

20 **Then he called them. So they left their father Zebedee in the boat along with the hired men and followed him.** The presence of **hired men** indicates that Zebedee & Sons was a small fishing business, perhaps even a modestly prosperous one. James and John, like Simon and Andrew, **left** behind their boat and nets in order to follow Jesus; James and John left behind their father, Zebedee, as well. For these disciples, following Jesus meant accompanying him as he traveled, and it inevitably meant some break with the past, some things left behind, some human relationships made secondary in order to make Jesus primary. There is a cost of discipleship, unique to each disciple. Mark holds up the ready response of Simon and Andrew and James and John as an example for his readers.

For reflection: What have I had to let go of in order to follow Jesus? Am I clinging to anything that is making me lag behind?

BACKGROUND: DISCIPLE Generally a first-century Jewish disciple was someone who studied for a period of time under a teacher. Once this training was complete, a disciple could in turn become a teacher, gathering disciples and passing on to them what he had learned. However, Jesus' call of men and women to follow him involved more than their studying under him. Jesus invited them into a lifelong personal relationship with him, not a temporary apprenticeship. Being a disciple of Jesus meant sharing his life and accompanying him as he traveled about, teaching and healing. Hence Jesus issued his invitations to discipleship by the calls "Come after me" (Mark 1:17) or "Follow me" (Mark 2:14). At the same time, some of Jesus' disciples did not accompany him in his travels: the Gospels of Luke and John portray Martha, Mary, and Lazarus as remaining at home and extending hospitality to Jesus. The Gospels show Jesus taking the initiative in inviting men and women to become his disciples, rather than would-be followers taking the first step toward discipleship. Becoming a disciple of Jesus could involve some break with one's family and livelihood, and potentially even giving up one's life. That was the cost of sharing the life of the one who would lay down his life for the sake of others.

Simon and Andrew and James and John, the first to respond to the call of Jesus, will form an inner circle among his disciples (1:29; 13:3; see also 5:37; 9:2; 14:33). Jesus will turn to them for support, and I suggest that as we read Mark's Gospel we would be justified in thinking of them as Jesus' best friends as well as his followers. Becoming friends with Jesus and following him are at the heart of what it means to enter the kingdom of God.

For reflection: How would I characterize my relationship with Jesus? Am I his servant? His friend?

ORIENTATION: *The scene shifts to the town of Capernaum, on the shore of the Sea of Galilee. Mark presents what can be read as a day in the life of Jesus (1:21–34).*

The Authority of Jesus

²¹ Then they came to Capernaum, and on the sabbath he entered the synagogue and taught. ²² The people were astonished at his teaching, for he taught them as one having authority and not as the scribes. ²³ In their synagogue was a man with an unclean spirit; ²⁴ he cried out, "What have you to do with us, Jesus of Nazareth? Have you come to destroy us? I know who you are—the Holy One of God!" ²⁵ Jesus rebuked him and said, "Quiet! Come out of him!" ²⁶ The unclean spirit convulsed him and with a loud cry came out of him. ²⁷ All were amazed and asked one another, "What is this? A new teaching with authority. He commands even the unclean spirits and they obey him." ²⁸ His fame spread everywhere throughout the whole region of Galilee.

Gospel parallels: Luke 4:31–37

21 Jesus and his disciples **came to Capernaum,** a fishing and farming village on the northwest shore of the Sea of Galilee with a population estimated at six hundred to fifteen hundred. Simon and Andrew lived in Capernaum (1:29), and apparently James and John did as well. Jesus called the fishermen to follow him, but he follows them home and will

make their home his home (1:29–33; 2:1). Even as Jesus' disciples leave behind their old lives to follow him, Jesus enters into their lives.

Capernaum: See page 37

And on the sabbath he entered the synagogue and taught. Remains of a first-century synagogue have been discovered in Capernaum beneath the ruins of a later synagogue. Sabbath synagogue worship included prayers, blessings, and readings from the books of the Mosaic law (Genesis through Deuteronomy) and from the prophets. Worship was led by laymen (priests presided only in the Temple in Jerusalem), and any man could be invited to comment on the readings. Jesus used the occasion to teach, but Mark does not spell out the content of his teaching. We can assume that Jesus' teaching was connected with his message, "This is the time of fulfillment. The kingdom of God is at hand" (1:15).

Synagogue: See page 57

22 While Mark does not present the content of Jesus' teaching, he does describe the reaction of those who heard it. **The people were astonished at his teaching, for he taught them as one having authority and not as the scribes.** Mark will repeatedly tell of people being astonished and amazed by Jesus. He taught **not as the scribes,** whose teaching was a matter of passing on and applying traditions that interpreted the law of Moses. The authority of scribes lay in the tradition they passed on; Jesus' authority rested in himself: **he taught them as one having authority.** Jesus' authority came directly from God, who authorized him to pronounce that the kingdom of God was at hand. The contrast between how others taught and how Jesus taught was so striking that those who heard Jesus were **astonished.**

Scribes: See page 40

23 **In their synagogue was a man with an unclean spirit.** Is this man sitting quietly as part of the congregation, to all appearances a normal person? Or does he suddenly enter the synagogue and interrupt Jesus? Mark doesn't tell us; his interest is in what happens next.

Demons, unclean spirits: See page 105

24 **He cried out**—shrieked or shouted. The shout is that of the unclean spirit, speaking through the man under its sway. **What have you to do with us, Jesus of Nazareth? Have you come to destroy us?** The unclean spirit speaks on behalf of other unclean spirits, challenging Jesus, **What have you to do with us** (meaning "Why are you meddling with us?"). **Have you come to destroy us?** is a rhetorical question; the spirit recognizes that Jesus has come to do precisely that. The confrontation that began in the desert continues in Capernaum. If we are right in assuming that Jesus had been teaching about the coming of the kingdom of God (see 1:15), then the demon's outburst was entirely appropriate: the establishment of God's reign meant the overthrow of Satan and the forces of evil, so evil spirits were right to feel threatened.

The unclean spirit first addresses Jesus as **Jesus of Nazareth,** which is how he was popularly known. But then the unclean spirit adds, **I know who you are—the Holy One of God!** Readers of Mark's Gospel have been told who Jesus is (1:1), but his full identity has not yet been made evident to those around him. **The Holy One of God** was not a standard title for the Messiah, but its meaning is clear: Jesus is God's agent, uniquely sharing God's holiness.

25 The unclean spirit was right in its assessment of Jesus, but **Jesus rebuked him and said, "Quiet!"** A more literal translation is "Be muzzled," employing a word used for the muzzling of animals. This is the first in a series of occasions in Mark's Gospel when Jesus does not allow his identity to be publicized, and scholars have pondered the reason for this. The best short answer seems to be that Jesus' identity could only be understood in light of the cross, and premature proclamations about him, even if true, would be misleading. Hence, even if we as readers of Mark's Gospel can appreciate the truth of what the unclean spirit says about Jesus, it is not a truth to be publicly announced at this point in Jesus' ministry.

Jesus not only **rebuked** the unclean spirit into silence but also commanded it, **Come out of him!** Jesus' casting out of this unclean spirit is a skirmish in Jesus' battle to establish God's reign; he has indeed come to destroy (verse 24) the hold that evil has on this man.

26 **The unclean spirit convulsed him and with a loud cry came out of him.** Jesus' command accomplishes what Jesus commanded. The unclean spirit makes a last-ditch show of its power by convulsing the man but leaves with a wail of defeat. In the confrontation between Jesus and the forces of evil, Jesus is the conqueror.

27 **All were amazed and asked one another, "What is this? A new teaching with authority. He commands even the unclean spirits and they obey him."** Mark again reports the amazement of **all** in reaction to Jesus, but now on two scores. First, as before, they are amazed by the **new teaching** that Jesus proclaims **with authority.** And second, they are amazed that Jesus' authority is not limited to his teachings but extends to his commands as well: **he commands even the unclean spirits and they obey him.** There were other Jewish exorcists who expelled demons through rituals and prayers, but Jesus' authority was such that unclean spirits were subject to his simple command. Jesus was no ordinary exorcist, just as he was no ordinary teacher. By asking, **What is this?** the people were in effect asking, "Who is this?"

Jesus' **new teaching with authority** and his vanquishing of **unclean spirits** are part of the coming of God's reign (1:15), as was Jesus' gathering of disciples to himself (1:16–20).

For reflection: What is my experience of the authority and power of Jesus? Has he spoken words of command that made a difference in my life?

28 **His fame spread everywhere throughout the whole region of Galilee.** Mark wraps up his account of what happened in the synagogue by noting that word of it spread to the surrounding area. Astonishing words and deeds are not easily kept secret. The impulse behind evangelism is less a sense of duty than an inability to keep quiet about the amazing.

Galilee: See page 30

Jesus Heals Simon's Mother-in-Law

²⁹ **On leaving the synagogue he entered the house of Simon and Andrew with James and John. ³⁰ Simon's mother-in-law lay sick with a fever. They immediately told him about her. ³¹ He**

approached, grasped her hand, and helped her up. Then the fever left her and she waited on them.

Gospel parallels: Matt 8:14–15; Luke 4:38–39

29 **On leaving the synagogue he entered the house of Simon and Andrew:** the remains of the first-century synagogue in Capernaum are about eighty-five feet from the remains of a house that archaeologists identify as that of Simon Peter. His brother Andrew and Andrew's family may have occupied one of the other small houses that shared a courtyard with Peter's house. The presence of **James and John** means that all of Jesus' followers so far mentioned are with him.

30 **Simon's mother-in-law lay sick with a fever.** That Simon had a mother-in-law means he was married; Paul indicates that Simon Peter's wife accompanied him on missionary journeys (see 1 Cor 9:5). A **fever** was more life threatening in the ancient world than in our world of potent medicines. The fever may have been a sign of malaria, which was endemic in northern Palestine until the nineteenth century. **They immediately told him about her.** Was this simply to inform Jesus that a member of Peter's extended family was ill, or was it an implied request that he heal her? We do not know if those around Jesus already looked upon him as a healer, for Mark has not yet described Jesus healing anyone of a physical illness.

31 **He approached, grasped her hand, and helped her up.** Whatever the nuances of what the disciples said to Jesus, he takes the initiative. He goes to her, since she cannot get up to go to him. He **grasped her hand,** touching her, making personal contact. He **helped her up;** literally, he raised her up. Mark will use the same Greek word for the raising of the dead, including Jesus' being raised from the dead (14:28; 16:6) and the resurrection of the dead in the next life (12:26). Jesus raised Simon's mother-in-law from her sickbed out of compassion for her, but his raising her up prefigured far greater raisings. **Then the fever left her:** Jesus had authority over illness, just as he had authority over unclean spirits (1:25–28), and his healings and exorcisms were first fruits of the coming of God's reign.

For reflection: How has Jesus bent down to me when I could not rise up to him?

The incident ends with what seems to be a homey note: **and she waited on them.** Now that she was no longer laid up, she could do what women did when guests arrived: get out the good dishes and prepare some food. But there is a deeper meaning as well: the Greek word for **waited on** can also be translated "served," and it is the word Jesus will use when he tells his followers that he has come not to be served but to serve (10:45), and that they likewise must become servants (10:43). Simon Peter's mother-in-law is the first person in Mark's Gospel to fulfill this teaching of Jesus. The fact that she puts herself at the service of **them** means that she does it for Jesus and his followers—for the whole Church, so to speak. She is not simply someone whom Jesus healed but a model of service for all.

For reflection: Have I experienced Jesus touching and raising me for service? How am I best able to serve Jesus and his followers?

BACKGROUND: PETER'S HOUSE In Capernaum, archaeologists have found the remains of an ancient neighborhood of rooms clustered around courtyards. An octagonal church was erected over some of the ruins in the fifth century; octagonal or circular churches were built to mark holy places. Beneath the center of the church are the remains of a room that was built around 65 BC. Its walls and floor were made of unworked basalt stones (basalt is black volcanic rock) and would have supported a roof of beams and tree branches covered with thatch and earth. The interior of this room measured about twenty by twenty feet, and it shared a courtyard with other rooms. Archaeologists have found evidence (fishhooks, broken kitchenware) indicating that it was used as a family home at the time of Jesus. Later in the first century this room was set aside for special use. Its walls and floor were plastered (unlike other houses discovered in Capernaum), and Christians began carving prayers in the plaster, which suggests that it was a venerated site and a place for Christian gatherings. An arch was added in the fourth century to support a more durable roof. Egeria, a European nun who came on pilgrimage to the Holy Land sometime around AD 380, wrote in her travel notes, "In Capernaum a house church was made out of the house of Peter, and its walls still stand today." Subsequently the octagonal church was built over the site. A modern church was dedicated in 1992, with a glass floor that allows worshipers to gaze down on the remains of Peter's house.

Healings in Simon's House

³² When it was evening, after sunset, they brought to him all who were ill or possessed by demons. ³³ The whole town was gathered at the door. ³⁴ He cured many who were sick with various diseases, and he drove out many demons, not permitting them to speak because they knew him.

Gospel parallels: Matt 8:16–17; Luke 4:40–41

32 By Jewish reckoning, a day ended not at midnight but at sunset (see Lev 23:32). On the Sabbath, Jesus taught in the synagogue and then went to Simon's house (1:21, 29); now **it was evening, after sunset,** that is, the Sabbath is over, and it is now the next day. Jesus freed a man of an unclean spirit in the sight of everyone in the synagogue, and word of it has spread quickly through Capernaum. Probably many have also heard of his healing of Simon Peter's mother-in-law. Now others want to be likewise freed and healed. The people of Capernaum waited until the Sabbath ended to carry their sick to Jesus, lest they violate the commandment forbidding work (such as carrying a load) on the Sabbath. But as soon as they could, **after sunset, they brought to him all who were ill or possessed by demons.** Jesus has healed one sick woman and freed one possessed man; now **all** those of Capernaum with such afflictions are brought to him.

33 **The whole town was gathered at the door** of Simon Peter's house. According to an archaeologist's reconstruction, this door opened onto an irregular courtyard that was far too small to hold the **whole town** of Capernaum. Perhaps the image we should form is of all who have afflicted relatives and friends trying to bring them to Jesus, crowding the narrow alleys and open spaces around Simon's house, patiently (or not so patiently) awaiting their turn with Jesus.

For reflection: Who are the afflicted that I would like to bring to Jesus for healing?

34 Jesus **cured many who were sick with various diseases, and he drove out many demons.** Jesus' curing of **many** does not mean that not all were cured; it indicates only that Jesus healed a large number of

people who were sick or demon afflicted. Jesus had complete authority over illnesses and demons, and he used it to bring health and wholeness. Jesus did not allow demons to proclaim his identity, although they correctly perceived it: he did not permit **them to speak because they knew him.** Those around Jesus will have to gradually grow in their realization of who he is, and their view of him will not be complete until it includes the cross.

For reflection: How am I most in need of physical or spiritual healing? Have I turned to Jesus to make me whole?

Jesus Goes from Village to Village

35 Rising very early before dawn, he left and went off to a deserted place, where he prayed. 36 Simon and those who were with him pursued him 37 and on finding him said, "Everyone is looking for you." 38 He told them, "Let us go on to the nearby villages that I may preach there also. For this purpose have I come." 39 So he went into their synagogues, preaching and driving out demons throughout the whole of Galilee.

Gospel parallels: Luke 4:42–43

35 Since the people of Capernaum brought a large number of afflicted people to Jesus after sunset (1:32–34), Jesus' healing of them presumably continued long into the night. Yet **rising very early before dawn, he left and went off to a deserted place, where he prayed.** Prayer was more important to Jesus than getting a good night's sleep. Mark does not tell us what Jesus prayed about. Later, in Gethsemane, Jesus will pray to his "Abba, Father" (14:36), and this was likely his usual form of address to God. Did Jesus need time to meditate on the amazing power he had exercised the previous day—the first exorcisms and healings recorded in Mark? Did Jesus seek God's will for what he should do next? Did Jesus simply want time to commune with his Father? Or did Jesus pray about all this and more?

For reflection: How important is prayer for me? What do I pray about? Am I willing to rearrange my schedule to make time for prayer?

Jesus goes out of Capernaum **to a deserted place** to pray. There were no wilderness areas around Capernaum, so Jesus did not go into a desert. He simply found a place where he could be by himself, away from the crowds, away even (for the moment) from his followers.

36 Jesus' privacy doesn't last. **Simon and those who were with him pursued him**—tracked or hunted him down. This was not what Jesus had in mind when he invited Simon and the others to follow him! Jesus has gone off by himself to a deserted place because he wants to be alone, but his disciples fail to grasp, or fail to honor, his intention. This is the first time, but far from the last time, that Jesus' followers do not understand him.

37 **And on finding him said, "Everyone is looking for you."** "Everyone" is the people of Capernaum, who look upon Jesus as one who can heal their sick and demon possessed. If Jesus wishes, he can be a local celebrity. **Everyone is looking for you:** the implication in Simon's words is "What are you doing here in a deserted place? You should be back in the midst of those who are clamoring for you."

38 Jesus, however, is not looking back on his success in Capernaum but ahead to his mission. **He told them, "Let us go on to the nearby villages that I may preach there also."** Jesus includes his disciples in his mission, telling them, "Let **us** go," inviting them to be with him as he travels. His efforts will be directed to the **villages** of Galilee; Mark does not describe Jesus going into any of Galilee's major cities. Jesus will go to **preach** to the men and women of these villages, that is, to proclaim to them the good news that the kingdom of God is at hand (1:14–15). If it is at hand, then it is urgent that Jesus get the message out. Jesus adds, **For this purpose have I come.** Jesus' mission is to proclaim the coming of the reign of God and to bring it about through his healings and exorcisms and all that he will do. There may also be another meaning in these words, a hint of Jesus implying that for this purpose he has come *from God* (see 9:37). Simon and the others likely missed this hint, but Mark's readers might have caught it, having been told that Jesus is the beloved Son (1:11).

39 **So he went into their synagogues, preaching and driving out demons throughout the whole of Galilee.** Mark does not tell us how long Jesus spent traveling from village to village in Galilee, but some span of time is implied by Jesus going into **synagogues,** for he would have found congregations gathered in them only on Sabbaths and feasts. Mark characterizes Jesus' efforts as **preaching and driving out demons;** this is a shorthand way of saying that Jesus did the same thing in the other villages of Galilee that he had done in Capernaum. Jesus' mission continues to be to proclaim and bring about the reign of God, overthrowing the forces of evil.

Synagogue: See page 57

Jesus goes **throughout the whole of Galilee.** This was not a vast area. Save for Jerusalem, most of the sites Jesus visits in Mark's Gospel were within a day's walk of Capernaum or a short boat ride away. Jesus

---

BACKGROUND: GALILEE was the northern region of ancient Palestine. Most of the Galilean sites mentioned in the Gospels were in what was considered "lower Galilee" in the time of Jesus: a roughly circular area twenty to twenty-five miles across, with the Sea of Galilee on the east and the coastal hills of the Mediterranean on the west. Nazareth was near the southern edge of lower Galilee, and Capernaum was in the northeast. The general character of Galilee was rural: the two most significant cities in lower Galilee—Sepphoris and Tiberias—seem to have had little cultural impact on those who did not live within them. Most of the inhabitants of Galilee made their living as farmers or fishermen and lived in villages or small towns. Galilee contained the estates of its ruler, Herod Antipas, and his wealthy supporters, and some Galileans worked as tenant farmers or day laborers on these estates. There was not much of a "middle class" in Galilee: there was a small wealthy elite and many ordinary and rather poor people. The Galilee of Jesus was primarily the Galilee of ordinary people: while Jesus' message reached members of the upper class, the Gospels never describe Jesus going into Sepphoris or Tiberias, even though Sepphoris lay only four miles from Nazareth, and Tiberias seven miles from Capernaum. Galilee during the ministry of Jesus has sometimes been described as a paganized area, a region of lax religious observance, and a hotbed of revolutionary nationalism, but none of these characterizations is accurate. In general the Jews of rural Galilee were relatively uninfluenced by Greek culture, traditional in their religious practices, and slow to heed calls to revolution. *Related topic: Herod Antipas (page 138).*

did not travel far and wide, as Paul did; Jesus focused his efforts on small villages in a small region.

For reflection: Why did Jesus limit his efforts to such a small area? Might it imply that his mission required face-to-face encounters with men and women as well as preaching to crowds?

Jesus Cleanses an Outcast

⁴⁰ A leper came to him [and kneeling down] begged him and said, "If you wish, you can make me clean." ⁴¹ Moved with pity, he stretched out his hand, touched him, and said to him, "I do will it. Be made clean." ⁴² The leprosy left him immediately, and he was made clean. ⁴³ Then, warning him sternly, he dismissed him at once. ⁴⁴ Then he said to him, "See that you tell no one anything, but go, show yourself to the priest and offer for your cleansing what Moses prescribed; that will be proof for them." ⁴⁵ The man went away and began to publicize the whole matter. He spread the report abroad so that it was impossible for Jesus to enter a town openly. He remained outside in deserted places, and people kept coming to him from everywhere.

Gospel parallels: Matt 8:1–4; Luke 5:12–16
OT: Lev 13–14

40 Leprosy rendered one ritually unclean; hence people with leprosy had to avoid contact with others, lest they infect them with their disease and ritual impurity (Lev 13:45–46). Yet **a leper came to** Jesus, ignoring this prohibition. He had apparently heard that Jesus healed the sick, and he needed healing. Some manuscripts of Mark's Gospel describe him **kneeling down** before Jesus. This is the posture of a person pleading for something from another person (2 Kings 1:13), but for Mark's first readers it was also a posture of worship (see Phil 2:10). The man **begged him and said, "If you wish, you can make me clean."** He expresses confidence in Jesus' ability to heal him rather than doubt that Jesus will be willing to do so. The man with leprosy implores Jesus to do what he is able to do.

31

> *The one who bears the sore of leprosy shall keep his garments rent and his head bare, and shall muffle his beard; he shall cry out, "Unclean, unclean!" As long as the sore is on him he shall declare himself unclean, since he is in fact unclean. He shall dwell apart, making his abode outside the camp.*
>
> Lev 13:45–46

41 The New American Bible reads that Jesus was **moved with pity** for the man; the Greek word means to be profoundly moved with compassion (or, more literally, to have a gut reaction of compassion). This is the first time Mark tells us of Jesus' emotions, and it is striking that it is a glimpse of Jesus being moved with compassion at the sight of a suffering person.

> *For reflection: How does Jesus look upon me? Do I believe that his attitude toward me is heartfelt compassion?*

Some ancient manuscripts of Mark's Gospel have Jesus moved not by pity but by anger at the sight of the man with leprosy. His anger would not have been directed at the man but at his condition and at the evil forces that had caused it. This would fit in with verse 43, which apparently portrays the healing of the man as an exorcism.

BACKGROUND: LEPROSY In the Old and New Testaments, "leprosy" refers to a variety of skin conditions and infections, one of which might have been what is called leprosy today (Hansen's disease). Some of these skin conditions went away in time; some did not. A skin condition that resulted in abnormal appearance made the afflicted person ritually impure or unclean, since purity was associated with normality, and impurity with abnormality. Old Testament regulations specified that priests were to determine whether a skin condition was leprosy; if it was, the person with the skin disease was excluded from the community as unclean (Lev 13). Priests likewise judged whether a person's leprosy had gone away, in which case the person underwent purification rituals before rejoining the community (Lev 14). These procedures indicate that what was at stake was ritual purity and not simply health. Exclusion of the afflicted person from the community had as much to do with preventing the spread of uncleanness as with preventing the spread of disease.

Jesus then **stretched out his hand** and **touched him.** Lepers were doubly untouchable for Jews: not only were people put off by their physical deformity, but touching a leper also made one unclean. Even worse than the physical effects of leprosy were the social consequences: lepers were untouchable outcasts. But Jesus breaks through the barriers, stretching out his hand to the leper, touching him, ending his isolation. Jesus **said to him, "I do will it. Be made clean."** Jesus has both the desire and the power to make this man whole—not only restored to physical health but also *cleansed* of ritual impurity and its social consequences.

> *For reflection: Do I have any untouchable areas in my life—darknesses that I cannot share with others? Do I believe that Jesus stretches out his hand in compassion to touch even what is untouchable in me?*

42 **The leprosy left him immediately.** Instantaneously the leprosy **left** the man, just as the unclean spirit had come out of the man in the synagogue (1:26). Jesus was not made unclean by touching the leper; the leper **was made clean** by Jesus' touch and command.

43 **Then, warning him sternly, he dismissed him at once.** This verse is an enigma, for in Greek it reads that Jesus was snortingly indignant and drove the man away, and there seems to be no reason for Jesus to have been so stern with the man. Some scholars suspect that in an early alternate version of the incident, Jesus' indignation was directed at an unclean spirit responsible for the man's condition, and that it was this spirit (rather than the man) that was ordered to leave (**dismissed** translates the same Greek word used in verses 34 and 39 for the driving out of demons). This would indicate that Jesus' encounter with the man was remembered in two forms, as a healing and as an exorcism, and Mark may have combined features of both. The story reads well if verse 43 is skipped. (Matthew and Luke will omit this sentence when they recount the incident: Matt 8:1–4; Luke 5:12–16.)

44 **Then he said to him, "See that you tell no one anything, but go, show yourself to the priest and offer for your cleansing what Moses prescribed; that will be proof for them."** Jesus has healed the man of his leprosy, but the man still has to follow the procedures

specified in the law of Moses in order to be ritually purified (Lev 14). Jesus tells the man to do what the law requires: **Go, show yourself to the priest and offer for your cleansing what Moses prescribed.** That will restore him to society, allowing him to have normal contact with others. Jesus' previous command, **See that you tell no one anything,** might be interpreted to mean "Don't go running up to people telling them of your cleansing and restoration to the community until it is compete; go first to a priest." But Jesus' command is more likely intended as a more lasting prohibition, for it fits in with his later commands to others whom he heals to keep quiet about it (5:43; 7:36; 8:26). Jesus' motive here is the same as his motive for silencing demons: too much publicity at this point will lead to misunderstanding. Jesus is far more than a wonder-worker.

Jesus tells the man to show himself to a priest and make the necessary offerings, for **that will be proof for them,** that is, evidence to the priests of his having been cured. Perhaps, more subtly, it will also be proof to them that Jesus respects the law of Moses, since he has instructed the leper to do all the law requires. The question of Jesus' attitude toward the law will soon arise.

45 **The man went away and began to publicize the whole matter. He spread the report abroad.** Mark does not tell us whether the man obeyed Jesus and first went to a priest. Mark does say that he began to tell others of his healing, despite Jesus' order. In the context of Jesus' ministry, this was disobedience. Yet we can have some sympathy for this man: how could a man who had been a leper and had been restored not only to health but also to the society of others keep it a secret?

If we move from the context of Jesus' ministry to the context of those for whom Mark writes, then, ironically, the healed man can serve as a model for what Mark's readers are to do: tell everyone what Jesus has done for them. The matter of his disobedience aside, the man who was cleansed is, in Mark's Gospel, the first missionary!

For reflection: Do I tell others what Jesus has done for me?

In the context of Jesus' ministry, however, this man's disobedience makes life more difficult for Jesus. **He spread the report abroad so that**

it was impossible for Jesus to enter a town openly. He remained outside in deserted places. Jesus and the man who has been cured of leprosy have switched places. Previously the man was forced to live in deserted areas, but now he has rejoined society. Previously Jesus went into towns to preach (1:38–39), but now his fame (in part a result of the healed man's loose lips) is such that he will be mobbed if he does so, and he has to take refuge in deserted areas. This is a foreshadowing of the cross, where Jesus and Barabbas will switch places, and Barabbas will live because Jesus dies (15:6–15).

Despite Jesus' remaining in deserted places, **people kept coming to him from everywhere.** Previously people from Capernaum searched him out (1:36–37); now it is people from **everywhere.** If Mark had ended his Gospel at this point, it would have been a story of triumph and success. Jesus has vanquished sickness and evil wherever he has encountered them, and crowds are streaming into the Galilean countryside to find him. Mark has kept his promise of telling us good news about Jesus (1:1).

For reflection: What is my impression of Jesus at this point in Mark's Gospel?

CHAPTER 2

ORIENTATION: *Jesus has received widespread acclaim but now begins to meet with opposition. Chapter 2 and the first six verses of chapter 3 describe rising tensions between Jesus and religious leaders, culminating in some of them plotting his death. The underlying issue is the question of Jesus' identity and authority.*

Jesus' Authority to Forgive Sin

¹ When Jesus returned to Capernaum after some days, it became known that he was at home. ² Many gathered together so that there was no longer room for them, not even around the door, and he preached the word to them. ³ They came bringing to him a paralytic carried by four men. ⁴ Unable to get near Jesus because of the crowd, they opened up the roof above him. After they had broken through, they let down the mat on which the paralytic was lying. ⁵ When Jesus saw their faith, he said to the paralytic, "Child, your sins are forgiven." ⁶ Now some of the scribes were sitting there asking themselves, ⁷ "Why does this man speak that way? He is blaspheming. Who but God alone can forgive sins?" ⁸ Jesus immediately knew in his mind what they were thinking to themselves, so he said, "Why are you thinking such things in your hearts? ⁹ Which is easier, to say to the paralytic, 'Your sins are forgiven,' or to say, 'Rise, pick up your mat and walk'? ¹⁰ But that you may know that the Son of Man has authority to forgive sins on earth"—¹¹ he said to the paralytic, "I say to you, rise, pick up your mat, and go home." ¹² He rose, picked up his mat at once, and went away in the sight of everyone. They were all astounded and glorified God, saying, "We have never seen anything like this."

Gospel parallels: Matt 9:1–8; Luke 5:17–26

1 Jesus had been traveling from village to village, proclaiming the good news of the reign of God (1:38–39) and taking respite in deserted places (1:45), but then he **returned to Capernaum after some days.** He makes Capernaum his base of operations in Galilee, staying in the

house of Peter. Word of his return spreads quickly through Capernaum: **it became known that he was at home.**

Peter's house: See page 26

2 Once before, Peter's house and courtyard were mobbed by those who wanted to hear and be healed by Jesus (1:33), and now it happens again: **many gathered together so that there was no longer room for them, not even around the door.** No wonder Jesus had to repeatedly search out deserted places to have a little privacy (1:35, 45)! Yet he did not turn away those who came to him, even though their constant presence and needs must have been a drain on his energy.

For reflection: What does Jesus' availability to others tell me about him? What does it say about his availability to me?

Jesus **preached the word to them:** the presence of a crowd is an opportunity for him to carry out the purpose for which he has come (1:38). He proclaims **the word:** he has returned to Galilee to proclaim

---

BACKGROUND: CAPERNAUM lay on the northwest shore of the Sea of Galilee, along a road that led from the Mediterranean to Bethsaida and ultimately Damascus. Since Capernaum was near the border between the territory governed by Herod Antipas and the territory governed by Philip, there was a customs post there to collect taxes on goods being transported between the territories. Capernaum was a fishing and farming village covering about twenty-five acres, with a population estimated to be between six hundred and fifteen hundred. Its houses were one story and small, with walls of unworked stones and flat thatched roofs; its narrow winding streets of packed earth would have been muddy during the rainy season and dusty the rest of the year. Archaeologists have not found signs of wealth in any of its houses; Capernaum was a village of ordinary rural Galileans. Nor have they found evidence of public buildings, other than what seems to be the remains of a synagogue, which probably served as a community center. Jesus moved from Nazareth to Capernaum and made Capernaum his base of operations for his public ministry; Mark and Matthew indicate that he stayed in the house of Peter. In later centuries there was a continuing Christian presence in Capernaum, alongside its Jewish population. Capernaum was abandoned in the seventh century, following the Islamic conquest of Palestine. *Related topics: Farming (page 80), Fishing (page 19), Galilee (page 30), Peter's house (page 26).*

the gospel of God, the good news that the reign of God is at hand (1:14–15). Later he will speak "the word" in parables (4:33); perhaps he used parables of the kingdom on this occasion as well.

3 **They came bringing to him a paralytic carried by four men.** The four are presumably relatives or friends of the paralyzed man. The man needs Jesus' healing of his paralysis, but his paralysis has kept him from coming to Jesus. Likewise, we can find ourselves spiritually paralyzed, keeping us away from the one who can forgive us and make us whole. Those who love the paralyzed man do for him what he cannot do for himself: they bring him to Jesus. We too may need the help of others to come to Jesus—and we too may be able to extend that help to others.

4 **Unable to get near Jesus because of the crowd, they opened up the roof above him.** The man's paralysis is not the only obstacle; there is also an impenetrable crowd surrounding Jesus. There is a way to get around the crowd, but it is not an easy one. Peter's house had a flat roof made of wooden beams overlaid with branches, thatch, and packed earth. An outside stairway or ladder led to the roof, which was used as a place to sleep on hot nights and to dry crops (see 13:15). Those carrying the paralyzed man take him up onto the roof, and **after they had broken through, they let down the mat on which the paralytic was lying.** It would have been easy to break through the clay and thatch and make an opening between two beams—but also very messy; some of the debris must have fallen on those inside Peter's house. Those who want to bring the paralyzed man to Jesus are willing to do whatever it takes.

For reflection: Whom do I want to bring to Jesus? What obstacles stand in the way? What am I willing to do to overcome these obstacles?

5 Jesus could have been annoyed by those who were interrupting his preaching by showering debris on him and his audience, but he is not. His focus is different: he **saw their faith,** a faith expressed by deeds rather than words. Their going to unusual lengths to bring the paralyzed man to Jesus for healing demonstrates their confidence in Jesus.

What Jesus does next seems puzzling: **he said to the paralytic, "Child, your sins are forgiven."** The four men have brought the paralyzed man to Jesus for healing, not for forgiveness of his sins; nothing has been said about this man being a sinner. Yet there are connections between healing and forgiveness. In Old Testament times, sickness was often viewed as evidence of and punishment for sin, and this belief was still held by some at the time of Jesus (see John 9:2). Jesus did not endorse this view, but neither did he hold that sickness and sin were completely unrelated: both were the presence of evil. Sin is a sickness deadlier than any physical illness; sin is a paralysis that keeps us from coming to God. Jesus was concerned for the whole person and discerned that forgiveness was the greatest need of the man who had been brought to him.

Jesus addresses the man as **child,** a term of affection. Jesus says, **Your sins are forgiven.** This might be interpreted as Jesus saying, "God has forgiven your sins," much as Nathan announced God's forgiveness to David (2 Sam 12:13). But what follows indicates that Jesus pronounced the man's forgiveness as if Jesus was the one doing the forgiving. Further, Jesus granted forgiveness apart from the procedures set down in the Old Testament for obtaining forgiveness, particularly through making sacrificial offerings at the Temple (Lev 4–7, 16). Something very new and very different has just happened in Peter's house.

> For reflection: Am I in any way paralyzed by sin? Does Jesus look on me with affection, despite my sins? How have I experienced his forgiveness?

6 **Now some of the scribes were sitting there.** This is the first mention of any interaction between **scribes** and Jesus. Scribes were scholars and teachers of the law of Moses. They react as if Jesus has just said something extraordinary, and they are **asking themselves** about it.

7 The scribes wonder to themselves, **Why does this man speak that way? He is blaspheming. Who but God alone can forgive sins?** Not only has Jesus pronounced forgiveness apart from all established procedures, but he is also claiming to do something that only God can

do. Consequently the scribes accuse Jesus of **blaspheming** by claiming a prerogative of God. The charge of blasphemy will also be leveled at Jesus during his hearing before the Sanhedrin (14:61–64). It is a serious charge: Leviticus prescribes that blasphemy be punished with death by stoning (Lev 24:15–16). **Who but God alone can forgive sins?** is indeed the issue, and the answer is that Jesus can. God forgives sins through Jesus.

8 **Jesus immediately knew in his mind what they were thinking to themselves.** Does this simply mean that their faces gave them away to a perceptive observer like Jesus? Jesus would have been well aware that his pronouncing forgiveness of sins would be jarring to Jewish scholars, for there was no basis in Jewish Scripture or tradition for a human being to grant divine forgiveness. Or is Mark hinting that Jesus had more than human knowledge of the thoughts of those around him? It is not easy to decide simply on the basis of this passage. However Jesus came to know what the scribes were thinking, **he said, "Why are you thinking such things in your hearts?"** and proposed a test.

9 **Which is easier, to say to the paralytic, "Your sins are forgiven," or to say, "Rise, pick up your mat and walk"?** We can interpret **easier**

BACKGROUND: SCRIBES The scribes encountered in the Gospels are scholars and teachers of the law of Moses, but the profession of scribe included others as well. A scribe was literally someone who could write, a literate person in a largely illiterate society. Scribes ranged from village scribes who handled routine correspondence and record keeping to high-ranking officials in governmental administrative positions. (Today we apply the title secretary both to a typist and to the secretary of state.) In the Gospel accounts, scribes are men who specialize in studying and teaching the law of Moses and are centered in Jerusalem. When Jesus proclaimed interpretations of the law different from those of scribes, conflicts arose between them and Jesus. Some scribes (a professional group) were Pharisees (a religious group), but not all scribes were Pharisees, and not all Pharisees were scribes. Likewise, some Jerusalem priests were also scribes, and some scribes were Sadducees (an aristocratic elite). Eventually some scribes took part in the reshaping of Judaism after the destruction of Jerusalem by Rome in AD 70 and were among those who became known as rabbis. *Related topics: Pharisees (page 163), Sadducees (page 318).*

in two senses. A physical healing, although miraculous, is in a sense easier than a spiritual healing. Elisha, the great wonder-worker of the Old Testament, performed some wonderful deeds but never claimed he could forgive anyone's sins. Neither had John the Baptist claimed he could forgive sins, despite his preaching of repentance. On the other hand, it is certainly easier to **say** to a paralytic, **Your sins are forgiven** than to say to him, **Rise, pick up your mat and walk,** for no one could observe the forgiveness of sins, but anyone could tell whether a paralyzed man got up and walked. Jesus proposes the latter as the test for the former: if he is able to heal the man of his paralysis, then that should be a sign that he is able to forgive his sins as well.

10 **But that you may know that the Son of Man has authority to for-give sins on earth.** This is the first time that Jesus refers to himself as **the Son of Man.** It is a description or title that Jesus will use often for himself, and it can carry different shades of meaning. Son of man is an Aramaic idiom for human being, and thus Jesus might be using it simply as a way of saying "I." But it also has other associations, particularly of a heavenly "one like a son of man" in the book of Daniel who is given authority by God (Dan 7:13–14). Jesus uses **the Son of Man** in a complex

---

BACKGROUND: SON OF MAN Jesus uses the expression *Son of Man* more than eighty times in the four Gospels; it is found only four times in the rest of the New Testament. In its origin it is a Hebrew and Aramaic idiom that means human being: Ezekiel, for example, is repeatedly addressed as "son of man" by God (see Ezek 2:1; 3:1; 4:1). It seems to have the same meaning in some passages where Jesus refers to himself as the Son of Man—that is, it simply means that he shares the human condition. Jesus also employs the expression as a way of referring to himself during his public ministry, even when he is doing things that by human standards are extraordinary (for example, forgiving sins: Mark 2:10). In other passages, Jesus uses the expression *the Son of Man* when speaking of his coming suffering and death. In still other passages, the Son of Man is the risen Jesus returning in glory at the end of time. These last instances echo the use of "one like a son of man" in Dan 7:13–14. Neither in Daniel nor in any other Jewish writing from before the time of Jesus is Son of Man used as a title for the Messiah. Jesus' referring to himself as the Son of Man was distinctive: others did not call him the Son of Man. It is also enigmatic: scholars have endlessly debated the complexities of this title.

way, referring to himself as a human who has been given extraordinary authority by God, the **authority to forgive sins on earth.** Jesus brings God's forgiveness to **earth** as God's unique agent. **That you may know** echoes Old Testament texts in which God says he will do something that will demonstrate his might (Exod 8:18; 9:14). Jesus is about to make a similar unmistakable demonstration of his **authority.**

11 **He said to the paralytic, "I say to you, rise, pick up your mat, and go home."** The word translated **rise** is the same word that will later be used for rising from the dead (12:26; 14:28; 16:6): the man's rising from his paralysis is a sign of much greater rising to new life in store for us through Jesus. **Pick up your mat,** for you will no longer need it to lie on all day long. **Go home** and begin your new life.

12 The man is able to do as Jesus commands because of Jesus' command. **He rose, picked up his mat at once, and went away in the sight of everyone.** He was carried in on a **mat;** now he leaves carrying it—a sign of the complete change Jesus has made in his life, spiritually as well as physically. His healing happens **at once,** and it is manifest **in the sight of everyone.** The people in turn **were all astounded and glorified God.** Again, people are astonished by what Jesus does (see 1:22, 27); they now have a somewhat fuller realization that he is God's agent, and consequently they **glorified God** for working through Jesus. They say, **We have never seen anything like this,** yet at least some of them had to have witnessed Jesus' previous healings and exorcisms in Capernaum (1:32–34). What sets this particular healing apart from Jesus' previous healings has to be its link with Jesus' forgiving the man's sins: no one had ever claimed to forgive sins and backed up that claim with a demonstration of authority.

We might wonder whether the scribes were among the **all** who were astonished by what Jesus had done and praised God for it. Subsequent events will indicate that they probably did not join in the acclaim for Jesus, despite his clear demonstration of authority.

For reflection: Has Jesus made a dramatic difference in my life—as life-changing as being freed of paralysis? Do I praise God for what he has done for me through Jesus?

The Call of Levi and Sinners

¹³ Once again he went out along the sea. All the crowd came to him and he taught them. ¹⁴ As he passed by, he saw Levi, son of Alphaeus, sitting at the customs post. He said to him, "Follow me." And he got up and followed him. ¹⁵ While he was at table in his house, many tax collectors and sinners sat with Jesus and his disciples; for there were many who followed him. ¹⁶ Some scribes who were Pharisees saw that he was eating with sinners and tax collectors and said to his disciples, "Why does he eat with tax collectors and sinners?" ¹⁷ Jesus heard this and said to them [that], "Those who are well do not need a physician, but the sick do. I did not come to call the righteous but sinners."

Gospel parallels: Matt 9:9–13; Luke 5:27–32
NT: Matt 11:19; Luke 3:12–13; 7:34; 15:1–2; 19:7–8

13 **Once again he went out along the sea.** Jesus was walking along the shore of the Sea of Galilee when he called his first disciples (1:16–20), and he does so **once again.** This time he is not alone, for now people are constantly flocking to him (1:33, 45; 2:2): **all the crowd came to him.** Mark writes that **he taught them** without saying what Jesus taught; we can speculate that Jesus used the opportunity to announce the reign of God (1:15).

14 **As he passed by, he saw Levi, son of Alphaeus, sitting at the customs post.** A road ran along the shore of the Sea of Galilee past Capernaum, connecting the territory ruled on behalf of Rome by Herod Antipas and the territory ruled by his brother Philip. Customs were collected on goods passing between these territories, and because Capernaum was the nearest town to the border, it had a **customs post.** Since **Levi** was a **son of Alphaeus,** he would have been the brother of "James the son of Alphaeus" (3:18) if it was the same Alphaeus.

Jesus **saw Levi,** just as he had earlier focused his gaze upon Simon and Andrew and James and John (1:16, 19), and **he said to him, "Follow me,"** just as he had called the four fishermen. Levi responds as they responded: **he got up and followed him.** But Levi leaves more behind: self-employed fishermen could pick up their work again, but Levi is resigning from Herod Antipas's tax administration, which might not give him his job back.

This is the only mention of Levi by name in the Gospel of Mark; he is not listed as one of the twelve apostles (3:14–19). Mark seems to be telling us of the call to discipleship of someone who will not later be made an apostle. This account has an element of realism: Jesus called many to be his disciples, only twelve of whom he chose to be apostles. And it offers a lesson in the importance of discipleship. Jesus does not call all disciples into positions of authority, but he does call all to enter into an intimate relationship with him and to serve him. In the Gospel of Mark, Levi is "merely" a disciple personally chosen by Jesus—as are the rest of us who are "merely" his followers.

For reflection: If Jesus has called me to be "merely" one of his followers, how important do I consider this calling to be?

15 Levi might not be mentioned by name again, but he does not immediately disappear. Mark writes, with some ambiguity, that Jesus was at table **in his house**—but whose house is **his house**? Grammatically it could be either Jesus' house or Levi's house, but Levi's house makes more sense. Jesus does not have a house; he stays in Simon Peter's modest dwelling (1:29; 2:1). Further, the Greek for **at table** literally describes Jesus reclining, as was the custom at banquets, when guests would lie on one elbow on cushions set around a low table (the arrangement portrayed in John's account of the Last Supper: John 13:23–25). As a customs collector, Levi may have had sufficient income to host a banquet and to afford a house with a dining area. Jesus ate at Peter's house after Peter became his follower (1:29–31), and now he eats with Levi, along with **many** other guests.

Banquets: See page 142

It is not the number of guests that is striking, however, but who they are: **many tax collectors and sinners sat with Jesus and his disciples; for there were many who followed him.** The sense of **tax collectors and sinners** is tax collectors and *other* sinners, for tax collectors were viewed as habitually dishonest and corrupt. The label **sinners** indicates that those gathered are guilty of serious sins—such as fraud, adultery, extortion, prostitution, theft, and the like (see 7:21–22)—and not simply ritually unclean. There are **many** of these notorious sinners sitting with—literally, reclining with—Jesus at this meal. The next phrase is ambiguous: **for there were many who followed him.** Does this refer to the **disciples,** meaning that by now Jesus had called many to follow him? Or does it mean that many **tax collectors and sinners** had become disciples of Jesus? Scholars are divided over what Mark meant. Perhaps we can take his words as deliberately ambiguous, conveying that Jesus now had many followers, many of whom were known to be sinners.

This is the first explicit mention of Jesus' **disciples** and indicates that Jesus had already called more than the five Mark has listed by name. (Mark's account of Jesus' ministry is compressed and does not record all of Jesus' actions or words.) It is also evident that some of those who followed Jesus had lived seriously sinful lives. They were not run-of-the-mill, salt-of-the-earth people; they were known to be criminals and irreligious people. We can also note that such people were attracted to Jesus and wanted to follow him—which should tell us something about Jesus.

Disciple: See page 20

16 Jesus' choice of companions upsets some people. **Some scribes who were Pharisees saw that he was eating with sinners and tax collectors and said to his disciples, "Why does he eat with tax collectors and sinners?"** The **Pharisees** were a religious group or movement that

---

BACKGROUND: TAX COLLECTORS Those who collected taxes were almost universally scorned by Jews at the time of Jesus, and they were spoken of in the same breath with sinners (Luke 7:34). They were despised for several reasons. First, the tax system lent itself to abuse. One arrangement was to auction off the right to collect taxes to the highest bidder and then allow the tax collector to keep anything he could collect over that amount. It was a license for greed and extortion, and many tax collectors took advantage of it. Second, there were many forms of taxation, and together they extracted a sizable portion of the income of ordinary people—up to 40 percent, by some estimates. Third, Jewish tax collectors were agents, directly or indirectly, of Rome. After about a century of Jewish self-rule, Rome had taken away Jewish independence in 63 BC and had imposed tribute or taxes. As a result of these factors, tax collectors were considered unscrupulous extortionists who worked on behalf of a foreign power and drained people's livelihoods.

had developed traditions for following the law of Moses in everyday life. They were particularly concerned with ritual purity and Sabbath observance. Their name, **Pharisees,** may come from a word that means separated; they did try to separate themselves from unclean people and sinners. Some of them were trained as scholars and teachers—these were the **scribes who were Pharisees** (not all scribes were Pharisees, nor were all Pharisees scribes). These scribes are disturbed that Jesus is **eating** with sinners and tax collectors. Meals had greater social significance in the world of Jesus than in our world of drive-through fast-food establishments. Sharing a meal with someone expressed fellowship and intimacy; shared food meant shared lives. How could Jesus—or anyone who took God's laws seriously—enter into an intimate relationship with **sinners and tax collectors?** The scribes' concern goes beyond Jesus' becoming ritually unclean by sharing a meal with sinners. For the scribes, Jesus' open friendship with sinners signals tolerance of their sins and thus disregard for God's law.

Scribes: See page 40

Pharisees: See page 163

Scribes earlier were upset that Jesus claimed authority to forgive sins, but they kept their thoughts to themselves (2:6–7). This time they voice their objection, but not directly to Jesus: they **said to his disciples, "Why does he eat with tax collectors and sinners?"** It is more a rhetorical question expressing disapproval than a genuine question seeking an answer.

17 **Jesus heard** of their disapproval of his associating with sinners and gave them an answer, telling them, **Those who are well do not need a physician, but the sick do.** This may be a proverb or simply a commonsense observation. A physician who avoids all contact with sick people is not only useless but perversely so; the mission of a physician is to the sick. So too, Jesus says, **I did not come to call the righteous but sinners.** The accent in Jesus' words is not on the **righteous,** whatever degree of righteousness they might have, but on **sinners:** Jesus is a physician who can cure sinners of their sins, as he demonstrated when he forgave and healed the paralytic (2:3–12). Their sins will not contaminate him any more than leprosy did (1:40–41). Jesus has **come to call** sinners to new

lives as his followers and to bring them into the kingdom of God. No one, no matter how sinful, is beyond the scope of his call.

Jesus' meal in the home of Levi amounts to a physician making a house call. It prefigures the Eucharist as a feast for sinners and prefigures as well the eternal banquet of heaven.

For reflection: What does it mean for me that Jesus ate with sinners? What does it mean for me that Jesus is a physician? Where am I in need of healing?

Feasting and Fasting and New Wine

18 The disciples of John and of the Pharisees were accustomed to fast. People came to him and objected, "Why do the disciples of John and the disciples of the Pharisees fast, but your disciples do not fast?" 19 Jesus answered them, "Can the wedding guests fast while the bridegroom is with them? As long as they have the bridegroom with them they cannot fast. 20 But the days will come when the bridegroom is taken away from them, and then they will fast on that day. 21 No one sews a piece of unshrunken cloth on an old cloak. If he does, its fullness pulls away, the new from the old, and the tear gets worse. 22 Likewise, no one pours new wine into old wineskins. Otherwise, the wine will burst the skins, and both the wine and the skins are ruined. Rather, new wine is poured into fresh wineskins."

Gospel parallels: Matt 9:14–17; Luke 5:33–39

OT: Judith 8:1–6

NT: Matt 11:18–19; Luke 7:33–34; 18:12; John 2:1–10; Acts 13:2–3; 14:23

18 To prepare the reader for this scene, Mark provides some background: **The disciples of John and of the Pharisees were accustomed to fast.** The Mosaic law required only one day of fasting a year, on the Day of Atonement (Lev 16:29), but some Jews did additional fasting for various reasons. **The disciples of John** the Baptist presumably imitated his example of austerity (1:6) and fasted as a sign of repentance. **Pharisees** adopted fasting as a pious practice and abstained from food on Mondays and Thursdays (see Luke 18:12).

Mark provides no setting but simply writes that **people came to Jesus and objected, "Why do the disciples of John and the disciples of the Pharisees fast, but your disciples do not fast?"** Since **disciples** imitated their teachers and followed their teachings, Jesus' disciples' not fasting indicated that Jesus neither instructed them to fast nor fasted himself. This was a striking departure from popular expectations: those serious about their relationship with God were expected to fast. Jesus' failure to fast and to advocate fasting is so puzzling that some unidentified **people** come to him and ask him about it.

19 **Jesus answered them** with a rhetorical question: **Can the wedding guests fast while the bridegroom is with them?** Weddings were times for feasting, not fasting. They did not involve a marriage ceremony as such but simply entailed a banquet at the bridegroom's house to celebrate the couple's beginning to live together as husband and wife (the scene portrayed in John 2:1–10). Jesus then answers his own question: **As long as they have the bridegroom with them they cannot fast.** Yet what is the relevance of this to Jesus and his disciples? Is Jesus comparing

---

BACKGROUND: FASTING In both the Old and New Testaments, fasting means abstaining from all food for a period of time. In its origins, fasting may have been a sign of mourning: David fasted following the deaths of Saul, Jonathan, and Abner (2 Sam 1:12; 3:31–35), and Judith fasted after the death of her husband as part of her mourning (Judith 8:2–6). Fasting out of grief was not necessarily a religious practice but a mark that one was so deeply sorrowful that he or she had lost all appetite for food. It seems that fasting as an expression of sorrow evolved to include fasting as an expression of sorrow for sin (Joel 2:12–13). The Day of Atonement is the only annual fast day prescribed in the Old Testament (Lev 16:29). Fasts could also be called in times of national crisis, as part of prayers of supplication (Joel 1:14). Prophets such as Isaiah warned that fasting was no substitute for upright and merciful conduct (Isaiah 58). Eventually fasting became a pious act, done not only in times of sorrow or crisis but also simply as an act of devotion. The book of Tobit, written about two centuries before Christ, lists fasting, prayer, and almsgiving as three pious Jewish practices (Tobit 12:8). Different Jewish groups at the time of Jesus had their own traditions of fasting. The *Didache*, a Christian writing dating from about a century after Christ, speaks of Jews fasting on Mondays and Thursdays and advises Christians to fast instead on Wednesdays and Fridays.

---

himself to a **bridegroom**? Does **as long as** imply that there will come a time when the bridegroom will no longer be **with them**? We might imagine Jesus' listeners nodding their heads in agreement with what he has said but waiting for him to finish making his point.

20 Jesus' next words are, on the surface, curious: **But the days will come when the bridegroom is taken away from them, and then they will fast on that day.** Bridegrooms didn't get **taken away;** they remained at the house, and it was the guests who left. Nor was the end of a wedding banquet a cause for fasting. Jesus is no longer speaking of wedding customs but is trying to convey something deeper. He is indeed referring to himself when he speaks of a **bridegroom,** even though this was not a traditional title for the Messiah. He indicates that there will come a time when he will be **taken away,** a veiled reference to his being put to death—the first time this ominous note is sounded in his ministry. And **on that day** when he is taken away, his followers will fast out of profound grief, just as Judith fasted to mourn the death of her husband (Judith 8:6).

> The widowed Judith remained three years and four months at home. . . . She put sackcloth about her loins and wore widow's weeds. She fasted all the days of her widowhood, except sabbath eves and sabbaths, . . . feastdays and holidays of the house of Israel.
>
> Judith 8:4–6

Jesus' being with his followers is cause for celebration, and fasting is more out of place than it would be at a wedding feast: how could one mourn while with the Son of God? But Jesus' physical presence with his followers will come to an end, and then fasting will be appropriate. By the end of the second century, a tradition had developed of commemorating the death of Jesus by fasting from Good Friday afternoon until Easter morning, a period of roughly forty hours. Lent later developed as a fast of forty days.

For reflection: Do I fast? How do I fast? Why do I fast?

21 Jesus goes on to make several commonsense observations to explain why he is not teaching his followers to fast. Jesus first notes that **no one sews a piece of unshrunken cloth on an old cloak. If he does, its fullness pulls away, the new from the old, and the tear gets worse.** New cloth shrinks when it is washed; to sew an unshrunken piece of cloth onto an old, already shrunken garment will only make matters worse the next time the cloth is washed. Once more we can imagine Jesus' listeners nodding in agreement with what he has said but wondering what it has to do with fasting.

22 Jesus makes a second observation, this one having to do with expansion rather than shrinking: **Likewise, no one pours new wine into old wineskins. Otherwise, the wine will burst the skins, and both the wine and the skins are ruined.** Leather wineskins become brittle with age; new wine is still fermenting, and the resulting pressure will burst old skins. Again, we can imagine nods of agreement along with raised eyebrows: where is this leading?

Jesus provides but the briefest of punch lines: **Rather, new wine is poured into fresh wineskins,** which have the flexibility to expand. On one level, this is simple common sense. But just as with Jesus' speaking of himself as a bridegroom, there is a deeper meaning here. There is something radically new about Jesus and what he is doing. He is proclaiming "a new teaching with authority" (1:27). He is doing unheard-of things: touching a leper and healing him (1:41–42), forgiving a paralyzed man's sins (2:5–7)—and now, not fasting, as others expect him to. Jesus is a new wine that cannot be bottled up in an old wineskin; he is a new piece of cloth that cannot be sewn onto an old garment. Jesus is not showing disdain for the old: his examples safeguard the old cloak and old skins. But neither can the old set limits for the new. Even a revered custom like fasting must give way to Jesus.

Jesus' words have implications far beyond the question of fasting. Coming in the third of five scenes of conflict (2:1–3:6), they convey that what is central to these conflicts is the radical newness of Jesus and scope of his authority. Jesus is teaching and acting as if he has divine authority for what he does, and some find this quite upsetting.

For reflection: Has Jesus been new wine and a breath of fresh air for me? Has he liberated me from old habits, old self-imposed limitations, old ways of thinking?

The Sabbath and Jesus' Authority

23 As he was passing through a field of grain on the sabbath, his disciples began to make a path while picking the heads of grain. 24 At this the Pharisees said to him, "Look, why are they doing what is unlawful on the sabbath?" 25 He said to them, "Have you never read what David did when he was in need and he and his companions were hungry? 26 How he went into the house of God when Abiathar was high priest and ate the bread of offering that only the priests could lawfully eat, and shared it with his companions?" 27 Then he said to them, "The sabbath was made for man, not man for the sabbath. 28 That is why the Son of Man is lord even of the sabbath."

Gospel parallels: Matt 12:1–8; Luke 6:1–5
OT: Exod 20:8–11; 23:12; 34:21; Lev 19:9–10; 23:22; 24:5–9; Deut 5:12–15; 23:26; 1 Sam 21:2–7
NT: Mark 7:8–13

23 **As he was passing through a field of grain on the sabbath, his disciples began to make a path while picking the heads of grain.** Jesus and his disciples are going through a grain field, and his disciples are snacking on the run—plucking some ripe grain, rubbing off the husks, and eating it, which was not only allowed in the law of Moses (Deut 23:26) but also provided for (Lev 19:9–10; 23:22). Grain crops (principally wheat and barley) grew over the winter rainy season; the springtime Feast of Unleavened Bread (Passover) celebrated the beginning of the barley harvest (Lev 23:5–6), and fifty days later the Feast of Weeks (Pentecost) celebrated the wheat harvest (Exod 34:22). The disciples' eating ripened grain provides the only clue in Mark's Gospel to the duration of Jesus' public ministry: it lasted at least from one grain harvest until the beginning of the next, since Jesus will be crucified at Passover.

> *When you go through your neighbor's grainfield, you may pluck some of the ears with your hand, but do not put a sickle to your neighbor's grain.*
>
> Deut 23:26

24 **At this the Pharisees said to him, "Look, why are they doing what is unlawful on the sabbath?"** The law of Moses clearly forbade work on the **sabbath** (Exod 20:8–11; 23:12; 34:21; Deut 5:12–15). What is at issue here is how work is defined. The **Pharisees** consider the disciples' casual plucking of grain to be reaping and therefore **unlawful on the sabbath.**

25 Jesus makes a two-part response to the Pharisees, with the beginning of each part signaled by **he said to them.** He asks, **Have you never read what David did when he was in need and he and his companions were hungry?** The words **have you never read** mean "have you never read in the Scriptures"; the passage Jesus is referring to is 1 Sam 21:2–7.

> *David went to Ahimelech, the priest of Nob, who came trembling to meet him and asked, "Why are you alone?*

BACKGROUND: SABBATH The Sabbath is the seventh day of the week in the Israelite calendar, our Saturday. *Sabbath* comes from a Hebrew verb that means to stop or cease, indicating an essential note of the Sabbath: it was a day on which all work was to cease. The third of the Ten Commandments spells this out: "Remember to keep holy the sabbath day. Six days you may labor and do all your work, but the seventh day is the sabbath of the LORD, your God. No work may be done then either by you, or your son or daughter, or your male or female slave, or your beast, or by the alien who lives with you" (Exod 20:8–10). Eventually the Sabbath became a day for prayer and study of Scripture as well as a day of leisure. By the time of Jesus, complex interpretations had been developed of what constituted work forbidden on the Sabbath—for example, walking more than roughly one thousand yards (the "sabbath day's journey" of Acts 1:12). Different Jewish groups had different interpretations of what constituted forbidden work, with the Essenes and some Pharisees taking a very rigorous approach. Jesus rejected rigorous Sabbath regulations as burdensome and instead emphasized the original meaning of the Sabbath, as a day of rest that God had given to his people. *Related topics: Essenes (page 297), Pharisees (page 163).*

---

*Is there no one with you?" David answered the priest:
"The king gave me a commission and told me to let no
one know anything about the business on which he sent
me or the commission he gave me. For that reason I have
arranged a meeting place with my men. Now what have
you on hand? Give me five loaves, or whatever you
can find." But the priest replied to David, "I have no
ordinary bread on hand, only holy bread." . . . So the
priest gave him holy bread, for no other bread was on
hand except the showbread which had been removed
from the LORD's presence and replaced by fresh bread
when it was taken away.*

1 Sam 21:2–5, 7

26 **How he went into the house of God when Abiathar was high priest
and ate the bread of offering that only the priests could lawfully
eat, and shared it with his companions?** The **bread of offering** was
twelve loaves that were set out on the Sabbath on a table in the **house
of God** (at that time, a tent). On the following Sabbath, new loaves were
offered, and priests ate the old loaves (Lev 24:5–9). David, being of the
tribe of Judah, was not a priest (priests came from the tribe of Levi), but
nevertheless he took some **bread of offering** as food when he was fleeing in haste from Saul (1 Sam 21:2–7, 11).

While Jesus is clearly referring to the incident described in 1
Samuel, there are discrepancies between how the text of Samuel reads
and what Jesus says. Among them: in Samuel the priest is not Abiathar
but his father, Ahimelech; David doesn't enter the house of God to take
the loaves but is given them by Ahimelech; David speaks of having
companions, but no companions appear in this or the following scene;
David's hunger is not as explicit.

There have been various attempts to explain the discrepancies
between Jesus' words and what is found in Samuel. My suggestion is that
Jesus did not have perfect instant recall of all the Old Testament. Nor
did he carry a Bible around with him: the Scriptures at that point were
an unwieldy collection of handwritten scrolls. Jesus had read the book of
Samuel in the synagogue (or had heard it read) but had not committed it

to memory. He recalled David being **in need** and **hungry** and obtaining bread reserved for priests for his companions. Details like the name of the priest involved were unimportant.

I offer this interpretation as nothing more than a possibility. But if Jesus was like us in all things save sin, then I do not see why a perfect memory has to be attributed to him. Rather, just as we often recall events that we experienced or read about in light of their significance for us (and may be fuzzy about the details), so too may have Jesus.

The significance for Jesus of the incident with David lies in its being an instance where human need and hunger carried more weight than the prescription that reserved the bread of offering for priests. Jesus implicitly approves of what David did and cites it as an instance where human need took precedence over the written law. By comparison, Jesus' hungry disciples have done something far less grave: they have violated only an interpretation of the law that elevates their snacking into the forbidden labor of reaping.

For reflection: Am I willing to consider the possibility that Jesus might not have had perfect recall of the Scriptures?

27 Citing the example of David is not Jesus' complete response. He offers another consideration, proclaiming, **The sabbath was made for man, not man for the sabbath.** The Greek word translated **man** means not only males but also human beings in general. **Was made** implies was made *by* God: God instituted the Sabbath. Work was forbidden on the Sabbath in order to provide a day of rest each week (Exod 23:12). God created the Sabbath to make life easier, not more difficult. Sabbath prescriptions that turned the casual plucking of a few heads of grain into forbidden reaping not only were misguided but also undercut the very purpose of the Sabbath. Jesus will later condemn other interpretations of the law that go against its intent (7:8–13).

For six days you may do your work, but on the seventh day you must rest, that your ox and your ass may also have rest, and that the son of your maidservant and the alien may be refreshed.

Exod 23:12

For reflection: Do I observe Sunday as a day of rest and worship each week? What do I do to relax? What is the purpose of Sunday for me?

28 Jesus concludes, **That is why the Son of Man is lord even of the sabbath.** The **that is why** connects Jesus' concluding statement with his previous statement, specifically with his proclamation that the Sabbath was made by God. Jesus is God's agent, authorized to declare on behalf of God how the Sabbath is to be observed in light of God's purpose in creating it. **The Son of Man is lord even of the sabbath,** just as "the Son of Man has authority to forgive sins" (2:10). Jesus has authority **even** over something set down in the law of Moses, since he speaks for and acts on behalf of God.

Son of Man: See page 41

For reflection: What glimpses into Jesus' identity am I given by this incident?

CHAPTER 3

Withered Hand, Hardened Hearts

¹ Again he entered the synagogue. There was a man there who had a withered hand. ² They watched him closely to see if he would cure him on the sabbath so that they might accuse him. ³ He said to the man with the withered hand, "Come up here before us." ⁴ Then he said to them, "Is it lawful to do good on the sabbath rather than to do evil, to save life rather than to destroy it?" But they remained silent. ⁵ Looking around at them with anger and grieved at their hardness of heart, he said to the man, "Stretch out your hand." He stretched it out and his hand was restored. ⁶ The Pharisees went out and immediately took counsel with the Herodians against him to put him to death.

Gospel parallels: Matt 12:9–14; Luke 6:6–11
OT: 1 Macc 2:27–41

1 **Again he entered the synagogue:** presumably this is the synagogue of Capernaum (1:21), and it is perhaps on the same Sabbath that his disciples plucked grain (2:23–28). What follows again demonstrates that the Sabbath is made for man (2:27) and that Jesus is lord of the Sabbath (2:28). **There was a man there who had a withered**—paralyzed and atrophied—**hand.** Some scholars suggest that the Greek word for **withered** indicates the result of an injury rather than a birth defect. In any case, a crippled hand was a serious disability in a society where most men made their living through manual labor, such as in fishing and farming.

2 **They watched him closely to see if he would cure him:** Mark implies that **they** were those who had been critical of Jesus (see 2:24); Mark will shortly identify them as Pharisees (verse 6). They **watched** Jesus **closely,** as police might watch a suspect under surveillance, **to see if he would cure** the man with the withered hand **on the sabbath so that they might accuse him.** Those keeping an eye on Jesus took it for granted that he had the power to heal this man. They also apparently thought that the sight of infirmity would move Jesus to act. They viewed healing **on the sabbath** as a violation of the law, and they were hoping

that Jesus' compassion would result in another charge against him. Jews commonly accepted that preserving life took precedence over Sabbath regulations (1 Macc 2:41), but a withered hand was not a life-threatening condition that demanded immediate medical treatment.

3 Jesus is aware of their scrutiny and intentions, just as he was earlier aware of what lay in the hearts of others (2:8), and he brings matters to a head. **He said to the man with the withered hand, "Come up here before us."** Jesus asks the man to stand up and come into the middle of the synagogue. While seated in the congregation, the **man with the withered hand** would have been no more noticeable than anyone else; once he stood in the middle of the synagogue he would have been the center of attention. The man does not volunteer to be in the limelight or ask Jesus to heal him; he is simply in the right place at the right time.

For reflection: Have I had the experience of being in the right place at the right time for God's grace to strike?

BACKGROUND: SYNAGOGUE The original meaning of the Greek word *synagogue* was a gathering or an assembly, but it came to mean the place of assembly—the building that served as a Jewish community center and place of prayer and study. Synagogues may have originated during the Exile, when Jews were deprived of Temple worship. At the time of Jesus, synagogues, at least in the sense of assemblies, were common in Galilee, in Jerusalem, and wherever Jews resided outside of Palestine. Synagogues were used for Scripture reading and prayer; sacrifices were offered only in the Temple in Jerusalem. Synagogues were also used for religious education and community gatherings, which sometimes included communal meals. After the time of Jesus, synagogues became more exclusively used for religious activities and less as general-purpose community centers. Archaeologists have discovered the remains of a few first-century synagogues. Such a synagogue consisted of a large room with one or two tiers of benches around the walls. In the center was a raised platform with a lectern for Scripture reading and teaching. Anything done in such a synagogue—such as Jesus' healings and exorcisms—would have been visible to the whole congregation. Ruins of a third- or fourth-century synagogue built of limestone can be found in Capernaum today; beneath the ruins are what seem to be the remains of a first-century synagogue built of basalt blocks—apparently the synagogue in which Jesus taught and healed.

---

4 Then he said to them, "Is it lawful to do good on the sabbath rather than to do evil, to save life rather than to destroy it?" Jesus poses a double question to those who are waiting for him to violate their understanding of Sabbath law. On one level, the question could be answered easily: of course good rather than evil should be done on the Sabbath—as on any other day of the week. Of course life should be saved rather than destroyed on the Sabbath, or any other day. Jesus' question shifts attention from whether an act counts as work on the Sabbath to what an act accomplishes—to whether it has good or evil results, to whether it saves or destroys life. One can do good on the Sabbath without violating Sabbath rest (for example, by sharing one's Sabbath meal with someone who is hungry), and one can do evil as well (words of slander would not count as work). Those hoping to accuse Jesus are concerned about a speed limit, as it were: would Jesus go more than thirty miles an hour? Jesus' question is more fundamental: Where are you headed? What will your trip accomplish?

Is Jesus asking about *his own* doing good on the Sabbath rather than doing evil and saving life rather than destroying it, or about the actions of those who are lying in wait for him? Is Jesus' question pointed toward him and his actions, or is it pointed at those who want to bring an accusation against him? Is it probing whether they are intent on good or evil, on saving or destroying?

Those to whom Jesus addresses his question do not want to face its implications. They do not want to shift attention away from Sabbath law to more fundamental issues of good and evil. Nor do they want to give Jesus an opening to apply his question to their own intentions for that Sabbath. Hence **they remained silent.**

5 Their silence reveals their stance as clearly as if they had spoken. **Looking around at them with anger and grieved at their hardness of heart, he said to the man, "Stretch out your hand."** Jesus first looks his opponents in the eye: the words translated **looking around at them** convey a confrontation rather than a casual glance. Jesus gazes on them **with anger and grieved at their hardness of heart.** Jesus feels **anger** because of their perversity in trying to turn a healing into a crime, a good act into an evil act. At the same time, Jesus is **grieved at their hardness of heart.** He is saddened that men who are serious about trying to walk in God's ways (and the Pharisees were certainly that) have gotten so far off the path. He diagnoses them as suffering from **hardness of heart.** The heart was considered the seat of thinking, willing, and feeling; the heart was one's inner self. Being hard of heart meant closing oneself off from God (see Jer 7:24; 13:10; 16:12). Jesus feels both angry and grieved that these Pharisees are rejecting what God is doing through him. Perhaps some of Jesus' sadness and anger is over his failure to break through their hardness of heart. The Gospels give us few glimpses of Jesus' emotions; this glimpse reveals his reaction to those who have closed their hearts to him.

> For reflection: Is there anything in my heart that angers and grieves Jesus? Is my heart in any way withered and hardened?

In response to Jesus' command, the man with the withered hand **stretched it out and his hand was restored.** The man was previously incapable of opening or extending his hand, and his doing so manifests his healing, just as the paralyzed man's getting up from his mat manifested his healing (2:12). Not only is the man's hand restored, but so too is his life as an able-bodied man. Jesus has done good and saved life.

6 Nevertheless, **the Pharisees went out and immediately took counsel with the Herodians against him to put him to death.** The Pharisees act **immediately:** their minds are made up. They **took counsel,** acting deliberately, plotting on the Sabbath to do evil and destroy life. The Pharisees were a religious group and had no authority to have anyone executed. In Galilee, Herod Antipas had such authority, and he would

---

BACKGROUND: HERODIANS Little is known of the Herodians other than what their name probably implies: they were supporters of Herod, that is, of Herod Antipas, who ruled Galilee and an area east of the Jordan River during Jesus' public ministry. The Herodians likely included men whom Herod Antipas had entrusted with royal estates or who served as his officials and administrators or who were in other ways dependent on him for their wealth and position. Their interests would have lain in keeping Herod Antipas in power and friendly to them. Since Herod Antipas ruled on behalf of Rome, they also would have been loyal to Rome and would have favored payment of taxes. *Related topic: Herod Antipas (page 138).*

---

use it to behead John the Baptist (1:14; 6:17–29). The **Herodians** were supporters of Herod Antipas, and the Pharisees turn to them, hoping that they will use their influence with Herod Antipas to arrange Jesus' death. Their quest will not succeed, but Jesus will later be crucified by another partnership of religious and civil leaders—the chief priests in Jerusalem and Pilate.

Pharisees: See page 163

Herod Antipas: See page 138

Why were these Pharisees so set on wanting Jesus dead? Even if Jesus had violated their interpretation of Sabbath law, did that justify a death penalty? Their grievances against Jesus were probably cumulative and most likely included not only his eating with sinners (2:16) and failure to fast (2:18), but also his claims to have the authority to forgive sins (2:6–7, 10) and to be lord of the Sabbath (2:28). The Pharisees' problem with Jesus was not merely that he disagreed with their teachings: many Jews, including the Sadducees, did not accept their teachings, and Pharisees admittedly debated their teachings among themselves. Rather, their problem was that Jesus claimed a divine authority, which overrode their authority.

Jewish religious diversity at the time of Jesus: See page 164

Whatever the motives of those who sought Jesus' death, there was also an element of perverse evil at work in these men who considered themselves good. Because of their hardness of heart, these opponents of Jesus were blind to what God was doing in their midst. That they could be so misguided despite their commitment to obeying God's laws is a sober warning to any of us who may feel sure that we are following God's ways. Perhaps God is not as satisfied with us as we are with ourselves.

Mark has told us that he is bringing us good news (1:1), but now the shadow of the cross has fallen over his Gospel. Some wish Jesus dead even as he restores life. Mark proclaims good news, but that does not mean that Jesus—and his followers—will not experience opposition and failure.

For reflection: What is my reaction to this notice that some wanted Jesus dead? What does it mean for my following of him?

ORIENTATION: *Now that Jesus lives in the shadow of death, he will increasingly turn his attention to forming his followers so that they may carry on his work.*

The Compassion and Identity of Jesus

⁷ Jesus withdrew toward the sea with his disciples. A large number of people [followed] from Galilee and from Judea. ⁸ Hearing what he was doing, a large number of people came to him also from Jerusalem, from Idumea, from beyond the Jordan, and from the neighborhood of Tyre and Sidon. ⁹ He told his disciples to have a boat ready for him because of the crowd, so that they would not crush him. ¹⁰ He had cured many and, as a result, those who had diseases were pressing upon him to touch him. ¹¹ And whenever unclean spirits saw him they would fall down before him and shout, "You are the Son of God." ¹² He warned them sternly not to make him known.

7 Jesus may have been aware that some were plotting his death (3:6), for he **withdrew toward the sea with his disciples.** The word **withdrew** can convey getting out of harm's way, but it can also simply convey getting away for some quiet time, as Jesus has repeatedly done (1:35, 45). Since Jesus withdrew **with his disciples,** we might surmise that he wanted some time with them (see 3:13–18). He **withdrew toward the sea,** that is, he left Capernaum and walked along the shore of the Sea of Galilee.

Jesus' desire to get away has been frustrated before (1:35–37, 45), and it is frustrated once again: **a large number of people [followed] from Galilee and from Judea.** The New American Bible prints **followed** in brackets because this word is missing in some ancient manuscripts, but the picture is clear: a **large number of people** pursue Jesus along the seashore, coming from **Galilee** and **Judea.** This is the first mention of **Judea** in Mark's Gospel; Judea was the region around Jerusalem, which was about seventy-five miles south of Galilee. Since Mark has not described Jesus visiting Judea, he implies that Jesus' reputation had spread to Judea, motivating many to travel to Galilee to see him.

Galilee: See page 30

Judea: See page 248

8 These Galileans and Judeans are not the only people flocking to Jesus. **Hearing what he was doing, a large number of people came to him also from Jerusalem, from Idumea, from beyond the Jordan, and from the neighborhood of Tyre and Sidon.** They had heard of **what he was doing,** namely, healing the sick and casting out demons. As will be shortly evident, this **large number of people came to him** because they were in need of healing. They came not only from Galilee and Judea (verse 7) but from surrounding regions as well, indicating that word of Jesus' healings had spread far and wide. **Jerusalem** was in the heart of Judea; **Idumea** was the region south of Judea. The people of Idumea were Edomite by ancestry but had been forcibly converted to Judaism in 129 BC (Herod the Great was an Idumean). The regions **beyond** (east of) **the Jordan** River were ruled in the south by Herod Antipas, the ruler of Galilee, and in the north by his brother Philip, and they had a mixed Jewish and Gentile population. **Tyre** and **Sidon** were cities northwest of Galilee on the Mediterranean coast; they were Gentile cities with a Jewish minority. Mark leaves it unclear whether those who came to Jesus from Gentile areas were Jews or included Gentiles as well.

Jesus has become more famous than John the Baptist: John's following came from "the whole Judean countryside" (1:5), but Jesus is attracting people from many other areas as well. Mark emphasizes that a **large number** came to Jesus along the seashore (3:7, 8). Some Pharisees are plotting with the Herodians to put Jesus to death (3:6), but Jesus has great popularity among ordinary people.

9 Jesus' popularity is so great that he risks being mobbed, as will happen shortly. Jesus foresees this, and **he told his disciples to have a boat**

BACKGROUND: JEWISH POPULATION IN PALESTINE AT THE TIME OF JESUS There are no records of the Jewish population of Judea and Galilee at the time of Jesus. Most modern scholarly estimates range between six hundred thousand and one million, although a few put the figure higher. Along with the Jewish population, there were a few hundred thousand Gentiles, mainly concentrated in Gentile areas and larger cities, and a smaller number of Samaritans living in Samaria. The villages of Galilee where Jesus carried out most of his public ministry were exclusively Jewish, but Jesus also traveled into some of the predominantly Gentile areas that ringed Galilee.

ready for him because of the crowd, so that they would not crush him. There were fringe benefits to having fishermen as disciples: they had boats and knew how to handle them. Jesus asks them to have a **boat ready for him** as a safety measure, so he can escape from the **crush** of the crowds should it become necessary. The boat will also come in handy later, as a pulpit (4:1) and for transportation across the Sea of Galilee (4:35–36; 5:21; 6:32, 45, 53).

For reflection: What do I have that I can make available to Jesus?

10 The crowd does indeed press in on Jesus: **he had cured many** (an expression that does not mean that Jesus left some uncured) **and, as a result, those who had diseases were pressing upon him to touch him.** The expression **pressing upon him** means literally falling upon him; **those who had diseases** were pushing their way to Jesus through the crowd, touching and jostling him in order to be healed through physical contact. This will not be the last time that people will push their way to Jesus in the hope that touching him or his garment will bring them healing (5:27–31; 6:56). These people are desperate for healing—the Greek word Mark uses for **diseases** literally means scourges—and they have traveled great distances in order to be healed by Jesus. It is a chaotic scene. Jesus is pushed and buffeted yet endures it so that the sick may be healed. The boat sits available for Jesus' escape, but Jesus stands available for those shoving their way to him. And surely Jesus knows that the more people he heals, the more he will be mobbed: **he had cured many *and, as a result,* those who had diseases were**

BACKGROUND: IDUMEA The southern portion of Palestine was the land of the tribe of Judah and part of the kingdom of David and Solomon. After Babylon conquered Jerusalem in 587 BC, Jewish control of this area was lost. Edomites, whose traditional homeland, Edom, lay southeast of the Dead Sea, migrated westward under pressure from an Arab tribe known as the Nabateans. Displaced Edomites settled in the southern part of Palestine, and the region then became known as Idumea. The Maccabean Jewish ruler John Hyrcanus I conquered Idumea in 129 BC and forcibly converted the Idumeans to Judaism. Herod the Great's father was Idumean, and his mother was Nabatean, making his Jewish identity suspect in the eyes of many. At the time of Jesus' public ministry, Idumea was part of the area governed by Pontius Pilate.

---

pressing upon him to touch him (emphasis added). We are given a glimpse of the compassion of Jesus that will lead him to accept the cross, enduring pain for the sake of others.

> *For reflection: Am I willing to help others even at my own discomfort? Am I willing to help others even though my helping may lead to greater demands on me?*

11 **And whenever unclean spirits saw him they would fall down before him and shout, "You are the Son of God."** The presence of **unclean spirits** implies that some of the healings involved exorcisms. We can interpret Mark's description **they would fall down before him and shout** as meaning that the **unclean spirits** convulsed men and women before Jesus and shouted through them, **You are the Son of God.** (The scene is similar to an earlier expulsion of an unclean spirit: 1:23–26.)

Demons, unclean spirits: See page 105

12 **He warned them sternly not to make him known.** Jesus literally *rebuked* the unclean spirits, as he earlier rebuked an unclean spirit and

---

BACKGROUND: SON OF GOD The title son (or sons) of God carries a variety of meanings in the Old Testament. It is applied to angels and members of the heavenly court (Psalm 89:7; Job 1:6; 2:1; 38:7). It is used to refer to the people of God (Exod 4:22; Deut 14:1). A king could be referred to as a son of God (2 Sam 7:14; Psalm 2:7), as could a devout Israelite (Wisd 2:18). It is not, however, a title associated with the Messiah: no prophecy of a coming messiah refers to him as the son of God. When the title Son of God is applied to Jesus in the Gospels or in Paul's letters, it carries a different and far greater meaning than in the Old Testament, since it refers to Jesus' unique relationship with God as his Father. This is particularly developed in the Gospel of John. Paul focuses on what Jesus is able to do to bring us salvation because he is the Son of God (Rom 5:10; 8:3, 32; Gal 4:4–5; Col 1:13). In later centuries the Church reflected on what Jesus' Sonship meant in terms of his divinity. The Council of Nicaea in AD 325 proclaimed that the "Lord Jesus Christ, the Son of God" is "true God from true God, begotten not made, consubstantial with the Father"—"one in Being with the Father" in the English wording of the Nicene Creed. The Council of Chalcedon, held in AD 451, proclaimed that Jesus Christ is one person with two natures, a divine nature and a human nature, so he is both fully divine and fully human.

---

commanded silence (1:25). Jesus does not want these spirits **to make him known,** that is, to make his identity as the Son of God known. As before (1:34), the unclean spirits know who Jesus is, and for that very reason Jesus commands their silence. As readers of Mark's Gospel, we know that Jesus is indeed the Son of God (1:1, 11), but this is a title that those around Jesus are not yet able to understand correctly. They look upon Jesus as a marvelous healer and would interpret his being the Son of God in terms of his being able to heal. While Jesus is a healer, he is also far more than that, and his full identity will become apparent only on the cross.

The Creation and Mission of the Twelve

¹³ He went up the mountain and summoned those whom he wanted and they came to him. ¹⁴ He appointed twelve [whom he also named apostles] that they might be with him and he might send them forth to preach ¹⁵ and to have authority to drive out demons: ¹⁶ [he appointed the twelve:] Simon, whom he named Peter; ¹⁷ James, son of Zebedee, and John the brother of James, whom he named Boanerges, that is, sons of thunder; ¹⁸ Andrew, Philip, Bartholomew, Matthew, Thomas, James the son of Alphaeus; Thaddeus, Simon the Cananean, ¹⁹ and Judas Iscariot who betrayed him.

> Gospel parallels: Matt 10:1–4; Luke 6:12–16
> NT: Acts 1:13

13 Mark does not tell us how long Jesus healed those crowding to him (3:7–12) but picks up his account again when Jesus is able to get away with his disciples. **He went up the mountain and summoned those whom he wanted.** Jesus went up **the mountain;** this could have been any of the hills that surround the northern end of the Sea of Galilee. **The mountain** provided a refuge from the crowds but can also bring to mind Mount Sinai, where the twelve tribes of Israel were forged into the people of God (Exod 19–20). Jesus **summoned those whom he wanted:** the emphasis is on Jesus and on his choosing whom he wants and calling them to himself. Those whom Jesus summons respond to his call: **they came to him** on the mountain.

14 **He appointed twelve [whom he also named apostles]:** it is unclear whether Jesus summoned only twelve to come up the mountain to be with him and now makes them apostles, or whether Jesus summoned a larger number and now selects twelve of them for a special role. The latter is more likely: Mark's Gospel reads as if Jesus had a number of disciples in addition to the special group of twelve (see 2:14–15). Jesus **appointed** these **twelve.** He is doing something new but based on the old: **twelve** was the number of sons of Jacob and tribes of Israel. Ten of the tribes had disappeared in an Assyrian deportation seven centuries earlier, and there were long-held hopes that God would restore these tribes when he finally rescued his people (Ezek 37:15–22; Sirach 36:10–11). Jesus' appointing of **twelve** for a special role symbolizes his renewal and restoration of Israel. Jesus is forming a new people of God, not as a replacement for what God has been doing through Israel but as its fulfillment.

Not all ancient manuscripts of Mark's Gospel have the words **whom he also named apostles,** but Mark refers to them as apostles later (6:30). The Greek word for apostle means one sent out as an authorized agent or representative—for example, a messenger or an ambassador. Jesus selects twelve as his apostles, but they remain disciples: he chooses them so **that they might be with him and he might send them forth.** Being **with** Jesus, sharing in his life, is the heart of discipleship. It is only on the basis of their being with him that Jesus can **send them forth,** giving them a share in his mission. Jesus will not send them forth until later (6:7). For now, they need to **be with him**—to be with him constantly, learning from him and modeling their lives on his.

Apostle: See page 146

For reflection: How does Jesus call me to be with him? What do I need to do to respond to his invitation?

Jesus appoints the Twelve so that he can **send them forth to preach,** that is, to proclaim the good news that he has proclaimed. They are to announce that now is the time of fulfillment and the kingdom of God is at hand; they are to invite men and women to accept this good news (1:14–15).

15 Jesus will send them forth not only to proclaim God's reign but to bring men and women into God's reign, freeing them from the power of evil. The apostles will **have authority to drive out demons,** sharing in Jesus' own authority. What Jesus did in the synagogue of Capernaum—teach with authority and command evil spirits (1:21–27)—the Twelve will also do. They will be sent forth to carry on Jesus' work as his agents.

> *For reflection: What has Jesus sent me to do? What has Jesus equipped me to do? How am I able to be his agent?*

Along with the symbolic significance, there are practical reasons for Jesus to share his mission with the Twelve. Jesus' ministry has become too big for one person to handle, as was evident when the crowd mobbed him along the seashore (3:7–12). Jesus also has the future in mind: after he has been "taken away" (2:20), the good news will need to be proclaimed to "all nations" (13:10). Appointing the Twelve is the first step toward bringing the gospel "to the whole world" (14:9).

16 **[He appointed the twelve:] Simon, whom he named Peter:** not all manuscripts include the words in brackets. **Simon,** the first disciple Jesus called (1:16–18), is listed first among the Twelve. His name is a form of the name Simeon, who was one of the twelve sons of Jacob. Mark notes that Jesus **named** him **Peter.** Jesus spoke Aramaic, and he gave Simon the Aramaic name Kepha, meaning rock or stone (Paul calls him Cephas—1 Cor 15:5; Gal 1:18). Translated into Greek, Kepha became Petros, a form of the Greek word for rock or stone, and this in turn became Peter in English. Mark does not tell us why Jesus gave the name Peter to Simon. It can be taken as a nickname ("Rocky") or as a hint that Peter will be a foundation stone upon which Jesus will build.

17 We might have expected that Mark would list Andrew next, since he was called at the same time as Peter (1:16–18). But instead Mark lists **James, son of Zebedee, and John the brother of James:** these were the second pair Jesus invited to become disciples (1:19–20). Jesus calls James and John **Boanerges, that is, sons of thunder.** This has the

ring of a nickname and probably indicates that they had a stormy temperament (see 9:38). Simon, James, and John are listed first among the Twelve and are the only ones to whom Jesus gives new names. They will be Jesus' closest associates, and he will want them at his side in critical moments (5:37; 9:2; 14:33).

18 **Andrew** is now listed; on at least one occasion he will join the select group of Peter, James, and John (13:3). Andrew and **Philip** bear Greek rather than Hebrew or Aramaic names. **Bartholomew** is Aramaic for "son of Talmai" and indicates who his father is. Mark lists a **Matthew** among the Twelve but does not identify him with Levi the customs collector (2:14). **Thomas** is Aramaic for twin, but we are not told who his twin is. **James** is identified as **the son of Alphaeus** to avoid confusion with James the son of Zebedee; Levi is also a son of an Alphaeus (2:14) and is perhaps James's brother. **Thaddeus** seems to be an Aramaic name but is of uncertain meaning. **Simon** was a very popular Hebrew name at the time, and this second Simon is called **the Cananean** to avoid confusion with Simon Peter. **Cananean** does not mean from Cana, nor does it mean Canaanite. Rather, it comes from an Aramaic word meaning zeal and probably indicates that Simon was intensely zealous about obeying the law of Moses and in insisting that others obey it. A revolutionary party known as the Zealots did not form until the revolt against Roman rule some decades later, so the theory that Simon was a political rebel is unlikely.

19 Listed last is **Judas Iscariot who betrayed him.** The name **Judas** comes from the Hebrew name Judah, the name of one of the sons of Jacob. **Iscariot** is probably Hebrew for "man of Kerioth," indicating that he came from the village of Kerioth (Joshua 15:25), some thirty miles south of Jerusalem.

Of the twelve apostles, we have heard of only four earlier in Mark's Gospel, and Mark will not mention seven by name again. Three—Bartholomew, Thaddeus, and Simon the Cananean—do not appear anywhere in the New Testament save in listings of the Twelve. Being called to an important service by Jesus does not necessarily mean that one will receive a lot of publicity.

For reflection: Has Jesus chosen me to play a largely anonymous role in his service? Does this anonymity lessen the importance of what I am called to do?

The final words in the list of the twelve who are specially appointed by Jesus, **Judas Iscariot who betrayed him,** cast a pall on our reading of Mark's Gospel. There is a cancer in the midst of Jesus' select followers, and it will prove fatal to him. The good news that Mark proclaims includes Jesus' meeting with opposition and betrayal—and Mark's readers will also experience opposition and betrayal because they are disciples of Jesus.

ORIENTATION: *After referring to "Judas Iscariot who betrayed him" (3:19), Mark tells of Jesus being profoundly misunderstood. Verses 20 through 35 form a single block of material in Mark's account, although Bibles often break it up into smaller sections for ease of reading. As he does elsewhere, Mark sandwiches one incident inside another.*

Jesus Is Misunderstood

20 He came home. Again [the] crowd gathered, making it impossible for them even to eat. 21 When his relatives heard of this they set out to seize him, for they said, "He is out of his mind." 22 The scribes who had come from Jerusalem said, "He is possessed by Beelzebul," and "By the prince of demons he drives out demons."

23 Summoning them, he began to speak to them in parables, "How can Satan drive out Satan? 24 If a kingdom is divided against itself, that kingdom cannot stand. 25 And if a house is divided against itself, that house will not be able to stand. 26 And if Satan has risen up against himself and is divided, he cannot stand; that is the end of him. 27 But no one can enter a strong man's house to plunder his property unless he first ties up the strong man. Then he can plunder his house. 28 Amen, I say to you, all sins and all blasphemies that people utter will be forgiven

them. **²⁹ But whoever blasphemes against the holy Spirit will never have forgiveness, but is guilty of an everlasting sin." ³⁰ For they had said, "He has an unclean spirit."**

³¹ His mother and his brothers arrived. Standing outside they sent word to him and called him. ³² A crowd seated around him told him, "Your mother and your brothers [and your sisters] are outside asking for you." ³³ But he said to them in reply, "Who are my mother and [my] brothers?" ³⁴ And looking around at those seated in the circle he said, "Here are my mother and my brothers. ³⁵ [For] whoever does the will of God is my brother and sister and mother."

Gospel parallels: Matt 12:22–32, 46–50; Luke 8:19–21; 11:14–23
NT: Mark 6:3; 10:28–30; 13:12–13; John 7:3–7, 20; 8:48–52; 10:20

20 **He came home:** coming down from the mountain (3:13), Jesus returns to Peter's house in Capernaum, which Jesus has made his **home** (1:29; 2:1). **Again [the] crowd gathered** in and around Peter's house, as they had done on previous occasions (1:32–33; 2:1–2). Ever more people are coming to Jesus to be healed (2:13; 3:7–10), and this time the **crowd** is so large and insistent that they make **it impossible for them** (Jesus and his disciples) **even to eat.** Jesus called the Twelve to be with him (3:14), but being with Jesus means being mobbed as Jesus is mobbed, to the point of not being able to take a break for a meal.

For reflection: Have I found that being a disciple of Jesus means also sharing in his suffering?

21 **When his relatives heard of this they set out to seize him, for they said, "He is out of his mind."** Jesus' relatives **heard of this,** that is, they have heard of Jesus being mobbed by crowds of sick and demon-possessed people (3:7–12, 20). **They set out,** presumably from Jesus' hometown of Nazareth (1:9; 6:1–6), to make the roughly twenty-mile journey to Capernaum in order to **seize** Jesus, **for they said, "He is out of his mind."** The Greek word translated **seize** is the same word that will be used for Jesus' arrest (14:1, 44, 46, 49), but here it connotes

taking Jesus into protective custody out of concern for his physical and mental health. Jesus' relatives think he has to be protected from himself because he is **out of his mind.** They apparently do not view his healings and exorcisms as evidence that God is working through him but take them as a sign that he has become mentally unbalanced.

22 Mark shifts attention away from Jesus' relatives, who are on their way to Capernaum, to a group that has already arrived in Capernaum: some **scribes who had come from Jerusalem.** Word of what Jesus is saying and doing has reached Jerusalem (3:8), and these scribes have come to check Jesus out. They carry more authority than the Galilean Pharisees who opposed Jesus: in Jerusalem, **scribes** were religious scholars associated with the Sanhedrin and the Temple. While Jesus' relatives think him out of his mind, these scribes go a step further and say, **He is possessed by Beelzebul.** The two charges are not completely unrelated, since insanity was often attributed to demonic influence (see John 10:20). **Beelzebul** is another name for Satan. Jesus is charged with being **possessed** by the chief and most powerful evil spirit! The scribes lodge a further charge against Jesus: he is not only possessed by

---

BACKGROUND: SATAN In Hebrew, the word *satan* means adversary or accuser. Satan (literally "the satan," the accuser) appears in the book of Job as an angelic prosecuting attorney who puts humans to the test (Job 1:6–12; 2:1–7). In Job this accuser is a member of God's heavenly court, not an evil spirit opposed to God (see also Zech 3:1–2). In late Old Testament times, however, "Satan" began to be thought of as an evil spirit (see 1 Chron 21:1). Nonbiblical writings from shortly before the time of Jesus describe the fall of some angels, the chief of whom is variously called Mastema, Satan, and Belial or Beliar. In the New Testament, this evil spirit is likewise called a variety of names, including Satan, the devil, Beelzebul (Matt 12:24–27; Mark 3:22; Luke 11:15–19), and Beliar (2 Cor 6:15), and is portrayed as the chief of evil spirits and demons (Matt 12:24; Luke 11:15). While demons are inferior to God, they can influence or control individuals and events. The Gospels present Satan as the ruler of this world (Matt 4:8–9; Luke 4:5–6; John 12:31; 14:30; 16:11); the coming of God's kingdom abolishes the reign of Satan. *Related topics: Demons, unclean spirits (page 105), Nonbiblical writings (page 243).*

Satan but is also his agent: **By the prince of demons he drives out demons.** The many exorcisms Jesus has performed (1:21–27, 34, 39; 3:11) are explained as his casting out demons through the power that Satan, **the prince of demons,** has over subordinate evil spirits.

Scribes: See page 40

Demons, unclean spirits: See page 105

This view of Jesus as a demon-possessed tool of Satan is so contrary to everything that Mark has told us about Jesus that it may take our breath away. The one whom God proclaimed to be his beloved Son (1:11), the one whom even demons acknowledged as the "Holy One of God" (1:24) and Son of God (3:11) is condemned as an instrument of Satan. Mark provides no explanation for why scribes from Jerusalem arrived at this judgment. Many of Mark's first readers, however, had also experienced seemingly irrational rejection by others. Jesus will warn his followers, "You will be hated by all because of my name" (13:13). Those suffering rejection could find solace in knowing that they shared in the rejection experienced by Jesus.

For reflection: Have I been misunderstood or rejected because I am a Christian? How did I react?

23 Jesus responds to the charges made against him, beginning with the charge that he drives out demons by the power of Satan. **Summoning them, he began to speak to them in parables, "How can Satan drive out Satan?"** That is, how can Satan drive out evil spirits subject to his control? Why would Satan work against his own interests? To show the absurdity of this, Jesus offers several **parables.** This is the first mention of **parables** in Mark's Gospel. The Greek word for parable means setting beside, placing two things side by side for comparison. Jesus has already used comparisons to make a point (2:19–22), and he now compares Satan's reign to that of a king over a kingdom and a householder over a house.

Parables: See page 79

24 **If a kingdom is divided against itself, that kingdom cannot stand.** A civil war would devastate any kingdom or country; no king would ever

start a rebellion against his own rule. If Satan instigates a civil war in his realm, his realm is doomed.

25 **And if a house is divided against itself, that house will not be able to stand.** What is true on the level of nations is also true on the level of households. Conflict and division within a family shatters the family, and no head of a family would want this. If Satan stirs up a conflict with those he rules, he destroys his rule.

26 **And if Satan has risen up against himself and is divided, he cannot stand; that is the end of him.** If Satan is using Jesus to drive out demons (as the scribes charge), then Satan is working against himself. The more demons Jesus drives out, the more Satan's influence is diminished. Thus it is absurd to charge that Jesus is acting as a tool of Satan when Jesus overcomes demons subject to Satan.

27 How then are Jesus' exorcisms to be understood? Jesus makes another comparison: **But no one can enter a strong man's house to plunder his property unless he first ties up the strong man. Then he can plunder his house.** No one can rob a house that a man is guarding without first overpowering him. Jesus compares Satan to a **strong man** who has certain possessions, namely, those possessed by evil spirits. Satan may be strong, but Jesus is stronger: Jesus is the mightier one who was announced by John (1:7). Jesus **ties up the strong man:** the binding of Satan by one stronger was portrayed in a Jewish writing of the time and is reflected in the book of Revelation (Rev 20:2–3). Because Jesus overpowers and ties up Satan, Jesus is able to **plunder his house** and take his possessions: Jesus' exorcisms dispossess Satan of those he possesses. Rather than working on behalf of Satan (as the scribes charge), Jesus is overthrowing Satan's dominion and replacing it with the reign of God. The battle against Satan that began in the desert (1:12–13) continues in Jesus' binding of Satan and freeing of those whom Satan holds captive. How could anyone be so blind as to think that Jesus is on Satan's side?

For reflection: Have I experienced Jesus freeing me from the bondage of evil? Where am I still most in need of being set free?

28 Jesus has addressed the accusation that it is through the prince of demons that he drives out demons, and he now addresses the previous charge that he is possessed by Beelzebul (verse 22). He proclaims, **Amen, I say to you, all sins and all blasphemies that people utter will be forgiven them.** The Hebrew word **amen** means truly; when uttered at the end of a prayer it expresses one's agreement with the prayer (see 1 Chron 16:36). Jesus uses the word **amen** at the beginning of a statement to emphasize the importance of what he is about to say. **Amen, I say to you** means "You need to pay attention to this." **All sins and all blasphemies that people utter will be forgiven them** seems to admit no exceptions. **All sins** might be interpreted as all sins against fellow human beings, and **all blasphemies** might signify all sins against God; together they encompass all possible sins. The words **will be forgiven** mean will be forgiven *by God.* Jesus solemnly pronounces the all-inclusive scope of God's mercy and willingness to forgive: *all* sins are forgivable.

29 There is one exception: **But whoever blasphemes against the holy Spirit will never have forgiveness, but is guilty of an everlasting sin.** How can there be an exception in God's mercy? In actuality, God's mercy has no exceptions, but our accepting God's mercy is another matter. The words **blasphemes against the holy Spirit** mean defiantly denies the action of the Holy Spirit. This is a blasphemy, expressed not so much in words as by an attitude of hostility to God and his workings. It is a refusal to accept God's mercy. Those who refuse forgiveness **will never have forgiveness.** They are **guilty of an everlasting sin** if they erect a permanent barrier between themselves and God.

Some in their misery wonder, *Have I committed sins that God will not forgive? Am I guilty of blasphemy against the Holy Spirit?* The very fact that one is concerned with forgiveness is a sign that one is forgivable. Only those who refuse forgiveness will not receive it.

The Spirit: See page 12

For reflection: Am I willing to accept God's forgiveness and transformation in every area of my life?

30 **For they had said, "He has an unclean spirit."** The power of the Holy Spirit is at work in Jesus, but those who are closed to Jesus attribute this power to an **unclean spirit** (verse 22). They interpret Jesus' exorcisms as evidence that he is demonically possessed. Their interpretation qualifies as blasphemy against the Holy Spirit: a deliberate blindness to what God is doing through Jesus.

Note that Jesus does not directly accuse the scribes of committing a sin that cannot be forgiven. Jesus' words are rather a warning to his critics that they are entertaining hazardous thoughts.

31 Jesus' relatives had earlier set out for Capernaum to seize him (verse 21), and now **his mother and his brothers arrived.** This is the only time in the Gospel of Mark that Mary comes on the scene, and Mark does not name her but simply refers to her as **his mother.** Mark will provide Mary's name later, as well as the names of **his brothers** (6:3). No mention is made of Jesus' father. **Standing outside they sent word to him and called him:** Jesus' relatives are **outside** the house in which Jesus is teaching and healing, and the press of the crowd (verse 20) makes it difficult for them to enter. So **they sent word to him** that they had arrived **and called him** to come out to them, away from his mission. They intend to take him away, for they think that he is mentally unbalanced (verse 21). They do not recognize that what Jesus is doing is the work of God.

32 **A crowd seated around him told him, "Your mother and your brothers [and your sisters] are outside asking for you."** This **crowd** includes Jesus' disciples (verse 20) and others who are **seated around him** to listen to his teaching. Word is passed to Jesus that his **mother** and **brothers** (some manuscripts include **sisters** as well: see 6:3) are **outside asking for** him. This is the second mention of **outside** in two verses, and it highlights the contrast between Jesus' family, who are **standing outside** (verse 31), and those **seated around** Jesus inside the house.

33 Jesus does not obey his family's summons. Instead, he continues speaking with those seated around him: **but he said to them in reply, "Who**

are my mother and [my] brothers?" The obvious answer is those who are standing outside calling for him. In the society of the time, blood ties and family relationships were all-important. One's identity was bound up with one's kinship. Family obligations took precedence over individual achievement in a way that we, in our culture of individualism, might have a hard time fathoming.

34 Jesus answers his own question, but not with the expected answer. **And looking around at those seated in the circle he said, "Here are my mother and my brothers."** As previously (3:5), **looking around at** signifies gazing steadily and deliberately; here it is gazing affectionately. Jesus looks at those **seated in the circle:** the Greek text literally reads "seated in the circle around him," repeating the "around him" of verse 32 for emphasis. Jesus proclaims of those gathered around him, **Here are my mother and my brothers.** Jesus is creating a new family, a web of relationships centered on himself. Membership in his new family is based not on blood ties but on discipleship. Those who respond to Jesus' call, those who enter into a personal relationship with him—they are his new family circle.

BACKGROUND: BROTHERS AND SISTERS OF JESUS Brothers of Jesus are mentioned in the Gospels as well as in Acts 1:14, 1 Cor 9:5, and Gal 1:19. Four brothers are listed by name in Matt 13:55 and Mark 6:3: James, Joses (or Joseph), Simon, and Judas; unnamed sisters are mentioned in Matt 13:56 and Mark 6:3. While these references might be interpreted to mean that Mary and Joseph had children after Jesus' birth, other passages indicate a different Mary as the mother of James and Joses (Matt 27:56; Mark 15:40), and the Church from early times has held to the perpetual virginity of Mary. One explanation, circulated in the second-century writings *Protoevangelium of James* and *Infancy Gospel of Thomas,* is that the brothers and sisters of Jesus were children of Joseph from a previous marriage. St. Jerome (lived about AD 342 to 420) proposed that the brothers of Jesus were his cousins, since the Hebrew word for brother can also mean cousin. Jerome's explanation became widely but not universally accepted (Greek has a word for cousin, used in Col 4:10: "Mark the cousin of Barnabas"). The Gospels present the brothers of Jesus as having no faith in him during his public ministry (Mark 3:21, 31; John 7:3–7). Paul lists a James, who was not one of the twelve apostles, as among those whom Jesus appeared to after his resurrection (1 Cor 15:5–7). "Mary the mother of Jesus, and his brothers" awaited Pentecost in the upper room (Acts 1:13–14). "James the brother of the Lord" (Gal 1:19) emerged as the leader of the Christian community in Jerusalem (Acts 12:17; 15:13–21; 21:18; Gal 1:19; 2:9, 12).

Jesus' apparent rejection of his natural family for a new family might shock us, and it would have been even more shocking in first-century Jewish culture. It will not be the last time that Jesus will elevate discipleship above family ties (10:29–30). As important as family ties are, Jesus is calling men and women to something more.

For reflection: Has my following Jesus strengthened or weakened my bonds with my family?

35 Jesus restates his pronouncement but from a different angle: **[For] whoever does the will of God is my brother and sister and mother.** Doing **the will of God** is another definition of discipleship, for discipleship involves recognizing that Jesus is God's agent who makes known God's will. The accent falls on *doing* God's will, not merely knowing it. **Whoever does the will of God** is part of Jesus' new family, and this could certainly include Jesus' natural family, although Mark portrays them as misunderstanding Jesus at this point in his ministry. Being part of Jesus' new family makes his disciples brothers and sisters of one another.

For reflection: Is my bond with the Church as strong as my bond with my family?

Some of Mark's first readers had experienced rejection by their natural families when they became Christians, but they had found a new family in the Christian community (10:29–30). This scene probably had special meaning for them as they came to grips with being estranged from one family and welcomed into another.

COMMENT: MARK AND MARY If we had only Mark's Gospel, we would not have much basis for devotion to Mary. It is the other Gospels that present a fuller view of her and her role in God's plans. To properly appreciate Mary we must pay attention to all that Scripture tells us about her. On the other hand, to appreciate the message that Mark is trying to convey through his Gospel, we must pay attention to what he has written and not read into it what he didn't write. Mark presents Jesus as being misunderstood even by his relatives. (Mark is not alone in this: the Gospel of John states that Jesus' brothers did not believe in him—John 7:5.) That Jesus was misunderstood by relatives indicates that he was not a stick figure but a person of such depth and mystery that some who knew him for many years did not really know him.

CHAPTER 4

ORIENTATION: *Why does Jesus meet with misunderstanding and rejection? If the reign of God is at hand, why isn't its triumph more complete? Jesus addresses these concerns in parables about "the mystery of the kingdom of God" (4:11).*

The Parable of the Sower

¹ On another occasion he began to teach by the sea. A very large crowd gathered around him so that he got into a boat on the sea and sat down. And the whole crowd was beside the sea on land. ² And he taught them at length in parables, and in the course of his instruction he said to them, ³ "Hear this! A sower went out to sow. ⁴ And as he sowed, some seed fell on the path, and the birds came and ate it up. ⁵ Other seed fell on rocky ground where it had little soil. It sprang up at once because the soil was not deep. ⁶ And when the sun rose, it was scorched and it withered for lack of roots. ⁷ Some seed fell among thorns, and the thorns grew up and choked it and it produced no grain. ⁸ And some seed fell on rich soil and produced fruit. It came up and grew and yielded thirty, sixty, and a hundredfold." ⁹ He added, "Whoever has ears to hear ought to hear."

Gospel parallels: Matt 13:1–9; Luke 8:4–8
OT: Gen 26:12

1 **On another occasion he began to teach by the sea.** The Greek words that the New American Bible translates as **on another occasion** simply read "and again," alluding to Jesus' previous teaching by the sea (2:13) and connecting what Jesus teaches now with the misunderstanding and rejection he has just experienced (3:21–22). **A very large crowd,** like the crowd that had earlier mobbed him along the seashore (3:7–10), **gathered around him.** Jesus had asked his disciples to have a boat ready for him (3:9); now **he got into a boat on the sea and sat down. And the whole crowd was beside the sea on land.** The boat not only kept Jesus away from the press of the crowd but also served as a pulpit: sound carries well over water.

2 **And he taught them at length in parables.** Jesus has taught on previous occasions (1:21–22, 27; 2:13), presumably about the reign of God (1:14–15), but Mark has not spelled out this teaching. Now Mark presents Jesus teaching **at length** in what might be thought of as a "Sermon on the Sea," and Mark will provide a sample of its contents. Jesus characteristically taught by means of **parables**—memorable comparisons and stories that conveyed a message and invited reflection. **And in the course of his instruction he said to them:** this is the third time in two verses that the word *teach* (or *instruct*) occurs in some form, alerting us that what follows is to be read as a significant teaching of Jesus.

3 **Hear this! A sower went out to sow.** In the Greek, Jesus' opening words read literally "Hear! See!"—a double instruction that invites us not only to listen carefully to what Jesus says but also to picture in our minds the scene he describes.

For reflection: How carefully do I pay attention to Jesus' words?

BACKGROUND: PARABLES Jesus did not invent the idea of conveying a message by means of a parable (see 2 Sam 12:1–7 for an Old Testament example), but parables are his favorite manner of teaching in the Gospels of Matthew, Mark, and Luke. The Greek word for parable means setting beside, placing two things side by side for comparison. This Greek word corresponds to a Hebrew word that has a range of meanings, including proverb, riddle, metaphor, story, fable, and allegory. Jesus' parables range from pithy sayings ("No one pours new wine into old wineskins"—Mark 2:22) to miniature stories (the parable of the prodigal son—Luke 15:11–32). What is common in Jesus' parables is his use of examples from everyday life as comparisons that throw light on what God is doing through him or how one should respond to what God is doing. Jesus' parables are vivid but sometimes enigmatic. They are meant to be thought provoking, to stimulate the listener's reflection. Sometimes they confront the listener with a decision: Make up your mind—where do you stand? Some scholars have claimed that each parable makes only one point, but that is an artificial restriction. Some parables are like diamonds, revealing new facets of meaning when examined from different angles.

A sower went out to sow: to picture the scene, we need some knowledge of Galilean farming practices. Most farmers had to make do with fields that consisted of a thin covering of soil over a rock base. Plots were usually small, and every area that might support a crop was sown. At the beginning of the annual winter rainy season, grain seeds were scattered by hand and later plowed in.

4 **And as he sowed, some seed fell on the path:** paths edged or criss-crossed fields; some hand-cast seeds fell (or were blown) onto these paths. Before the seed could be plowed under, **the birds came and ate it up.** These seeds had no chance even to sprout.

5 **Other seed fell on rocky ground where it had little soil.** Since the rocky base under the soil was uneven, some soil was thin and some was deeper. A farmer could not tell at a glance how thick or thin the soil was and so cast seeds over his whole plot of land. The seeds that landed on thin soil **sprang up at once because the soil was not deep:** thin soil does not make seeds grow any faster, but in shallow soil seeds are near

---

BACKGROUND: FARMING Farmers made up most of the population of rural Galilee. Unlike American farmers, who tend to live in isolated houses on their farms, Galilean farmers lived together in small towns and villages and went out to work their fields. They grew grain crops, including wheat and barley; fruits, such as grapes, olives, and figs; and vegetables, such as lentils, beans, peas, and cucumbers. Galilee contained some prime farmland in its valleys, including the broad valleys north and south of Nazareth. Virtually all the prime land had been expropriated, and the ruler (Herod Antipas at the time of Jesus) either had it managed for him or entrusted it to his influential supporters. Some farmers worked as tenant farmers or day laborers on these estates. Most farmers owned their own plots of land, which were often small and were sometimes on a rocky hillside that had to be terraced to provide cropland. Farmers were subject to tithes and taxes on their crops, which by some estimates added up to 40 percent of their harvests. These farmers were better off than day laborers, but a few bad harvests could lead to indebtedness and loss of land. There was not much of a "middle class" in Galilee, and a wide gap separated the few wealthy people from the large number of ordinary farmers, craftsmen, and day laborers.

---

the surface after being plowed in and hence sprout through faster than seeds plowed into deeper soil.

6 **And when the sun rose, it was scorched and it withered for lack of roots.** Roots in thin soil have little room to grow and cannot sustain a mature plant. Nor can thin soil retain much water—as a result, plants wither in the sun. This second category of seeds were able to sprout, but the plants soon withered.

7 **Some seed fell among thorns, and the thorns grew up and choked it:** we should probably picture these seeds not landing in the middle of thorn plants but being sown on soil that contains thorn seeds. The grain seeds and the thorn seeds sprouted together, but the thorns choked the grain stalks, and they **produced no grain.** These grain plants almost made it to maturity but yielded no crop.

8 **And some seed fell on rich soil and produced fruit.** Despite all the obstacles facing farmers, they still were able to grow crops. While some seeds never produced a harvest, other seeds did: they **came up and grew**—sprang up through the soil and grew to maturity—**and yielded thirty, sixty, and a hundredfold** harvests. Jesus' first listeners would have been struck by these numbers: a thirtyfold harvest was very good, and a hundredfold harvest was quite extraordinary, just short of a miracle (see Gen 26:12). Any farmer would have been wowed.

9 **He added, "Whoever has ears to hear ought to hear."** Jesus prefaced this parable with the admonition "Hear!" (verse 3), and he repeats it at the end in even stronger terms: "If you have ears, use them!" Everyone **ought to hear** what Jesus has just said. But what has he said? He has told a story about farming, a story in which there was an abundant harvest despite obstacles and failures. Since this story is characterized as a parable (verse 2), it has another level of meaning; it is not simply a report that might appear in the *Farm Journal.* Jesus wants his listeners to **hear** and comprehend the true meaning of his words.

Jesus' ministry has had its failures as well as its successes. His preaching has fallen on some deaf ears and has borne no fruit. He has been accused of blasphemy (2:7); some want him dead (3:6), while others think he is out of his mind (3:21), demon possessed (3:22), and a tool of Satan (3:22). Yet at the same time, ever-increasing crowds are flocking to him (1:32–33; 2:2, 13; 3:7–10, 20; 4:1), a thirty-, sixty-, even hundred-fold response that prefigures the ultimate success of Jesus' mission. Just as the farmer harvested a bumper crop despite all the setbacks, so Jesus will reap a great harvest for the reign of God. We are given a glimpse of what Jesus will call "the mystery of the kingdom of God" (4:11), a mystery that encompasses failure as well as success, a mystery that will include the cross.

Jesus' listeners didn't expect God to establish his reign in a manner that involved failure as well as success. Some of them thought that God would raise up a general to lead a Jewish army to victory over Rome, reestablishing Jewish independence. Some thought that God would utterly transform their present world, eliminating all evil and death, creating a new heaven and a new earth (Isaiah 25:7–8; 65:17–25). All of the various expectations envisioned divine triumph. Yet most of Jesus' parable is devoted to failure, not triumph. There is an element of mystery in how God is acting through Jesus: why are his words and deeds not more successful?

Jewish expectations at the time of Jesus: See page 339

There is as well an element of mystery in how God acts in the world today. Why, after two thousand years, is his reign not more firmly established on earth? Why are there still wars and genocides? Why is good not more triumphant over evil? Why are Christians sometimes so un-Christlike?

For reflection: Do I question why God is not more in control today? What meaning does Jesus' parable have for me?

Jesus' parable indicates that there will be failure as well as success in his ministry and in the coming of the reign of God: that is a fact, like the fact that not all seeds sown by a farmer produce a harvest. But *why* is this so? Why is there failure? Mark introduces a parenthesis into the "Sermon on the Sea" in order to address these *whys*.

ORIENTATION: *Mark interrupts his account of the "Sermon on the Sea" to jump ahead to a time after the crowd has departed, leaving Jesus alone with his followers. In response to their questions about the meaning of his parables, Jesus explains his teachings.*

The Mystery of the Kingdom of God

¹⁰ And when he was alone, those present along with the Twelve questioned him about the parables. ¹¹ He answered them, "The mystery of the kingdom of God has been granted to you. But to those outside everything comes in parables, ¹² so that

> **'they may look and see but not perceive,**
> **and hear and listen but not understand,**
> **in order that they may not be converted and be**
> **forgiven.'"**

Gospel parallels: Matt 13:10–15; Luke 8:9–1
OT: Isaiah 6:9–10
NT: Matt 11:25–26; Luke 10:21; John 12:37–40

10 **And when he was alone, those present along with the Twelve questioned him about the parables.** The scene shifts to a time when Jesus is **alone** with **those present** (literally, those around him—see 3:32, 34) **along with the Twelve.** Jesus had told a number of **parables** during his "Sermon on the Sea" (Mark will recount more of them shortly), and his followers **questioned him about the parables.** The implication is that they were puzzled by his parables and wanted Jesus to explain them. It will not be the last time that they ask Jesus the meaning of one of his parables or cryptic sayings (7:17).

11 **He answered them, "The mystery of the kingdom of God has been granted to you."** The word **mystery** can have different nuances of meaning; one is the secret purpose of God (Paul will use the word *mystery* in the same sense: Rom 11:25; 16:25; see also 1 Cor 2:7). God's purpose or plan, which up until now has been veiled, is to establish **the kingdom of God** through Jesus. Knowledge of this **has been granted** to Jesus' disciples: they have been let in on the secret. Something that could not have been known

except through revelation—namely, that the reign of God has come in the person and work of Jesus—is now being made known by Jesus.

But to those outside everything comes in parables. Standing in contrast to those who are around Jesus (verse 10) are those who are on the **outside.** Jesus' ministry has resulted in a division between those who are quite literally with him and those who are against him (the crowds seem to fall somewhere in the middle). His opponents neither understand nor accept his teachings; for them **everything comes in parables.** Here the word **parables** means riddles: Jesus' teaching is an enigma to them. It is not that Jesus deliberately teaches in a manner that his listeners cannot understand: Jesus wants his parables to be understood (see 4:13, 33). But if his parables are puzzling to some of his followers, they are completely obscure to those who reject him.

12 Why do some utterly fail to understand Jesus' teachings? Jesus applies a prophecy of Isaiah to the situation. Jesus' teaching is a riddle **so that / "they may look and see but not perceive, / and hear and listen but not understand, / in order that they may not be converted and be forgiven."** These words are troubling: they can seem to say that God wants some people to misunderstand Jesus so that they will not accept his message and receive forgiveness. But that is difficult to reconcile with everything else Jesus teaches about God's willingness to forgive (for example, Jesus' pronouncement that all sins can be forgiven—3:28).

In pondering this apparent conflict, it is helpful to consider Isaiah's prophecy in its original context. Isaiah has seen a vision of God and responded to God's call to become a prophet. God warns Isaiah that his words will fall on deaf ears. In keeping with an Old Testament emphasis on the supreme sovereignty of God, this warning is expressed as if it is God's will that some reject Isaiah's message. No attempt is made in this prophecy to reconcile God's sovereignty with the Old Testament's teaching that men and women are able to choose between good and evil and are responsible for their choices (see, for example, Deut 30:19; Ezek 18).

Go and say to this people:

Listen carefully, but you shall not understand!
Look intently, but you shall know nothing!

> *You are to make the heart of this people sluggish,*
>   *to dull their ears and close their eyes;*
> *Else their eyes will see, their ears hear,*
>   *their heart understand,*
>   *and they will turn and be healed.*
>
> Isaiah 6:9–10

Jesus invokes Isaiah's prophecy without resolving the question of how human responsibility is reconciled with God's sovereignty. Jesus seems to make the point that just as the rejection of Isaiah's message fit into God's plans, so does some people's rejection of Jesus' teachings. This does not answer all questions. Why do some reject Jesus and his message—a rejection that will culminate in Jesus' being put to death? Even if God's plan is able to incorporate rejection, why does it happen? The early Church continued to wrestle with these thorny questions, sometimes invoking Isaiah's prophecy (see Acts 28:23–28).

For reflection: How do I understand Jesus' words about his teachings being misunderstood and rejected?

An Interpretation of the Parable of the Sower
¹³ Jesus said to them, "Do you not understand this parable? Then how will you understand any of the parables? ¹⁴ The sower sows the word. ¹⁵ These are the ones on the path where the word is sown. As soon as they hear, Satan comes at once and takes away the word sown in them. ¹⁶ And these are the ones sown on rocky ground who, when they hear the word, receive it at once with joy. ¹⁷ But they have no root; they last only for a time. Then when tribulation or persecution comes because of the word, they quickly fall away. ¹⁸ Those sown among thorns are another sort. They are the people who hear the word, ¹⁹ but worldly anxiety, the lure of riches, and the craving for other things intrude and choke the word, and it bears no fruit. ²⁰ But those sown on rich soil are the ones who hear the word and accept it and bear fruit thirty and sixty and a hundredfold."
Gospel parallels: Matt 13:18–23; Luke 8:11–15

13 The disciples have questioned Jesus about several parables (4:10), but Jesus' primary concern is that they understand the parable of the sower (4:3–9). Mark's Gospel presents this parable as the first teaching of Jesus; it is also the first of many times that Jesus' disciples fail to understand his teaching: **Jesus said to them, "Do you not understand this parable?"** Jesus thinks that they should have understood this parable, especially since the mystery of the kingdom of God is being revealed to them (4:11). If you do not understand the parable of the sower, he tells them, **then how will you understand any of the parables?** Jesus is not holding up the parable of the sower as a typical parable, implying that if they can't understand it, they can't understand parables in general. Rather, Jesus considers the parable of the sower the key to understanding parables: it is a parable about understanding parables and all of Jesus' teachings. Jesus goes on to give an interpretation of its meaning for his followers.

14 **The sower sows the word.** Jesus will assign a meaning to virtually every element in the parable of the sower, but he does not do so for **the sower.** All we are told is that the sower **sows the word,** but who is the **sower,** and what is the **word**? Is the sower God? Is the sower Jesus, who sows the word that the kingdom of God is at hand (1:15; 2:2; 4:33)? Is the sower any later Christian apostle who sows the word of the gospel (Acts 6:4; Col 1:5; 1 Thess 1:6)? By leaving the identity of **the sower** unspecified, Jesus allows his explanation of the parable to be applied to many different situations in which **the word** is preached, including Jesus' own teaching by means of parables.

15 Jesus focuses on the different types of soil on which the seeds fall in the parable of the sower, and he interprets these different soils as different responses to the word that is sown. First **are the ones on the path where the word is sown. As soon as they hear, Satan comes at once and takes away the word sown in them.** These listeners never give the word of God a hearing; it does not penetrate them. Consequently, **as soon as** they hear, Satan comes **at once** and snatches the word away, like a sparrow pecking seeds off a sidewalk. Jesus and Satan are contending for men and women, and Satan's binding is not yet complete (3:27).

Satan: See page 71

16 **And these are the ones sown on rocky ground who, when they hear the word, receive it at once with joy.** These listeners respond at **once** to the word that is proclaimed to them and welcome it **with joy.** They receive the good news of Jesus as good news indeed.

17 **But they have no root; they last only for a time. Then when tribu‑ lation or persecution comes because of the word, they quickly fall away.** Jesus presents this category of listener as having to endure **tribu‑ lation or persecution,** not merely the hardships of life that every human being faces. They are subject to these tribulations or persecutions **because of the word**—precisely because they are disciples of Jesus. Jesus will warn his followers that they will be persecuted on account of him (10:29–30; 13:9–13). Tragically, some of them will **quickly fall away** from their allegiance to Jesus when faced with trials and persecutions. The Greek translated **fall away** literally means to be tripped up by an obstacle. The joy with which the gospel message is received can be snuffed out by trials and persecutions unless the gospel becomes deeply rooted within us.

18 **Those sown among thorns are another sort. They are the people who hear the word** and respond to it—at least for a time.

19 **But worldly anxiety, the lure of riches, and the craving for other things intrude and choke the word, and it bears no fruit.** The phrase **worldly anxiety** literally means the cares of this world or age, in contrast to concerns about the age to come. We cannot escape the cares of this world as long as we are in it, but neither can we allow them to smother our following of Jesus and our concern for the next life. **The lure of riches** can likewise be fatal to discipleship, as Jesus will point out on a later occasion (10:23–25). So too can **craving for other things,** such as power and honor (10:42–44; 12:38–40). Some who hear and respond to the word end up choked by anxieties and cravings, and the word **bears no fruit** in their lives.

20 **But those sown on rich soil are the ones who hear the word and accept it and bear fruit thirty and sixty and a hundredfold.** In contrast to how he has spoken of the preceding types of ground, Jesus gives little explanation of the final category. By not saying more in his

interpretation of the parable about those who bear fruit, Jesus seemingly throws the spotlight more on failure than on success. This is sobering, and it foreshadows Jesus' meeting with more failure than success in sowing the word during his public ministry.

From another point of view, however, Jesus' interpretation of the parable is evenly balanced. There are basically only two categories of ground: that in which the word does not bear fruit, and that in which it does. This parallels the distinction between those outside the circle of Jesus and those on the inside (4:11). Each of these two types of ground is in turn divided into three categories. The unfruitful ground includes the pathway, the rocky soil, and the thorny soil. The fruitful ground includes that which yields a **thirty**fold harvest, that which yields **sixty,** and that which yields a **hundredfold.**

Implicit in these descriptions of types of soil are questions for Jesus' listeners: Which type of soil are you? If you are unfruitful, why are you unfruitful? Have you never given the word of God a hearing? Have you fallen away when the going got tough? Are your concerns as a disciple being choked by other concerns? And if you are fruitful, how much fruit are you bearing? Are you yielding a thirtyfold harvest when you are capable of a sixty- or hundredfold?

For reflection: What kind of ground am I? Am I hearing God's word and acting on what I hear? What harvest is my life bearing?

Some of Mark's first readers would have found particular meaning in Jesus' interpretation of the parable of the sower. These readers had tried to bring the gospel message to others, but their words had often fallen on deaf ears. Some of their fellow Christians had abandoned their faith to escape persecution, which was demoralizing to those who were struggling to remain faithful. Other Christians had succumbed to the lures of wealth and worldly success and had become lukewarm disciples at best. Jesus' explanation of the parable assured readers who were trying to spread the gospel message that God's kingdom would ultimately triumph in a rich harvest, despite all the setbacks they were experiencing.

If this parable is the key to understanding all of Jesus' teachings (verse 13), then the central point is that it is not enough to listen to Jesus' words. One must grasp their meaning and make an enduring response.

Jesus' first invitation to his listeners was "Repent, and believe in the gospel" (1:15)—align your thinking with what I am telling you, and change your behavior accordingly. Jesus' message can be grasped only through a change of mind and heart. True understanding of Jesus' words sprouts from acting upon them. The letter of James will make a similar point (James 1:22–25). It is those who *do* the will of God who form the new family of Jesus (3:35).

> For reflection: James writes, "Be doers of the word and not hearers only, deluding yourselves" (James 1:22). Am I a doer as well as a hearer?

The Parable of the Lamp

²¹ He said to them, "Is a lamp brought in to be placed under a bushel basket or under a bed, and not to be placed on a lampstand? ²² For there is nothing hidden except to be made visible; nothing is secret except to come to light. ²³ Anyone who has ears to hear ought to hear."

Gospel parallels: Matt 5:15; 10:26; Luke 8:16–17; 11:33; 12:2

21 **He said to them, "Is a lamp brought in to be placed under a bushel basket or under a bed, and not to be placed on a lampstand?"** Jesus continues to instruct his disciples in private, although with parables and sayings that he may have used many times in the course of his public ministry (every teacher has a favorite stock of examples). Jesus asks rhetorical questions whose answers are obvious: **Is a lamp brought in to be placed under a bushel basket or under a bed?** The kind of **lamp** used at the time of Jesus was a small fired-clay container that held olive oil; a cloth wick dipped in the oil burned with a candlelike flame. The **bushel basket** was a grain measure that held about two gallons. It would be pointless to light a lamp only to hide it under a basket. It would also be pointless to put a lamp **under a bed** (and dangerous as well: the bed might catch fire). Jesus asks, "Don't you bring in a lamp in order to place it **on a lampstand** so that it can illuminate the room?" The answer is obvious: yes.

What point does Jesus want to make by asking these obvious questions? What is he comparing with a lamp? One clue lies in the way the first question is phrased: the Greek literally reads "Does the lamp come in order that it may be put under the measure?" Oil lamps don't come on their own but are carried. This phrasing, with mention of the lamp's *coming,* subtly alludes to the coming of Jesus (see 1:7, 9, 14, 24, 38; 2:17) and to the coming of the kingdom of God (1:15). Jesus has come to reveal the coming of God's reign; Jesus illuminates what God is doing. Just as a lamp is meant to give light, so Jesus' parables are meant to enlighten.

22 **For there is nothing hidden except to be made visible; nothing is secret except to come to light.** Another translation might be "Nothing is hidden except in order to be made visible; nothing is secret except in order that it come to light." These paradoxical statements seem to contradict what Jesus has just said. What does it mean to hide something (like a lamp) *in order* to make it visible? How can you keep something a secret *in order* to bring it to to light?

These paradoxes apply to Jesus' ministry and the reign of God. Jesus has refused to let his identity be publicized up to this point (1:25, 44; 3:12). The very fact that Jesus calls God's reign a mystery (4:11) indicates that there is something hidden and elusive about it, and Jesus will shortly address this in a parable (4:26–29). Yet these elements of hiddenness are there for a purpose: somehow they are there "in order" for all that God wants revealed to ultimately be revealed. If the light of Jesus seems to be under a basket, it is only so that it can later be put on a lampstand. If the coming of God's kingdom is mysterious, that is part of its coming.

23 Yet why there should be these elements of hiddenness in Jesus' ministry and God's reign is still not clear; these are matters to be pondered. That is what Jesus invites his followers to do: **Anyone who has ears to hear ought to hear.** As before (4:3, 9), Jesus indicates that his words demand attentive listening and careful reflection.

> *For reflection: What elements of my faith are most mysterious for me? How carefully do I ponder them?*

The Measure of Understanding
²⁴ **He also told them, "Take care what you hear. The measure with which you measure will be measured out to you, and still more will**

be given to you. ²⁵ To the one who has, more will be given; from the one who has not, even what he has will be taken away."

Gospel parallels: Matt 7:2; 13:12; Luke 8:18
NT: Luke 6:38; 19:26

24 **He also told them, "Take care what you hear."** During his "Sermon on the Sea," Jesus twice exhorted his listeners to grasp what he was telling them (4:3, 9), and now during his private instructions to his followers he twice does the same (4:23, 24). **Take care what you hear** is literally "See what you hear," recalling earlier expressions (4:3, 12). Jesus has been telling parables, and he exhorts his followers to perceive their meaning. Take care, he tells them, that you do not hear my parables simply as stories about everyday matters like farming; take care that you understand their deeper significance.

The meaning of Jesus' next words depends on the context in which Jesus speaks them. In this context, **the measure with which you measure will be measured out to you** means the measure to which you ponder my words is the measure of what you will get out of them. If you give my words a superficial hearing, you will take away a superficial understanding. If you make an effort to hear and understand and respond to what I am saying, then you will profit accordingly. In fact, **still more will be given to you:** you will reap a harvest greater than your efforts have sown. The words **will be given to you** imply will be given to you *by* God. Those who pay careful attention to Jesus will be rewarded far beyond what their efforts deserve.

For reflection: How have I experienced God blessing me far more than I deserve?

25 Jesus adds another observation that likewise can have different meanings in different contexts. **To the one who has, more will be given; from the one who has not, even what he has will be taken away** could simply be an observation like "The rich get richer and the poor get poorer" or "It takes money to make money." In this context, the meaning is "It takes understanding to grow in understanding; ignorance breeds even greater ignorance." Hearing and doing the words of Jesus leads to deeper insight into their meaning, but what one gains from a casual listening is

soon forgotten. Take care then what you hear (verse 24), for hearing well leads to even better hearing, and hearing poorly leads to deafness.

This is the conclusion of Jesus' private instruction to his followers, an instruction that began with their questioning him about the meaning of his parables (4:10). In the course of this instruction Jesus has told them that he is revealing the mystery of the kingdom of God to them, but they will not begin to grasp it if they give his words a superficial hearing or if they are distracted by other concerns. They must listen carefully to Jesus' words and wrestle with their meaning, for his words deal with the mystery of God's reign being hiddenly established amid setbacks and failures. If they begin to grasp what Jesus is talking about, then they will be able to grow in understanding.

> For reflection: What does Jesus' exhortation "Take care what you hear" mean to me? What is my understanding of the mystery of the reign of God?

ORIENTATION: *Mark resumes his account of Jesus teaching from a boat in a "Sermon on the Sea." Jesus uses parables to teach the crowds about the mystery of the reign of God.*

Seed Grows of Itself

26 He said, "This is how it is with the kingdom of God; it is as if a man were to scatter seed on the land 27 and would sleep and rise night and day and the seed would sprout and grow, he knows not how. 28 Of its own accord the land yields fruit, first the blade, then the ear, then the full grain in the ear. 29 And when the grain is ripe, he wields the sickle at once, for the harvest has come."

OT: Joel 4:11–16

26 If we read this scene as coming directly after the telling of the parable of the sower (4:3–9), we can see a connection between that parable and this one. The parable of the sower threw light on the mystery of the kingdom of God, and Jesus follows it up with a similar parable. **He said, "This is how it is with the kingdom of God; it is as if a man were to scatter seed on the land."** The **kingdom of God** is a unique, complex

reality that defies simple description. Rather than try to define the kingdom of God, Jesus uses parables, or comparisons, to speak about different aspects of it. Here Jesus says that the kingdom, or reign, of God **is as if** a series of events happened, beginning with **a man** scattering **seed on the land.** The parable of the sower also began with seed being sown, and Jesus' next parable will be about a mustard seed (4:30–32). Jesus based his parables on the everyday experiences of his listeners, and we can presume that many in his audience were farmers.

Kingdom of God: See page 96

Farming: See page 80

27 After the seed had been sown, the farmer **would sleep and rise night and day and the seed would sprout and grow, he knows not how.** In Jesus' description of the farmer's normal life as a pattern of sleeping and rising, **night and day** reflects the Jewish view of days running from sunset to sunset. Jesus seems to say that once the farmer had sown the seed, he didn't have much to do except sleep well at night. We might imagine one of Jesus' listeners, a farmer with a weatherworn face, raising his hand and saying, "That might be how farming looks to a carpenter, but let me tell you, it's a lot of hard work day after day, clearing fields of rocks and plowing and weeding and a lot more." Jesus' response would be "To be sure! But the key thing is that once you plant the seed, it does the growing, and in a manner beyond your comprehension." The farmer knew **not how** the marvel of life and growth was in the seed. He couldn't make it grow. Nor did he need to make it grow.

28 **Of its own accord the land yields fruit, first the blade, then the ear, then the full grain in the ear.** The seed grew **of its own accord,** at first in a hidden manner beneath the earth, then breaking through and maturing. It may take some months for a seed to grow into a full seed-bearing plant, but it does, and **of its own accord.**

29 **And when the grain is ripe, he wields the sickle at once, for the harvest has come.** Jesus brings the farmer back on the scene to harvest the crop **when the grain is ripe.** Despite the farmer's presence, the seed still has the starring role. The seed grew of its own accord, and it was up to the seed-become-a-plant to determine the time of harvest.

Crops cannot be harvested until they are ripe, nor can they be coaxed into growing faster so that they may be harvested sooner. But **when the grain is ripe,** the harvest takes place **at once,** without delay.

If this comparison tells "how it is with the kingdom of God" (verse 26), then how is it? The parable's spotlight is on the seed, so Jesus is comparing the reign of God to a seed that has been planted, is growing, and will come to final harvest. At first the seed grows hiddenly, beneath the ground, and so too there is a hiddenness to God's reign during the public ministry of Jesus. The seed grows of its own accord, without the farmer really understanding how; so too the kingdom of God is coming through God's power and in a manner that we cannot fully comprehend. The seed does not instantaneously transform itself into a harvest-ready plant; its growth takes time, as does the coming of God's reign. But just as the seed will in its own time be ready for harvest, so too will God's reign be definitively established at an appointed time. The concluding words of the parable point toward this culmination, echoing Joel's prophecy of a final judgment (Joel 4:13).

> Let the nations bestir themselves and come up
>   to the Valley of Jehoshaphat;
> For there will I sit in judgment
>   upon all the neighboring nations.
>
> Apply the sickle,
>   for the harvest is ripe. . . .
> For near is the day of the LORD
>   in the valley of decision.
>
> Joel 4:12–14

In the context of Jesus' public ministry, the parable of the seed growing by itself indicates that the reign of God has been planted and is beginning to grow through the words and deeds of Jesus—but still in a largely hidden manner. There will be much about the coming of God's reign that Jesus' followers will not understand, but it will come despite their lack of understanding: an assured harvest lies ahead.

This parable would have encouraged Mark's first readers to continue their sowing of the word of the gospel, even if they were not seeing much in the way of results. The growth of God's reign on earth depends on God, and the timing of the final harvest is up to him. Even if they were perplexed by how God's reign was coming (or seeming not to come), they could be assured that it was coming and that the ultimate harvest lay ahead.

For reflection: What is the message of this parable for me? Am I confident that my prayer "Thy kingdom come" is being answered?

The Mustard Seed

30 He said, "To what shall we compare the kingdom of God, or what parable can we use for it? 31 It is like a mustard seed that, when it is sown in the ground, is the smallest of all the seeds on the earth. 32 But once it is sown, it springs up and becomes the largest of plants and puts forth large branches, so that the birds of the sky can dwell in its shade."

Gospel parallels: Matt 13:31–32; Luke 13:18–19

30 **He said, "To what shall we compare the kingdom of God, or what parable can we use for it?"** Jesus proclaimed, "This is the time of fulfillment. The kingdom of God is at hand" (1:15). Some probably responded, "It is? Where? I don't see it." Jews expected radical changes to occur when God established his active, direct rule. At a minimum it would mean the end of Roman domination. Some expected nothing less than an end to the present age, with all its evils, and the inauguration of a new age. Jesus' achievements didn't seem to amount to much compared with these expectations. He had a small group of followers, and a larger number came to him for his healing and teaching, but this was not making much of a dent in Roman domination or all the evils of the age. Jesus tells a parable that addresses people's doubts about the coming of God's kingdom. He says, **To what shall we compare the kingdom of God?** What is a good image for the reign of God? A general on a white stallion leading an army against the Romans? An angel coming down from heaven with a fiery sword, destroying all the wicked of the earth? **What parable can we use** for the coming of the reign of God so that you can recognize that it is happening?

95

31 The comparison Jesus makes is surprising. The kingdom of God **is like a mustard seed that, when it is sown in the ground, is the smallest of all the seeds on the earth.** In the world of Jesus, a mustard seed was thought of as the ultimate in tininess. Jesus' saying that God's reign could be compared to a mustard seed would have raised some eyebrows. Shouldn't God's reign be like something spectacular, perhaps a powerful lightning bolt or a mighty earthquake?

32 The comparison Jesus makes is not only with what a mustard seed is, but also with what it becomes: **But once it is sown, it springs up and becomes the largest of plants and puts forth large branches, so that the birds of the sky can dwell in its shade.** Mustard is an annual herb that usually grows to a height of two to six feet, and sometimes to eight feet or more. In Palestine at the time of Jesus, its seeds were crushed to make mustard oil, which was used as a flavoring. A mustard plant grows rapidly: **it springs up** and becomes so large **that the birds of the sky** can dwell in its shade. Some scholars hear an echo of a prophecy

---

BACKGROUND: KINGDOM OF GOD The central theme of Jesus' preaching was that God was establishing his kingly rule: "The kingdom of God is at hand" (Mark 1:15). When Jesus spoke of the kingdom of God, he invoked Old Testament images of God reigning as king (Psalm 97:1; Isaiah 52:7), and his listeners would have had some grasp of what he was talking about. Yet the expression *kingdom of God* never occurs in the Hebrew Scriptures and is rarely found in the New Testament except on the lips of Jesus. The coming of the kingdom of God meant the coming of God's final triumph over evil; it meant the coming of God's direct, manifest reign over everyone and everything. Jesus' listeners would not necessarily have understood this to mean the end of space and time, but they would at least have understood it as the end of the world as they knew it, the end of a world shot through with evil and suffering, a world in which God's people were in bondage to their sins and to foreign domination. The kingdom of God was the fulfillment of hopes engendered by Old Testament prophecies and by nonbiblical writings of the two centuries before Jesus. Because of the richness and diversity of these prophecies and writings, Jesus' listeners had no single blueprint in mind for what the reign of God would be like. Some expected God to free them from Roman rule; others expected God to accomplish a good deal more. Jesus used parables to convey what the reign of God was like. *Related topics: Jewish expectations at the time of Jesus (page 339), Messiah, Christ (page 204), Nonbiblical writings (page 243).*

of Ezekiel in which a majestic cedar tree that shelters birds is a symbol for God's people becoming a great nation and offering shelter for other peoples (Ezek 17:22–23).

The chief point of Jesus' comparison lies in the contrast between how tiny a mustard seed is and how large a bush it becomes. The first stirrings of the reign of God on earth are small, taking place among ordinary men and women in rural Galilee. No generals on horses, no angels with flaming swords—just Jesus walking from village to village, healing and teaching. But this humble beginning will develop into something far greater, just as the mustard seed becomes a sizable bush. Even if the ministry of Jesus does not seem to amount to much compared with the scope of evil in the world, it is the seed from which God's victory over evil and his rule over all peoples will grow.

Although this primary significance of the parable of the mustard seed is reassuring, the parable also has its disquieting elements. Mustard plants are large compared with mustard seeds but small compared with trees. Why didn't Jesus say, "The kingdom of God is like an acorn, from which a mighty oak grows"? Or, if Jesus had Ezekiel's prophecy in mind, "The kingdom of God is like a towering cedar of Lebanon, sprung forth from a seed but now sheltering flocks of birds"? There is humbleness in mustard, in its full growth as well as in its seed. Mark's first readers might have applied this to themselves. The mustard seed of Jesus' ministry, death, and resurrection had grown into the Church, but the Church was still pretty small potatoes compared with the population and power of the Roman Empire.

Some scholars suggest that first-century farmers viewed wild mustard as a noxious, fast-growing weed that choked out more useful plants (the need for wheat far exceeded the need for mustard oil). Birds may well have enjoyed its shade, but farmers would have rooted it out. Did those who followed Jesus find themselves viewed by others as a weed to be rooted out, rather than hailed as part of the coming of God's reign on earth?

A Roman view of Christians: See page 347

For reflection: What light does the parable of the mustard seed shine on Jesus? On the Church? What elements of it match up with my own experiences and hopes?

Jesus' Use of Parables

³³ With many such parables he spoke the word to them as they were able to understand it. ³⁴ Without parables he did not speak to them, but to his own disciples he explained everything in private.

Gospel parallels: Matt 13:34–35

33 **With many such parables he spoke the word to them:** Jesus' normal manner of teaching was through parables. Out of the **many** parables Jesus told, Mark has presented three seed parables in a "Sermon on the Sea" (4:3–8, 26–29, 30–32). Through parables like these, Jesus **spoke the word to them:** the **word** that Jesus preached was the message that the kingdom of God was at hand (1:14–15), and each of the three seed parables cast light on some aspect of the coming of God's reign. Jesus **spoke the word** to the crowds **as they were able to understand it** (literally, as they were able to hear it). The ability of Jesus' audience to understand his teachings depended on their willingness to embrace them.

34 **Without parables he did not speak to them, but to his own disciples he explained everything in private.** If Jesus taught the crowds exclusively through parables, then the implication is that the "mystery of the kingdom of God" (4:11) can only be spoken of through parables or comparisons. Jesus did not say what the reign of God was but what it was like. Understanding the meaning of Jesus' parables is not always easy: God's kingdom is a mystery, and parables about it may be enigmatic or have more than one interpretation. Parables demand pondering: what does it mean that the kingdom of God is like a mustard seed? Jesus' disciples asked him to explain the meaning of his parables (4:10), and **to his own disciples he explained everything in private** (4:11–25). For us, as for the first disciples, the key to understanding Jesus' teachings lies in having a personal relationship with him. We must ponder his words as words he speaks to us. Jesus' teachings are not abstract principles but invitations to enter into and remain within the reign of God. Only those who respond to Jesus' invitation will grasp his message (4:24–25).

For reflection: Do I prayerfully ponder Jesus' words as his words to me? What insight have I gained from pondering the seed parables Jesus told in his "Sermon on the Sea"?

ORIENTATION: *After the "Sermon on the Sea," Jesus continues his confronta-*
tion with the forces of evil and death. Who is this who wields
divine authority?

Jesus Calms a Storm at Sea

**35 On that day, as evening drew on, he said to them, "Let us cross to
the other side." 36 Leaving the crowd, they took him with them in
the boat just as he was. And other boats were with him. 37 A violent
squall came up and waves were breaking over the boat, so that it
was already filling up. 38 Jesus was in the stern, asleep on a cushion. They woke him and said to him, "Teacher, do you not care
that we are perishing?" 39 He woke up, rebuked the wind, and said
to the sea, "Quiet! Be still!" The wind ceased and there was great
calm. 40 Then he asked them, "Why are you terrified? Do you not
yet have faith?" 41 They were filled with great awe and said to one
another, "Who then is this whom even wind and sea obey?"**

Gospel parallels: Matt 8:23–27; Luke 8:22–25
OT: Psalms 4:9; 65:8; 69:2–3, 15–16; 89:10; 107:29; Jonah 1

35 **On that day, as evening drew on, he said to them, "Let us cross
to the other side."** Jesus preached his "Sermon on the Sea" from a boat
anchored just offshore of the northwest coast of the Sea of Galilee near
Capernaum. At the conclusion of his teaching he tells his disciples, **Let
us cross to the other side.** The **other side** of the Sea of Galilee was a
predominantly Gentile region (see 5:1, 20). Up until now Jesus has taught
and healed in Jewish areas, but now he takes the initiative to go to a
pagan, Gentile area. He brings his disciples with him: let **us** cross. Jesus
came to restore and renew Israel (symbolized by his choice of the Twelve
for a special role—3:14); by crossing the Sea of Galilee he extends his
ministry to Gentiles, and by bringing along his disciples he foreshadows
the early Church's mission to Gentiles.

36 **Leaving the crowd, they took him with them in the boat just as he
was.** The disciples took Jesus **just as he was,** indicating that they cast
off immediately, without Jesus first going onto the shore. **The crowd** that
has been listening to Jesus' teachings is left behind on the shore, but a
number of Jesus' disciples apparently accompanied him across the lake,

for **other boats were with him.** Mark will not mention these other boats again; his spotlight will be on the boat carrying Jesus.

37 **A violent squall came up and waves were breaking over the boat, so that it was already filling up.** Sudden storms are common on the Sea of Galilee because of the high hills and steep valleys that border it. This **violent** (literally, great) **squall** sends waves crashing over the bow of the commercial fishing boat, **filling** and swamping it.

Boat: See *Fishing*, page 19

38 **Jesus was in the stern, asleep on a cushion.** The front and stern sections of fishing boats of the time were often decked; a rudderman would sit on a cushion on the stern deck. Jesus uses such a **cushion** as a pillow and falls asleep in the stern of the boat. This incident is the only time that the Gospels describe Jesus being **asleep.** It is evening (verse 35), and Jesus has had a long day and is tired—fatigued enough to sleep in a boat being tossed about by a violent storm. Jesus' being able to sleep though a storm is also a sign of his complete trust in God's care for him in all circumstances, a trust Jesus professed when he prayed the psalms.

> In peace I shall both lie down and sleep,
> for you alone, LORD, make me secure.
>
> Psalm 4:9

Those in the boat with Jesus are anything but relaxed and trustful, however. Some of them have spent their lives fishing on the Sea of

---

BACKGROUND: SEA OF GALILEE Luke aptly calls the Sea of Galilee a lake (Luke 5:1; 8:22), for it is a freshwater body thirteen miles long and seven miles wide at most, with a maximum depth of two hundred feet. The Jordan River empties into the northern end of the lake and flows out from its southern end. In the time of Jesus the lake was ringed with fishing villages, and it is still commercially fished today. The Sea of Galilee lies seven hundred feet below sea level and is bordered by high hills that are cut by steep valleys. Strong winds can blow through these valleys and down onto the Sea of Galilee and stir up sudden storms. The Sea of Galilee is called the Sea of Chinnereth (or Kinneret) in the Old Testament, the Sea of Tiberias by John, and the Lake of Gennesaret by Luke.

Galilee and know well the dangers of its storms; they realize that the boat is sinking. **They woke him and said to him, "Teacher, do you not care that we are perishing?"** They address Jesus as **Teacher** (the first time he is called a teacher in Mark's Gospel): he taught at length that day. But shouldn't the disciples have perceived that Jesus was far more than a teacher? Their question, **Do you not care that we are perishing?** is a rather sharp reproach. The sense of it seems to be "How can you sleep at a time like this? Are you indifferent to our drowning?" The disciples' later reactions will indicate that they did not expect that Jesus could do much to save them (except maybe help bail); they were just irked that he was sleeping peacefully while they were scared witless.

For reflection: What does Jesus' sleeping through a storm tell me about him? What does his disciples' reproaching him tell me about their relationship with him?

39 He woke up, rebuked the wind, and said to the sea, "Quiet! Be still!" Jesus does not pray that God will calm the storm, nor does he even invoke God's name; Jesus commands the storm himself, rebuking it and ordering it to be quiet in the same way that he commanded demons (1:25). The chaos of the sea was a traditional image for evil forces (Psalm 69:2–3, 15–16), and control over such storms was a manifestation of God's power (Psalms 65:8; 89:10; 107:29). Jesus wields such power: **the wind ceased and there was great calm.** Choppy waves usually persist for a while after a wind dies down, but both the wind and the waves vanish at Jesus' word, and the great squall (verse 37) is instantly replaced by a **great calm.**

> You still the roaring of the seas,
> the roaring of their waves,
> the tumult of the peoples.
>
> Psalm 65:8

40 Then he asked them, "Why are you terrified? Do you not yet have faith?" Jesus realizes that it is quite normal to be terrified by the prospect of drowning in a violent storm at sea. He reproaches his followers for reacting normally when they should have recognized that they were no longer leading normal lives. They have been called by Jesus to take part in the establishment of God's reign, and Jesus is in the boat with them. Their despairing of surviving the storm treats Jesus' call of them as pointless: why would Jesus recruit them only to let them drown? Their fear is a sign of lack of faith in God's care for them (fear and faith are opposites: 5:36). Yet Jesus knows that a faith that overcomes normal human fears is not an easy achievement: his asking whether they do not **yet** have such faith implies that at some point they can.

41 **They were filled with great awe:** that the great storm suddenly became a great calm fills them with **great awe**—awe in the face of divine power at work in a manner that is beyond human comprehension. Only God has the power to make violent storms vanish—but Jesus has just done so. They **said to one another, "Who then is this whom even wind and sea obey?"** Who is this in the boat with us? Who is this to whom we have committed our lives? Who is this who sleeps so soundly and commands so mightily?

> *For reflection: Once again Mark's Gospel raises the question, Who is Jesus? What light does the incident of the storm at sea throw on Jesus' identity?*

From ancient times, the storm-tossed boat bearing the disciples and the sleeping Jesus has been used as an image of the Church. Storms and persecutions buffet the Church, to the point that its survival may seem in doubt. Jesus surely must be present with his Church, yet he sometimes seems to be asleep as the winds howl and the waves batter it. Mark's first readers would have been encouraged by his account of Jesus preserving his followers from the storm and would have taken it as a call to replace their fears with faith. Certainly, though, faith that Jesus can calm storms is easier when the winds are not blowing; faith is put to the test when the boat is swamping.

> *For reflection: What storms buffet the Church—or buffet me—today? What do my fears reveal about my faith?*

CHAPTER 5

ORIENTATION: *After rescuing his disciples from a tempest at sea, Jesus enters a Gentile region and rescues a man engulfed in a demonic tempest.*

The Healing of the Gerasene Demoniac

¹ They came to the other side of the sea, to the territory of the Gerasenes. ² When he got out of the boat, at once a man from the tombs who had an unclean spirit met him. ³ The man had been dwelling among the tombs, and no one could restrain him any longer, even with a chain. ⁴ In fact, he had frequently been bound with shackles and chains, but the chains had been pulled apart by him and the shackles smashed, and no one was strong enough to subdue him. ⁵ Night and day among the tombs and on the hillsides he was always crying out and bruising himself with stones. ⁶ Catching sight of Jesus from a distance, he ran up and prostrated himself before him, ⁷ crying out in a loud voice, "What have you to do with me, Jesus, Son of the Most High God? I adjure you by God, do not torment me!" ⁸ (He had been saying to him, "Unclean spirit, come out of the man!") ⁹ He asked him, "What is your name?" He replied, "Legion is my name. There are many of us." ¹⁰ And he pleaded earnestly with him not to drive them away from that territory.

¹¹ Now a large herd of swine was feeding there on the hillside. ¹² And they pleaded with him, "Send us into the swine. Let us enter them." ¹³ And he let them, and the unclean spirits came out and entered the swine. The herd of about two thousand rushed down a steep bank into the sea, where they were drowned. ¹⁴ The swineherds ran away and reported the incident in the town and throughout the countryside. And people came out to see what had happened. ¹⁵ As they approached Jesus, they caught sight of the man who had been possessed by Legion, sitting there clothed and in his right mind. And they were seized with fear. ¹⁶ Those who witnessed the incident explained to them what had happened to the possessed man and to the swine. ¹⁷ Then they began to beg

him to leave their district. **¹⁸ As he was getting into the boat, the man who had been possessed pleaded to remain with him. ¹⁹ But he would not permit him but told him instead, "Go home to your family and announce to them all that the Lord in his pity has done for you." ²⁰ Then the man went off and began to proclaim in the Decapolis what Jesus had done for him; and all were amazed.**

Gospel parallels: Matt 8:28–34; Luke 8:26–39
OT: Lev 11:1–8

1 **They came to the other side of the sea, to the territory of the Gerasenes.** It was evening when Jesus and his disciples set out from near Capernaum for **the other side** of the Sea of Galilee (4:35), but what happens when they land seems to take place during daylight. Even allowing for a storm at sea (4:37–39), crossing the Sea of Galilee would not have taken all night. Mark may be linking two separate events to imply that they have an underlying connection: a (demonic) storm at sea is followed by a demonic storm on land. (The chapter break between these incidents should be ignored. Mark wrote his Gospel with no chapter divisions; these were not added until centuries later.) We do not know where on the eastern shore of the lake Jesus and his disciples landed. The designation that Mark gives, **the territory of the Gerasenes,** indicates that Jesus entered the region of the Decapolis (see verse 20), a grouping of Gentile cities that included Gerasa. This is the first time in Mark's Gospel that Jesus has traveled into Gentile—pagan—territory.

Decapolis: See page 112

2 **When he got out of the boat, at once a man from the tombs who had an unclean spirit met him.** All indications point to this man being a Gentile, making this Jesus' first direct encounter with a Gentile in Mark's Gospel. This man comes to Jesus **at once,** as soon as Jesus gets out of the boat. This man lives in **tombs:** caves in hillsides were used as burial places and could be taken over by squatters desperate enough to dwell among the dead. For Jews, graves were ritually impure and a source of ritual impurity (see Matt 23:27), but this man is possessed by **an unclean spirit** and cannot get any uncleaner.

3 Mark pauses in his account of Jesus' encounter with the possessed man to spell out how thoroughly this man was in the grip of evil. **The man had been dwelling among the tombs, and no one could restrain him any longer, even with a chain.** He was an outcast from society, cut off from his family, living among the dead. He was also violent, and for his own protection as well as the protection of others he needed to be restrained. But restraints were useless: **no one could restrain him any longer,** not **even with a chain.** In modern idiom we might say "no way, no how" could he be tied.

4 Mark emphasizes the impossibility of controlling this possessed man despite many attempts to do so: **in fact, he had frequently been bound with shackles and chains.** The words translated **shackles and chains** indicate that the man had been bound hand and foot, **but the chains had been pulled apart by him and the shackles smashed.** This man was possessed by a superhuman power, and human restraints were useless. Hence **no one was strong enough to subdue him:** he was out of control and beyond help. **No one was strong enough** is a faint echo of Jesus' words about Satan ("No one can enter a strong man's house to plunder his property unless he first ties up the strong man"—3:27): the possessed man derived his great strength from the unclean spirit.

BACKGROUND: DEMONS, UNCLEAN SPIRITS The New Testament takes the existence of demons for granted but does not describe their origin and says little about their nature. The chief emphasis lies on their influence and effects on human beings. Both mental and physical illnesses (including epilepsy, blindness, deafness, muteness, and curvature of the spine) are sometimes ascribed to the influence of demons, and healing takes place through casting out the demon causing the illness. But not every illness is attributed to the influence of demons, and some healings are presented simply as healings. Likewise, some exorcisms are simply exorcisms, with no mention of any accompanying physical healing. Demons are also referred to as unclean spirits and evil spirits, and they are under the authority of Satan (also called Beelzebul). Jesus' casting out of demons was an assault on the kingdom of Satan and evidence that the kingdom of God was breaking into this world through the power of Jesus. *Related topic: Satan (page 71).*

When the man broke his bonds he experienced not freedom but rather greater slavery to the unclean spirit, which was freer to do with him as it wished. Similarly for us, casting off all restraints does not make us free but capricious; true freedom comes, paradoxically, from the bonds of commitments.

5 **Night and day among the tombs and on the hillsides he was always crying out and bruising himself with stones.** The expression **night and day** follows the Jewish reckoning of a day beginning at sundown, but days and nights had become an indistinguishable jumble for this man as he roamed around, **always crying out,** continually shrieking and howling in torment. It will shortly be evident that he went about naked, stripped of human dignity, reduced to living as an animal. He was self-destructive, **bruising himself with stones.** He had been created in the image of God, as is every human, but that image was now warped beyond recognition.

It would be hard to imagine a person being in more desperate straits.

For reflection: What are the most desperate straits I have been in? Is there anything in my life that distorts God's image in me?

6 Mark resumes his account of this man's encounter with Jesus. **Catching sight of Jesus from a distance, he ran up and prostrated himself before him.** This might seem straightforward on first reading, but the more we ponder it, the more puzzling it becomes. Jesus is making his first visit to the area—how does this man, in his demented state, recognize Jesus from a distance? Does this man run to Jesus of his own accord, or is he impelled by the unclean spirit? Is he running to Jesus to confront and combat him or to seek his help? Why does this out-of-control man prostrate himself before Jesus? There are no clear answers to these questions at this point in Mark's account. We are simply given an image: as Jesus gets out of the boat, a naked wild man runs to him and prostrates himself—like a lion furiously charging someone but stopping inches short and dropping to the ground.

7 The prostrate man is **crying out in a loud voice,** but it is the unclean spirit that speaks: **What have you to do with me, Jesus, Son of the**

Most High God? The expression **What have you to do with me?** means "Mind your own business" and was the expression used by the unclean spirit that Jesus expelled from the man in the Capernaum synagogue (1:24). If it is the unclean spirit that speaks, then presumably it was this spirit that impelled the man to run to Jesus. But why would the unclean spirit come to Jesus only to beg Jesus to leave it alone? Apparently the unclean spirit recognizes who has come to the region and the threat he poses: this is **Jesus, Son of the Most High God.** Once again an unclean spirit makes a true statement about who Jesus is (see 1:24; 3:11). This time it is a confession spoken through a Gentile; **the Most High God** was a name Gentiles used to refer to the God of Israel (Gen 14:18–20; Num 24:16; Acts 16:17).

The unclean spirit impels the man to come to Jesus because it recognizes Jesus as the one who is assaulting the forces of evil, and it prostrates the man before Jesus in acknowledgment of Jesus' superior power. It not only begs Jesus to leave it alone but also says, **I adjure you by God, do not torment me!** The unclean spirit's saying, **I adjure you by God** is deeply ironic. The expression was a formula used by Jewish exorcists; the unclean spirit tries to turn words of exorcism into protection against exorcism. Furthermore, it invokes God against the one it recognizes as the Son of God! Likewise ironic is the unclean spirit's begging Jesus, **Do not torment me** after it has done so much to torment the man it possesses. Evil twists everything to its own purposes.

8 Mark remarks parenthetically that Jesus **had been saying to him, "Unclean spirit, come out of the man!"** In Mark's account, after Jesus began his public ministry, his first deed among Jews was an exorcism in the synagogue of Capernaum, and now his first deed among Gentiles is also an exorcism. Jesus' mission is to overthrow the reign of Satan and replace it with the reign of God, beginning among Jews but extending to all peoples. Yet this unclean spirit did not depart immediately at Jesus' command, for Jesus **had been saying to him**—perhaps more than once—**Come out of the man!**

9 When the unclean spirit did not depart, Jesus **asked him, "What is your name?"** While knowing a person's name might put one in a position of power over the person (see Gen 32:29), Jesus never acts as

though he needs to know the names of evil spirits in order to cast them out, as can be seen in this very incident: the demon does not really tell him its name, and Jesus casts it out anyway. The spirit **replied, "Legion is my name. There are many of us."** A Roman **legion** was made up of three thousand to six thousand foot soldiers; the unclean spirit replies that there are a great many unclean spirits in this man. (Other Gospel passages also speak of possession by multiple demons: Matt 12:45; Luke 8:2; 11:26.) Jesus addressed his command, **Unclean spirit, come out of the man!** (verse 8), to a single spirit, but Jesus is faced with an army of evil spirits.

10 Despite their numbers, these unclean spirits recognize that Jesus is the more powerful and try to negotiate the terms of their surrender. **And he pleaded earnestly with him not to drive them away from that territory.** The unclean spirit pleads on behalf of itself and the legion of other unclean spirits in the man, asking that Jesus not **drive them away from that territory.** They have given up hope of remaining in the man but want to remain in the region. Demons were viewed as having to have a place of residence (see Matt 12:43–45; Luke 11:24–26), and these unclean spirits apparently felt at home in the pagan territory of the Gerasenes (verse 1), amid the tombs where the possessed man took shelter.

11 **Now a large herd of swine was feeding there on the hillside.** The presence of a **herd of swine** is another indication that Jesus has entered a Gentile area, for Jews were forbidden to eat—and presumably did not raise—pigs (Lev 11:1–8).

> *Their flesh you shall not eat, and their dead bodies you shall not touch; they are unclean for you.*
>
> Lev 11:8

12 **And they pleaded with him, "Send us into the swine. Let us enter them."** The unclean spirits beg to be sent into unclean animals. Their pleading acknowledges Jesus' authority to send them wherever he chooses.

13 Jesus does not command the spirits to enter the swine but simply gives them permission to do so: **and he let them, and the unclean spirits came out** of the man **and entered the swine.** Just as there were a large number of unclean spirits in the man, so there are a large number of pigs on hand to receive them—**about two thousand.** This was roughly ten times the number of pigs usually herded together, and the large number reflects the magnitude of the evil that Jesus is defeating. The **two thousand rushed down a steep bank into the sea, where they were drowned** (literally, where they were choked in the sea). Just as the presence of evil spirits in the man led to self-destructive behavior, their presence in the swine does as well. Jesus has allowed the unclean spirits to determine the course of their own destruction. We may wonder what became of the unclean spirits after the pigs drowned. Mark likely intends for us to understand that they were consigned to the depths of the sea, since he mentions the sea twice in this verse. The sea was considered an abode for evil: Jesus rebuked the storm at sea as if he was commanding a demon (4:39).

14 After seeing the two thousand swine rush into the sea and drown, **the swineherds ran away and reported the incident in the town and throughout the countryside.** We might have expected Mark to write "The swineherds reported the fate of the pigs to their owners, who came to Jesus demanding compensation for their financial loss." But Mark makes no mention of the pigs' owners, nor does he raise the question of whether Jesus did them financial harm by allowing the unclean spirits to destroy their livestock. This might be a legitimate question in our eyes, but it was not Mark's concern. Mark could not explore every facet of every incident in the confines of his Gospel. Mark mentions the swineherds only because they witnessed what happened, and it was natural for them to tell others **throughout the countryside** about it, with the result that **people came out to see what had happened.**

15 **As they approached Jesus, they caught sight of the man who had been possessed by Legion, sitting there clothed and in his right mind.** The one who had roamed about shrieking, the one whom no

chains could restrain, is now **sitting there** quietly by Jesus. He had gone about naked but now is **clothed.** (Mark doesn't explain where the clothes came from; that is not his concern either.) The man had been so demented that he had gashed and bruised himself with stones, but now he is **in his right mind.** Mark focuses on the contrast between the man before he was freed and after, and on Jesus as the one who changed him. Before, this man had been in an unbreakable grip of destructive evil; now Jesus has shattered the grip of evil and restored him to full human life.

For reflection: Has Jesus made a before-and-after difference in my life? Am I still in the grip of any evil whose hold I cannot break? Does Jesus' freeing of this man hold out any hope for me?

They caught sight of the man who had been possessed by Legion, sitting there clothed and in his right mind. Mark's Greek text literally reads that those who come to Jesus see the "possessed-by-demons" sitting clothed and of sound mind: they still look upon him as controlled by demons. Yet here is this possessed man, sitting calmly, clothed and rational. **And they were seized with fear,** the same fearful awe that the disciples felt when Jesus calmed the storm at sea (4:41), awe in the face of an incomprehensible power at work. A berserk man behaving normally—what is going on? Who is this who came ashore and in whose presence a possessed man is self-possessed?

16 Naturally they want an explanation. **Those who witnessed the incident explained to them what had happened to the possessed man and to the swine.** The swineherds give an account of what they saw: the possessed man ran to Jesus and prostrated himself and shrieked a bit, and the swine stampeded into the sea. With the man now evidently demon-free, it seems clear that the unclean spirits that controlled him had gotten control of the swine instead. But who could order demons around, particularly the powerful demons that possessed this man? Again they likely wonder, *Who is this who has come into our midst?*

17 **Then they began to beg him to leave their district.** Shouldn't they have been grateful that Jesus had freed the possessed man and begged Jesus to stay and heal others? Were they worried about losing more pigs?

Or did such concerns pale in light of the fear that gripped them (verse 15), the awe they experienced over the great power of Jesus? Were they unwilling to risk Jesus' upsetting the way things were? Did they fear that he might strike out at other evils in their midst, dispossessing them of that which they wanted to cling to? Did they fear Jesus as a force even more uncontrollable than the possessed man had been? Whatever the content of their fears, they beg Jesus to go away.

For reflection: Am I fearful of what Jesus might do with me if I get too close to him? Am I fearful of what might happen if I completely abandon myself into his hands?

18 **As he was getting into the boat, the man who had been possessed pleaded to remain with him.** Jesus is content to leave: his primary mission lies elsewhere. But in contrast to the people of the Gerasene region who do not want Jesus to remain with them, the restored man wants to **remain with** Jesus. That is the heart of discipleship: being with Jesus, accompanying him on his travels (1:17; 2:14; 3:14). The man **pleaded** to become a disciple of the one who had given him back his life.

For reflection: Have I asked Jesus to draw me closer to him? What has he done for me that would give him a claim on my life?

19 **But he would not permit him** to become a disciple who accompanied him on his travels. We might wonder why Jesus would turn away someone who wanted to remain with him. A possible reason is that disciples are not volunteers but are chosen and called by Jesus. There may be a better explanation: Jesus calls each person to the specific service she or he is best able to carry out. Jesus' primary mission during his public ministry was among Jews, and this Gentile was ill suited to help with that. He was suited, however, to do something else. Jesus **told him instead, "Go home to your family and announce to them all that the Lord in his pity has done for you."** This man who has lived in tombs as an outcast is now able to **go home** again, back **to his family,** literally "to his own," an expression that encompasses friends as well as relatives. Jesus tells him to **announce to them** what has happened to him, **all that the Lord in his pity** has done for him. The title **Lord** here means

the Lord God, who **in his pity** has freed him from his horrible state and restored him to normal life. God did so out of sheer mercy: this Gentile who had been swallowed up by evil spirits was hardly capable of earning God's favor.

Lord: See page 332

For reflection: How have I experienced God's sheer mercy? What am I able to say about it to others?

Jesus has not previously asked anyone he has healed to proclaim it publicly. Rather, Jesus told the man he healed of leprosy to be quiet about it (1:44), and he silenced demons who blurted out his identity (1:25; 3:11–12). Jesus' ministry until now has been among Jews, who might take him to be the wrong kind of messiah if they focus only on his deeds of power. There is less danger of this happening among Gentiles, who have no expectations that God will send someone to establish his reign on earth. Hence Jesus can tell the man he has freed of unclean spirits to go to "his own" fellow Gentiles and **announce to them all that the Lord in his pity has done for you.**

20 This the man does. **Then the man went off and began to proclaim in the Decapolis what Jesus had done for him.** The word here translated **proclaim** (or preach) is the same word used earlier for the mission of the Twelve, whom Jesus chose so that he could send them out to preach (3:14). Jesus sends this man out on mission, as he will send the Twelve. Jesus tells him to announce what the Lord has done for him, but he proclaims **what Jesus had done for him.** This Gentile probably had

BACKGROUND: DECAPOLIS The Greek word *decapolis* means ten cities, and it originally referred to a confederation of ten cities chiefly situated east of the Jordan River. At the time of Jesus the Decapolis was an administrative district attached to the Roman province of Syria. The cities of the Decapolis had a predominantly or entirely Gentile population, were Greek in their culture and religion, and were wealthy compared with the Jewish villages of Galilee. Archaeologists have uncovered colonnaded paved streets, theaters, temples, sports facilities, and other evidence of Greek lifestyle in cities of the Decapolis. *Related topic: Greek language and culture (page 179).*

little knowledge of God, but he knew firsthand what happened to him because of Jesus. Mark would have expected his readers to understand that God works through Jesus and that the title Lord can be applied to Jesus as well as to God (see 1:3). As a result of the man telling what has happened to him, **all were amazed**—astonished, filled with wonder. The man plays a role similar to that of John the Baptist, preparing the way for Jesus among Gentiles, as John did among Jews. Jesus will return to this Gentile area, and after his death the Church will proclaim the gospel to Gentiles. The man who had been freed from his demonic state was equipped as no one else was to tell others what Jesus had done for him, and this is what Jesus asked of him.

For reflection: In light of my life experience or abilities, what am I best equipped to do? What is the highest service I can offer Jesus?

ORIENTATION: *After rescuing his disciples from drowning and freeing a man from a life among tombs, Jesus saves two women from the power of death. Mark's account is a three-scene drama.*

Scene One: A Deeply Concerned Father

²¹ When Jesus had crossed again [in the boat] to the other side, a large crowd gathered around him, and he stayed close to the sea. ²² One of the synagogue officials, named Jairus, came forward. Seeing him he fell at his feet ²³ and pleaded earnestly with him, saying, "My daughter is at the point of death. Please, come lay your hands on her that she may get well and live." ²⁴ He went off with him, and a large crowd followed him and pressed upon him.

Gospel parallels: Matt 9:18–19; Luke 8:40–42

21 **When Jesus had crossed again [in the boat] to the other side, a large crowd gathered around him, and he stayed close to the sea.** Jesus crosses by boat back to the western shore of the Sea of Galilee, possibly returning to the region of Capernaum. A crowd on the eastern shore rejected him, begging him to leave (5:17), but he is warmly welcomed by a **large crowd** upon his return to Galilee. They **gathered around him**

on the seashore, as they had done before (3:7–10; 4:1), mobbing him with their needs. Wherever Jesus goes, he is the center of attention.

22 **One of the synagogue officials, named Jairus, came forward.** A **synagogue official** was a layman who had been elected to supervise the synagogue building and the activities that took place within it. A synagogue usually had one supervising official but could have more (see Acts 13:15). Jesus received a hostile response from religious leaders in another synagogue (3:1–6), but at least one synagogue official turns to Jesus in his need. He is **named Jairus,** and he **came forward,** pushing through the crowd around Jesus. **Seeing him he fell at his feet,** a posture of supplication. Jairus does not discretely seek out Jesus at night, in private, but does so in the full view of others. Heedless of his dignity as a synagogue official, he prostrates himself before Jesus.

Synagogue: See page 57

23 Jairus **pleaded earnestly with him, saying, "My daughter is at the point of death."** Jairus has little concern for himself because he is more concerned for someone else: his **daughter.** He literally calls her "my little daughter," but she is twelve years old (5:42) and practically an adult in the culture of the time; "my little daughter" is a term of affection. She is ill and **at the point of death,** and because of his love for her, he **pleaded earnestly** with Jesus: **Please, come lay your hands on her that she may get well and live.** A second reason for Jairus being heedless of himself is his faith that Jesus can heal his daughter.

> *For reflection: Do I love anyone so much that I am willing to forsake everything for that person? Do I intercede for those I love, asking Jesus to touch them and make them well?*

Jairus asks Jesus to **lay your hands on her.** There is no mention in the Hebrew Scriptures of healing through the laying on of hands, but this practice is mentioned in one of the Dead Sea Scrolls, religious writings from the time of Jesus. Jesus sometimes lays his hands on those he healed (6:5; 7:32–35; 8:23–25), and the early Church will continue the practice (Acts 9:12, 17; 28:8). Jairus is confident that if Jesus does lay his hands on his daughter, she will **get well and live.** The Greek word translated **get well** literally means be saved from death or be kept alive and can broadly refer to any rescue from danger and distress. In Mark's Gospel, this word is sometimes used for physical healing (its meaning on Jairus's lips), but it is also used for a more fundamental rescue from everlasting death (8:35; 10:26; 13:13). Jairus wants his daughter to **live,** and this word likewise has a richness of meaning. Jairus is asking Jesus to heal his daughter of her sickness so that she might continue on with her life, but Mark's first readers would have perceived a greater significance in his words: through Jesus we are saved and live—given salvation and eternal life.

Dead Sea Scrolls: See page 245

24 Jesus responds to Jairus's request: **he went off with him, and a large crowd followed him and pressed upon him.** We can imagine Jairus trying to clear a way through the crowd for Jesus, anxious for Jesus to reach his daughter as quickly as possible, since she is at the point of death. **A large crowd followed** them **and pressed upon** Jesus, as had happened before (3:7–10, 20). Jairus is not the only one seeking a healing from Jesus.

Scene Two: A Woman of Courageous Faith

²⁵ There was a woman afflicted with hemorrhages for twelve years. ²⁶ She had suffered greatly at the hands of many doctors and had spent all that she had. Yet she was not helped but only grew worse. ²⁷ She had heard about Jesus and came up behind him in the crowd and touched his cloak. ²⁸ She said, "If I but touch his clothes, I shall be cured." ²⁹ Immediately her flow of blood dried up. She felt in her body that she was healed of her affliction. ³⁰ Jesus, aware at once that power had gone out from him, turned around in the crowd and asked, "Who has touched my clothes?" ³¹ But his disciples said to him, "You see how the crowd is pressing upon you, and yet you ask, 'Who touched me?'" ³² And he looked around to see who had done it. ³³ The woman, realizing what had happened to her, approached in fear and trembling. She fell down before Jesus and

told him the whole truth. **³⁴ He said to her, "Daughter, your faith has saved you. Go in peace and be cured of your affliction."**
    Gospel parallels: Matt 9:20–22; Luke 8:43–48
    OT: Lev 15:19–30; 17:11–14; 20:18; Deut 12:23

25 Jesus and Jairus are making their way to Jairus's house, accompanied by a large crowd that is pressing upon Jesus (5:24). In this crowd **there was a woman afflicted with hemorrhages for twelve years.** Strictly speaking, she should not have been there, bumping into other people. She suffered from chronic vaginal bleeding, which made her perpetually unclean according to the law of Moses (Lev 15:25), and anyone who came into physical contact with her would be made unclean as well (Lev 15:19). She could not sit on a cushion or lie on a bed without making them unclean and a source of uncleanness for others (Lev 15:26–27); if she was married, she and her husband were forbidden to have sexual intercourse (Lev 20:18). She could not enter the Temple precincts to worship, nor would those who wished to maintain ritual purity have welcomed her presence in a synagogue. Her continual loss of blood may have left her anemic. And this had been going on for twelve years!
    Clean and unclean: See page 173

In the biology of the Old Testament, "the life of a living body is in its blood," and blood is "the seat of life" (Lev 17:11). Or, more simply, "blood is life" (Deut 12:23). This woman's life had been draining away for twelve years.

For reflection: Is anything draining away my life? Is anything cutting me off from others?

26 Naturally she had done everything she could to rid herself of her affliction, going to one doctor after another. Ancient medicine had no cure for her condition; the remedies were sometimes bizarre and painful. This woman **had suffered greatly at the hands of many doctors:** their treatments had been not merely futile but also extremely unpleasant. A person needed financial resources to pay doctors' fees (the poor could not afford much medical care), but whatever savings this woman once had were gone, for she **had spent all that she had** on doctors.

Despite enduring painful treatments and impoverishing herself, **she was not helped but only grew worse.** Just as the Gerasene demoniac was beyond human help (5:1–5), so too is this woman.

27 But **she had heard about Jesus.** She has heard reports of his curing the afflicted (see 1:28; 3:8), and she joins the crowd of those who are seeking his healing. She knows that she is doing something forbidden: she should avoid jostling crowds lest she make others unclean. But this woman, like the man with leprosy who came to Jesus in his need and faith despite his quarantine (1:40), joins those who are pressing upon Jesus with their needs. She does not want to make Jesus unclean, so she tries to have as little physical contact with him as possible. She **came up behind him in the crowd** so that he would not see her, and she **touched his cloak,** his outer garment, probably trying to touch it so gently that he would not notice.

28 **She said** to herself, **If I but touch his clothes, I shall be cured.** Mark has described an earlier occasion when "those who had diseases were pressing upon him to touch him" (3:10) and be cured; later Mark will relate that some who were sick "begged him that they might touch only the tassel on his cloak; and as many as touched it were healed" (6:56). This woman comes to Jesus with the same faith. Jesus does not have to lay hands on her for her to be healed; it is sufficient for her to lay her hand on him, even just on his cloak. She is confident that if she does so, she will **be cured:** the Greek word used here is again the word that

---

BACKGROUND: CLOTHING The two basic items of clothing at the time of Jesus were the tunic and the cloak. The tunic was an inner garment often made by folding a rectangle of cloth (sometimes linen) over on itself and stitching the sides, with openings for the head and arms. The cloak (often wool) was an outer garment, perhaps a loose-fitting robe or a rectangular cloth that one draped around oneself. These garments were worn by both men and women, with only color and decoration distinguishing them. A Jewish man's cloak would have tassels (Num 15:37–40; Deut 22:12). Belts were used to cinch tunics and cloaks. A head covering could be simply a cloth draped or tied around the head; leather sandals protected the feet. The upper class could afford imported silk and dyes, and their clothing proclaimed their status.

---

means be saved. She has come to Jesus for physical healing, but she will receive far more from him.

29 **Immediately her flow of blood dried up.** Her twelve-year condition is gone in an instant as soon as she touches Jesus' cloak. **She felt in her body that she was healed of her affliction.** She knows she is healed, somehow physically feeling the change. The word Mark uses for **affliction** literally means scourge and alludes to the suffering that her condition had caused her.

> *For reflection: What is the biggest difference Jesus has made in my life? In the life of someone I love?*

30 **Jesus, aware at once that power had gone out from him, turned around in the crowd and asked, "Who has touched my clothes?"** Just as the woman immediately "felt in her body" that she had been healed, so Jesus is immediately aware that his power has gone forth. Mark does not explain how Jesus knew this; he simply tells us that Jesus was certain that **power had gone out from him.** Jesus apparently realized that his power had flowed to someone who had been behind him and brushed against him, for he stopped and **turned around** and **asked, "Who has touched my clothes?"** This is a genuine question: Jesus does not know the identity of the person who has touched his clothes and is the beneficiary of his power.

31 **But his disciples said to him, "You see how the crowd is pressing upon you, and yet you ask, 'Who touched me?'"** The woman knows what happened to her, and Jesus knows what happened to him, but Jesus' disciples are oblivious to what is going on. Their response to Jesus is a little sarcastic but expresses their appraisal of the situation: since Jesus is being pushed and shoved by many people, how can anyone be singled out for touching him? This is the third time the disciples chide Jesus or speak to him with less-than-respectful words (see 1:37; 4:38).

32 **And he looked around to see who had done it.** Jesus searches the faces of those who have been walking behind him, gazing at them deliberately and steadily (see 3:5, 34). Yet it does not seem that Jesus

can tell at a glance who has touched his cloak and drawn forth his power: there is no indication that Jesus identifies the woman or invites her to step forward.

33 Rather, the woman who has been healed steps forward of her own account. She sees that Jesus has stopped walking, has turned around, and is searching the crowd for someone. She realizes that he must be looking for her, for she is aware that her healing occurred when she touched his cloak. **The woman, realizing what had happened to her, approached in fear and trembling. She fell down before Jesus and told him the whole truth.** Her **fear** was not that Jesus would criticize her for mingling in a crowd in her unclean condition or that he would scold her for touching him. Rather, she trembled with awe because she realized **what had happened to her:** she had been healed by the power of Jesus. Just as the disciples were "filled with great awe" when Jesus calmed the storm at sea (4:41) and just as the crowd was "seized with fear" when Jesus freed the possessed man (5:15), so this woman is overcome with awe at what has happened to her (Mark uses the same word for fear/awe in all three instances). In gratitude she **fell down before Jesus and told him the whole truth**—the story of her affliction and of being cured when she touched his cloak.

34 **He said to her, "Daughter, your faith has saved you."** Jesus addresses her as **daughter,** a term of affection but also a proclamation that there is a bond between them: Jesus welcomes to himself one who had been cut off from human relationships. He tells her that her **faith has saved** her. Many people bumped up against Jesus in the crowd, but this did not in itself bring them healing. Her touch was an expression of her **faith** in him, and through it she was **saved:** the physical healing of her life-draining affliction foreshadows a far greater healing that followers of Jesus will receive in response to their **faith.** Jesus tells her, **Go in peace,** a traditional parting blessing (1 Sam 1:17). The Hebrew word translated **peace** means not simply an absence of conflict but a state of wholeness: Jesus tells the woman to go forth in her new wholeness. Jesus adds, **And be cured of your affliction.** This is a ratification of the cure she has already received but looks to the future and has the meaning of "Continue to be well and remain healthy."

Jesus, by stopping and identifying the woman who touched him, makes her healing public. She no longer has to live as an unclean untouchable; she can go about living a normal life now. Jesus also highlights the reason she has received healing and new life: it is her **faith** that has **saved** her. She believed that Jesus could heal her, and she reached out to touch him, not allowing the crowd or her uncleanness or anything else to stop her. She is a model of courageous faith for everyone, including Jairus, who at this point must have been worrying that if Jesus kept stopping to heal people, he would not reach his house in time to save his daughter.

For reflection: How can this woman serve as an example for me? Am I in need of the courage to act on my faith?

Scene Three: The Daughter of Jairus

35 While he was still speaking, people from the synagogue official's house arrived and said, "Your daughter has died; why trouble the teacher any longer?" 36 Disregarding the message that was reported, Jesus said to the synagogue official, "Do not be afraid; just have faith." 37 He did not allow anyone to accompany him inside except Peter, James, and John, the brother of James. 38 When they arrived at the house of the synagogue official, he caught sight of a commotion, people weeping and wailing loudly. 39 So he went in and said to them, "Why this commotion and weeping? The child is not dead but asleep." 40 And they ridiculed him. Then he put them all out. He took along the child's father and mother and those who were with him and entered the room where the child was. 41 He took the child by the hand and said to her, *"Talitha koum,"* which means, "Little girl, I say to you, arise!" 42 The girl, a child of twelve, arose immediately and walked around. [At that] they were utterly astounded. 43He gave strict orders that no one should know this and said that she should be given something to eat.

Gospel parallels: Matt 9:23–26; Luke 8:49–56

OT: Num 19:11–22

35 Jesus was talking with the woman who had been healed of her hemorrhage (5:33–34), and **while he was still speaking, people from**

the synagogue official's house arrived and said, "Your daughter has died." These messengers were probably at Jairus's house when his daughter died, and they arrive bearing the sad message. Jesus did not reach Jairus's house in time to heal his daughter, for he was slowed down by the crowd and stopped to speak with the woman who had been healed. Since the girl is now dead, the messengers suggest to Jairus, **Why trouble the teacher any longer?** From their point of view, there is nothing Jesus can do now: they have no expectation that Jesus can raise the dead.

36 Jesus overheard their words to Jairus, but **disregarding the message that was reported, Jesus said to the synagogue official, "Do not be afraid; just have faith."** Jesus disregards the news of the girl's death, but Jairus does not: his heart falls on hearing the message. Jesus addresses Jairus's loss of hope by telling him, **Do not be afraid:** in Greek, the expression conveys "Stop being fearful." Instead of being fearful, Jairus needs to revive the faith with which he came to Jesus. **Just have faith** means "Keep on believing, keep on trusting in me; that is the only thing you need to do." Jairus should have been encouraged by the example of the woman of faith whom Jesus had just healed, yet even greater faith is asked of him: his beloved daughter is not simply ill but dead.

> For reflection: What is the greatest act of faith that has ever been asked of me?

37 Once they arrived at the house of Jairus, Jesus **did not allow anyone to accompany him inside except Peter, James, and John, the brother of James.** Jesus singles out these three disciples, the first he called (1:16–20) and the first listed among the Twelve (3:16–17), to be with him as he deals with the death of Jairus's daughter. Jesus will also ask these three to be with him during his transfiguration (9:2) and his prayer in Gethsemane (14:33) and to hear (along with Andrew) his discourse about the coming of the Son of Man (13:3–37). We might take this to mean that Peter, James, and John were Jesus' closest friends, the ones he particularly wanted at his side. But there is a deeper significance: the occasions when Jesus asks Peter, James, and John to be with him provide privileged glimpses of who Jesus is.

38 **When they arrived at the house of the synagogue official, he caught sight of a commotion, people weeping and wailing loudly.** If Jairus was an ordinary Galilean, the mourners would have been in a courtyard shared by a number of one- or two-room houses. Since Jairus was the leader of a synagogue, he may have been relatively well-to-do and able to afford a multiroom house laid out around an atrium or interior courtyard. In any case, the mourners would have gathered outside the room in which the deceased person lay, for contact with a corpse or entering the room in which a corpse lay rendered one unclean (Num 19:11–22).

> *Whoever touches the dead body of any human being shall be unclean for seven days. . . .*
>
> *When a man dies in a tent, everyone who enters the tent, as well as everyone already in it, shall be unclean for seven days.*
>
> Num 19:11, 14

Whether in an outside courtyard or an interior atrium, the scene is one of **commotion,** with **people weeping and wailing loudly.** In ancient Middle Eastern cultures, as still today in such cultures, the response to death was not a stiff upper lip and sad reserve but a torrential outpouring of emotion and grief. Professional mourners were often hired

---

BACKGROUND: HOUSES First-century Palestinian houses ranged from the very small to the truly sumptuous. Ordinary people often lived in one-room houses that usually shared an open courtyard with other one-room houses. Much of life was lived outdoors; cooking was done in the courtyard. Rooms were dark and sometimes windowless and used for sleeping and shelter from the elements. In eastern Galilee (for example, in Capernaum), house walls were built of basalt, a volcanic stone common in the area. Floors were made of basalt cobblestones; roofs were made of beams overlaid with thatch and clay. In Jericho, a city in the lower Jordan River valley, mud brick was used for the walls of ordinary dwellings. The wealthy elite lived in fine houses with mosaic floors, frescoed (painted plaster) walls, and elegant columns. The remains of several mansions belonging to the wealthy have been excavated in Jerusalem. One of these houses had several stories and more than six thousand square feet under its roof; it probably belonged to a member of a high-priestly family.

to add to the wailing, and this may have been the case at Jairus's house. Neither the presence of hired mourners nor the loud volume of the weeping meant that the grief was insincere: this was simply how profound grief was customarily expressed.

39 **So he went** into the midst of the grievers **and said to them, "Why this commotion and weeping? The child is not dead but asleep."** Jesus' words strike the mourners as profoundly ignorant. **Why this commotion and weeping?**—obviously because someone has died. **The child is not dead but asleep**—but she *is* dead, or we would not be mourning. Does Jesus pretend that he can diagnose the medical condition of someone he has yet to see and pronounce that a corpse is really a sleeping person? That is not Jesus' claim. Jesus accepts the truth of the report that the girl has died. But Jesus can raise the dead as easily as we can awaken someone from a nap. (When Paul refers to the dead as fallen asleep, it is not a euphemism but a statement of faith: 1 Cor 15:20; 1 Thess 4:13–15.)

> *For reflection: How do I refer to those who have died, particularly family members and friends? What does my choice of words indicate about my beliefs?*

40 **And they ridiculed him:** the mourners misunderstand Jesus' words and insist that the girl is really dead and any claim to the contrary is ridiculous. Jesus does not enter into a useless debate with them but gets on with what he has come to do. **Then he put them all out:** Jesus disperses the mourners, for he does not want what he is going to do to turn into a sideshow. **He took along the child's father and mother and those who were with him**—Peter, James, and John—**and entered the room where the child was.** Jesus shows his concern for Jairus and his wife by inviting them to be present. There is again a contrast between those who are with Jesus and those who are on the outside (see 3:31; 4:11), and now those with Jesus are face-to-face with death, the ultimate human calamity.

41 **He took the child by the hand,** just as he had taken Simon Peter's mother-in-law by her hand to raise her up from her sickbed (1:30–31), touching her, making personal contact. Jesus **said to her,** *"Talitha koum,"* **which means, "Little girl, I say to you, arise!"** Jesus spoke

Aramaic, and Mark includes a number of Aramaic expressions in his Gospel, usually translating them for the benefit of his Greek-speaking readers (see also 7:11, 34; 14:36; 15:22, 34). *Talitha* is an affectionate term, meaning little lamb or little girl; **koum** is the common Aramaic word for arise or get up. On many mornings Jairus or his wife had probably spoken this very word, **koum,** to their sleeping daughter, telling her, "Get up, breakfast is ready, you'll be late." Jesus speaks this word to her in the sleep of death, telling her, **Little girl, I say to you, arise,** his personal word accompanying his personal touch. Jesus issued the same command to **arise** to a paralyzed man lying on a mat, and that man sprang up from his paralysis (2:11–12). Now Jesus commands a girl to arise from the infinitely greater paralysis of death.

42 **The girl, a child of twelve, arose immediately and walked around.** She **arose immediately,** healed of death as quickly as the woman was healed of her bleeding (5:29). She **walked around,** making it obvious that she was alive. Mark adds the note that she was **a child of twelve,** perhaps simply to indicate that she was practically an adult in the culture of the time, even though Jairus and Jesus affectionately referred to her as a little girl (5:23, 41). Perhaps too Mark noticed the coincidence

---

BACKGROUND: WHAT LANGUAGES DID JESUS SPEAK? The language of ancient Israel was Hebrew, and most of the Old Testament was written in Hebrew. Jesus would have had to have a reading knowledge of Hebrew in order to read aloud from the scroll of Isaiah in the synagogue in Nazareth (Luke 4:16–21). Aramaic, a related language, was the international language of the Babylonian and Persian Empires. Jews adopted Aramaic as their ordinary language after the Exile, when they were under the rule of Persia. (Some chapters of the books of Ezra and Daniel, written during or after this period, are in Aramaic.) Jesus grew up speaking Aramaic, the ordinary language of Jews in Palestine in the first century. The Gospels preserve a few Aramaic words that Jesus used, such as *Talitha koum* (Little girl, arise—Mark 5:41) and *Abba* (Father—Mark 14:36). Following the conquests of Alexander the Great around 330 BC, Greek became widely used throughout the eastern Mediterranean world, especially for commerce. Some scholars believe that Jesus picked up some Greek. Whether Jesus taught in Greek is a different question; it is highly probable he taught in Aramaic, the language in which both he and the rural people of Galilee were most at home. *Related topic: Greek language and culture (page 179).*

between the girl being twelve and the woman having hemorrhaged for twelve years (5:25) and wanted his readers to note it as well, as a hint that the two incidents had connections. A woman whose life had been draining away and a young woman whose life had drained away had been healed (and, in a deeper sense, saved: 5:23, 28, 34) and given life through faith in Jesus (5:34, 36).

At the sight of the girl getting up and walking around, Jairus and his wife and Peter, James, and John **were utterly astounded**—even more astounded than those who had seen the paralytic rise from his mat (2:12). They must have wondered, *Who is this who raises the dead?* The disciples may also have asked themselves, *Who is this to whom we have given our lives—and what will he do next?*

43 Jesus then makes two requests, one seemingly impossible and one quite easy. First, **he gave strict orders that no one should know this.** But how could it be kept quiet? Could anyone expect that a twelve-year-old girl wouldn't talk with her friends? Were Jairus and his wife to pretend that nothing unusual had happened that day? Wouldn't the mourners ask how the dead girl had come back to life? Jesus' **strict orders** seemingly demanded the impossible, and he had to know that it was impossible, so we must wonder why he made this demand. I know of no totally satisfactory answer. The best answer seems to be that what Jesus did during his public ministry could not be fully understood except in light of his death and resurrection, and the more spectacular his deeds, the more open they were to misunderstanding. The most Jesus could reasonably hope for in this instance was that Jairus and his family would not publicize the restoration of the girl's life any more than they absolutely had to—in modern terms, they wouldn't give press conferences, do TV talk shows, or fly banners on their house proclaiming, "See the Girl Brought Back to Life!" Still, Jesus' demanding **strict** silence remains somewhat puzzling.

Jesus' second request is far easier: he **said that she should be given something to eat.** Presumably she did not eat much as she lay dying; now she is healthy but hungry, and the commonsense thing to do is give her something to eat. Jesus doesn't want her family to overlook her ordinary human needs in their jubilation over her return from death.

Mark has shown Jesus ever more directly confronting and overcoming death. He rescued his disciples from possible death at sea (4:35–41), he restored to normal life a man who was living in tombs (5:1–20), he healed a woman of a life-draining affliction (5:25–34), and he has now raised a dead girl back to life. The words translated "arise" (verse 41) and "arose" (verse 42) in the account of Jesus' raising up of the girl are the same words that will be used later in this Gospel for Jesus' rising from the dead (8:31; 9:9, 31; 10:34; 14:28; 16:6). Jesus' ultimate battle is with death itself, and he will conquer death through his own resurrection. Jesus' raising of the daughter of Jairus foreshadows his raising of men and women to eternal life.

For reflection: What glimpse into who Jesus is does the raising of Jairus's daughter give me? What hope does it give me?

CHAPTER 6

ORIENTATION: *After confronting and overcoming the powers of death, Jesus travels to Nazareth, where he is rejected by those who think they know him.*

Jesus Meets with Rejection in His Hometown

¹ He departed from there and came to his native place, accompanied by his disciples. ² When the sabbath came he began to teach in the synagogue, and many who heard him were astonished. They said, "Where did this man get all this? What kind of wisdom has been given him? What mighty deeds are wrought by his hands! ³ Is he not the carpenter, the son of Mary, and the brother of James and Joses and Judas and Simon? And are not his sisters here with us?" And they took offense at him. ⁴ Jesus said to them, "A prophet is not without honor except in his native place and among his own kin and in his own house." ⁵ So he was not able to perform any mighty deed there, apart from curing a few sick people by laying his hands on them. ⁶ He was amazed at their lack of faith.

Gospel parallels: Matt 13:54–58; Luke 4:16–30
NT: Mark 3:20–21, 31–35; John 6:42; 7:5

1 **He departed from there and came to his native place, accompanied by his disciples.** Jesus is at the house of Jairus (5:38–43), and he travels **from there** to his **native place** of Nazareth, the village in which

---

BACKGROUND: NAZARETH was an insignificant farming village located on a saddle in a hill overlooking the Jezreel Valley in southern Galilee. Archaeologists tell us that it was no more than ten acres in size at the time of Jesus and had less than four hundred inhabitants—likely only around two hundred. The scanty remains from the first century suggest that its houses were rather insubstantial, with fieldstone walls and thatched roofs. No luxury items of any kind have been found on the site. Nazareth is not mentioned in the Old Testament; its unimportance is reflected in Nathanael's question "Can anything good come from Nazareth?" (John 1:46). There was nothing to distinguish Nazareth from other small farming villages in Galilee during the years Jesus called it home.

---

he grew up (1:9, 24). Since he is **accompanied by his disciples,** Jesus is not making a private visit to see family and friends but is carrying on his mission, "preaching and driving out demons throughout the whole of Galilee" (1:39). Mark's Gospel has not previously described Jesus going back to Nazareth after the beginning of his public ministry.

2 **When the sabbath came he began to teach in the synagogue,** as was his custom (1:21–27, 39; 3:1–5). Mark does not tell us what he taught. Jesus may have commented on a reading from the Hebrew Scriptures (as was customary to do on the Sabbath: see Luke 4:16–21; Acts 13:14–15). He likely taught about the coming of the kingdom of God, for that was the basic theme of his preaching (1:14–15). He may have taught in parables, as he did on other occasions (4:1–9, 21–34). Whatever the specific form and content of his teaching, **many who heard him were aston-ished.** On a previous occasion when Jesus taught in a synagogue, "the people were astonished at his teaching" (1:22), and there is astonishment in Nazareth as well.

This time the astonishment has overtones of skepticism, for **they said, "Where did this man get all this? What kind of wisdom has been given him? What mighty deeds are wrought by his hands!"** To properly understand these questions we need to know the tone in which they were asked. We can come upon someone and innocently ask out of curiosity, "What are you doing?" Or we can challenge someone with a shriek of protest: "What are you doing!" The questions raised about Jesus are more challenges than inquiries. The people speak of Jesus as **this man,** an expression with a disparaging edge: "Who does this guy think he is?" **Where did** he **get all this**—his teachings and his power to work mighty deeds? **What kind of wisdom has been given him?**—is his "new teaching with authority" (1:27) valid or a dangerous novelty? **What mighty deeds are wrought by his hands!**: the people of Nazareth have heard reports of what Jesus has been doing (1:45; 3:8) and have probably witnessed it themselves, but what is the source of his power? These are legitimate questions, but they are asked in the wrong spirit. The people of Nazareth cannot reconcile the Jesus who is now with them—teaching with authority, healing, and casting out unclean spirits—with the Jesus they have known since he was a child.

3 They ask one another, **Is he not the carpenter?** speaking as if the small village of Nazareth needs and has only one carpenter. The Greek word translated **carpenter** applies to one who works in stone as well as wood, a manual laborer who has the ability to erect the stone walls of houses and has the skills to fashion wooden door frames and furniture. Jesus had been the village craftsman until he left to go to John in the desert to be baptized (1:9) and then began preaching and healing. Mark gives no indication of how many years Jesus worked as a craftsman before beginning his second career, but it had been long enough to firmly establish his identity as **the carpenter** in the eyes of the people of Nazareth. Yet now Jesus is not acting like a village carpenter; he is teaching as if he has authority and is performing deeds that require great power. What is going on?

There is a second stumbling block to the people of Nazareth accepting the new Jesus: they have not only known him for many years, but they know his entire family as well. In their village of a few hundred people, many of them are probably related to Jesus in one way or another. They know beyond a doubt that he is **the son of Mary** and **the brother of James and Joses and Judas and Simon** and that **his sisters** live in their midst. Usually a man was identified in terms of his father (even if his father was dead), but Jesus is called **the son of Mary.** The significance in Mark's Gospel of Jesus being thought of as **the son of Mary** is uncertain. Today's readers might take this to be a hint of Jesus' conception in Mary through the Holy Spirit, but there is no awareness of this

---

BACKGROUND: CARPENTER The Greek word *tekton*, used to describe Jesus (Mark 6:3) and Joseph (Matt 13:55), is usually translated carpenter. A *tekton*, however, worked not just with wood but with any hard and lasting material, including stone. Houses in Nazareth usually had unworked stone walls; wood was used sparingly for roof beams, doors, and door frames. Jesus spoke of building on rock (Matt 7:24) and laying a cornerstone (Mark 12:10), and he might have had firsthand experience of doing both. A *tekton* would also have been expected to have the skills to make and repair plows, yokes, and furniture. Wooden beams (and sometimes stone blocks) were shaped with hand tools; a man who spent his life working as a *tekton* would have callused hands and hard muscles. Our mental image of Jesus the carpenter should be of a skilled manual laborer.

elsewhere in Mark's Gospel. **Mary** and the brothers bear traditional Jewish names—perhaps a sign that they were traditional Jews, relatively uninfluenced by Greek culture (devotees of Greek ways often gave Greek names, such as Philip and Alexandra, to their children). **Mary** was named after Miriam, sister of Moses; **James** is a form of Jacob, the name of the father of the twelve tribes of Israel. **Joses and Judas and Simon** were named after Joseph, Judah, and Simeon, sons of Jacob. A James and Joses are mentioned again in Mark's Gospel as sons of Mary, but this Mary is apparently not the Mary who is the mother of Jesus (15:40). On the relationship of Jesus to these brothers and sisters, see the background information on brothers and sisters of Jesus, page 76. Whatever the degree of relationship between Jesus and his relatives, the people of Nazareth are sure they know him: Jesus did not drop down out of the sky but grew up in their midst, as one of them.

And they took offense at him: they are scandalized by Jesus, tripped up by him, as one stumbles over a rock (Paul uses a form of the same Greek term for offense in speaking of the scandal of the cross: 1 Cor 1:23). They cannot reconcile the ordinariness of the Jesus they have known for many years with the man filled with "wisdom" and the worker of "mighty deeds" who now stands before them.

> For reflection: Some people who had known Jesus for many years thought he was simply a carpenter. Do I have so exalted an image of Jesus that no one could mistake him for an ordinary person?

Not everyone in Nazareth took offense at Jesus. Mark writes that "many" were astonished and skeptical (verse 2), but it will shortly appear that some people in Nazareth did have faith in Jesus. We can also note that while the relatives of Jesus are mentioned, they do not appear on the scene; Mark gives no indication of their reactions to Jesus that day.

4 **Jesus said to them, "A prophet is not without honor except in his native place and among his own kin and in his own house."** There were proverbs similar to this in circulation in the ancient world, so Jesus may have invoked a common observation but modified it to fit his situation. A modern counterpart might be "An expert is someone from out of town." This is the first time in Mark's Gospel that Jesus refers to himself

as a **prophet** or is described that way, although he has been carrying out a prophet's mission of speaking for God (1:14–15; 2:27–28). Prophets often met with hostility and rejection, dramatically so in the case of Jeremiah. Jesus sharpens the proverb by giving it a progressively narrower application: a prophet receives no honor **in his native place** (his hometown) and from **his own kin** (his relatives) and **in his own house** (from his immediate family). To be **without honor** means to be dishonored.

Jesus uses this proverb as a sad acknowledgment of the rejection he has met with in Nazareth but not as a justification for it. Many of Mark's first readers probably experienced similar rejection by associates and relatives because they had become Christians. Jesus' experience meant that he understood what they were going through, and he was not asking them to endure anything that he had not first endured himself.

For reflection: Have I had to endure any misunderstanding or rejection because of my Christian beliefs? Has my following Christ meant honor or dishonor for me?

5 **So he was not able to perform any mighty deed there.** This does not mean that the people of Nazareth were able to rob Jesus of his power by their skepticism and rejection. Rather, Jesus' mighty deeds were done in response to faith (5:34) and as an integral part of Jesus' establishing the reign of God. If Jesus was not recognized as one authorized by God to do what he did, his mighty deeds were nothing but sideshow spectacles. Jesus **was not able to perform any mighty deed there** because the faith that gave meaning to his mighty deeds was lacking.

Mark quickly modifies his statement: Jesus could not do anything in Nazareth **apart from curing a few sick people by laying his hands on them.** Although many in Nazareth reject Jesus, some accept him as authorized by God. Consequently he is able to cure them, because their faith provides the context in which their cures have meaning. Once again Jesus heals through his personal touch, **laying his hands** on those who are sick.

6 The few who turned to Jesus in faith were exceptions. Most of the people of Nazareth refused to recognize that God's power was at work though Jesus, and **he was amazed at their lack of faith.** This was not the

response Jesus had been expecting when he came to Nazareth. That Jesus could experience surprise and disappointment is another indication of his full humanity: Jesus did not have absolute knowledge of the future, and his expectations could be dashed.

> *For reflection: Who is Jesus? Who is this man who earned his living as a carpenter and raised the dead, who had astonishing wisdom but could still be amazed and disappointed?*

Mark's Gospel paints a mixed picture: Jesus performs mighty deeds, even raising the dead, but he is rejected by many religious leaders and even by relatives and friends he lived among for many years. The truth and power of the message of Jesus does not guarantee that it will be welcomed and embraced by everyone.

ORIENTATION: *Jesus continues to carry out his mission and begins to involve his disciples in it.*

Jesus Sends Out the Twelve

⁶ He went around to the villages in the vicinity teaching. ⁷ He summoned the Twelve and began to send them out two by two and gave them authority over unclean spirits. ⁸ He instructed them to take nothing for the journey but a walking stick—no food, no sack, no money in their belts. ⁹ They were, however, to wear sandals but not a second tunic. ¹⁰ He said to them, "Wherever you enter a house, stay there until you leave from there. ¹¹ Whatever place does not welcome you or listen to you, leave there and shake the dust off your feet in testimony against them." ¹² So they went off and preached repentance. ¹³ They drove out many demons, and they anointed with oil many who were sick and cured them.

Gospel parallels: Matt 10:1–15; Luke 9:1–6
NT: Mark 3:13–19; James 5:14–15

6 **He went around to the villages in the vicinity teaching.** The conclusion of verse 6 summarizes what Jesus did after being rejected in Nazareth: he continued with his mission (1:38–39), visiting villages around

Nazareth. The setback in Nazareth did not slow him down. Mark characterizes Jesus' activity as **teaching,** but it probably included casting out demons and healing as well, as it had when Jesus taught in Capernaum (1:21–34).

7 Jesus decides it is now time to involve his disciples in his work. **He summoned the Twelve and began to send them out two by two.** Jesus called his first followers to be "fishers of men" (1:17), but they have yet to do such fishing. Jesus appointed **the Twelve** "that they might be with him and he might send them forth to preach and to have authority to drive out demons" (3:14–15). The Twelve have been with Jesus ever since, listening to his teachings (4:1–34) and observing his actions in preparation for sharing in his mission. Now Jesus **began to send them out,** having them actively participate in his mission for the first time, beginning their in-service training. The Greek word translated **send out** gives us the word *apostle,* which means one who is sent as a messenger or an authorized representative. Jesus sends them out **two by two:** in the Old Testament, two witnesses were required in legal proceedings (Deut 19:15; see 1 Tim 5:19), particularly when life was at stake (Num 35:30; Deut 17:6). The message that the Twelve will proclaim is so important that it deserves no less authentication.

Apostle: See page 146

There is another reason for the Twelve to go out two by two: their mission is to gather men and women into a community, and the communal goal of their mission needs to be reflected in shared ministry. Jesus extends this even to simple tasks that one person can do (11:1–3; 14:13–16). The early Church will follow the same pattern, sending out Barnabus and Paul as a team (Acts 13:1–3). After Paul and Barnabus have a falling out, Paul will not continue on his own but will choose Silas to accompany him in place of Barnabus (Acts 15:36–40).

For reflection: How has my working with others helped me carry out Christian service?

As Jesus sent out the Twelve, he **gave them authority over unclean spirits.** Jesus has repeatedly cast out unclean spirits as part of his mission to establish the reign of God; now he shares his authority and power over evil spirits with the Twelve. They are empowered to do as he has done. The power to heal the sick is also conveyed, as will be evident shortly.

8 Those being sent out are to rely on the power that Jesus has entrusted to them and on God's providence rather than on their own resources. Consequently Jesus tells them to travel light: **he instructed them to take nothing for the journey but a walking stick—no food, no sack, no money in their belts.** In a world without fast-food restaurants, travelers usually carried **food** with them, but Jesus tells the Twelve not to follow ordinary practice. They are not even to bring along a **sack** for carrying food, which also means that they cannot accept traveling provisions from others. Nor are they to take **money** with them. The word used here for **money** literally means copper, copper coins being the least valuable minted; those whom Jesus is sending out are not even to carry loose change. Self-sufficiency is ruled out for those who bear Jesus' authority. The Twelve can, however, carry a **walking stick,** which will help them cross the uneven terrain of Palestine and can serve as well for defense against robbers and wild animals.

9 **They were, however, to wear sandals,** which would make it easier to walk long distances on rough ground, **but not a second tunic.** A **tunic** was the basic undergarment, worn beneath a robe. Wearing a second tunic was a way of carrying a spare item of clothing. That too Jesus tells the Twelve to forgo; they are allowed only the bare essentials.

Clothing: See page 117

10 Traveling so light meant that those being sent out would be very dependent on others—on God's providence and on the hospitality of those who would provide them with food and lodging. Those traveling on main roads would find an occasional inn for caravans, with food and shelter for travelers and animals. But off the beaten path and in villages, there were no hotels. Rather, there was a long tradition of personal hospitality, of welcoming travelers (even strangers) into one's home. Jesus relied on the hospitality of others during his journeys (9:28; 10:10), and he instructed the Twelve to do the same. **He said to them, "Wherever you enter a house, stay there until you leave from there."** This implies a stay

of at least several days in each village they visit. Why did Jesus instruct them to remain in the same house? Scholars often suggest that Jesus was prohibiting them from upgrading their accommodations if an offer of better housing came along. My own hunch is that it reflected Jesus' practice as well as his expectations of the impact they would have in villages. When Jesus lodged with Peter on the night that Jesus cured Peter's mother-in-law, "the whole town was gathered at the door" of Peter's house, bringing "all who were ill or possessed by demons" (1:32–33). If the Twelve are successful in casting out demons and healing the sick, they too will be besieged wherever they lodge; there will be no need for them to go from house to house to carry out their mission.

11 Even as Jesus sends the Twelve out with his authority, he knows that this authority is no guarantee of a warm reception. The Twelve have witnessed Jesus being rejected on a number of occasions (3:6, 21–22; 5:17), most recently in Nazareth (6:1–6), and they will experience rejection as well. Jesus tells them what to do when it happens: **Whatever place does not welcome you or listen to you, leave there and shake the dust off your feet in testimony against them.** If they find no **welcome** or hospitality in a village, if no one in a village will **listen** to the message

---

BACKGROUND: HOSPITALITY The practice of welcoming guests, including strangers, into one's home for meals and lodging is common in the Old and New Testaments. Abraham provides an example of generous hospitality when he begs three traveling strangers to accept a snack from him but then serves them a banquet (Gen 18:1–8). Abraham's nephew Lot pleads with passing strangers to spend the night in his house rather than sleep in the town square (Gen 19:1–3). Job lists hospitality among his upright deeds: "No stranger lodged in the street, / but I opened my door to wayfarers" (Job 31:32). Those who traveled usually had to rely on the hospitality of others. Caravan inns on main routes provided shelter for travelers and animals (Luke 10:34–35), but there were no hotels in ordinary towns and villages. Jesus depended on the hospitality of his followers, including Peter (Mark 1:29–34; 2:1) and Martha and Mary (Luke 10:38–42). Jesus included hospitality among his concerns on judgment day: "I was . . . a stranger and you welcomed me" (Matt 25:35). The practice of hospitality is evident in Acts (Acts 10:21–23; 16:15; 28:7), and the letters of the New Testament hold hospitality in high regard (Rom 12:13; 1 Tim 3:2; 5:10; Titus 1:8; Heb 13:2).

they bear, then they are to **leave** that village and go on to the next, as Jesus did after his rejection in Nazareth (verse 6). Just as the setback in Nazareth did not slow Jesus down, neither should setbacks prevent his followers from continuing in the mission he has given them.

> For reflection: How do I react to setbacks and disappointments, particularly in my service of Jesus? How persevering am I when the results seem meager?

Jesus tells the Twelve that as they leave an inhospitable and unresponsive village, they are to **shake the dust off your feet in testimony against them.** Shaking the dust off one's feet was a symbolic gesture of disassociation (Acts 13:51), akin to washing one's hands (Matt 27:24) or shaking out one's garments (Acts 18:6). It conveyed "We have nothing further to do with you; we don't even want the dust of your village on our sandals." Shaking off dust **in testimony against** those who reject the Twelve may mean that the gesture conveys to the rejecters that they are being bid good riddance. Is this a harsh and unwarranted response for the Twelve to make to unresponsiveness? Not in light of what is at stake: the kingdom of God is at hand, and the response that men and women make to its coming is of great gravity.

12 **So they went off and preached repentance.** Both John the Baptist (1:4) and Jesus (1:15) preached **repentance** in preparation for what God was about to do, and the Twelve follow in their wake. There is an element of John's preaching in what the Twelve do, for they too are preparing the way of Jesus (1:2–3). But those whom Jesus sends forth are also sharing in his mission and authority, so they are able to accomplish more than John the Baptist did.

Repentance: See page 17

13 With the authority and power of Jesus, **they drove out many demons, and they anointed with oil many who were sick and cured them.** It should not have surprised the Twelve that demons were subject to them as they had been subject to Jesus and that they were able to heal as he had healed. Still, this was the first time that they had experienced the power of Jesus working through them in such manifest ways, enabling

them to drive out **many** demons and heal **many** who were sick, and we can suspect it made a powerful impression on the Twelve.

For reflection: How have I most clearly experienced the power or grace of Jesus working through me? What impact has this had on me?

The Twelve **anointed with oil many who were sick and cured them.** This is the only mention of anointing with oil for the sake of divine healing in the Gospels; Jesus is not described as doing so. Olive oil was used to ceremonially anoint kings and high priests in Old Testament times, and it was also used to soothe wounds (see Luke 10:34). The Twelve's anointing the sick with olive oil draws on its religious and medicinal uses. The early Church will continue the practice (James 5:14–15), and it will be the basis for the sacrament of anointing of the sick.

ORIENTATION: *While the people of Nazareth are sure they know who Jesus is, others are puzzled.*

Jesus the Enigma

¹⁴ King Herod heard about it, for his fame had become widespread, and people were saying, "John the Baptist has been raised from the dead; that is why mighty powers are at work in him." ¹⁵ Others were saying, "He is Elijah"; still others, "He is a prophet like any of the prophets." ¹⁶ But when Herod learned of it, he said, "It is John whom I beheaded. He has been raised up."

Gospel parallels: Matt 14:1–2; Luke 9:7–9
OT: Sirach 48:9–12; Mal 3:1, 23–24
NT: Mark 8:27–28; 9:11–13

14 Mark turns his attention from the Twelve (who are out on mission: 6:12–13) to rumors that are circulating about Jesus and to the impact of these rumors on Herod Antipas, the ruler of Galilee. **King Herod heard about it, for his fame had become widespread, and people were saying, "John the Baptist has been raised from the dead; that is why mighty powers are at work in him."** Mark literally writes that **King Herod heard;** *about it* is supplied in the translation

for smoother reading. What did Herod hear? He might have heard about the Twelve going about healing and casting out demons, for that is described in the immediately preceding verses. However, Mark adds **for his fame had become widespread,** indicating that Herod had heard about Jesus. Herod had probably heard reports about what Jesus was doing and what his followers were doing in his name. Herod was the type of ruler who stayed informed of what was happening, lest he be caught off guard by an uprising.

There is another way to interpret what **Herod heard:** he heard not only what Jesus was doing but also various popular opinions about Jesus' identity. The two went together: there was speculation about who this person was who could do such extraordinary things. Herod heard that some **people were saying, "John the Baptist has been raised from the dead; that is why mighty powers are at work in him."** This is a puzzling view. Granted, Jesus did not begin his public ministry until after John was arrested (1:14). But John was not a wonder-worker like Jesus: no **mighty powers** were evident in John's ministry. Nor was there anything in first-century Jewish belief that associated coming back from the dead with having mighty powers. Those who believed in a resurrection of the dead thought it would

---

BACKGROUND: HEROD ANTIPAS Two individuals are called Herod in the Gospels: Herod the Great, who was the ruler when Jesus was born, and his son Herod Antipas, who ruled Galilee during Jesus' public ministry. In 40 BC, Rome made Herod the Great king of Judea, Samaria, Galilee, and some territories to the east and south; his actual rule began in 37 BC. Herod Antipas's mother, Malthace, one of Herod the Great's ten wives, was a Samaritan. After the death of Herod the Great in 4 BC, Rome divided his kingdom among three of his sons. Herod Antipas was made tetrarch (ruler of a fourth of a kingdom) of Galilee and of a region east of the Jordan River; he is simply called Herod in the Gospel of Mark. Herod Antipas executed John the Baptist, but he was not as paranoid and ruthless as his father, and Galilee was generally tranquil during his more than forty years of rule. Antipas was deposed by Rome and exiled in AD 39. His brother Philip was made tetrarch of a territory northeast of the Sea of Galilee that included Bethsaida and Caesarea Philippi, which he ruled well until his death, around AD 34. A third brother, Archelaus, was made ruler of Judea, Samaria, and Idumea but ruled so incompetently that Rome removed him in AD 6 and appointed a Roman governor in his place.

---

happen only at the end of this age. All in all, the idea that Jesus might be **John the Baptist . . . raised from the dead** indicates that some people were so puzzled by Jesus that they would entertain outlandish rumors of who he was.

15 Herod Antipas also heard that **others were saying, "He is Elijah."** This makes more sense than a risen John the Baptist. **Elijah** had worked wonders (1 Kings 17–18), and at the end of his life he had been taken up to heaven in a flaming chariot (2 Kings 2:11). Malachi prophesied that Elijah would return to herald a "day of the LORD," when God would judge his people (Mal 3:1, 23–24; see also Sirach 48:9–12; Mark 9:11). If people were scratching their heads trying to figure out who Jesus was, Elijah was a possibility.

Still others thought that Jesus was neither John the Baptist nor Elijah but **a prophet like any of the prophets** of the Old Testament. There had been no prophets for several centuries; if Jesus was a prophet sent by God, it meant that God was once again speaking to his people.

These different views of Jesus reveal that Jesus was an enigma to many, and people could not find the right label for him. Note that Mark does not report that anyone was saying, "He is the Messiah we have been expecting."

16 **But when Herod learned of it, he said, "It is John whom I beheaded. He has been raised up."** When the various views of who Jesus is reach Herod Antipas, he seizes on the most outlandish of them. He has executed John and cannot shrug off the fear that John has come back from the dead to plague him. An uneasy conscience can conjure up irrational dreads.

For reflection: Mark's Gospel again raises the question "Who is Jesus?" What might I learn from the various views of Jesus that were circulated in his time?

ORIENTATION: *Mark provides a flashback that explains how Herod came to behead John the Baptist.*

The Death of John the Baptist

17 Herod was the one who had John arrested and bound in prison on account of Herodias, the wife of his brother Philip, whom he had married. 18 John had said to Herod, "It is not lawful for you to have your brother's wife." 19 Herodias harbored a grudge against him and wanted to kill him but was unable to do so. 20 Herod feared John, knowing him to be a righteous and holy man, and kept him in custody. When he heard him speak he was very much perplexed, yet he liked to listen to him. 21 She had an opportunity one day when Herod, on his birthday, gave a banquet for his courtiers, his military officers, and the leading men of Galilee. 22 Herodias's own daughter came in and performed a dance that delighted Herod and his guests. The king said to the girl, "Ask of me whatever you wish and I will grant it to you." 23 He even swore [many things] to her, "I will grant you whatever you ask of me, even to half of my kingdom." 24 She went out and said to her mother, "What shall I ask for?" She replied, "The head of John the Baptist." 25 The girl hurried back to the king's presence and made her request, "I want you to give me at once on a platter the head of John the Baptist." 26 The king was deeply distressed, but because of his oaths and the guests he did not wish to break his word to her. 27 So he promptly dispatched an executioner with orders to bring back his head. He went off and beheaded him in the prison. 28 He brought in the head on a platter and gave it to the girl. The girl in turn gave it to her mother. 29 When his disciples heard about it, they came and took his body and laid it in a tomb.

Gospel parallels: Matt 14:3–12; Luke 3:19–20

17 **Herod was the one who had John arrested and bound in prison on account of Herodias, the wife of his brother Philip, whom he had married.** There was some intermarriage in the dynasty spawned by Herod the Great and his ten wives. **Herodias** was the daughter of one of Herod Antipas's half brothers and had been the wife of another half brother, whom Mark names as **Philip** (the Jewish historian Josephus

calls Herodias's first husband Herod and says that it was their daughter Salome whom Philip married). Herod Antipas had divorced his first wife to marry Herodias, who was his sister-in-law and niece. Herodias thus was successively married to two of her uncles, both of whom, according to Josephus, were called Herod. Relationships within the Herodian dynasty were quite tangled when John the Baptist came along.

18 **John had said to Herod, "It is not lawful for you to have your brother's wife."** The law of Moses prohibited a man from marrying his (living) brother's wife (see Lev 18:16), branding it incest (Lev 20:21). John may also have criticized Herod Antipas for other things, for Antipas was not noted for obedience to the Mosaic law.

19 **Herodias harbored a grudge against him and wanted to kill him but was unable to do so.** Presumably only Herod Antipas could order the execution of John the Baptist. Herodias bided her time, waiting for an opportunity that would allow her to permanently silence John.

20 **Herod feared John, knowing him to be a righteous and holy man, and kept him in custody.** John the Baptist lived in the wilderness and dressed in rough garments, while Herod Antipas had three palaces and lived in luxury. The ruler Herod, however, was in awe of the prophet John, afraid of him yet fascinated by him. Herod had John arrested (1:14) and **kept him in custody.** Herod visited John in prison, for **when he heard him speak he was very much perplexed, yet he liked to listen to him.** Herod was ambivalent toward John, rejecting his condemnation of his marriage but drawn to this man who was the opposite of him in every way. Herod recognized that John was a **righteous and holy man,** even if he was also a thorn in his side.

21 Herodias's waiting paid off. **She had an opportunity one day when Herod, on his birthday, gave a banquet for his courtiers, his military officers, and the leading men of Galilee.** Celebrating a **birthday** with a banquet was a pagan rather than a Jewish practice. Herod threw a large **banquet,** inviting his **courtiers** (the inner circle of his government), his high-ranking **military officers,** and **the leading men of Galilee** (wealthy aristocrats). Some of these people were likely those

whom Mark referred to earlier as Herodians, who were considering how they might arrange Jesus' death (3:6). We can note that this was an all-male banquet and would have included ample wine.

Herodians: See page 59

22 **Herodias's own daughter came in and performed a dance that delighted Herod and his guests.** Herodias's **own daughter** (unnamed by Mark but called Salome by Josephus) was from her first marriage. The banquet turned into a stag party: the word translated **delighted** can carry sexual overtones, and Hollywood has probably been right to portray the **dance** as lascivious. A princess displaying herself to her stepfather and his cronies would have been highly extraordinary and scandalous. However, they were the Herods, and nothing can be ruled out.

Herod was galvanized by the girl's dance and, probably having drunk freely, handed her the equivalent of a blank check: **the king said to the girl, "Ask of me whatever you wish and I will grant it to you."** Herod wanted to dazzle his guests with his magnanimity.

23 Not content to simply make an extravagant promise, Herod confirmed it with oaths, like a man who cannot shut off his bluster. **He even swore [many things] to her, "I will grant you whatever you ask**

BACKGROUND: BANQUETS or feasts played important social and religious roles at the time of Jesus. Banquets were not only a chance for ordinary people to enjoy ample food and meat and wine (which they otherwise rarely did), but also a form of entertainment in a world that offered few diversions compared with the modern world. Banquets marked special occasions, such as weddings (Matt 22:2; John 2:1–3) or a wayward son coming home (Luke 15:23). Those who were wealthy could feast every day (Luke 16:19). Banquets were also used to celebrate religious feasts, such as Passover (Exod 12:1–28). It was the custom at Greek banquets for diners to recline on their left side on cushions around the outside of a U-shaped arrangement of low tables; those serving the food worked inside the U. Jews adopted the custom of reclining during banquets, as John portrays in his account of the Last Supper (John 13:12, 23–25). The prophets spoke of God providing a banquet for his people (Isaiah 25:6), and Jesus used a feast as an image for the reign of God (Matt 8:11; 22:1–14; Luke 13:28–29; 14:15–24). Having plenty of good food to eat would have sounded heavenly to Jesus' listeners. *Related topic: Diet (page 150)*

---

of me, even to half of my kingdom." His offer to give her **half** of his **kingdom** was not intended literally: Rome, not subordinate rulers like Herod, disposed of kingdoms. Rather, giving half of one's kingdom was a cliché for regal generosity (found, for example, on the lips of King Ahasuerus in the book of Esther—Esther 5:3, 6; 7:2). Today someone might say, "I'd give my right arm for tickets to the Super Bowl" and likewise not expect to be taken literally.

24 **She went out and said to her mother, "What shall I ask for?"** Herodias did not have to spend a lot of time mulling over Herod's offer, for this was the opportunity she had been waiting for. **She replied, "The head of John the Baptist."** Herodias wanted incontrovertible evidence that John was dead, and this was a sure, if gruesome, way to obtain it.

25 **The girl hurried back to the king's presence and made her request, "I want you to give me at once on a platter the head of John the Baptist."** Herodias's daughter not only demanded the head of John the Baptist but also specified **on a platter,** served up, as it were, as one more offering at the banquet. She demanded it **at once,** not allowing time for Herod to have second thoughts about what he was doing (perhaps after he had sobered up).

26 **The king was deeply distressed, but because of his oaths and the guests he did not wish to break his word to her.** However **deeply distressed** Herod might have been over being asked to kill a man he recognized as righteous and holy (verse 20), his desire to save face won out. He would have found it very embarrassing to renege on his promise to give this girl whatever she asked for, a promise confirmed with oaths and made in the presence of his administrators and military officers and the leading men of Galilee. Herod's honor (or his twisted idea of what honor meant) was more important to him than an innocent man's life.

27 **So he promptly dispatched an executioner with orders to bring back his head. He went off and beheaded him in the prison.** The setting for Herod's birthday party was most likely his palace in Tiberias, a new city he had built on the western shore of the Sea of Galilee as his capital (note that the "leading men" of Galilee attended: verse 21).

Herod also had an old palace in Sepphoris (not far from Nazareth) and a palace/fortress at Machaerus, east of the Dead Sea. The historian Josephus writes that John the Baptist was imprisoned and executed at Machaerus, a two- or three-day journey from Tiberias. There have been various suggestions for how the accounts of Mark and Josephus can be reconciled. Both accounts agree on the important point: Herod Antipas had John the Baptist put to death.

28 **He brought in the head on a platter and gave it to the girl. The girl in turn gave it to her mother.** Mark's account might be interpreted to imply that John was imprisoned not far from the banquet and that it took only a matter of minutes for him to be executed and for his head to be brought to Herodias's daughter. However, there is no mention of John's head being brought into the banquet. We are told only that it was given to the girl, who gave it to her mother, with no indication of the time involved.

29 **When his disciples heard about it, they came and took his body and laid it in a tomb.** John's disciples (2:18) gave him a proper burial. The forerunner of Jesus had run his course to its end.

Mark has told the story of John's death in some detail because John was the forerunner of Jesus in death as well as in life. John had preached repentance (1:4), but this was a hazardous occupation when power was in the hands of people like Herod Antipas. Jesus also preached repentance (1:15), and now Jesus' disciples are doing the same (6:12). John's death had ominous implications for them. Those who

---

BACKGROUND: JOSEPHUS ON THE DEATH OF JOHN THE BAPTIST The Jewish historian Josephus (lived from AD 37 to roughly AD 100) attributed John's death to Herod Antipas's fear of his popularity: "When others crowded around John and were deeply moved by his preaching, Herod became afraid. John's ability to sway the people might lead to some kind of uprising, for they seemed willing to act on John's advice. So Herod thought it best to take action, not wanting to be caught by surprise and face problems that would make him regret his hesitation. Because of Herod's suspicions, then, John was taken in chains to the fortress called Machaerus and put to death" (*The Antiquities of the Jews*, XVIII, 5, 2).

proclaim the reign of God might meet with violent opposition from those whose allegiance is to the reign of Rome or any other earthly power. Jesus' message is not a matter of safe "religious" sentiments but a challenge to how this world is run.

For reflection: Do I see any of my own sins writ large in Herod and Herodias and her daughter? What meaning does the death of John the Baptist have for me?

ORIENTATION: *Mark returns to his account of the Twelve, who had been sent out on mission by Jesus (6:7–13).*

The Twelve Rejoin Jesus

³⁰ The apostles gathered together with Jesus and reported all they had done and taught. ³¹ He said to them, "Come away by yourselves to a deserted place and rest a while." People were coming and going in great numbers, and they had no opportunity even to eat. ³² So they went off in the boat by themselves to a deserted place. ³³ People saw them leaving and many came to know about it. They hastened there on foot from all the towns and arrived at the place before them.

Gospel parallels: Luke 9:10–11

30 **The apostles gathered together with Jesus and reported all they had done and taught.** The word *apostle* means one who is sent out as an authorized representative; this is the only time (with the possible exception of 3:14) that Mark calls the Twelve **apostles.** Jesus had sent out the Twelve bearing his authority over unclean spirits (6:7), and now, after an unspecified period of time, they have returned and **gathered together with Jesus** again. They **reported all they had done and taught.** They **had done** the same things that Jesus had done during his public ministry: driven out demons and healed the sick (6:13). And just as Jesus had taught on many occasions, most recently in the villages near Nazareth (6:6), those whom he had sent out had also **taught.** Jesus had given them a share in his mission; what they did was an extension of what he had been doing, multiplying its effects.

Some try to change the world by the force of their ideas; others try to gain political or military power. Jesus used a different method to achieve world-shaking results: he took ordinary people and asked them to carry on his work, empowering them to battle the evils that afflicted others, authorizing them to speak in his name. The sending out of the Twelve prefigures the mission of every follower of Jesus.

For reflection: What particular share in Jesus' mission has he entrusted to me?

31 Jesus periodically sought refuge from the clamor of crowds by going off to deserted places (1:35, 45), and the Twelve now need some quiet time themselves after having worked hard. **He said to them, "Come away by yourselves to a deserted place and rest a while."** Jesus knows well the toll his work takes on him, and he has compassion for his apostles in their weariness. The Twelve have been so successful in carrying out Jesus' mission that they are being mobbed as he was mobbed (3:7–10): **people were coming and going in great numbers.** And just as Jesus was so constantly besieged by those in need that there was no time for meals (3:20), so too the Twelve **had no opportunity even to eat.** Sharing in Jesus' mission means sharing his burdens—and ultimately sharing his cross.

For reflection: What toll has doing the work of Jesus taken on me? How has Jesus rejuvenated me?

BACKGROUND: APOSTLE The Greek word for apostle comes from a verb meaning to send out. In secular usage, an apostle is an ambassador or a messenger. Jesus was sent by God (Mark 9:37; John 20:21), and so the letter to the Hebrews calls Jesus an apostle (Heb 3:1). Jesus in turn sent out twelve specifically chosen followers as his envoys, commissioned to bear his message and carry out his work. The Gospels refer to this group most often as the Twelve and less often as apostles, indicating that their significance lay in their being a symbol of Jesus' restoration of all Israel (which was made up of twelve tribes—Matt 19:28) as much as in their being sent out. The early Church used the term *apostle* for a select few of those who went out on mission for Christ (Rom 1:1; 16:7).

32 **So they went off in the boat by themselves to a deserted place.** The setting is the Sea of Galilee, where there is a **boat** at Jesus' disposal (3:9). But Mark gives no precise indication of either their point of departure or their destination, save saying that the latter is a **deserted place.** Jesus and his followers go **by themselves:** Jesus wants to spend some time apart with them, as he has done before (4:10).

33 **People saw them leaving and many came to know about it.** Many see Jesus and his disciples leave in the boat, but this crowd still has unmet needs and doesn't want to go away empty-handed. **They hastened there on foot from all the towns and arrived at the place before them.** Presumably Jesus and the disciples sailed not across the Sea of Galilee but only to another landing along the same shore. A crowd of people **from all the towns** runs to the landing point and is waiting there when the boat lands. Perhaps a headwind had made for slow rowing. Jesus' hopes for getting away with his disciples are frustrated. What will he do now?

Boat: See *Fishing*, page 19

The Feeding of Five Thousand

³⁴ **When he disembarked and saw the vast crowd, his heart was moved with pity for them, for they were like sheep without a shepherd; and he began to teach them many things. ³⁵ By now it was already late and his disciples approached him and said, "This is a deserted place and it is already very late. ³⁶ Dismiss them so that they can go to the surrounding farms and villages and buy themselves something to eat." ³⁷ He said to them in reply, "Give them some food yourselves." But they said to him, "Are we to buy two hundred days' wages worth of food and give it to them to eat?" ³⁸ He asked them, "How many loaves do you have? Go and see." And when they had found out they said, "Five loaves and two fish." ³⁹ So he gave orders to have them sit down in groups on the green grass. ⁴⁰˜The people took their places in rows by hundreds and by fifties. ⁴¹ Then, taking the five loaves and the two fish and looking up to heaven, he said the blessing, broke the loaves, and gave them to [his] disciples to set before the people; he also divided**

the two fish among them all. **42 They all ate and were satisfied.
43 And they picked up twelve wicker baskets full of fragments and
what was left of the fish. 44 Those who ate [of the loaves] were five
thousand men.**

Gospel parallels: Matt 14:14–21; Luke 9:11–17; John 6:5–13
OT: 2 Kings 4:42–44
NT: Matt 15:32–38; Mark 6:52; 8:1–9, 14–21; 14:22

34 **When he disembarked and saw the vast crowd, his heart was
moved with pity for them, for they were like sheep without a
shepherd.** Jesus tried to get away with his disciples to give them a
much-needed rest (6:30–32), but his plans are frustrated: a **vast crowd**
is awaiting them on the shore when their boat lands. Had we been in
Jesus' place, we might well have been irritated and petulantly told the
people to go away. Jesus reacts differently: **his heart was moved with
pity for them.** This is one of the occasional glimpses Mark gives us of
Jesus' emotions. The Greek word translated by the phrase **his heart was
moved with pity** means to have a gut reaction of compassion: Jesus is
profoundly moved by the condition of the crowd. They are **like sheep
without a shepherd.** Flocks of sheep were a common sight in the world
of Jesus; everyone knew what would happen if the shepherd dozed off.
(Today we might use the comparison "like a class of kindergartners in a
shopping mall without adult supervision.") **Sheep without a shepherd**
scatter and become prey for wild animals. The Old Testament uses this as
an image for the vulnerability of God's people without proper leadership
(Num 27:17; 1 Kings 22:17). Jesus realizes that those who are flocking
to him need direction and guidance, and he responds to their need: **he
began to teach them many things.** Mark doesn't spell out what these
many things were; we might suspect that they had to do with the coming of God's kingdom and how these people were called to respond to
what God was doing (see 1:15).

35 The many things Jesus spoke about took some time; by the time he was
finished, **it was already late and his disciples approached him and
said, "This is a deserted place and it is already very late."** It was
probably near sunset, around the time when the evening meal was usually eaten.

36 The disciples consequently suggest that Jesus **dismiss them so that they can go to the surrounding farms and villages and buy themselves something to eat.** This is a reasonable suggestion. Although they are in a deserted area, there are places nearby to buy food. Perhaps the disciples are also thinking, *If Jesus sends the crowd away, then we will finally get some quiet time.*

37 Jesus is not willing to send away empty-handed those who come to him with spiritual and physical needs. **He said to them in reply, "Give them some food yourselves."** Jesus has involved his disciples in his mission (6:7–13), and he wants them to continue their active involvement. But while the disciples' suggestion was reasonable, Jesus' request seems unreasonable. A vast crowd (verse 34) could consume a vast quantity of food, surely far more than the disciples could be expected to have at their disposal. The disciples point this out to Jesus in a less-than-respectful manner: **but they said to him, "Are we to buy two hundred days' wages worth of food and give it to them to eat?"** Ordinary people usually did not have much savings; **two hundred days' wages** was a large sum for Jesus' followers. The disciples address Jesus rather sharply, as if he doesn't understand the situation as well as they do (which they have thought before: 1:37; 4:38; 5:31). Yet they should have had an inkling that Jesus was not demanding the impossible. He had sent them on mission without food or money (6:8), and none of them had starved. He had given them power to heal the sick and demonized. Shouldn't they have realized by now that being a disciple of Jesus meant being stretched beyond their limits?

For reflection: Has Jesus ever asked the seemingly impossible of me? How did I respond? How has being a disciple of Jesus stretched me beyond my limits?

38 **He asked them, "How many loaves do you have? Go and see."** Having returned from their mission, the disciples were again following the common practice of carrying some food with them as they traveled about. Jesus asks them to tally up their supplies. **And when they had found out they said, "Five loaves and two fish."** Bread was the staple food in the diet of ordinary people; **loaves** were usually round and flat, about an inch high and eight inches in diameter. The **fish** that they were

carrying on their travels were likely dried or salted and were eaten to flavor bread more than as a main dish. **Five loaves and two fish** might have sufficed for a sparse evening meal for the Twelve and Jesus.

39 **So he gave orders to have them sit down in groups on the green grass.** The word translated **sit down** literally means to recline, as was customary at banquets; the word **groups** has the connotation of fellowship. Although they are in a deserted place (6:32), it is not a desert; there is **green grass,** making it a nice site for a picnic.

40 **The people took their places in rows by hundreds and by fifties.** That they **took their places in rows** conveys that everything was orderly; their grouping together **by hundreds and by fifties** means that they gathered in clusters to share the meal that Jesus was about to provide. The expression **by hundreds and by fifties** echoes Old Testament descriptions of how God's people were organized (Exod 18:21, 25; Deut 1:15), but it is unclear how much should be made of this. People gathering together in clusters for a meal could have resonated with Mark's first readers as a foreshadowing of their own gatherings for the Eucharist.

BACKGROUND: DIET Bread was the basic food of ordinary people at the time of Jesus and provided a substantial part of their daily calorie intake. Most families baked their own bread daily in an outdoor oven and ate bread at every meal. Bread was usually made from wheat; barley bread was cheaper but less desirable. Bread made up so much of the diet that the word *bread* could be used to refer to food in general. Grain was also eaten parched ("roasted"—Ruth 2:14). Vegetables, such as beans, lentils, cucumbers, and onions, rounded out meals, along with fruits, such as grapes, figs, dates, and pomegranates. Grapes could be processed into wine or raisins. Olives were crushed for oil, which was used in cooking as well as in oil lamps. Goats and sheep provided milk, yogurt, and cheese. Fish were usually dried or salted to preserve them and were eaten more often as a condiment for bread than as a main course. Herbs, spices, and salt added taste to even simple meals. Ordinary people ate meat only on special occasions, such as feasts. Meals were eaten with the fingers, with bread used as edible spoons to scoop up porridges and soak up sauces (Ruth 2:14; John 13:26), as is still the custom in some traditional Middle Eastern cultures today. Members of the wealthy upper class ate much better than ordinary people: imported wines graced their tables, along with ample meat. *Related topic: Banquets (page 142).*

41 **Then, taking the five loaves and the two fish and looking up to heaven, he said the blessing, broke the loaves, and gave them to [his] disciples to set before the people; he also divided the two fish among them all.** Jesus takes the **five loaves** and **two fish** from his disciples and acts as a host at a Jewish meal would, making the customary **blessing** that was offered before eating. **Looking up to heaven** is a gesture of prayer (see also 7:34). The **blessing** said before Jewish meals is not a blessing of the food but a thanksgiving to God for providing the food. The traditional Jewish blessing over bread is "Blessed are you, O Lord our God, King of the universe, who brings forth bread from the earth." Jesus then **broke the loaves** and **gave them to [his] disciples** to distribute to the crowd, along with the **fish.** Bread and fish was a simple meal, peasants' fare. The disciples are able to carry out Jesus' charge to feed the crowd themselves (verse 37) because of what they have put in the hands of Jesus.

> *For reflection: What have I entrusted to Jesus so that he might have me give it to others?*

Mark's choice of words to describe Jesus' actions foreshadows what Jesus will do at the Last Supper, when he will again take bread, say a blessing, break the bread, and give it to his disciples (14:22). Jesus' feeding of the crowd is an image for Jesus' nourishing of his followers in the Eucharist.

42 Mark does not describe the mechanics whereby five loaves and two fish became sufficient to feed a crowd. He simply recounts Jesus giving the food to his disciples to distribute and then jumps ahead to the results: **they all ate and were satisfied.** No one in the crowd was left out: they **all** ate. No one was still hungry afterward: they all were **satisfied.** Jesus did not send anyone away half-satisfied.

> *For reflection: How completely has Jesus satisfied my needs and longings?*

We can note what is missing from this scene. There are no shouts of amazement from the crowd at the marvelous multiplication of food, no falling down before Jesus in worship, no proclamations that he is someone extraordinary. It is as if the crowd gives no thought to where the food distributed by the disciples has come from—nor does the crowd seem to notice anything out of the ordinary. Jesus fed the crowd in a manner that made no spectacular display of his power. Yet Jesus' disciples could not help but be aware that something extraordinary had taken place. There was a lesson here for them—but would they get the message (see 6:52; 8:14–21)?

For reflection: What lesson might I find in the way Jesus fed the crowd?

43 Mark notes the bountiful results of Jesus' actions. Not only did everyone eat until they were satisfied, but there are also leftovers. **And they picked up twelve wicker baskets full of fragments and what was left of the fish.** The **wicker baskets** were used for carrying food and other items when traveling. That there are **twelve** baskets matches up with the Twelve, who distributed the bread and fish and are now collecting the left-overs. There is more food at the end than there was at the beginning.

44 **Those who ate [of the loaves] were five thousand men.** Mark doesn't tell us whether Jesus also fed some women and children that day; Mark only wants to make the point that a lot of people had been fed—**five thousand** hungry **men.** The prophet Elisha fed a hundred men with twenty loaves of bread, with some left over (2 Kings 4:42–44), but Jesus has done something far greater: he has fed five thousand with five loaves and two fish, with twelve baskets of leftovers.

Mark's first readers may have understood the great number fed by Jesus as a foreshadowing of the Church. The little clusters of people gathering together to celebrate the Eucharist were part of a larger number being fed by Jesus.

Mark has told tales of two banquets (6:17–29, 34–44). One banquet took place in a palace and was hosted by Herod Antipas for his influential friends and "the leading men of Galilee." Herod undoubtedly served the finest foods and imported wines available. This banquet ended in a decadent dance and the death of John the Baptist. The second banquet took place in a grassy field and was hosted by Jesus for ordinary people. The food was also as ordinary as could be. This second banquet did not end in a death, but it foreshadowed another meal that would. The bread that Jesus provided on the shore of the Sea of Galilee anticipated his giving of himself in the Eucharist and on the cross. The two banquets provide a vivid contrast between the kingdoms of this world and the kingdom of God.

ORIENTATION: *After telling of Jesus' feeding of the crowd, Mark recounts one of the most enigmatic episodes in his Gospel.*

Jesus Walks on the Sea of Galilee

⁴⁵ Then he made his disciples get into the boat and precede him to the other side toward Bethsaida, while he dismissed the crowd. ⁴⁶ And when he had taken leave of them, he went off to the mountain to pray. ⁴⁷ When it was evening, the boat was far out on the sea and he was alone on shore. ⁴⁸ Then he saw that they were tossed about while rowing, for the wind was against them. About the fourth watch of the night, he came toward them walking on the sea. He meant to pass by them. ⁴⁹ But when they saw him walking on the sea, they thought it was a ghost and cried out. ⁵⁰ They had all seen him and were terrified. But at once he spoke with them, "Take courage, it is I, do not be afraid!" ⁵¹ He got into the boat with them and the wind died down. They were [completely] astounded. ⁵² They had not understood the incident of the loaves. On the contrary, their hearts were hardened.

Gospel parallels: Matt 14:22–33; John 6:15–21
OT: Exod 3:13–14; 33:18–22; 34:6; 1 Kings 19:9–11; Job 9:8

45 **Then he made his disciples get into the boat and precede him to the other side toward Bethsaida, while he dismissed the crowd.** Jesus wants **his disciples** to **precede him to the other side** of the Sea of Galilee, **toward Bethsaida.** The town of **Bethsaida** lay near the point where the Jordan River flows into the northern end of the Sea of Galilee; the disciples set out from somewhere on the western shore of the lake. As the disciples rowed off, Jesus **dismissed the crowd:** the disciples had earlier asked Jesus to dismiss the crowd (6:36), but Jesus had refused to do so before they had been fed. Jesus operates by his own priorities and timetable.

Bethsaida: See page 197

46 **And when he had taken leave of them, he went off to the mountain to pray.** Jesus previously went off by himself before dawn to pray (1:35); now he finds privacy by dismissing the crowd and sending the disciples off in a boat. He goes **off to the mountain** to pray: the Sea of Galilee is ringed by hills, some of them steep. Mark speaks of Jesus going to **the mountain** as if Jesus went to a specific hill, but there is no way of identifying it. Some scholars suggest that Mark wants his readers to recall another mountain, Mount Sinai, which Moses climbed to be in the presence of God (Exod 24:12–18). Jesus goes to the mountain **to pray,** and as will be evident from verse 48, he spends almost the entire night in prayer.

47 **When it was evening, the boat was far out on the sea and he was alone on shore.** It was late in the day when Jesus fed the crowd (6:35); now the sun is over the horizon, and the disciples are **far out on the sea** (literally, in the middle of the sea), while Jesus is **alone on shore,** atop a hill overlooking the lake.

48 From his vantage point Jesus could see the lake, and either in the dwindling daylight or by the light of the moon he **saw that they were tossed about while rowing, for the wind was against them.** The hills surrounding the Sea of Galilee provide a panoramic view of the lake, which is only seven miles across at its widest. The disciples are **tossed about while rowing** or, more literally, are being tormented in the rowing, straining to make progress despite a strong headwind blowing **against them.** Earlier Jesus tried to take the disciples to a lonely place to give them a much-needed rest (6:31), but his efforts were frustrated by an eager crowd (6:33–34). Now it is night, and instead of having them get some sleep, Jesus has sent them to row into a headwind. In their weariness they must have wondered what Jesus had in mind and why they had to go ahead of him to Bethsaida despite the unfavorable wind. They are in no danger of drowning (as they were during an earlier storm at sea: 4:35–38), but they are exhausted and make little progress. They battle the headwind until **about the fourth watch of the night.** Romans divided the period from 6:00 p.m. to 6:00 a.m. into four watches; the **fourth watch** ran from 3:00 a.m. to 6:00 a.m. Rowing into a headwind and making little progress from evening (verse 47) until

between 3:00 and 6:00 in the morning would be a hard way to spend a night, particularly if one was tired before setting out.

Some of Mark's first readers may have identified with the disciples' frustrating situation. They may have felt that they too were engulfed in darkness, with Jesus off someplace else. As hard as they tried to do what Jesus asked of them, they made little progress. Their efforts to spread the good news about Jesus met with opposition. Why was Jesus asking them to endure hardship and even persecution? Why didn't he provide them with a strong tailwind to fill their sails instead of expecting them to row into a headwind?

For reflection: Has my life as a follower of Jesus ever seemed like a hard journey through darkness without getting anywhere?

About the fourth watch of the night, he came toward them walking on the sea. The people of Nazareth who had known Jesus for many years were sure that he was an ordinary person (6:3). Yet Jesus has done extraordinary things: he has healed the sick, expelled demons, raised a dead girl to life, and now walks on the Sea of Galilee. It is difficult to keep both his ordinariness and his extraordinariness in mind at the same time (a difficulty the people of Nazareth experienced—6:2–3). How can someone who is one of us do things that none of us can do? Once again Mark's Gospel raises the question "Who is Jesus?" Who is this who is **walking on the sea**?

Scripture scholars draw attention to Old Testament passages that speak of God treading on the sea (Job 9:8; Psalm 77:20; Isaiah 43:16) and suggest that Jesus' walking on the Sea of Galilee was meant to be a manifestation of his divinity. Whether these passages would have popped into the minds of the disciples in the boat, or into the minds of Mark's first readers, is another question.

He alone stretches out the heavens
and treads upon the crests of the sea.

Job 9:8

Mark writes that as Jesus was walking on the Sea of Galilee toward his disciples in the boat, **he meant to pass by them.** These are among the most enigmatic words in Mark's Gospel. Jesus intended to walk past his disciples straining at the oars, but why? What was the point of his walking on the water toward his disciples but then walking past them?

The most common explanation that scholars give is that Jesus' passing by his followers echoes Old Testament texts in which God manifests himself by passing by Moses (Exod 33:19, 22; 34:6) and Elijah (1 Kings 19:11). These scholars maintain that this makes Jesus' passing by the disciples a manifestation of his divinity. While these Old Testament parallels exist, I do not think they provide a satisfactory explanation. Consider the event from the point of view of the disciples. They were rowing hard and saw a figure apparently walking on the water, and as the next verses will indicate, they thought it was a ghost and were terrified. They didn't have a copy of Mark's Gospel in their hands to inform them that it was Jesus and that he **meant to pass by them,** so the Old Testament parallels would not have occurred to them. Now consider the event from the point of view of Mark's first readers. Mark does not treat his readers as if they are thoroughly familiar with the Hebrew Scriptures and Judaism. Rather, Mark explains Jewish practices (7:3–4) and translates Hebrew words (7:11), as if this is necessary. I therefore think it doubtful that Mark expected his readers to make a connection between Jesus' passing by and a few Old Testament references to God's passing by. (We can also note that Matthew wrote his Gospel for an audience more familiar with Judaism, and that when Matthew incorporated into his Gospel Mark's account of Jesus walking on the water, he dropped the enigmatic words *He meant to pass by them,* which he wouldn't have done if he had thought that they made an important connection with the Old Testament: see Matt 14:25.)

> *When my glory passes I will set you in the hollow of the rock and will cover you with my hand until I have passed by.*
>
> Exod 33:22

> *Then the* LORD *said, "Go outside and stand on the mountain before the* LORD; *the* LORD *will be passing by."*
>
> 1 Kings 19:11

But why then was it that Jesus **meant to pass by them**? My suggestion (and it may be fanciful) is that Jesus might have thought that the disciples were doing fine under the circumstances and there was no need for him to stop on his way to Bethsaida to help them, despite the fact that they were rowing into a headwind and were stalled in the middle of the Sea of Galilee. Jesus had not sent the headwind, but neither will he remove all headwinds that assail his followers. He will ask far harder things of them than a night's rowing (8:34–35); in carrying on his mission, they will face opposition (13:9–13). This was not the last difficult situation Jesus' disciples would find themselves in, and it would be best for them to get used to headwinds.

For reflection: What do I understand to be the meaning of Jesus intending to pass by his disciples in the boat?

49 **But when they saw him walking on the sea, they thought it was a ghost and cried out.** The disciples see a figure **walking on the sea,** but they do not recognize it as Jesus. Who or what could be able to walk on the sea? **They thought it was a ghost and cried out** in terror. One more thing going awry that night: now a ghost has come to haunt them.

50 **They had all seen him and were terrified. But at once he spoke with them, "Take courage, it is I, do not be afraid!"** Whatever Jesus' reason for intentionally passing by his followers, when he sees their terror he **at once** tries to reassure them, calling out to them, **It is I.** This is the kind of expression we use with those who know us well and recognize our voice; for example, a daughter phoning her parents might leave a message on their answering machine that says, "It's me; give me a call when you have time." Jesus knows that his disciples merely need to hear his voice to realize that it is him. Jesus tells them, **Take courage, . . . do not be afraid!** They are afraid: they think they are seeing a ghost. But Jesus tells them, "It's me; you have nothing to worry about."

Here too Scripture scholars find parallels with the Hebrew Scriptures. The Greek for **it is I** can also be translated "I am." God names himself or speaks of himself as "I am" in the Old Testament (Exod 3:14; Isaiah 43:10–13; 51:12), and scholars suggest that Jesus' use of this expression

157

points to his divinity. Again, though, I wonder if this is a subtlety that would have escaped the disciples and Mark's first readers, since Jesus can simply be understood to be saying, "It's me; your fears are groundless."

> "But," said Moses to God, "when I go to the Israelites and say to them, 'The God of your fathers has sent me to you,' if they ask me, 'What is his name?' what am I to tell them?" God replied, "I am who I am." Then he added, "This is what you shall tell the Israelites: I AM sent me to you."
>
> Exod 3:13–14

For reflection: Is there a relationship between my fears and my lacking a sense of Jesus' presence? How does my relationship with Jesus give me courage?

51 Perhaps to give greater reassurance to his disciples, or perhaps because it was now pointless to continue walking by them, Jesus **got into the boat with them and the wind died down.** It previously took a rebuke by Jesus to still a storm at sea (4:39); now his simple presence brings calm. Mark tells us that the disciples **were [completely] astounded.** We may wonder whether they were more astounded by Jesus walking on the sea or by the wind dying down once he got into the boat. We might also question whether they should have been astonished by anything Jesus did, given all the extraordinary things they had already witnessed.

52 Mark thinks that they should not have been astounded, for the reason they were astounded was that **they had not understood the incident of the loaves.** This too is enigmatic. What was it about **the incident of the loaves** that, if they had understood it, would have prevented them from being astounded when Jesus came walking to them on the sea and the wind then died down? Mark does not provide an answer. I suggest that the broad lesson of the **incident of the loaves** is that Jesus takes care of needs. Jesus is someone to be relied on in difficult situations, even when there does not seem to be an answer or a way out. A second lesson might be that Jesus told his followers to do something they thought was pointless and useless (6:37–39), but when they did it everything worked

out fine (6:41–44). Then Jesus told his disciples to go ahead of him in the boat toward Bethsaida, which also seemed to be an unrealistic demand once a headwind began to blow. But in the end, Jesus was in the boat with them, and all was calm. Should they have been surprised? Shouldn't they have had more trust in Jesus' concern for them and in his power to care for them in every circumstance?

For reflection: How firm is my faith that Jesus cares for me? What are the limits to my trust in him?

Yet the disciples were surprised, even astounded, because they had not learned a lesson from the incident of the loaves. Mark notes that **on the contrary, their hearts were hardened.** This too is a surprising assertion. We might understand him saying that the disciples missed the point because they were not very observant or because they hadn't reflected on the significance of the incident of the loaves. But instead Mark writes that **their hearts were hardened,** a spiritual condition, a refusal to accept what God was doing through Jesus (Mark used the same expression to characterize the willful obtuseness of Jesus' opponents—3:5). Mark seems to be saying that the cause of the disciples' lack of understanding lay not in their not being smart enough but in their not wholeheartedly accepting Jesus. If they had truly given themselves to him and entrusted themselves into his hands, nothing he did would astound or dismay them, and nothing would cause them to fear or doubt.

Despite the meaning we can find in this episode, its enigmatic elements remain. Perhaps they too are part of its message. When we find ourselves rowing against a stiff headwind in the dark, there is much we do not understand. We can only rely on Jesus, understanding that we do not understand.

Jesus Heals Many

53 After making the crossing, they came to land at Gennesaret and tied up there. 54 As they were leaving the boat, people immediately recognized him. 55 They scurried about the surrounding country and began to bring in the sick on mats to wherever they heard he was. 56 Whatever villages or towns or countryside he entered,

they laid the sick in the marketplaces and begged him that they might touch only the tassel on his cloak; and as many as touched it were healed.

Gospel parallels: Matt 14:34–36
OT: Num 15:37–39; Deut 22:12

53 The final enigma in the episode of Jesus walking on the Sea of Galilee is that while Jesus sent the disciples by boat toward Bethsaida (6:45), **after making the crossing, they came to land at Gennesaret.** Bethsaida is on the northern end of the Sea of Galilee; **Gennesaret** is a region along the western shore. Mark provides no explanation for this apparent change in Jesus' itinerary. Perhaps the boat had been blown back toward Gennesaret, making it the nearest landfall. In any case, they landed **and tied up there.** Gennesaret lies between Capernaum and Magdala (the home of Mary Magdalene); it is a fertile plain that stretches about three miles along the shore of the Sea of Galilee and a mile inland.

54 **As they were leaving the boat, people immediately recognized him.** Jesus' reputation has spread far and wide, making it difficult for him to go anywhere without being recognized. Perhaps some of these **people** had been in the crowd that had been doggedly seeking Jesus (6:31–33).

55 Earlier, four men brought a paralyzed man on a mat to Jesus for healing (2:1–4); that is now repeated many times over by those who **scurried about the surrounding country and began to bring in the sick on mats to wherever they heard he was.** Jesus is traveling—or trying to travel—but **wherever** he goes word gets out that he is there, and people bring their sick to him, as they have been doing since the beginning of his ministry (1:32–34).

56 **Whatever villages or towns or countryside he entered, they laid the sick in the marketplaces.** No matter where Jesus goes, he attracts those in need of healing. **Marketplaces** were open areas where vendors offered produce and goods for sale. Villages usually had narrow streets; marketplaces provided space for the sick on their mats to await Jesus. When he came, they **begged him that they might touch only the tassel on his cloak.** The law of Moses specified that Jewish men were

to have tassels on the four corners of their cloaks as a reminder to keep God's commandments (Num 15:37–39; Deut 22:12). Jesus' wearing of such tassels indicates that he observed the law of Moses, obeying even what we might think of as its ritualistic requirements.

Cloak: See Clothing, page 117

> The LORD said to Moses, "Speak to the Israelites and tell them that they and their descendants must put tassels on the corners of their garments, fastening each corner tassel with a violet cord. When you use these tassels, let the sight of them remind you to keep all the commandments of the LORD."
>
> Num 15:37–39

Those lying sick on mats in marketplaces **begged** Jesus to allow them to **touch only the tassel on his cloak.** They cannot reach up very far from their mats, but they don't ask Jesus to bend down to touch them. They ask **only** to be able to touch a tassel on his cloak as he walks by. There is nothing magical about these tassels, nor is there anything superstitious in wanting to touch them. Rather, these sick men and women reach out to Jesus with the same faith shown by the woman with a hemorrhage, who said to herself, "If I but touch his clothes, I shall be cured" (5:28). She was cured, and Jesus commended her faith (5:34). Jesus similarly honors the faith of those who now reach out to him for healing: **and as many as touched** the tassel on his cloak **were healed.** All who seek healing from Jesus receive it.

For reflection: Have I implored Jesus for healing, for myself or someone I love? What was Jesus' response to my prayer?

CHAPTER 7

ORIENTATION: *Jesus addresses questions about Jewish laws and traditions—matters that will have a bearing on relations between Jews and Gentiles in the early Church.*

Washed Hands, Distant Hearts

¹ Now when the Pharisees with some scribes who had come from Jerusalem gathered around him, ² they observed that some of his disciples ate their meals with unclean, that is, unwashed, hands. ³ (For the Pharisees and, in fact, all Jews, do not eat without carefully washing their hands, keeping the tradition of the elders. ⁴ And on coming from the marketplace they do not eat without purifying themselves. And there are many other things that they have traditionally observed, the purification of cups and jugs and kettles [and beds].) ⁵ So the Pharisees and scribes questioned him, "Why do your disciples not follow the tradition of the elders but instead eat a meal with unclean hands?" ⁶ He responded, "Well did Isaiah prophesy about you hypocrites, as it is written:

> **'This people honors me with their lips,**
> > **but their hearts are far from me;**
> **⁷ In vain do they worship me,**
> > **teaching as doctrines human precepts.'**

⁸ You disregard God's commandment but cling to human tradition."

Gospel parallels: Matt 15:1–3, 7–9
OT: Isaiah 29:13

1 **The Pharisees with some scribes who had come from Jerusalem gathered around him.** The **Pharisees** were a religious group or movement who had developed particular traditions for observing and applying the law of Moses. **Scribes** in this instance were scholars who studied and taught the law of Moses. Some Pharisees were also trained as scribes (2:16), but most were not; likewise, not all scribes belonged to the Pharisee party. These particular **scribes** were in sufficient agreement with the Pharisees to join them in confronting Jesus. **Jerusalem**

was the religious center of Judaism, and **scribes who had come from Jerusalem** may have had some amount of status in the eyes of Galilean Jews. Some Pharisees, along with some scribes from Jerusalem, **gathered around** Jesus, ganging up on him.

Scribes: See page 40

2 These Pharisees and scribes **observed that some of his disciples ate their meals with unclean, that is, unwashed, hands.** Nothing is said about whether Jesus ate with unwashed hands; the focus is on the behavior of **his disciples.** As their leader and teacher, Jesus could be held responsible for their behavior, but Mark's framing the issue in terms of Jesus' **disciples** is a hint that Mark is writing with an eye to the situation of his readers, who are later disciples of Jesus. The Pharisees and scribes see that **some of** Jesus' first **disciples** do not wash their hands before eating. This might indicate that some of Jesus' disciples did wash, which in turn might imply that there were divisions in Mark's community over

---

BACKGROUND: PHARISEES were a group or movement, primarily of laymen, who had developed particular traditions for how God's law was to be observed. They were influential but were only one group within first-century Judaism. An ancient historian reports that there were about six thousand Pharisees at the time of Jesus, out of a total Jewish population estimated at a half million to one million in Judea and Galilee. The Pharisees' traditions spelled out how a Jew should observe the Mosaic law, particularly regarding food, tithing, Sabbath observance, and ritual purity. Pharisees had their origin about 150 years before the birth of Jesus, and their rules for observing the law of Moses were handed on as "the tradition of the elders" (Mark 7:3, 5)—traditions established by earlier Pharisees. Pharisees accepted recent developments within Judaism, such as the belief in an afterlife (Acts 23:6–10). Jesus' outlook was closer to that of the Pharisees than to that of any other group we know of in first-century Judaism, but he also had some serious disagreements with them. These disagreements carried over into the early Church, which found itself in competition with the Pharisees for the allegiance of Jews. Since the Pharisees were concerned with daily life rather than Temple worship, their influence survived the destruction of the Temple in AD 70, and Pharisees were among those who shaped the future course of Judaism. The Judaism of today is not identical to the Judaism of the Pharisees of the time of Jesus, but the traditions of the Pharisees are part of the roots of modern Judaism. *Related topic: Jewish religious diversity at the time of Jesus (page 164).*

---

issues about Jewish practices. The Pharisees and scribes observe some of the disciples eating with **unclean** hands: the Greek word used here for **unclean** means common and is the opposite of holy, that which is set apart. Mark explains for his Gentile readers that common or **unclean** hands means **unwashed** hands. The washing in question is not for hygiene but for ritual cleanness.

Clean and unclean: See page 173

3 Mark thinks it necessary to explain some Jewish ritual practices to his readers, many of whom are not Jews. **For the Pharisees and, in fact, all Jews, do not eat without carefully washing their hands, keeping the tradition of the elders.** Earlier generations of **Pharisees** had developed traditions for observing and applying the law of Moses: these are referred to as **the tradition of the elders.** Nowhere did the law of Moses require ordinary Jews to ritually purify their hands before eating. The Mosaic law required priests to wash their hands and feet before offering sacrifice (Exod 30:17–21) and required them to be ritually clean (which usually entailed ritual washing) before eating their share of the sacrifice (Num 18:11–13). In order to sanctify the lives of Jews

---

BACKGROUND: JEWISH RELIGIOUS DIVERSITY AT THE TIME OF JESUS While all Jews shared certain fundamental beliefs and observances, there was considerable diversity when it came to specific views and practices. All Jews revered the law of Moses and the Temple, but different groups, such as the Pharisees, Sadducees, and Essenes, developed different traditions for observing the law. These groups also had differing views on such matters as the kind of messiah or messiahs God would send and whether there would be an afterlife or resurrection of the dead. The vast majority of Jews belonged to no religious group or party: Pharisees, the largest and most influential party, numbered only about six thousand. There were also degrees of compliance with God's laws, however these laws were interpreted. Only the highly dedicated tried to completely separate themselves from potential sources of ritual uncleanness. On the other end of the spectrum were those considered sinners because of their laxity in observing even basic commands of the law. Most Jews fell somewhere in the middle, observing the law as best as their circumstances allowed but without adopting the rigorous practices of the Pharisees. The Judaism of today has roots in the Pharisees of the time of Jesus but reflects a considerable development of traditions and practices. *Related topics: Essenes (page 297), Pharisees (page 163), Sadducees (page 318).*

---

who were not priests, Pharisees tried to extend to everyday life the ritual purity required of priests serving in the Temple. Hence they developed traditions for how hands were to be ritually washed before eating. Mark simplifies matters when he writes that **all Jews** followed the traditions of the Pharisees: many Jews did to varying degrees, but other Jewish groups (such as the Sadducees and the Essenes) had their own traditions, which were not identical to the traditions of the Pharisees. Mark is providing a short parenthetical explanation for his Gentile readers; going into the diversity of Jewish practices at the time of Jesus is beyond his scope.

4 Mark continues his parenthetical explanation: **And on coming from the marketplace they do not eat without purifying themselves.** Going into a **marketplace** meant bumping up against other people and handling merchandise, and there was no way of knowing whether all these people and things were ritually clean. Hence a ritual washing before a meal was necessary after a shopping trip. **And there are many other things that they have traditionally observed:** the tradition of the elders covered many aspects of life. Among the traditions were ritual washings, and among the ritual washings was **the purification of cups and jugs and kettles [and beds].** Anything used to prepare or serve food had to be ritually clean. Some ancient manuscripts of Mark's Gospel mention **beds,** which could become unclean for a variety of reasons (Lev 15:2–5, 19–27.) The goal of sanctifying all of life was noble, but the traditions for doing so had become ever more complex as practice was added onto practice.

For reflection: What do I do to sanctify my daily life?

In providing background information for his Gentile readers, Mark has made the connection between the Pharisees' ritual washing of their hands before eating and the "tradition of the elders." Now Mark can return to his account of some Pharisees and scribes confronting Jesus.

5 **So the Pharisees and scribes questioned him, "Why do your dis-ciples not follow the tradition of the elders but instead eat a meal with unclean hands?"** The **Pharisees and scribes** pose two questions

to Jesus. Both questions have an edge: these Pharisees and scribes are not merely seeking information from Jesus but are criticizing him. The first question is broad: why doesn't Jesus have his disciples **follow the tradition of the elders,** that is, comply with the prescriptions established by earlier generations of Pharisees? At issue is the status of these traditions: are they to be considered authoritative applications of the law of Moses, binding on all, or just options? The second question focuses on one of the traditions of the elders: why does Jesus allow his disciples to **eat a meal with unclean hands?** Mark has explained that this means eating without first ritually washing (verse 2).

6 Jesus takes up the first question posed to him and rejects the traditions of the elders in no uncertain terms. They are not authoritative applications of the law; they are in fact a hindrance to observing God's law. **He responded, "Well did Isaiah prophesy about you hypocrites."** The Greek word **hypocrite** means actor, someone who plays a part on a stage. As used here, it refers to those whose lives betray a disconnect between the outward and the inward, between appearance and reality. Jesus invokes words of **Isaiah** and applies them to his questioners: **As it is written, / "This people honors me with their lips, / but their hearts are far from me."** Isaiah addressed his prophecy to the people of Jerusalem and Judea, accusing them of giving only lip service to God.

> *For reflection: Am I aware of gaps between appearance and reality in my life? Where is my heart in relation to God?*

7 **In vain do they worship me, / teaching as doctrines human precepts.** Isaiah's prophecy condemned the people of Jerusalem and Judea for worshiping God only superficially, because their hearts were not in it and because their religious practices were based on what they wanted to do rather than on what God wanted them to do. Mark follows a Greek translation of Isaiah that contains the nuance of **teaching as doctrines** of God **precepts** and requirements that are only **human.**

> *This people draws near with words only*
> *and honors me with their lips alone,*
> *though their hearts are far from me,*

And their reverence for me has become
routine observance of the precepts of men.

Isaiah 29:13

Mark does not record the expressions on the faces of the Pharisees and scribes when they heard Jesus call them "hypocrites" and tell them that Isaiah's scathing prophecy applied to them. We can imagine that their reaction was a mixture of shock and anger. They considered themselves men who took God's laws so seriously that they had adopted detailed practices for applying and obeying God's laws. Jesus tells them that they are playacting, that they are giving God only lip service, that their hearts are far from God, and that their traditions are human prescriptions that they are passing off as teachings from God.

8 In case the Pharisees and scribes missed the significance of Jesus' application of Isaiah's prophecy to them, he spells it out: **You disregard God's commandment but cling to human tradition.** Jesus draws two contrasts: between what God requires and what humans require, and between obeying and disregarding. He tells them that they have things backward: instead of shaping their lives by God's commands and ignoring merely human customs, they are ignoring what God wants and following human traditions.

Jesus has thrown down the gauntlet. At issue is not simply whether some of Jesus' disciples have properly washed their hands; at issue is the legitimacy of the Pharisees' "tradition of the elders" as an authoritative interpretation and application of the law of Moses. Jesus has pronounced these traditions to be human customs that substitute for obedience to God's law.

A Case in Point

⁹ He went on to say, "How well you have set aside the commandment of God in order to uphold your tradition! ¹⁰ For Moses said, 'Honor your father and your mother,' and 'Whoever curses father or mother shall die.' ¹¹ Yet you say, 'If a person says to father or mother, "Any support you might have had from me is qorban"' (meaning, dedicated to God), ¹² you allow him to do

nothing more for his father or mother. ¹³ You nullify the word of God in favor of your tradition that you have handed on. And you do many such things."
Gospel parallels: Matt 15:3–6
OT: Exod 20:12; 21:17; Num 30:3

9 **He went on to say:** Jesus continues to address the Pharisees and scribes from Jerusalem who have confronted him (7:1–2), responding to their questioning of why his disciples do not follow the traditions of the elders (7:5). Jesus previously accused them of disregarding God's commandment by clinging to human traditions (7:8), and now he repeats this charge in stronger terms: **How well you have set aside the commandment of God in order to uphold your tradition!** On the one hand is **the commandment of God;** on the other hand is their **tradition.** Jesus accuses these Pharisees and scribes of having **set aside** what God commands **in order to uphold** their own traditions.

10 Jesus provides an example of what he is talking about. **For Moses said, "Honor your father and your mother," and "Whoever curses father or mother shall die."** God gave commandments to Moses on Mount Sinai. **Honor your father and your mother** is one of the Ten Commandments (Exod 20:12), the most basic statement of God's law. **Whoever curses father or mother shall die** is also in the law of Moses (Exod 21:17) and indicates the great importance of proper respect for parents (a death penalty is the ultimate in sanctions). Giving **honor** to one's parents was understood to include supporting them materially should that be necessary.

> Honor your father and your mother, that you may
> have a long life in the land which the Lord, your God,
> is giving you.
>
> Exod 20:12

> Whoever curses his father or mother shall be put
> to death.
>
> Exod 21:17

11 **Yet you say:** the **you** is emphatic and highlights the contrast between what Moses said (verse 10) and what these Pharisees and scribes are saying. They hold that **if a person says to father or mother, "Any support you might have had from me is *qorban*" (meaning, dedicated to God).** The word *qorban* is Hebrew for offering, which Mark explains as meaning **dedicated to God.** Whether what was dedicated to God was immediately given to the Temple treasury is unclear; declaring something *qorban* may have been a way of making a deferred gift of property or money. But what happens if one's father or mother needs help, and one's resources have been dedicated to God?

12 Jesus says to the Pharisees and scribes, **You allow him to do nothing more for his father or mother.** An offering to God was made through a vow, and God commanded that vows be fulfilled (Num 30:3; Deut 23:22–24). Some Pharisees, following a tradition of strict observance of vows, judged that the vow of *qorban* took precedence over the obligation to materially support one's parents, and they would not permit a man to use resources vowed to the Temple to help his father and mother. (In later times other Pharisees would disagree with this ruling.)

> When a man makes a vow to the LORD or binds
> himself under oath to a pledge of abstinence, he shall
> not violate his word, but must fulfill exactly the promise
> he has uttered.
>
> Num 30:3

13 Jesus judges that allowing a *qorban* vow to have precedence over one of the Ten Commandments is completely wrong. Jesus tells these Pharisees and scribes, **You nullify the word of God in favor of your tradition that you have handed on.** This is the third time that Jesus has made this charge, each time in stronger terms (verses 8, 9, 13). Those he is speaking to not only disregard God's commands in favor of human traditions but also **nullify the word of God,** cancel it, **in favor of your tradition that you have handed on.** A sharp contrast is again drawn between **the word of God** and what has been **handed on** as a **tradition.** A case in point is the *qorban* issue. Could anything be clearer

than the intent of the command to honor one's father and mother? Yet this clear intent of God's law has been nullified, supposedly in the name of observing God's law.

The *qorban* issue is not an isolated instance, for Jesus concludes his words to the Pharisees and scribes by saying, **And you do many such things.** Jesus does not provide additional examples of these **many such things,** but we can suspect that regulations regarding Sabbath observance were among them. Earlier when Jesus' disciples plucked heads of grain as Sabbath snacks, some Pharisees judged it a violation of Sabbath law (2:23–24). Jesus reminded them that the intent of Sabbath law was to make it a day of rest and relaxation, not a day of onerous restrictions (2:27). Likewise, Jesus reminded those critical of his healing on the Sabbath that the Sabbath was meant for doing good and saving life, all their interpretations of the law notwithstanding (3:1–4).

Jesus called those who nullified God's law by means of human traditions "hypocrites" (7:6), meaning that there was a gap between appearance and reality in their lives. The traditions of the Pharisees appeared to implement God's law, while in reality they subverted and nullified it.

> *For reflection: Have I in any way substituted my interpretations of what God wants for what God wants? How can I tell?*

What Defiles? What Divides?

¹⁴ He summoned the crowd again and said to them, "Hear me, all of you, and understand. ¹⁵ Nothing that enters one from outside can defile that person; but the things that come out from within are what defile." [¹⁶]

¹⁷ When he got home away from the crowd his disciples questioned him about the parable. ¹⁸ He said to them, "Are even you likewise without understanding? Do you not realize that everything that goes into a person from outside cannot defile, ¹⁹ since it enters not the heart but the stomach and passes out into the latrine?" (Thus he declared all foods clean.) ²⁰ "But what comes out of a person, that is what defiles. ²¹ From within people, from their hearts, come evil thoughts, unchastity, theft, murder,

²² adultery, greed, malice, deceit, licentiousness, envy, blasphemy, arrogance, folly. ²³ All these evils come from within and they defile."

> Gospel parallels: Matt 15:10–20
> OT: Lev 11
> NT: Acts 10–11, 15; Rom 14; Gal 2:1–14

14 Some Pharisees and scribes asked Jesus two questions: why didn't his disciples follow the tradition of the elders, and, specifically, why did they eat with unclean hands (7:5)? Jesus responded to the first question with a scathing attack on the tradition of the elders (7:6–13). Mark does not tell us the reaction of the Pharisees and scribes to Jesus' words, but it could hardly have been favorable. Jesus goes on to address the second question, but to a different audience. **He summoned the crowd again and said to them, "Hear me, all of you, and understand."** Jesus prefaced his telling of the parable of the sower with an exhortation to **hear** (4:3); his doing so again indicates the importance of what he is going to say and that it is urgent that his listeners **understand.** Jesus says, "Hear **me**": he is the authority behind his words. Jesus says, "Hear me, **all of you**," a hint that his words will be important to later generations as well as to his first audience.

15 **Nothing that enters one from outside can defile that person; but the things that come out from within are what defile.** Jesus broadens the issue from eating with unclean hands to what one eats—everything that **enters one from outside.** Jesus proclaims that **nothing** that enters one from the outside **can defile** a person. The Greek word for **defile** is a form of the word that was previously translated "unclean" (7:2, 5). **Nothing** that enters one renders one unclean: the word **nothing** seems all-inclusive, admitting no exceptions. Jesus' words seemingly fly in the face of numerous injunctions in the law of God given through Moses (see chapter 11 of Leviticus, for example). Jesus goes on to say that there are things that defile: **the things that come out from within.** Jesus' meaning is not immediately obvious. What are **the things that come out from within**?

> *This is the law for animals and birds and for all the*
> *creatures that move about in the water or swarm on*

> *the ground, that you may distinguish between the clean*
> *and the unclean, between creatures that may be eaten and*
> *those that may not be eaten.*
>
> Lev 11:46–47

16 (Some manuscripts of Mark's Gospel include at this point the verse "Anyone who has ears to hear ought to hear." These words are not found in the most reliable manuscripts and were probably added by a scribe who copied them from Mark 4:23. The New American Bible omits this verse.)

17 **When he got home away from the crowd his disciples questioned him about the parable.** Jesus' words (verse 15) were a **parable**—a cryptic saying, not a story. As had happened previously when Jesus told parables, his disciples did not understand the meaning of this parable and so **questioned him** once they were alone with him (4:10, 34). The Greek for **when he got home** means literally "when he entered into a house" and does not imply that Jesus returned to Peter's house in Capernaum. Jesus went into someone's house, away from the crowd, and his disciples asked him to explain his words about things that enter and leave a person.

Parables: See page 79

18 **He said to them, "Are even you likewise without understanding?"** Jesus urged his listeners to understand his words (verse 14), but neither the crowd nor the disciples did so. This is not the first time Jesus' disciples lack understanding (4:13; 6:52), nor will it be the last. Jesus may be a little surprised at their obtuseness, for he exclaims to them, "Are **even you** without understanding?"

Jesus explains his cryptic words about what goes in and comes out of a person. He begins with what goes in—**Do you not realize that everything that goes into a person from outside cannot defile?**—restating in slightly different words what he has already said (verse 15).

19 Jesus explains why what goes into a person cannot defile: **It enters not the heart but the stomach and passes out into the latrine.** In one sense, this is simple physiology: the heart is not part of the digestive system, and what is taken by mouth makes no direct contact with the heart as it passes through the human body. But Jesus is not giving an anatomy

lesson. In biblical thought, the **heart** was the seat of emotions and will; it was the core of one's personality and the source of moral acts. "Hardness of heart" (3:5; 6:52) is not arteriosclerosis but a spiritual condition. Jesus says that what is eaten goes into the digestive system but does not enter the heart: nothing taken by mouth goes into the core of the person.

Jesus is not finished with his explanation, but Mark interrupts his account to draw an implication from what Jesus has said. Mark interjects **Thus he declared all foods clean.** This is a bold claim in light of the Old Testament's detailed prescriptions regarding clean and unclean foods. But is the matter so simply and clearly settled as Mark thinks it is? Before we can properly consider this, we need to hear the rest of Jesus' explanation of his words.

20 Jesus continues to explain his words, taking up the second element of his argument: **But what comes out of a person, that is what defiles.**

BACKGROUND: CLEAN AND UNCLEAN The Old Testament contains complex regulations regarding the clean and the unclean (e.g., chapters 11 through 15 of Leviticus). The clean could come in contact with the holy, and the unclean could not; an unclean person could not worship in the Temple. A person could become unclean either through sin or for a variety of reasons that had nothing to do with sin. Virtually all sexual activity (even if perfectly moral) rendered one unclean, as did certain diseases, contact with a corpse, or eating certain forbidden foods. Some types of uncleanness were contagious. In these cases, contact with an unclean person or object rendered another person unclean. An unclean person could be made clean through remedies that depended on the type of uncleanness; washing with water and the passage of a certain amount of time were required, along with sacrifice in the Temple for more serious types of uncleanness. Most Jews were probably ritually unclean much of the time but could remedy their condition in order to enter the Temple area. Maintaining or restoring cleanness was important for priests because they served the Temple, and special rules pertained to them. Ritual cleanness was a particular concern for the Pharisees, and their program aimed at maintaining in everyday life the ritual purity, or cleanness, required for Temple worship. Archaeologists have found widespread evidence of concern for ritual cleanness in Galilee and Judea (baths for ritual washing; cups and bowls carved from stone, which made them impervious to uncleanness), but most Jews did not observe the detailed traditions of the Pharisees. *Related topics: Pharisees (page 163), Social boundaries (page 176).*

Again he basically restates what he previously said (verse 15) in order to go on and explain its meaning.

21 **From within people, from their hearts, come evil thoughts.** Defilement comes not from without but from **within people,** specifically **from their hearts.** The heart in biblical idiom is the source of one's intentions and actions. From it can **come evil thoughts:** the Greek word translated as **thoughts** has connotations of intentions and designs. The root of **evil** lies in our intentions, in our devising to do wrong. From **evil thoughts** flow all sorts of evil acts and vices; Jesus goes on to list twelve of them. He first mentions **unchastity** (sexual sins), **theft,** and **murder.**

22 The list continues with **adultery** and **greed** (greedy acts rather than simply greedy feelings). **Malice** is a general term for wicked deeds. Next are **deceit, licentiousness** (or debauchery), **envy, blasphemy** (abusive speech, whether against God or another person), **arrogance** (or pride), and **folly.** This is neither a systematic nor an exhaustive listing but simply a sample of serious sins.

23 **All these evils come from within and they defile.** These various **evils** proceed from the intentions of the human heart, and they **defile** a person. In Jesus' view, the defilement one should worry about is moral defilement resulting from sins, rather than ritual uncleanness resulting from diet.

For reflection: What flows from my heart? Have I in any way brought defilement on myself?

If what one eats does not bring moral defilement, then was Mark right to proclaim that Jesus "declared all foods clean" (verse 19)? Did Jesus, after upholding God's law against human traditions that nullified it (7:9–13), go on to nullify God's law regarding food?

In pondering this it is helpful to distinguish between the situation of Jesus and the situations of Mark and the early Church. There is no evidence that Jesus ever violated any of the food laws of the Old Testament. If Jesus had eaten ham, for example, his opponents would surely have condemned him for this direct violation of the Mosaic law (Lev 11:4–8).

Jesus was criticized for eating with the wrong people (2:16) but not for eating the wrong food. He was assailed for allowing his disciples to eat too much (2:18) and with unwashed hands (7:5) but not for allowing them to eat forbidden foods. Had Jesus ever given his critics any grounds for accusing him of violating food laws, they would have done so: Jesus' opponents kept him under a microscope (3:2).

Another consideration: if Jesus had directly declared that his followers were freed from the food laws of the Old Testament, it should have settled the matter. Yet these laws remained a hotly debated issue in the early Church for some years, along with other questions about the applicability of the law of Moses. Some Jewish and Gentile Christians thought that the entire Mosaic law was binding on all Christians, Jew and Gentile alike. Others thought that injunctions regarding circumcision and food were not binding on Gentile converts. Some of the story is told in chapters 10, 11, and 15 of Acts and in chapter 2 of Galatians. It is clear that the early Church wrestled with Jewish food laws as if the issue had not been settled by an explicit teaching of Jesus.

For reflection: What are the implications of Jesus not settling every issue during his public ministry but leaving questions for the Church to resolve?

What then was the meaning of Jesus proclaiming, **Nothing that enters one from outside can defile that person; but the things that come out from within are what defile** (verse 15)? Perhaps his words are best understood as a prophetic pronouncement, akin to God's statement through Hosea that "it is love that I desire, not sacrifice" (Hosea 6:6). Was God abolishing the laws that required sacrifices? No, God was saying, "I value your love far more than your animal sacrifices."

Jesus' words can be understood to mean "It is not so much what enters a person that defiles; the evil that comes out of a person is far more defiling." Jesus was not explicitly overturning food laws; he was teaching that there were more important laws. Just as Jesus upheld the commandment to honor one's father and mother (7:10–13), he also upheld the laws that followed it in the Ten Commandments, covering murder, adultery, theft, lying speech, and covetousness (Exod 20:13–17). By listing serious sins that flow from evil intentions (verses 21–22), Jesus put his finger on the real source of defilement and separation from God.

Jesus' words took on a fuller meaning for Mark. Mark wrote his Gospel about forty years after Jesus' public ministry, and there had been a lot of discussion in the meantime over the continuing validity of Old Testament injunctions. The Holy Spirit had guided the leaders of the Church into a realization that Gentile converts should not be required to follow all of the prescriptions of the law of Moses (Acts 15:28–29). This still left a lot of details to be worked out, and one of them was the question of whether Christians who observed Jewish food laws could eat with Christians who did not observe such laws. Paul and James differed on the issue, and Peter was caught in the middle (Gal 2:11–14). Mark wrote for a Church that may have been divided over food laws (see Rom 14) and perhaps over who could eat with whom. It was important that all Christians be able to eat together, because the Eucharist was celebrated as a meal.

Mark addressed the issues plaguing his audience by drawing an implication from Jesus' words. From Jesus' proclamation that what entered one from the outside could not make one unclean, Mark deduced that Jesus

---

BACKGROUND: SOCIAL BOUNDARIES Religious practices done out of obedience to God can have social consequences. The law of Moses commanded circumcision, Sabbath observance, not eating certain foods, and avoiding anything considered unclean. By observing these commandments, Jews were set apart from those who did not observe them. Because of laws and traditions that specified what could be eaten, Jews could not dine at Gentiles' tables. When Gentile converts began to be added to an originally Jewish Christian Church, it raised issues about how these ordinances should be observed. Some Jewish Christians were shocked by Peter's association with the Gentile convert Cornelius: "You entered the house of uncircumcised people and ate with them" (Acts 11:3). Later, when Peter was pressured into not eating with Gentile Christians, Paul scathingly criticized him (Gal 2:11–14). Since the Eucharist was celebrated as a meal, Jewish food laws—functioning as a barrier between those who adhered to such laws and those who did not—threatened to split the Church in two. Hence there was intense debate over the bindingness of Jewish laws that created social boundaries (Acts 15:1–29). The letter to the Ephesians proclaims that Christ broke down the barriers between Jew and Gentile: "For he is our peace, he who made both one and broke down the dividing wall of enmity, through his flesh, abolishing the law with its commandments and legal claims, that he might create in himself one new person in place of the two" (Eph 2:14–15; see also Eph 3:1–6). *Related topic: Clean and unclean (page 173).*

---

had "declared all foods clean" (verse 19). Jesus, as part of his "new teaching with authority" (1:27), had laid down a principle about the clean and the unclean (7:15). Mark, writing with the knowledge of how the Church was resolving the issue of Jewish food laws, drew a conclusion from Jesus' words: food could not defile, nor should it set up a barrier between Christian and Christian.

For reflection: What are the barriers that still divide Christian from Christian?

ORIENTATION: *Jesus' mission is primarily to Jews, but he also travels into Gentile areas outside Galilee.*

A Gentile Woman Tells Jesus a Parable

²⁴ From that place he went off to the district of Tyre. He entered a house and wanted no one to know about it, but he could not escape notice. ²⁵ Soon a woman whose daughter had an unclean spirit heard about him. She came and fell at his feet. ²⁶ The woman was a Greek, a Syrophoenician by birth, and she begged him to drive the demon out of her daughter. ²⁷ He said to her, "Let the children be fed first. For it is not right to take the food of the children and throw it to the dogs." ²⁸ She replied and said to him, "Lord, even the dogs under the table eat the children's scraps." ²⁹ Then he said to her, "For saying this, you may go. The demon has gone out of your daughter." ³⁰ When the woman went home, she found the child lying in bed and the demon gone.

Gospel parallels: Matt 15:21–28

24 **From that place he went off to the district of Tyre.** Mark doesn't specify the location of **that place,** but it would have been the place in Galilee where Jesus spoke about defilement (7:1–23). **From** there Jesus travels into **the district of Tyre,** a town northwest of Galilee in what is today Lebanon. **Tyre,** a Mediterranean seaport about forty miles from Capernaum, was a large, predominantly Gentile city; some Jews lived in the region. Jesus **entered a house and wanted no one to know about it.** He has previously gone off by himself for prayer

(1:35; 6:46). He apparently again wants some quiet time, and he goes into a Gentile area to escape the Jewish crowds who are following him (6:31–34). No mention is made of Jesus bringing his disciples along. Jesus' hopes for some time alone, however, are frustrated: **he could not escape notice.** Jesus' fame as a healer and an exorcist has spread even to pagan Tyre (3:8); it is hard for him to go anywhere anonymously.

For reflection: What insight into Jesus might I be given by his wanting some time by himself?

25 **Soon a woman whose daughter had an unclean spirit heard about him.** It doesn't take long for word of Jesus' whereabouts to reach **a woman whose daughter had an unclean spirit.** Out of concern for her afflicted daughter, this woman hunts down Jesus. **She came and fell at his feet,** a gesture of supplication.

For reflection: What needs do I bring to Jesus? Do I have any need so pressing that I am willing to prostrate myself at his feet?

26 What set this woman apart from those who had previously come to Jesus in need was that she **was a Greek, a Syrophoenician by birth.** She was **Greek,** not by nationality but by language and culture, as were many people living along the eastern Mediterranean coast. Her nationality is indicated by her being **a Syrophoenician by birth.** This means that she was a Phoenician living in Syria, as opposed to a Phoenician living in Carthage, on the North African coast, the other historic Phoenician center. From a Jewish point of view, this Gentile woman was an unclean woman with a daughter possessed by an unclean spirit.

She begged Jesus **to drive the demon out of her daughter.** Two parents have thrown themselves at the feet of Jesus on behalf of their daughters: Jairus, the Jewish synagogue official (5:22–23), and now this unnamed pagan woman. We are given a glimpse of the wide range of people who come to Jesus. She **begged** Jesus to free her daughter of the evil spirit, as she was confident he could.

27 Yet Jesus rebuffs her! **He said to her, "Let the children be fed first. For it is not right to take the food of the children and throw it to**

the dogs." Jesus invokes a parable, or comparison: just as parents would not make their children go hungry by throwing their food to dogs, so too Jesus cannot divert food to Gentiles that is meant for the children of Israel, whom he has a mission to feed. Jesus' words compare this woman to a dog; to call someone a dog was an expression of contempt. Some scholars point out that the Greek word for **dogs** used here means little dogs, perhaps puppies, and these scholars suggest that Jesus said these words with a twinkle in his eye, as if he was teasing and testing the woman. Perhaps this is so, but virtually all references to dogs in the Old Testament are negative: dogs are not tame household pets but mongrels that run wild as scavengers (Exod 22:30; 1 Kings 14:11; 21:23–24; 2 Kings 9:33–36). The image of throwing food to the dogs is that of tossing refuse outside the house, where dogs act as roving garbage-disposal units. It is hard to understand Jesus' response to the woman as anything other than a put-down: the children's food cannot be treated as garbage for scavengers.

For reflection: How do I understand Jesus' words and his turning this woman away?

BACKGROUND: GREEK LANGUAGE AND CULTURE Alexander the Great (ruled 336–323 BC) of Macedonia (northern Greece) conquered the eastern Mediterranean world, bringing in his wake Greek culture. Thereafter the Greek language became the common international language and the language of many of the lands he conquered. Many Jews living outside Palestine adopted Greek as their language; Jews living in Egypt translated the Hebrew Scriptures into Greek in the third and second centuries BC. Most Jews in Palestine kept Aramaic as their spoken language. The New Testament was written in Greek, the most commonly understood language (even Paul's letter to Rome was written in Greek, not Latin). The early Church, being overwhelmingly Greek-speaking, used the Greek translation of the Old Testament as its Scripture. Scholars debate whether Jesus knew any Greek. The common view is that he probably picked up some Greek words used in commerce but taught in Aramaic, his mother tongue. Greek culture (including philosophy, architectural styles, and enjoyment of the theater) had its Jewish adherents in some of the larger cities of Palestine (including Jerusalem) but does not seem to have penetrated the small villages and rural areas of Galilee. *Related topics: What languages did Jesus speak? (page 124).*

28 This woman came to Jesus out of concern for her daughter, and she is not willing to go away empty-handed. She takes Jesus' parable and reworks it into a new parable. **She replied and said to him, "Lord, even the dogs under the table eat the children's scraps."** She addresses Jesus as **Lord** and is the only person in Mark's Gospel to call Jesus by this title. Her addressing him as **Lord** means that she recognizes him as one with authority; for Mark's readers, the title **Lord** carries a fuller meaning. She speaks of **the dogs under the table:** Greeks did keep dogs as pets, and the woman changes Jesus' image of wild scavenger dogs into an image of docile household pets sitting under the table, waiting for scraps of food to fall. She knows, as every parent knows, that when children eat, scraps of food do fall. And sometimes children slip bites of food to their pets when their parents aren't looking. This woman is not willing to wait for her daughter to be freed until the children of Israel are done eating; she wants Jesus to heal her daughter now, just as pets get their scraps **even** while the meal is in progress. She does not try to give dogs the same status as children but implicitly pleads, "Even if we Gentiles are dogs, can't you treat us as friendly companions rather than as wild mongrels?"

Lord: See page 332

29 Jesus recognizes that she has trumped his parable, and if he didn't have a twinkle in his eye before, he probably has one now. **Then he said to her, "For saying this, you may go":** Jesus does not commend her faith or her determination, although he could well have done so. Instead Jesus commends her words: **For saying this,** for beating me at my own parable game, you get your wish and **may go.** In his earlier exorcisms, Jesus confronted possessed people face-to-face and commanded that demons depart (1:25, 34; 3:11; 5:8). But now Jesus assures this woman that **the demon has gone out of your daughter,** expelled by Jesus even though he has not seen the girl or pronounced an exorcism over her. This might be the most powerful demonstration in Mark's Gospel of Jesus' power over evil spirits—and it is done after Jesus has his mind changed by a quick-witted woman who would not take no for an answer.

For reflection: Have I ever asked Jesus to change his mind? What arguments did I use?

30 **When the woman went home, she found the child lying in bed and the demon gone.** Mark wraps up his account by telling us that it happened just as Jesus said: when the woman got back home, she found that the demon had left her daughter. The daughter was **lying in bed,** perhaps exhausted by the ordeal but whole again.

By recounting this incident, Mark shows that the Church's mission to the Gentiles has a precedent in the ministry of Jesus. Even though Jesus was sent to the children of Israel, he allowed himself to be won over by this remarkable Gentile mother.

Jesus Opens a Man's Ears

[31] **Again he left the district of Tyre and went by way of Sidon to the Sea of Galilee, into the district of the Decapolis. [32] And people brought to him a deaf man who had a speech impediment and begged him to lay his hand on him. [33] He took him off by himself away from the crowd. He put his finger into the man's ears and, spitting, touched his tongue; [34] then he looked up to heaven and groaned, and said to him, "Ephphatha!"** (that is, **"Be opened!"**) [35] **And [immediately] the man's ears were opened, his speech impediment was removed, and he spoke plainly. [36] He ordered them not to tell anyone. But the more he ordered them not to, the more they proclaimed it. [37] They were exceedingly astonished and they said, "He has done all things well. He makes the deaf hear and [the] mute speak."**

OT: Isaiah 35:4–6

31 **Again he left the district of Tyre and went by way of Sidon to the Sea of Galilee, into the district of the Decapolis** (literally, into the middle of the district of the Decapolis). The seaport city of **Sidon** was twenty-two miles north of **Tyre,** while the **Sea of Galilee** and the **Decapolis** lay considerably south and east. To travel from Tyre to the Decapolis **by way of Sidon** is very indirect, so much so that some scholars suggest that Mark had his geography confused. But there is another explanation: Jesus may have purposely chosen a roundabout route that skirted Galilee. Going north from Tyre to Sidon, then east toward Damascus, and finally south to the Decapolis region would have allowed

Jesus to remain in Gentile areas throughout his journey. He would have had to cover more than one hundred miles on foot, and it would have taken about a week (or longer if he made any stops along the way, as he did near Tyre). Mark makes no mention of the disciples accompanying Jesus on this journey, nor are we told that they were present when Jesus reached the Decapolis.

Decapolis: See page 112

Why would Jesus want to make an extended journey through Gentile areas, possibly by himself? Some suggest that Jesus sometimes left Galilee because he thought his life was in danger, but Mark gives no indication of this. We might speculate that Jesus wanted an extended time by himself (see 7:24), away from the crowds, away perhaps even from his disciples, so that he could reflect on his mission and on what lay ahead and prepare himself for it in prayer. But Mark doesn't spell this out, and in the end we are unsure of Jesus' motives.

The unknowns about Jesus' journey from Tyre to the Decapolis are a reminder that Mark provides only a limited account of what Jesus did during his public ministry and does not relate all of Jesus' thoughts. Just as the early years of Jesus' life are hidden, much is also hidden from us during the period of Jesus' life covered by Mark's Gospel.

For reflection: What significance do I see in Jesus making an extended trip through Gentile areas? What lesson might I learn in there being elements of Jesus' life that are hidden from me?

32 At the end of his journey Jesus is in the Decapolis region, a predominantly Gentile area that Jesus briefly visited before (5:1–20) and that lay generally southeast of the Sea of Galilee. **People brought to him a deaf man who had a speech impediment and begged him to lay his hand on him.** Mark made a point of telling us that the woman who approached Jesus in Tyre was a Gentile, but he doesn't tell us the nationality of this **deaf man who had a speech impediment.** Since Jesus was in a heavily Gentile area, we might conclude that this man was a Gentile, but since some Jews lived in the region, we can't be sure. Perhaps Mark's intent is that we take the man to be a Gentile, since the region was Gentile, but that we also recognize that the matter of Jewish/Gentile

identity is of fading importance. Ultimately it will not matter whether those who come to Jesus are Jews or Gentiles, and Mark might be giving a hint of this by leaving the man's nationality unspecified.

Some **people brought** this man to Jesus. After Jesus' previous visit to the Decapolis area, a man whom Jesus had freed of a legion of demons "began to proclaim in the Decapolis what Jesus had done for him" (5:20). When Jesus returned, some recognized him as one with amazing power, and they brought an afflicted person to him. He was a **deaf man who had a speech impediment:** presumably he had not been born deaf (or he would not have been able to speak at all) but had become deaf at an early age, and now his speech was indistinct, as is often the case with those who have not been able to hear themselves speak. Those who brought this man to Jesus **begged him to lay his hand on him.** Previously people of the Decapolis begged Jesus to leave the region (5:17), but now they beg Jesus for a healing. What changed them? Perhaps it was the continuing witness of the man whom Jesus had freed of demons (5:20). They beg Jesus **to lay his hand** on the deaf person so that he might be healed. Jairus had also asked Jesus to lay his hands on his sick daughter (5:23).

33 **He took him off by himself away from the crowd.** Was this simply to get some privacy, or did Jesus want to downplay the spectacular element in what he was going to do? The latter seems more probable, in light of what follows (verse 36) and in light of Jesus also wanting to downplay the spectacular when he raised Jairus's daughter (5:37, 40). **He put his finger into the man's ears:** Jesus thrust or stuck his finger into the deaf man's ears as if opening up a passage for sound. Then Jesus, **spitting, touched his tongue.** The image we should probably have is of Jesus **spitting** on his finger and then touching the man's tongue with his finger, thus making contact with the man's afflicted organs, tongue as well as ears. Why would Jesus use spittle? Some maintain that in the time of Jesus, spittle was thought to have natural healing properties. But Jesus did not need to rely on natural means for his healings, so the significance of his using his spittle is uncertain. All Mark tells us is that Jesus did it, and on more than one occasion (8:23; see also John 9:6), even though it might strike some today as a bit crude and unhygienic. Mark has often described Jesus touching those whom he heals (1:31, 41; 5:41; 6:5) but never in such graphic detail.

34 **Then he looked up to heaven and groaned.** Jesus had also **looked up to heaven** in an attitude of prayer when he blessed the five loaves and two fish (6:41). Jesus **groaned,** sighing with deep feeling and compassion; his groan could also have been a form of prayer (Paul will write of the Holy Spirit interceding with inexpressible "groanings" to help us in our weakness—Rom 8:26). Jesus **said to him, *"Ephphatha!"* (that is, "Be opened!").** Since *Ephphatha* is an Aramaic word, Mark translates it for his Greek-speaking readers: **that is, "Be opened!"** Jesus commands the man's ears to be opened and his tongue released, and more broadly that the man be opened up to full life. Jesus speaks this word to a man who is deaf and cannot hear Jesus speak!

What languages did Jesus speak? See page 124

For reflection: Am I a bit hard of hearing when Jesus speaks to me? How has Jesus opened my ears to his words?

35 Jesus has gone to some lengths to heal this man—touching his ears and tongue, praying, speaking a healing command—as if deafness and impaired speech are difficult conditions to remedy, but the resulting healing is quick and complete. **And [immediately] the man's ears were opened, his speech impediment was removed, and he spoke plainly.** He could now hear, and the fact that he **spoke plainly** shows that **his speech impediment was removed.** When Jesus speaks, even the deaf can hear.

This healing is not recorded in the other Gospels, and it is the only instance in Mark's Gospel of Jesus healing a person who is deaf. Those of Mark's first readers who were familiar with the book of Isaiah might have recalled Isaiah's prophecy that when God came to save his people, "the ears of the deaf {will} be cleared; / . . . the tongue of the dumb will sing" (Isaiah 35:5–6). Jesus fulfills Isaiah's prophecy; God has come in Jesus to save his people.

> *Here is your God,*
> *he comes with vindication;*
> *With divine recompense*
> *he comes to save you.*

> *Then will the eyes of the blind be opened,*
> *the ears of the deaf be cleared;*
> *Then will the lame leap like a stag,*
> *then the tongue of the dumb will sing.*

Isaiah 35:4–6

36 **He ordered them not to tell anyone.** This is almost as unrealistic as Jesus' commanding that his raising of Jairus's daughter be kept secret (5:43). Those who had brought the deaf man to Jesus, as well as everyone who knew him, could not have helped but notice that he could now hear and speak clearly. Word of how this happened would inevitably get around. Jesus' intent again seems to be to downplay the spectacular lest it distract from the essentials of what he was about. **But the more he ordered them not to, the more they proclaimed it.** This may indicate that Jesus remained for a time in the Decapolis region. The word translated **proclaimed** was used for Jesus' proclamation that the reign of God was at hand (1:14–15), for the Gerasene demoniac's proclamation of what Jesus had done for him (5:20), and for the disciples' proclaiming of repentance (6:12). Those who proclaim the healing of the deaf man are doing what disciples of Jesus should do, but they are doing so before they have the complete picture of Jesus' identity and mission.

37 **They were exceedingly astonished** by what Jesus had done, absolutely overwhelmed that a deaf man could hear and speak clearly. **They said, "He has done all things well. He makes the deaf hear and [the] mute speak."** Mark has told us of the healing of only one deaf man. Perhaps there were others, or perhaps these words are a generalization. **He has done all things well:** Jesus receives a very favorable response from people living in a Gentile region. For Mark it is a foreshadowing of Gentiles responding positively to Jesus and becoming part of the Church.

For reflection: Can I say that Jesus has done all things well for me?

CHAPTER 8

The Feeding of Four Thousand

¹ **In those days when there again was a great crowd without anything to eat, he summoned the disciples and said,** ² **"My heart is moved with pity for the crowd, because they have been with me now for three days and have nothing to eat.** ³ **If I send them away hungry to their homes, they will collapse on the way, and some of them have come a great distance."** ⁴ **His disciples answered him, "Where can anyone get enough bread to satisfy them here in this deserted place?"** ⁵ **Still he asked them, "How many loaves do you have?" "Seven," they replied.** ⁶ **He ordered the crowd to sit down on the ground. Then, taking the seven loaves he gave thanks, broke them, and gave them to his disciples to distribute, and they distributed them to the crowd.** ⁷ **They also had a few fish. He said the blessing over them and ordered them distributed also.** ⁸ **They ate and were satisfied. They picked up the fragments left over—seven baskets.** ⁹ **There were about four thousand people.**

He dismissed them ¹⁰ **and got into the boat with his disciples and came to the region of Dalmanutha.**

Gospel parallels: Matt 15:32–39
NT: Mark 6:34–44

1 **In those days when there again was a great crowd without anything to eat:** Mark has not described Jesus leaving the Decapolis district (7:31); Mark relates what happened **in those days,** during Jesus' visit to the region. On a previous occasion in Galilee Jesus had fed a crowd of five thousand (6:34–44), and now **there again was a great crowd without anything to eat.** The previous crowd had been made up of Jews, but since the Decapolis was a Gentile region with a Jewish minority, the present crowd was presumably mostly Gentile. Mark doesn't make this explicit, however; perhaps his unspoken message is that the distinction between Jews and Gentiles will fade because of Jesus. Jesus **summoned the disciples:** there has been no mention of the disciples being with Jesus since they questioned him about defilement (7:17). Since then

Jesus has traveled to the district of Tyre (7:24) and through other Gentile regions to the Decapolis (7:31).

Decapolis: See page 112

2 When his disciples arrive, Jesus tells them, **My heart is moved with pity for the crowd, because they have been with me now for three days and have nothing to eat.** Mark continues to leave a lot unsaid. What had Jesus been doing during those **three days**? Had he been healing the sick who were brought to him, as he had healed a man who was deaf (7:32–35)? Had he been teaching, as he habitually did when crowds of Jews came to him (2:2; 4:1–2; 6:34)? We cannot imagine crowds flocking to him unless he was meeting their needs. Mark implies that Jesus ministered to this crowd but provides no details.

Jesus' **heart** is again **moved with pity for the crowd,** this time **because they have been with me now for three days and have nothing to eat.** Previously Jesus felt compassion for a crowd because "they were like sheep without a shepherd" (6:34), an image the Old Testament uses for the vulnerability of God's people without proper leadership. Now Jesus is profoundly moved because those who have been with him for three days are hungry. Food is a universal human need; hunger affects Gentile as well as Jew. Jesus has compassion for those who are in physical need as well as for those in spiritual need, which means that Jesus has compassion for all.

For reflection: How moved am I by the hunger and needs of others?

3 Jesus continues to speak to his disciples about the needs of the crowd: **If I send them away hungry to their homes, they will collapse on the way, and some of them have come a great distance.** This is simple common sense and an indication that Jesus is in touch with the realities of life (lofty religious sentiments sometimes ignore practical realities: see James 2:15–16). **Some of them have come a great distance:** people have come to Jesus from far and wide and are a long way from **their homes.**

4 **His disciples answered him, "Where can anyone get enough bread to satisfy them here in this deserted place?"** Jesus previously fed a

sizable crowd in a deserted area (6:32–44), but the disciples respond as if it has never happened. One commonly proposed explanation is that the story of Jesus feeding a large crowd was circulated in several different traditions; Mark knew of two of these traditions and took them to be two different incidents rather than two traditions about one incident. Thus there are similarities between Mark's accounts of the two feedings, including the disciples' bafflement over how the crowd could be fed. While this explanation has plausibility, we still need to read Mark's Gospel as he wrote it and draw meaning out of what he tells us. Mark writes of Jesus feeding two crowds, one a crowd of Jews and the other presumably largely Gentile. Mark portrays the disciples as having forgotten a lesson they should have learned when Jesus first fed a crowd, which is why they ask, **Where can anyone get enough bread to satisfy them here in this deserted place?** The disciples should have known **where,** but they learn slowly and forget quickly.

For reflection: How quickly do I learn from experience? How often do I repeat the same old mistakes?

5 Jesus must repeat the lesson. **He asked them, "How many loaves do you have?" "Seven," they replied.** Bread was made from wheat (or sometimes barley) and commonly baked in round **loaves** about an inch high and eight inches in diameter. The disciples have enough for a simple meal for themselves, but it is a crumb in a basket for a crowd. Will the disciples get the point this time—that what they have, however little, is sufficient to meet needs when it is placed in the hands of Jesus?

Bread: See Diet, page 150

6 **He ordered the crowd to sit down on the ground.** Mark's second account is sketchier, and he does not describe seating arrangements, possibly because the previous seating arrangements echoed Old Testament descriptions of how God's people were organized (6:39–40), and this **crowd** is made up of Gentiles. But Mark does include what he sees as being at the heart of Jesus' actions. **Then, taking the seven loaves he gave thanks, broke them, and gave them to his disciples to distribute, and they distributed them to the crowd.** Jesus does what the host at a Jewish meal would do, **taking** bread in his hands, giving **thanks**

to God for providing it, and breaking and distributing it. The parallels with what Jesus will do at the Last Supper are unmistakable (14:22). The Greek word Mark uses for **gave thanks** comes into English as the word *Eucharist*. The feeding of this crowd foreshadows Gentiles eventually being nourished by the Eucharist.

7 **They also had a few fish. He said the blessing over them and ordered them distributed also.** Mark mentions this as an afterthought: the significance of what Jesus did lies with the bread, as a foreshadowing of the Eucharist. The **fish** would have been dried or salted and eaten as flavoring for the bread rather than as the main course.

8 **They ate and were satisfied.** Jesus has addressed the needs of this hungry crowd and **satisfied** them. Jesus' compassion has tangible results. **They picked up the fragments left over—seven baskets.** The number **seven** has a biblical connotation for fullness and also matches up with the seven loaves of bread the disciples had on hand. The Greek word used here for **baskets** refers to large baskets, big enough to hold a

---

COMMENT: JESUS AND GENTILES Mark was faced with a delicate balancing act. On the one hand, Jesus had directed his efforts toward Jews during his public ministry. But on the other hand, the early Church, after considerable debate, had extended its mission to Gentiles, baptizing them and welcoming them as Christians without insisting that they become Jews (Acts 10–11, 15). In writing his Gospel, Mark wanted to be faithful to what Jesus had done and said, but Mark also wanted to provide as much basis as he could for the Church's acceptance of Gentiles. Mark therefore devoted a section of his Gospel (Mark 7:1–8:10) to teachings and actions of Jesus that provided foundations for the Church's acceptance of Gentiles. The first part of this section (Mark 7:1–23) includes teachings of Jesus that allowed the Church to set aside Jewish traditions for applying God's laws and provided a basis for Gentile converts not obeying Jewish food laws. The remainder of this section (Mark 7:24–8:10) describes encounters between Jesus and Gentiles: a woman who demands the crumbs from the food that Jesus is feeding the children of Israel, a deaf man from a Gentile area, and a largely Gentile crowd that Jesus feeds as he fed a Jewish crowd. Thus, while Jesus had devoted most of his attention to Jews, Mark could point out that Jesus had had some encounters with Gentiles and had cared for their needs. Eventually the Church would understand that the death and resurrection of Jesus had broken down the barrier separating Jew and Gentile (Eph 2:11–3:6).

man (Acts 9:25). Not only is the crowd satisfied, but there are plenty of leftovers as well. Jesus can take the little we have and make it not only sufficient but abundant.

For reflection: How has Jesus taken the little I have put at his disposal and turned it into an abundance?

9 **There were about four thousand people.** Previously Jesus fed five thousand men (6:44); now he has provided for four thousand. There is no note of their reaction to having been fed; Mark simply tells us that Jesus **dismissed them.** Mark's focus is on Jesus feeding them, not on the aftermath.

10 Jesus then **got into the boat with his disciples:** there is once again a boat handy when Jesus has need of it (3:9). The Decapolis region bordered the eastern shore of the Sea of Galilee, and Jesus and his disciples left by boat from there **and came to the region of Dalmanutha.** This is the only mention of **Dalmanutha** in the Bible, and its location is unknown; the common speculation is that it was on the western shore of the Sea of Galilee. Jesus left the Decapolis and apparently returned to Galilee, but his visit there will turn out to be brief.

The Demand for a Sign from God

11 The Pharisees came forward and began to argue with him, seeking from him a sign from heaven to test him. 12 He sighed from the depth of his spirit and said, "Why does this generation seek a sign? Amen, I say to you, no sign will be given to this generation." 13 Then he left them, got into the boat again, and went off to the other shore.

Gospel parallels: Matt 12:38–39; 16:1–4; Luke 11:16, 29
OT: Psalm 95:8–10

11 Jesus crossed the Sea of Galilee by boat and landed at Dalmanutha (8:10), somewhere on the western shore, and **Pharisees came forward and began to argue with him, seeking from him a sign from heaven to test him.** What exactly were they looking for? They were surely aware of

Jesus' healings and exorcisms, possibly even of his raising Jairus's daughter from the dead (5:41–42). It is doubtful that these Pharisees were simply demanding that Jesus do something even more spectacular. Rather, they wanted proof that Jesus' power and authority came from God. They come **seeking from him a sign from heaven,** that is, a sign from God that Jesus can produce as compelling evidence that he is God's agent. Did Jesus' power to expel demons come from the prince of demons (3:22) or from God? Was Jesus speaking for God when he interpreted the law of Moses (2:27; 7:15)? There is an edge to their demand: they come to **argue with him** and to dispute any claim Jesus has made for divine authorization. They are out **to test him** in the hope that he cannot produce a sign from God and will fail their test.

12 Jesus **sighed from the depth of his spirit:** Jesus is distressed by the Pharisees' skepticism; his sigh can convey pain, sorrow, anger, or anguish. This is not the first time that Jesus is angered and grieved by the hardness of heart of those who seek to trip him up (3:5). Jesus **said, "Why does this generation seek a sign?"** We might ask, Why not seek a sign? What is wrong with wanting to know whether God is behind Jesus? Why does Jesus find this so upsetting? A clue lies in the phrase **this generation.** This can mean the people who were alive at the time of Jesus, but it also recalls an Old Testament generation that was hard-hearted and rejected God no matter what God did (Psalm 95:8–10). Jesus knew that there was no sign, no matter how spectacular, that could convince those who did not want to be convinced. Wanting to know whether God stood behind Jesus was legitimate, but these Pharisees had already made up their minds that Jesus wasn't God's agent. Jesus **sighed from the depth of his spirit** over their continued hardness of heart (3:5).

> Do not harden your hearts as at Meribah,
>   as on the day of Massah in the desert.
> There your ancestors tested me;
>   they tried me though they had seen my works.
> Forty years I loathed that generation;
>   I said: "This people's heart goes astray;
>   they do not know my ways."
>
> Psalm 95:8–10

Jesus continues, **Amen, I say to you, no sign will be given to this generation.** When Jesus prefaces a pronouncement with the words **Amen, I say to you,** it indicates the seriousness of what follows. **No sign will be given** means no sign will be given *by* God. God will not authenticate Jesus **to this generation,** to those who have hardened their hearts against Jesus.

13 **Then he left them:** Jesus apparently judged that further discussion would be pointless, and he **got into the boat again, and went off to the other shore.** Jesus and the disciples will land at Bethsaida (8:22), in a territory east of Galilee that was ruled by Philip, a son of Herod the Great. Jesus leaves Galilee after having barely arrived (8:10), and he will return only in secret (9:30). In Mark's account, Jesus' public ministry in Galilee has come to an end; from now on Jesus will devote himself to training his disciples and preparing them for what lies ahead.

Jesus' ministry in his native Galilee concludes rather ingloriously, in a standoff between Jesus and skeptical Pharisees. Jesus has relatively little to show for all his preaching and healing in Galilee. He can draw crowds, but he hasn't won over religious leaders. He has a small band of disciples, but they have not demonstrated much understanding of what he is about.

For reflection: How do I react when my efforts produce disappointing results?

The Disciples Don't Get It
14 They had forgotten to bring bread, and they had only one loaf with them in the boat. 15 He enjoined them, "Watch out, guard against the leaven of the Pharisees and the leaven of Herod." 16 They concluded among themselves that it was because they had no bread. 17 When he became aware of this he said to them, "Why do you conclude that it is because you have no bread? Do you not yet understand or comprehend? Are your hearts hardened? 18 Do you have eyes and not see, ears and not hear? And do you not remember, 19 when I broke the five loaves for the five thousand, how many wicker baskets full of fragments you picked up?" They

answered him, "Twelve." ²⁰ "When I broke the seven loaves for the four thousand, how many full baskets of fragments did you pick up?" They answered [him], "Seven." ²¹ He said to them, "Do you still not understand?"

Gospel parallels: Matt 16:5–12; Luke 12:1
OT: Jer 5:21; Ezek 12:2

14 The disciples are in the boat with Jesus, crossing from Dalmanutha (8:10, 13) to Bethsaida (8:22), at the northern tip of the lake. **They had forgotten to bring bread, and they had only one loaf with them in the boat:** they have a single loaf of bread, not enough for a meal for everyone in the boat. **They had forgotten** to replenish their provisions.

15 Jesus may have been mulling over the Pharisees' demand for a sign from heaven to authenticate him as God's agent (8:11); he may also have been aware of Herod's view of him (6:14–16), and he certainly knew of Herod's treatment of John the Baptist (6:17–29). Somewhat out of the blue Jesus tells his disciples to be careful: **he enjoined them, "Watch out, guard against the leaven of the Pharisees and the leaven of Herod."** The disciples are to be vigilant and to protect themselves from **the leaven of the Pharisees and the leaven of Herod.** What might that be?

Bread dough, made from flour and water, was commonly leavened by mixing in a small amount of leavened dough kept unbaked from the previous batch. Even a little leavened dough could transform a whole new batch of dough (Gal 5:9). The presence of leaven was desirable if one wanted dough leavened (Matt 13:33; Luke 13:20–21) but undesirable if one wanted to get rid of old dough and start afresh with an unleavened batch (1 Cor 5:6–8), as was necessary at Passover (Exod 12:15).

Jesus is comparing something to **leaven;** his words are a miniparable or a riddle. Implicit in Jesus' comparison is that the leaven in question is undesirable, something to be guarded against. What is it about **the Pharisees** and **Herod** that Jesus compares to **leaven?** Leaven permeates and transforms dough: Jesus is warning his disciples about characteristics or tendencies of the Pharisees and Herod that can be contagious and corrupting. Jesus does not spell out what these characteristics are but gives his disciples something to think about.

Jesus gave biblical scholars something to think about as well, and there have been many suggestions for what the leaven of the Pharisees and the leaven of Herod might be: hardness of heart, unbelief, evil inclinations, corruption, godlessness, hypocrisy. Perhaps Jesus did not have a single meaning in mind but wanted his disciples to ponder what it was about the Pharisees and Herod that could have a bad influence on them. Jesus invoked a parable instead of putting his message in more direct words because he wanted his disciples to **watch out** for and **guard against** that which could harm them, and this would take ongoing attention and reflection.

For reflection: What influences do I need to guard against?

16 The disciples' thoughts are elsewhere (verse 14), and they completely miss what Jesus is talking about. **They concluded among themselves that it was because they had no bread.** Almost by free association their minds jump from Jesus' mention of leaven to leavened bread and then to their worry that they do not have enough bread along for their next meal: Will we be able to buy bread when we land? Do we have enough money with us? Jesus proposed a riddle for their reflection, but their minds are a million miles away.

For reflection: If I had tape-recorded all my thoughts during the last Mass or service I attended, what would I find on the tape?

17 **When he became aware of** his disciples' preoccupations, Jesus became impatient with their obtuseness and challenged them with a series of stinging questions. **He said to them, "Why do you conclude that it is because you have no bread?"** Why do you think I am talking about your next meal? **Do you not yet understand or comprehend** what I have been trying to teach you? You have missed the point before (4:13, 40; 6:52; 7:18; 8:4), and you are **not yet** getting it, even now. **Are your hearts hardened?** Is your obtuseness willful (6:52)? Have you no more understanding of me than those who are not my disciples (4:11–12)?

18 **Do you have eyes and not see, ears and not hear?** Jesus' words echo prophecies that decried the spiritual blindness and deafness of God's

people (Jer 5:21; Ezek 12:2). The disciples have seen what Jesus has been doing but have not understood the significance of his actions. They have heard Jesus' words of instruction but have not grasped their meaning. They have been with Jesus since the beginning of his public ministry but with unseeing eyes and unhearing ears, oblivious to what has been going on.

> Pay attention to this,
>   foolish and senseless people
> Who have eyes and see not,
>   who have ears and hear not.
>
> Jer 5:21

> Son of man, you live in the midst of a rebellious house; they have eyes to see but do not see, and ears to hear but do not hear.
>
> Ezek 12:2

Jesus prompts them to grasp at least one lesson they should have learned already. He asks them, **And do you not remember,**

19 **when I broke the five loaves for the five thousand, how many wicker baskets full of fragments you picked up?** Jesus does not ask his disciples about how he multiplied bread (6:35–44) but only about its ultimate outcome: do they remember how many baskets of leftovers there were? They did, and **they answered him, "Twelve."**

20 Jesus continues, turning their attention to the second occasion on which he fed a crowd (8:1–9). **When I broke the seven loaves for the four thousand, how many full baskets of fragments did you pick up?** Again, the focus is on the leftovers. The disciples again remember: **they answered [him], "Seven."**

The disciples know the facts, but they do not grasp the significance of these facts. They earlier demonstrated that they missed this significance, when Jesus' walking on the water astounded them (6:48–52).

21 They still don't get it. **He said to them, "Do you still not understand?"** This is not a question so much as an exclamation of disappointment.

The disciples should have realized that if Jesus could feed five thousand people with five loaves of bread and feed four thousand with seven loaves—and feed them so completely that there were leftovers—then he could certainly feed his disciples with the loaf they had with them (verse 14), with leftovers to boot. And if Jesus could do this, why were they preoccupied with where their next meal was coming from—so preoccupied that they missed the point of Jesus' warning about the leaven of the Pharisees and Herod? Don't they understand that Jesus can take care of them? Have they no insight into who he is?

Jesus reacts to his disciples' obtuseness as if time is running out. It is urgent that the disciples begin to understand Jesus, for he will not be around forever to take them through the same lessons over and over—hence his rapid-fire questions, expressing his disappointment in his followers, and his impatience for them to open their eyes and unstop their ears.

For reflection: How do I interpret the tone of Jesus' questions? What insight into Jesus do his questions give me?

There is a ray of hope: Jesus' repeated question to his disciples is "Do you not yet understand?" (verses 17, 21). Even if the disciples do not yet understand, they might in the future. Their ears might be opened, as the ears of the deaf man were opened in the Decapolis by Jesus (7:31–37), and their eyes given sight.

Mark does not recount this event to denigrate the disciples: he is not a tabloid journalist out to discredit pillars of the Church. Rather, Mark knows that later generations of disciples will not be immune from the failings that beset the first followers of Jesus. Mark's message is that we are all in the same boat. If the eyes of great figures like Peter and the rest of Jesus' chosen disciples were unseeing and their ears unhearing, perhaps we need to check our own eyes and ears. Maybe we too know facts about Jesus and can recount his teachings from memory but are still missing their significance for us.

For reflection: How well do I see and hear spiritually?

ORIENTATION: *Jesus travels with his disciples into the region northeast of Galilee. His public ministry in Galilee is over; he will return there only surreptitiously.*

Eyes Are Gradually Opened

22 When they arrived at Bethsaida, they brought to him a blind man and begged him to touch him. 23 He took the blind man by the hand and led him outside the village. Putting spittle on his eyes he laid his hands on him and asked, "Do you see anything?" 24 Looking up he replied, "I see people looking like trees and walking." 25 Then he laid hands on his eyes a second time and he saw clearly; his sight was restored and he could see everything distinctly. 26 Then he sent him home and said, "Do not even go into the village."

22 **When they arrived at Bethsaida, they brought to him a blind man and begged him to touch him.** Jesus and his disciples have gone by boat from Dalmanutha (8:10, 13) to Bethsaida, on the northern tip of the lake. Bethsaida lay outside of Galilee and was a village with a mixed Jewish and Gentile population. **They brought to him a blind man,**

BACKGROUND: BETHSAIDA was only four miles from Capernaum but lay in the territory ruled by Philip (a son of Herod the Great) during Jesus' public ministry. Bethsaida was built on a hilltop near where the Jordan River flows into the northern end of the Sea of Galilee; boats could be moored below the village. Archaeologists estimate that the population of Bethsaida at the time of Jesus was a couple of hundred people. The village may have had a mixed pagan and Jewish population, with Greek commonly spoken. Some first-century houses have been discovered there, several with evidence that their occupants were wealthy. Fishhooks and other fishing gear have been found (the name Bethsaida may mean "house of the fisher"). John's Gospel tells us that one of Jesus' disciples, named Philip, "was from Bethsaida, the town of Andrew and Peter" (John 1:44). The other Gospels portray Peter and Andrew living in Capernaum during Jesus' public ministry; perhaps they moved from Bethsaida to Capernaum. Bethsaida was apparently destroyed by an earthquake in AD 115; it was never rebuilt.

---

leading him because his blindness made it difficult for him to come to Jesus on his own. Once again a person in need will be healed because relatives or friends bring him to Jesus (see 1:32; 2:3–5; 6:55; 7:32). They **begged** Jesus **to touch him** and heal him, as those who had brought a deaf man to Jesus had begged Jesus to lay his hand on him (7:32). Their begging is an index of their concern for the blind man and of their faith that Jesus can heal him.

For reflection: Whom do I bring to Jesus in my prayers? What needs of theirs do I lay before him?

23 Jesus **took the blind man by the hand and led him outside the village:** Jesus leads him as a friend leads one who is blind, guiding him, helping him over uneven terrain. We are not told why Jesus took the man **outside the village** and away from others; we can suspect that it was once again to avoid making a public spectacle of a healing (see 5:37, 40; 7:33).

For reflection: How has Jesus led me when I could not see where I was going?

Putting spittle on his eyes he laid his hands on him: Mark literally writes that he spit in his eyes. Jesus had also used his spittle in his healing of the man who was deaf and had a speech impediment (7:33), but we do not know why Jesus sometimes used his spittle to heal and sometimes did not (Jesus will later give sight to another blind man simply by pronouncing him healed—10:52). Jesus lays his hands on him, touching his eyes (see verse 25). Jesus **asked, "Do you see anything?"** This is the only instance in the Gospels where Jesus asks someone he is healing whether the healing is complete. It seems to be a genuine question; Jesus asks it because he does not know the answer. While Jesus at times demonstrates extraordinary knowledge and insight, he is not omniscient (see also 5:30).

For reflection: What does Jesus' asking, "Do you see anything?" tell me about Jesus?

24 **Looking up he replied, "I see people looking like trees and walking."** The man who was blind can now see, but not clearly. His vision is so blurred that he cannot distinguish between **people** and **trees,** but he knows that people can walk and trees cannot, so if a figure is moving around it must be a person and not a tree. This is a marked improvement over total blindness but not yet a complete healing.

25 **Then he laid hands on his eyes a second time** because his first efforts had not brought complete healing. Jesus' previous healings seem to have been immediate and complete, as Mark has sometimes made explicit (5:29, 42). Such is not the case with the healing of this blind man. This is the only two-stage healing described in the Gospels, and we are not told why Jesus' first efforts were not fully effective. (One of Jesus' exorcisms may also have required repeated efforts—5:8.)

For reflection: What significance do I find in Jesus' first touch not being fully effective?

Jesus' second touch has the desired effect, and Mark emphasizes the completeness of the man's healing: **he saw clearly; his sight was restored and he could see everything distinctly.** Whereas the man's vision had been blurred after Jesus' first touch, now **he saw clearly.** An implication of his sight being **restored** might be that he had not been born blind but had become blind. **He could see everything distinctly:** the word **distinctly** has the connotation of something at a distance appearing clear. The man's eyesight is now perfect.

26 **Then he sent him home and said, "Do not even go into the village."** Jesus can send him off on his own because he no longer needs anyone to guide him. Jesus' command to him to go **home** without even going **into the village** seems to indicate that he did not live in Bethsaida. Jesus gives no reason for commanding the man to avoid Bethsaida; from what follows we can suspect it was because Jesus wanted to get away for some time alone with his disciples before word of the man's healing got around and every sick person in Bethsaida was brought to him (see 3:10). If this is the correct interpretation, then it means that Jesus realized that

he did not have the time to heal every sick person everywhere; he had to be about the mission God had given him, even if it meant leaving good works undone.

Jesus' restoring the sight of this blind man has its unique elements, particularly its occurring in stages, but it also shares features with Jesus' healing of the deaf man with a speech impediment (7:31–37). Both took place outside of Galilee; in each case an afflicted person was brought to Jesus by others who asked Jesus to lay his hands on him; Jesus took the person aside; he employed spittle and touch; he seemingly wanted to keep the healing quiet. Between these two healings Jesus berated his disciples for their lack of understanding (8:17–21), accusing them of having eyes that didn't see and ears that didn't hear (8:18). These two physical healings have a spiritual message. Even if the disciples are blind to who Jesus is and what he is about, there is hope that he will open their eyes and they will finally understand (8:21). Even though their coming to see has not been instantaneous, that is no reason for discouragement: it will happen in stages, as did Jesus' healing of the blind man. Even if the disciples are a bit deaf to Jesus' teachings, there is hope that he will open their ears to the meaning of his words and free their tongues to proclaim his message clearly to others. These two healings are parables-in-action, providing an image for what Jesus wants to do for his followers: open their eyes and ears to him.

For reflection: How has Jesus gradually opened my eyes and ears to him? Am I still spiritually nearsighted and hard of hearing?

ORIENTATION: *Jesus and his disciples travel north from Bethsaida toward Caesarea Philippi, passing through a mixed Jewish-Gentile region.*

Who Is Jesus?

²⁷ Now Jesus and his disciples set out for the villages of Caesarea Philippi. Along the way he asked his disciples, "Who do people say that I am?" ²⁸ They said in reply, "John the Baptist, others Elijah, still others one of the prophets." ²⁹ And he asked them, "But who do you say that I am?" Peter said to him in reply, "You are the Messiah." ³⁰ Then he warned them not to tell anyone about him.

31 He began to teach them that the Son of Man must suffer greatly and be rejected by the elders, the chief priests, and the scribes, and be killed, and rise after three days. **32** He spoke this openly. Then Peter took him aside and began to rebuke him. **33** At this he turned around and, looking at his disciples, rebuked Peter and said, "Get behind me, Satan. You are thinking not as God does, but as human beings do."

Gospel parallels: Matt 16:13–23; Luke 9:18–22
NT: Mark 6:14–16; 9:9, 12, 31–32; 10:33–34

27 **Now Jesus and his disciples set out for the villages of Caesarea Philippi.** Jesus and his disciples went by boat to Bethsaida (8:22), on the eastern bank of the Jordan River near the Sea of Galilee. From there they **set out for the villages of Caesarea Philippi,** about twenty-five miles to the north. **Caesarea Philippi** lay on the southern slope of Mount Hermon and was the site of a powerful spring that formed one of the sources of the Jordan River. Jesus and his disciples journey through a mixed Jewish-Gentile region ruled by Philip, one of the sons of Herod the Great; **Caesarea Philippi** was his capital. The **villages** of Caesarea Philippi were small settlements in the vicinity of the larger city. Mark does not describe Jesus going into Caesarea Philippi itself. Jesus has

---

BACKGROUND: CAESAREA PHILIPPI (not to be confused with Caesarea, a city on the Mediterranean coast that is mentioned in Acts) lay about twenty-five miles north of the Sea of Galilee, in the northern portion of the territory ruled by Philip at the time of Jesus. (Today this region is called the Jaulan or Golan Heights.) The site of Caesarea Philippi had long been a place of pagan worship, centered on a powerful spring that poured forth from the mouth of a cave and was one of the sources of the Jordan River. In the centuries immediately before the time of Jesus the site was dedicated to the Greek nature god Pan and called Paneas. Herod the Great built a temple at Paneas dedicated to the Roman emperor Caesar Augustus. After the death of Herod the Great in 4 BC, rule over the region northeast of the Sea of Galilee passed to his son Philip. Philip enlarged Paneas, renaming it Caesarea in honor of the Roman emperor. It came to be called Philip's Caesarea (Caesarea Philippi) to distinguish it from other cities named in honor of the emperor. At the time of Jesus, Caesarea Philippi was largely Gentile in population and pagan in religion; only a small minority of Jews lived in the city and nearby villages.

---

traveled near a number of large cities in the course of his public ministry but apparently without entering any of them.

Why would Jesus take his disciples on a journey through a largely Gentile region? One explanation might be that he wanted to spend some time with his disciples away from the crowds that mobbed him in Galilee (1:32–34; 3:7–10, 20; 4:1; 5:21; 6:31–34, 53–56) and to be free from confrontations with Jewish religious leaders (2:6–7, 16, 24; 3:1–6, 22; 7:5; 8:11). Jesus knew that his disciples did not yet have an adequate understanding of him and of what he was about (8:17–21), and he needed to continue their education. **Along the way,** as they walked from Bethsaida toward Caesarea Philippi, **he asked his disciples, "Who do people say that I am?"** Who does the public at large think I am?

28 **They said in reply, "John the Baptist, others Elijah, still others one of the prophets."** The disciples are aware of speculations about Jesus, just as Herod Antipas earlier was aware of such speculations (6:14–16). Some thought that Jesus was **John the Baptist** come back from the dead (6:14, 16), perhaps because John was the most striking religious figure in recent memory and because Jesus had been baptized by John. **Others** thought that Jesus was **Elijah,** a prophet who had worked wonders (6:15; 1 Kings 17–18) and had been taken up to heaven (2 Kings 2:11–12). Elijah was expected to return to earth to herald a "day of the LORD," when God would judge his people (Mal 3:1, 23–24; Sirach 48:9–12). **Still others** thought that Jesus was **one of the prophets** (6:15), which could simply mean that Jesus was viewed as a spokesman for God, as Isaiah and Jeremiah had been. Jesus had referred to himself as a prophet (6:4) and had made pronouncements as if he spoke for God (2:27; 7:14–15).

To think that Jesus was John the Baptist or Elijah was grasping at straws, for Jesus did not embrace the austere lifestyle of John and Elijah (1:6; 2:18; 2 Kings 1:8). It is striking that the disciples do not report any popular opinion that Jesus might be the Messiah, even though many Jews expected that God would send some sort of messiah.

29 **And he asked them, "But who do you say that I am?"** The **you** in Jesus' question is emphatic: Who do **you** say that I am? You know what others say about me, but what do **you** say? After I calmed the storm at

sea, you wondered, "Who then is this whom even wind and sea obey?" (4:41). Have **you** arrived at an answer?

This is the central question of Mark's Gospel: who is Jesus? Mark wants his readers to be among the **you** whom Jesus asks, **Who do you say that I am?**

For reflection: How do I answer Jesus' question? Who do I proclaim him to be?

Peter said to him in reply, "You are the Messiah." There were different expectations at the time of Jesus of who **the Messiah** would be and what he would do. The most common expectation was that he would be a descendant of David, a warrior king who would defeat the enemies of Israel and restore rule to the house of David. Beyond that, expectations varied considerably. Peter's profession that Jesus was **the Messiah** represented a different view of Jesus than the opinions in circulation (John the Baptist, Elijah, a prophet). But why did Peter think that Jesus was **the Messiah**? Jesus had proclaimed that the kingdom of God was at hand (1:15) but had never spoken of himself as a king or given any indication that he was going to overthrow Roman rule and reestablish the dynasty of David. Rather, Jesus had devoted himself to teaching, healing, and exorcising, which popular opinion did not associate with what **the Messiah** would do.

30 In Mark's Gospel, Jesus does not endorse Peter's identification of him as the Messiah. Nor does Jesus explicitly reject the title. He does forbid his disciples from talking about him as the Messiah: **then he warned them not to tell anyone about him.** Jesus is issuing a strong warning to his disciples, commanding **them not to tell anyone about him.** What is it that Jesus does not want them to **tell anyone about him**? It clearly seems that he does not want them to tell people that he is the Messiah. There are two likely reasons for this. First, it could have been dangerous: Roman authorities and their client rulers did not look kindly on anyone whose mission was to overthrow their rule and reestablish the dynasty of David—and that was the mission they would have attributed to Jesus on the basis of popular expectations of the Messiah. The fate of

John the Baptist demonstrated that those in power could do away with religious leaders even if they enjoyed great popularity. Second and more important, Jesus did not want to be called the Messiah because popular notions of the Messiah did not match up with his mission and the kind of Messiah he was.

BACKGROUND: MESSIAH, CHRIST There is a temptation to define the meaning of the title Messiah (Christ) in terms of who Jesus is, and to presume that this is the meaning that the word *messiah* had for Jews at the time of Jesus. The situation was more complex, however. The Hebrew word *messiah* is an adjective meaning anointed or smeared, as with olive oil. Israelite kings were ceremonially anointed, as were high priests. Thus a king could be referred to as God's "anointed" (Psalm 2:2). Based partly on a prophecy of the prophet Nathan, an expectation developed that an anointed descendant of David would play a decisive role in God's plans for his people; Nathan had prophesied to David that his throne would "stand firm forever" (2 Sam 7:16). David's dynasty came to an end with the Babylonian conquest of 587 BC, and Jews were under foreign rule for the next four centuries. In the two centuries before Jesus there was a resurgence of hopes for rule by a descendant of David—a messiah. Alongside various expectations for a kingly messiah, Jewish writings from this period also spoke of other messianic figures; there was no single clearly defined picture of a messiah. One Jewish group, the Essenes, expected God to send two messiahs: a kingly messiah descended from David and a priestly messiah descended from Aaron. Most messianic hopes had a political dimension: God would bring an end to Roman domination. Some expected God to bring the present age to an end and to usher in a new age. There was no expectation that a messiah would suffer: the "servant" of Isaiah 52:13–53:12 was not identified with the Messiah before the time of Jesus.

Jesus was ambivalent about being called the Messiah. On the one hand, he was establishing the reign of God as God's agent. On the other hand, popular understandings of what a messiah would do usually included the overthrow of Roman rule, and that was not Jesus' mission. Jesus clarified what it meant for him to be called the Messiah through his teachings, death, and resurrection. The New Testament, written in Greek, uses the Greek word for anointed: *christos*, which gives us the word *Christ*. The early Church embraced the word *Christ* as its most common title for Jesus, so much so that it evolved from being a title (Jesus the Christ) to being virtually a second name (Jesus Christ). *Related topics: The age to come (page 267), Essenes (page 297), Jewish expectations at the time of Jesus (page 339), Kingdom of God (page 96), Nonbiblical writings (page 243), Psalms of Solomon (page 207).*

By the time Mark wrote his Gospel, the Greek word for Messiah had become the common way of identifying Jesus: Jesus was the Christ, as Mark proclaims in the first verse of his Gospel. In order for the word *Messiah* (or *Christ*) to be an appropriate title for Jesus, it had to be purged of its political and military connotations and take on new meaning. This had not yet happened when Peter first professed Jesus to be the Messiah.

31 **He began to teach them that the Son of Man must suffer greatly.** Jesus begins to steer the disciples toward a clearer understanding of him by avoiding the term *messiah* and referring to himself instead as **the Son of Man.** Jesus perhaps adopted this enigmatic way of speaking of himself (2:10, 28) precisely because it was enigmatic and did not carry undesirable associations, as did the term *messiah*. The first thing Jesus says is that he **must suffer greatly.** There was no expectation that the Messiah would suffer, but Jesus will **suffer greatly.** Indeed, Jesus **must** suffer. This **must** might be interpreted to mean that Jesus would inevitably suffer, that the course he was pursuing would lead him into conflict with those who would do him harm (just as harm had befallen John the Baptist). But Jesus is speaking about more than inevitability; he is speaking of the necessity of his suffering in God's plan: he **must** suffer because this is God's will for him (14:36), an essential aspect of his mission. Jesus does not explain why it is God's will that he suffer or what his suffering will accomplish. These are matters for his disciples to ponder—and for the readers of Mark's Gospel to ponder as well.

Son of Man: See page 41

Jesus will **suffer greatly** because he will **be rejected by the elders, the chief priests, and the scribes.** The Jewish religious ruling body in Jerusalem, the Sanhedrin, was made up of **elders** (lay leaders), **chief priests** (including the high priest), and **scribes** (scholars of the law of Moses). Jesus has aroused the opposition of religious leaders in Galilee to the point where they are seeking his death (3:6), and he also will be opposed by religious leaders in Jerusalem. That someone who went about freeing people from evil and teaching on behalf of God should be rejected by religious leaders is profoundly ironic and tragic.

Elders: See page 303

High priest, chief priests: See page 403

Scribes: See page 40

The opposition of these religious leaders will lead to Jesus' death: he will **be killed.** Jesus previously hinted that he would be "taken away" (2:20), but this is his first clear statement that his mission will end in death. This is a chilling prediction; it must have been utterly shocking to his disciples. They have left their occupations to become his disciples and travel with him, and now he tells them that he is going to **be killed.** What will become of his mission if he is killed? What will become of his followers?

That Jesus would be killed was at odds with all expectations for the Messiah. The Messiah would defeat his enemies, not be defeated by them.

Jesus' death will not be the end, however. Jesus tells his disciples that he will **rise after three days.** The expression **three days** was an idiom for a short lapse of time (see Hosea 6:1–2). Many but not all Jews looked forward to a resurrection of the dead, when God would establish his reign, bringing the present age to an end and inaugurating the age to come. Will the rising of Jesus mark the beginning of the age to come and the resurrection of all who have died? If not, what will it mean for Jesus to **rise** before the arrival of the age to come?

Resurrection: See page 320

For reflection: If I had been among the disciples that day and heard Jesus speak of his suffering, dying, and rising, how would I have reacted?

32 **He spoke this openly:** Jesus usually taught by means of parables and riddles, but he spoke of his coming suffering, rejection, death, and rising in plain words, words that his disciples were able to understand. Peter grasps what Jesus is saying and is horrified by it. **Then Peter took him aside and began to rebuke him.** That Peter **took him aside** might indicate that Peter wanted to set Jesus straight quietly, without making a scene in front of the other disciples. For Peter to

rebuke Jesus was sheer effrontery: masters teach disciples and correct them when necessary, but disciples should not presume to lecture and **rebuke** their masters. This is far from the first time that a disciple has spoken boldly to Jesus (4:38; 5:31; 6:37; 8:4).

Mark does not spell out the content of Peter's **rebuke.** Since Peter had just professed Jesus to be the Messiah, Peter might have said, "That is not what happens to the Messiah: the Messiah triumphs over opposition. Since you are the Messiah, you can't be put to death." If Peter said something like that, he would have been echoing popular views of the Messiah, as found, for example, in some Jewish hymns written about a century earlier (the *Psalms of Solomon*—not in the Bible).

33 Jesus has spoken solemnly to his disciples about his coming suffering, death, and rising, and he does not appreciate Peter responding to his words with a rebuke. **At this he turned around and, looking at his disciples, rebuked Peter and said, "Get behind me, Satan."** Peter had taken Jesus aside, but Jesus turns and looks at all his disciples as he responds to Peter, for his words to Peter are a message for all of them.

BACKGROUND: PSALMS OF SOLOMON Eighteen hymns called the *Psalms of Solomon* were written around 50 BC, probably in Jerusalem. While not part of Scripture, they shed light on the messianic expectations of some Jews around the time of Jesus. One psalm speaks of a messiah who will deliver Jews from Roman rule and lead them into holiness: "See, Lord, and raise up for them their king, the son of David, to rule over your servant Israel in the time you have chosen, O God. Gird him with strength to shatter unrighteous rulers, to cleanse Jerusalem from gentiles who trample and destroy it. . . . He will have gentile nations serving under his yoke . . . and he will cleanse Jerusalem and make it holy as it was in the beginning. . . . For all shall be holy, and their king shall be the Lord Messiah. He will not trust in horse and rider and bow; he will not multiply gold and silver for war. . . . He himself will be free from sin so as to rule over a great people. He will put officials to shame and drive out sinners by the strength of a word. And he will not weaken during his days because of his God, for God has made him powerful with a holy spirit. . . . This is the majesty of the king of Israel, whom God knew, to raise him over the house of Israel" (PsSol 17:21–22, 30, 32–33, 36–37, 42). The "Lord Messiah" of this psalm, while sinless, is a human being, and his rule takes place on this earth. *Related topics: Jewish expectations at the time of Jesus (page 339), Messiah, Christ (page 204), Nonbiblical writings (page 243), Son of David (page 281).*

Peter had rebuked him, and now Jesus **rebuked Peter,** telling him, **Get behind me, Satan.** The expression **Get behind me** might mean "Get out of my sight!" It more likely means "Get back in line: you are to be my follower, walking behind me."

To call Peter **Satan** might be to identify Peter with the prince of evil spirits. But it is possible that Jesus calls Peter satan, with a small s, characterizing Peter as an adversary who is testing him (the Hebrew word *satan* means adversary or accuser). Biblical Aramaic and Greek did not have uppercase and lowercase letters, so whether Jesus called Peter Satan or satan is a matter of interpretation.

Satan: See page 71

Jesus explains why he called Peter satan: **You are thinking not as God does, but as human beings do.** Peter's thoughts are human, not demonic. But human thoughts are not God's thoughts (Isaiah 55:8–9), and human thoughts are prey to deception. Jesus, in speaking of his coming death and rising, is telling his followers what God's will is for him; Peter, in rebuking Jesus, is opposing God's will.

For reflection: To what degree is my thinking in line with God's thinking? How can I tell?

ORIENTATION: *We are now not only at the midpoint of Mark's Gospel but also at its heart. Who is Jesus? He is the Son of God (1:1, 11), who will suffer and die and rise (8:31). What does it mean to be his follower? It means sharing his destiny.*

Who Are Disciples of Jesus?
34 He summoned the crowd with his disciples and said to them, "Whoever wishes to come after me must deny himself, take up his cross, and follow me. 35 For whoever wishes to save his life will lose it, but whoever loses his life for my sake and that of the gospel will save it. 36 What profit is there for one to gain the whole world and forfeit his life? 37 What could one give in exchange for his life? 38 Whoever is ashamed of me and of my words in this faithless and

sinful generation, the Son of Man will be ashamed of when he comes in his Father's glory with the holy angels."

Gospel parallels: Matt 16:24–27; Luke 9:23–26

NT: Matt 10:32–33, 38–39; Mark 13:26–27; 14:62; Luke 12:8–9; 14:27; 17:33; John 12:25

34 **He summoned the crowd with his disciples:** Jesus set out for Caesarea Philippi with his disciples (8:27), presumably to spend time with them, but Jesus' fame has spread to this region "beyond the Jordan" (3:8), and he has no difficulty gathering a crowd. Jesus **summoned** a crowd because what he was going to say applied to everyone, not just to his first disciples. Jesus **said to them, "Whoever wishes to come after me must deny himself, take up his cross, and follow me."** The **whoever** admits no exceptions and includes the readers of Mark's Gospel. Jesus addresses every person who **wishes to come after** him, everyone who accepts Jesus' invitation and chooses to become his disciple. The expression translated **after me** is the same expression translated "behind me" in Jesus' rebuke of Peter (8:33): a disciple is one who follows behind Jesus and goes where he goes. Jesus has just told his disciples where he is going: he is headed for suffering and rejection, death and resurrection (8:31). This is God's will for Jesus, an essential aspect of his mission. A disciple of Jesus is someone who shares Jesus' life, not someone who merely learns from him or accompanies him as a spectator. For a disciple, a necessary step in sharing Jesus' life is to **deny** himself or herself. In legal contexts, the Greek word for **deny** meant to disavow any relationship with a person. Here the person in question is oneself: to follow after Jesus, a person must disown his or her self. Jesus is talking not about acts of self-denial (like turning down seconds of dessert) but about rejecting self-centeredness, relinquishing control over one's life, abandoning oneself completely to the will of God. As Jesus does, so whoever wishes to follow him must do.

For reflection: What does Jesus' requirement that I deny myself mean to me? Where do I struggle the most in denying myself?

The idea of denying oneself is a little abstract, and our ingrained self-centeredness can craftily turn self-denial into self-promotion (Oh, how holy I am: look at how I deny myself!). Jesus makes self-denial crudely concrete by saying that whoever wishes to come after him must **take up his cross,** which assuredly means also her cross. Mark's first readers knew, as we know, how Jesus died: he suffered crucifixion, a degrading and painful torture that Rome employed to execute rebels and those who were regarded as the dregs of society. Jesus' command to **take up his cross** demands that his followers join him in giving their lives for God, even to the extent of enduring a horrible death. This was a real possibility for Mark's first readers: many Roman Christians died, some by crucifixion, during Nero's persecution. For Mark's first readers, Jesus' words were an assurance that he had foreseen their suffering, and it was part of his call to them.

Crucifixion: See page 429

Nero's persecution: See A Roman view of Christians, page 347

What meaning did **take up his cross** have for the disciples and the crowd who heard Jesus speak these words? Jesus had told his disciples that he was going to be killed (8:31), but he had not specified how. Jesus had said that he was going to be rejected by religious leaders (8:31), but these leaders did not have the authority to crucify. Hence Jesus' first listeners might not have connected taking up one's cross with what lay ahead for Jesus. But they certainly knew what the expression meant: crucifixions were not rare occurrences in the first century. The condemned person was forced to carry a crossbeam to the place of execution, where it was fastened to an upright beam already in place. To take up a cross—carry a crossbeam—meant to be on one's way to the most painful and degrading form of death the ancient world could devise. Jesus' demand that whoever wanted to follow him had to **take up his cross** can be understood as a parable or comparison: his followers had to be willing to shoulder shame, suffering, and death. This Jesus will do, and so too must whoever wishes to follow him.

For reflection: Where do I draw the line: what am I willing to endure for the sake of Jesus, and what is too much for him to ask of me?

Jesus says that whoever wishes to **come** after him must deny himself, take up his cross, and **follow** him: **come** and **follow** are different translations of the same Greek verb. A translation could just as well have Jesus saying, "If anyone wants to follow me, he (or she) has to follow me." But Jesus' words are more than a simplistic equation. They mean "If you want to be my follower, then you actually have to follow: it is not a matter of pasting a label on yourself but a matter of action. If you want to be my follower, then you have to let me lead; you don't get to decide where you go. If you want to follow me, then you have to follow my path, a path of denying one's very self, a path that leads to a cross. If you wish to come after me, then do so!"

For reflection: How firm is my desire to follow Jesus? How absolute is my commitment to him?

35 If this was all Jesus had to say about following him, then the good news of the gospel would seem pretty grim. But Jesus goes on to explain why following him is the best thing his followers can do for themselves: **for whoever wishes to save his life will lose it.** The **for** connects what Jesus is saying with what he has just said about following him (verse 34). The word translated as **life** could also be rendered as "self." Self-seeking is self-destructive. Those who prize life in this present age above all else will not have life in the age to come.

This paradox of loss is complemented by a paradox of gain: **but whoever loses his life for my sake and that of the gospel will save it.** Denying oneself (verse 34) and losing one's life is the way to preserve oneself. Jesus is not advocating self-denial for the sake of self-denial (as if suffering in itself were good); Jesus is speaking of denying oneself and losing one's life for his **sake and that of the gospel.** We relinquish our lives, even taking up a cross, **for** the **sake** of Jesus, out of allegiance to him. Being a disciple is a matter of personal commitment to Jesus, just as being a husband or a wife is a matter of personal commitment to one's spouse. Jesus' followers give their lives for the **sake** of **the gospel.** During the ministry of Jesus, **the gospel** was the good news that the kingdom of God was at hand (1:15). For Mark, **the gospel** is also the good news about Jesus (1:1). Our personal allegiance to Jesus is expressed by our taking on his work and spreading the good news.

Losing our lives for Jesus and in his service means that we will **save** our lives. We will experience fuller life here and now (see 10:29–30), although not without the pain entailed by self-denial. Our full experience of the life we receive through losing our lives will be in the age to come.

36 Jesus adds other considerations that explain why following him, despite the self-denial it requires, is the best course for his followers. **What profit is there for one to gain the whole world and forfeit his life?** The Greek text literally begins *"For* what profit is there," again connecting what Jesus is saying with his words about following him in verse 34 (a *for* also prefaces the verses that follow). Jesus uses the language of commerce in order to get to the bottom line. Nothing we can **gain** in this life is adequate compensation if, in gaining it, we **forfeit** our lives and eternal life.

37 *For* **what could one give in exchange for his life?** Jesus repeats the question in different words. The exchange in question might be imagined in these terms: "How much money would you demand—payable only to you, not to your heirs or friends—as payment for your ceasing to exist?" No amount of recompense could be adequate; money is of no use to one who does not exist.

38 Jesus hints that a fate worse than nonexistence can befall us. *For* **whoever is ashamed of me and of my words in this faithless and sinful generation, the Son of Man will be ashamed of when he comes in his Father's glory with the holy angels.** His first disciples will be tempted to be **ashamed** of Jesus and his message when Jesus' prediction of his rejection, suffering, and death is born out in Jerusalem. Will they stand with Jesus against those who oppose him, whom he characterizes as a **faithless and sinful generation**? Mark's first readers faced a similar challenge: would they maintain their allegiance to Jesus despite his shameful death on a cross, or would they be **ashamed** of him, **ashamed** to admit that they were his followers? Mark's readers today may also face temptations to be **ashamed** to be known as Jesus' followers, **ashamed** to let his **words** guide their lives when his message is contrary to the values and practices of society today.

For reflection: Have I ever soft-pedaled my identity as a Christian because of social pressure? What do I do when there is a conflict between the words of Jesus and the morals of the society in which I live?

Jesus says that **whoever is** ashamed of him, **the Son of Man will be ashamed of when he comes in his Father's glory with the holy angels.** Jesus referred to himself as **the Son of Man** when he spoke of his coming suffering, death, and rising (8:31); he uses this same designation for himself when he speaks of coming **in his Father's glory with the holy angels.** This is the first time that Jesus speaks of God as his Father, but he does not elaborate on it. Likewise, this is the first time Jesus speaks of his coming in **glory,** but he does not explain what it involves. Nonetheless, there is an unmistakable note of finality in Jesus' words, as if his coming in **glory** accompanied by **angels** is going to wrap everything up. And at the wrap-up, Jesus **will be ashamed** of **whoever** has been **ashamed** of him. What this will mean for them is left unspoken, but it does not bode well. Nothing is said of what will happen to those who have denied themselves, taken up crosses, and not been ashamed of Jesus.

Son of Man: See page 41

Angels: See page 321

Jesus has not fully explained everything he has said, including his relation to God as his Father, his coming in glory, and the aftermath of his coming. At the same time, Jesus has made some things clear. Whoever wants to follow him must disavow his or her own interests, and indeed his or her very self. Discipleship means identification with Jesus in his suffering and dying. This may seem a harsh reality, but there are no good alternatives. We cannot preserve our lives by holding on to them; we can preserve them only by relinquishing them for Jesus.

Mark does not report the reaction of the disciples or the crowd to Jesus' words. If the disciples were stunned that Jesus would suffer and die, they were probably speechless at the prospect of having to do so themselves, as the condition for being his followers.

For reflection: Does Jesus set the cost of discipleship too high for me?

CHAPTER 9

ORIENTATION: *The first verse of chapter 9 continues the teaching Jesus began in 8:34. Mark wrote his Gospel with no chapter divisions; these were added much later.*

When Will the Kingdom of God Come in Power?
¹ He also said to them, "Amen, I say to you, there are some standing here who will not taste death until they see that the kingdom of God has come in power."
Gospel parallels: Matt 16:28; Luke 9:27
NT: Mark 13:30, 32; 14:25

1 **He also said to them:** Jesus is still speaking to the disciples and the crowd he summoned (8:34). He has just spoken of the Son of Man coming in the Father's glory with the holy angels (8:38). **Amen, I say to you** is Jesus' characteristic way of indicating that what he is about to say is important. **There are some standing here who will not taste death until they see that the kingdom of God has come in power.** The expression **taste death** is an idiom for dying (used also in Heb 2:9). Jesus proclaims that **there are some standing here**—some in his audience—who will not die before **they see that the kingdom of God has come in power.** Jesus proclaimed that **the kingdom of God** was at hand (1:15), and through Jesus' healings and exorcisms, his teaching and calling disciples, Jesus was establishing God's reign. However, God's reign is not yet fully established. That some of Jesus' listeners will be able to **see that the kingdom of God has come in power** seems to mean that they will be able to observe that God's reign has been fully and unmistakably established. In the context of what Jesus has just said, this will apparently involve Jesus as the Son of Man coming "in his Father's glory with the holy angels" (8:38). Jesus' words seem to be a solemn assurance that this will happen before all in his audience have died.

This obviously raises questions for readers of Mark's Gospel today. What did Jesus proclaim would happen? Was he speaking about the end of this age and the beginning of the age to come? If so, it seems that he was mistaken, for it did not happen before the last people in his audience died. Perhaps, however, Jesus was talking about something else when he spoke of **the kingdom of God** coming **in power.** Jesus will return to this topic again (in chapter 13), and it is best to defer our questions until then.

Kingdom of God: See page 96

A Glimpse of a Transformed Jesus
² After six days Jesus took Peter, James, and John and led them up a high mountain apart by themselves. And he was transfigured before them, ³ and his clothes became dazzling white, such as no fuller on earth could bleach them. ⁴ Then Elijah appeared to them along with Moses, and they were conversing with Jesus. ⁵ Then Peter said to Jesus in reply, "Rabbi, it is good that we are here! Let us make three tents: one for you, one for Moses, and one for Elijah." ⁶ He hardly knew what to say, they were so terrified. ⁷ Then a cloud came, casting a shadow over them; then from the cloud came a voice, "This is my beloved Son. Listen to him." ⁸ Suddenly, looking around, they no longer saw anyone but Jesus alone with them.

Gospel parallels: Matt 17:1–8; Luke 9:28–36
OT: Exod 19:9, 16; 24:15–16; 1 Kings 8:10–12
NT: Mark 1:10–11; 5:37; 13:3; 14:33; 2 Pet 1:16–18

2 **After six days Jesus took Peter, James, and John and led them up a high mountain apart by themselves.** It is **six days** after Peter professed that Jesus was the Messiah while they were traveling toward Caesarea Philippi (8:27–9:1). Jesus selects **Peter, James, and John** to accompany him, leaving the other disciples behind. Jesus chose these same three disciples to be with him when he raised the daughter of Jairus (5:37), and he will want them at his side on later occasions (13:3; 14:33); each occasion gives them a privileged glimpse of who Jesus is. Jesus **led them up a high mountain apart by themselves:** ascending a **high mountain** allowed them to be alone, which Mark emphasizes by saying that they were **apart** from others and **by themselves.** What is going to happen is not for public consumption but only for the inner circle of Jesus' followers. Jesus had previously gone up a mountain to pray (6:46), and this may have been his intent again, but this is not made explicit.

Mark does not identify the **mountain** that Jesus and the three disciples climbed, except to characterize it as a **high** mountain. There were a number of mountains around Caesarea Philippi, the highest being Mount Hermon, twelve miles to the northeast. Since Jesus and his disciples could have walked some distance in six days, the exact mountain cannot be identified.

On the mountain **he was transfigured before them:** Mark writes that Jesus was transformed and uses the same Greek word that Paul uses for our being transformed into the image of the risen Jesus (2 Cor 3:18). Jesus' transformation presumably entailed a change in appearance, but Mark does not describe what the transformed Jesus looked like. Mark's saying that Jesus **was transfigured** means that he was transfigured *by* God.

3 **And his clothes became dazzling white, such as no fuller on earth could bleach them.** In Jewish imagination, heavenly beings wore heavenly clothes: in Daniel, God, the "Ancient One," wears

---

BACKGROUND: MOUNT OF TRANSFIGURATION The Gospel of Mark tells of Jesus taking Peter, James, and John "up a high mountain apart by themselves" (Mark 9:2; see also Matt 17:1). According to Mark, Jesus and his disciples had been traveling to Caesarea Philippi (Mark 8:27), which was on the southernmost slope of Mount Hermon, the highest peak in the region. Mount Hermon lies on the border between present-day Lebanon and Syria; it has an elevation of 9,232 feet and is covered with snow for most of the year. Since the Gospels do not name the mountain on which Jesus was transfigured, we cannot be sure of its location. Mount Hermon certainly qualifies as a "high mountain." On the other hand, some days passed between Jesus' traveling to Caesarea Philippi and his ascending a mountain (Mark 9:2), allowing time for him to have gone to another region. Uncertainty over the site of the Transfiguration led to speculation about various locations. Eusebius (a bishop, Church historian, and geographer who died around AD 340) thought it was either Mount Hermon or Mount Tabor in Galilee. In AD 348, Bishop Cyril of Jerusalem advocated Tabor, and St. Jerome subsequently supported his choice. Tabor is a majestic rounded hill rising 1,485 feet above the Jezreel Valley. There was apparently a village on Tabor's summit at the time of Jesus, making it a less-private location than Mount Hermon. Cyril and Jerome might have had pilgrims in mind when they proposed Tabor, for it lay only six miles from Nazareth and was far more convenient for pilgrims to visit than the rugged heights of Hermon.

---

clothing that is "snow bright" (Dan 7:9). The clothing of the transformed Jesus is **dazzling white,** whiter than the best **fuller** (bleacher) **on earth could bleach them,** an indication that their whiteness is of heavenly origin. Jesus' transformed clothes, like his changed form, are the work of God.

4 **Then Elijah appeared to them along with Moses.** The presence of Elijah and Moses at Jesus' transfiguration is often interpreted as symbolic of "the law and the prophets"—but if that is the significance of their presence, why doesn't Mark list Moses, representing the law, first? **Moses** was the great lawgiver but was considered a prophet as well (Deut 18:15, 18; Hosea 12:14). **Elijah** was a wonder-working prophet who was expected to return before "the day of the LORD" (Mal 3:23). Significantly, **Moses** and **Elijah** are the only two individuals described in the Old Testament as ascending Mount Sinai (Moses: Exod 19:1–3, 12, 20–21; Elijah: 1 Kings 19:8–18, which uses the name Horeb for Sinai.) Their presence here may be an indication that what happens on this mountain is to be compared with what happened on Mount Sinai. Elijah and Moses **were conversing with Jesus;** Mark does not tell us what they were talking about.

5 **Then Peter said to Jesus in reply, "Rabbi, it is good that we are here!"** Peter addresses Jesus as **rabbi,** which is a term of respect but hardly an adequate title for one who is transformed and in heavenly clothing. We can note that Peter does not address Jesus as Messiah, perhaps because he realizes that Jesus does not want to be hailed by this title (8:29–30). **It is good that we are here:** seeing a transformed Jesus speaking with Elijah and Moses is quite an experience for the disciples.

BACKGROUND: RABBI The Hebrew word *rab* means big or great; with a first-person possessive ending it becomes *rabbi,* my great one, which was used as a respectful way of addressing another person. Eventually this respectful form of address came to be used as a title for those with teaching authority within Judaism, which is the meaning that the title rabbi has today. Some of this shift from being simply a respectful form of address to being also a title for a teacher is reflected in the Gospels. Usually Jesus is called rabbi in response to a miracle he has performed and not in response to his teaching. Yet the later meaning is reflected in some passages, where rabbi is equated with teacher (Matt 23:8; John 1:38; 3:2).

Peter may prefer that Jesus remain in transformed glory instead of suffer the rejection and death that Jesus said lay ahead for him (8:31). **Let us make three tents: one for you, one for Moses, and one for Elijah.** The word for **tents** can mean shelters made from branches. However, neither the transformed Jesus nor Moses or Elijah is in need of shelter from the elements or a place to stay.

Peter, James, and John are being given a glimpse of Jesus' identity, but it hasn't sunk in yet. Peter's suggestion of three shelters (rather than, say, one throne and two chairs of honor) puts Jesus, Moses, and Elijah on the same level. To elevate a carpenter from Nazareth to the ranks of Moses and Elijah would be a promotion, but Jesus is far greater than Moses and Elijah, as will be clear shortly.

6 **He hardly knew what to say, they were so terrified.** The disciples are awestruck by what they see, just as they were filled with fear and awe when Jesus calmed the storm at sea (4:40–41). Holy awe is good, but the disciples' terror is a sign of their incomprehension (see 4:40; 6:50–52).

For reflection: Have I ever had a religious experience that filled me with awe? Did this experience have a lasting effect on me?

7 **Then a cloud came, casting a shadow over them:** the expression **casting a shadow over** means cover or envelop. The **cloud** envelops **them**—Jesus, Moses, and Elijah—obscuring them from the disciples' view. What follows makes it clear that this **cloud** is a manifestation of God's presence, just as a cloud manifested God's presence on Mount Sinai (Exod 19:9, 16; 24:15–16) and in the Temple (1 Kings 8:10–12). **Then from the cloud came a voice, "This is my beloved Son. Listen to him."** God spoke from heaven after Jesus' baptism by John, telling Jesus that he was his **beloved Son** (1:11); now God speaks to Peter, James, and John, proclaiming to them Jesus' identity as his **beloved Son.** Jesus is not merely a lawgiver or a prophet on the order of Moses or Elijah; Jesus is uniquely the Son of God.

Son of God: See page 64

God tells the disciples, **Listen to him.** This could mean "Listen to all that my beloved Son teaches" but may have the more specific meaning of "Listen to what my beloved Son is telling you about his coming suffering, death, and rising, and about what you must do to be his disciples." This is what Jesus has been speaking about (8:31–38), and he will continue to speak of it in the days ahead. God puts an exclamation point after Jesus' words: **Listen to him.** In Hebrew idiom, to **listen** to someone's voice means to not only hear but also obey.

For reflection: How seriously do I take the words of Jesus?

What happens on the mountain takes place for the benefit of Peter, James, and John. Jesus "led them" up the mountain, where he was transformed "before them" (verse 2); Elijah and Moses appeared "to them" (verse 4); the heavenly voice addresses them; and when all this is over Jesus will be alone "with them" (verse 8). Jesus didn't need to be transformed to understand who he was, but his disciples needed to see him transformed and to hear God's words to grasp Jesus' identity as the Son of God. They are given a glimpse of the risen Jesus, the Jesus who will return "in his Father's glory" (8:38). This glimpse should help sustain their faith in the difficult days ahead. Jesus will indeed be rejected, suffer, and be put to death—but this will lead to his rising from the dead. The Transfiguration prefigures the Resurrection.

For reflection: What glimpse into Jesus' identity do the events on the mountain give me?

8 **Suddenly, looking around, they no longer saw anyone but Jesus alone with them.** The disciples' mountaintop experience ends abruptly: it was a moment of revelation for the three disciples but not a moment to be prolonged. **Jesus is alone with** Peter, James, and John: Jesus is to be the focus of attention for his disciples.

Commentators both ancient and modern suggest that Mark intended the transfiguration of Jesus to be understood as a fulfillment of Jesus' promise "There are some standing here who will not taste death until they see that the kingdom of God has come in power" (9:1). The transfigured Jesus was an anticipation of the risen Jesus, who would come "in his Father's glory with the holy angels" (8:38) to establish the complete reign of God. Yet it seems theatrical for Jesus to have promised that some in his audience would not taste death (9:1) until they had witnessed an event that took place a mere six days later (9:2). Jesus' transfiguration on the mountain did not usher in the kingdom of God in all its power, even if it foreshadowed it. We are still unsure of the meaning of Jesus' words in the first verse of chapter 9.

The Coming of Elijah

9 As they were coming down from the mountain, he charged them not to relate what they had seen to anyone, except when the Son of Man had risen from the dead. 10 So they kept the matter to themselves, questioning what rising from the dead meant. 11 Then they asked him, "Why do the scribes say that Elijah must come first?" 12 He told them, "Elijah will indeed come first and restore all things, yet how is it written regarding the Son of Man that he must suffer greatly and be treated with contempt? 13 But I tell you that Elijah has come and they did to him whatever they pleased, as it is written of him."

Gospel parallels: Matt 17:9–13

OT: 1 Kings 19:1–2, 10; 2 Kings 2:11; Psalm 22:7–8; Sirach 48:10; Isaiah 53:3; Dan 7:13; Mal 3:1–3; 23–24

NT: Mark 1:2–8; 6:17–29

9 **As they were coming down from the mountain:** Jesus does not remain atop the mountain, basking in the afterglow of his transfiguration. He descends to continue his mission. Jesus **charged them not to relate what they had seen to anyone,** not even the other disciples, **except when the Son of Man had risen from the dead.** Jesus' transfiguration, as an anticipation of his resurrected glory, could not be understood apart from his dying and rising. The disciples might eagerly accept a glorified Jesus, but they were slow to understand a Jesus who must suffer and die on the way to glorification. Too much attention on the final outcome could hinder their coming to grips with the necessity of the cross for Jesus—and for them.

For reflection: Am I more focused on rising with Jesus than dying with him?

10 **So they kept the matter to themselves, questioning what rising from the dead meant.** Peter, James, and John keep Jesus' transfiguration quiet but discuss among themselves what Jesus meant when he spoke of the Son of Man rising from the dead. Why would Jesus have to rise from the dead—why would he have to die? If he was the Messiah whom many were expecting, he would defeat his enemies and enjoy a secure life. Jews who expected that there would be a resurrection of the dead thought that it would occur at the end of the present age, when all the dead would rise and be judged by God. Was Jesus talking about his rising from the dead before the end of the age? Or would his rising signal the end of the age? Did Jesus' proclamation that "this is the time of fulfillment" (1:15) mean that the present age had reached its end?

Resurrection: See page 320

11 Peter, James, and John have just seen Elijah with the transfigured Jesus (verse 4), and this apparently reminds them that Elijah (who was taken up into heaven: 2 Kings 2:11) is expected to return before the day of the Lord and the end of this age. If the end of the age is at hand, where is Elijah? **Then they asked him, "Why do the scribes say that Elijah must come first?"** Malachi prophesied that Elijah would return (Mal 3:1–3, 23–24). Ben Sira, a scribe who lived two centuries before Jesus, wrote of Elijah's return (Sirach 48:10), and later **scribes** also apparently discussed it.

Scribes: See page 40

> *Lo, I will send you*
> > *Elijah, the prophet,*
> *Before the day of the LORD comes,*
> > *the great and terrible day,*
> *To turn the hearts of the fathers to their children,*
> > *and the hearts of the children to their fathers.*
> > > Mal 3:23–24

You {Elijah} are destined, it is written, in time to come
to put an end to wrath before the day of the LORD,
To turn back the hearts of fathers toward their sons,
and to re-establish the tribes of Jacob.

Sirach 48:10

12 **He told them, "Elijah will indeed come first and restore all things":** Jesus accepts that Elijah will return. The expectation that Elijah will **restore all things** is not explicit in Malachi; Jesus' words more closely echo Ben Sira, who wrote that Elijah would "re-establish"—that is, restore—"the tribes of Jacob" (Sirach 48:10).

But Elijah is of secondary importance: Jesus is more interested in his disciples understanding him and his role in God's plan. So Jesus asks the disciples, **Yet how is it written regarding the Son of Man that he must suffer greatly and be treated with contempt?** When he says, **How is it written?** Jesus is referring to what is written in Scripture. What passage or passages does Jesus have in mind? No text in the Old Testament explicitly says that **the Son of Man must suffer greatly and be treated with contempt.** The most notable "Son of Man" passage speaks rather of his coming on the clouds and receiving dominion, glory, and kingship from God (Dan 7:13–14). It is therefore best to understand Jesus' mention of **the Son of Man** simply as his way of referring to himself. Jesus is saying that he must **suffer greatly and be treated with contempt** and that this is foreshadowed in Scripture, even if it is not explicit in passages that use the term *Son of Man.* Jesus may have in mind Isaiah 53 and Psalm 22. Jesus previously indicated that he must suffer and be rejected and killed (8:31); now he teaches that this is in accordance with Scripture.

Son of Man: See page 41

He was spurned and avoided by men,
a man of suffering, accustomed to infirmity,
One of those from whom men hide their faces,
spurned, and we held him in no esteem.

Isaiah 53:3

> But I am a worm, hardly human,
>> scorned by everyone, despised by the people.
> All who see me mock me;
>> they curl their lips and jeer;
>> they shake their heads at me.
>
> Psalm 22:7–8

13 Jesus will continue to teach his disciples about his suffering and death, but he returns to the disciples' question about Elijah. **But I tell you that Elijah has come and they did to him whatever they pleased, as it is written of him.** Mark began his Gospel by invoking a prophecy about Elijah preparing the way for God in order to describe John the Baptist preparing the way for Jesus (1:2; Mal 3:1). By saying that **Elijah has come,** Jesus implies that John the Baptist fulfilled Elijah's preparatory role. Those who felt threatened by John **did to him whatever they pleased,** making his head the prize for a shameless dance (6:17–29). Jesus says that John's fate was **as it is written of him** in Scripture. Once again we must do a little searching, for the Scripture passages that speak of Elijah's return say nothing about his being put to death. However, a parallel does exist between an unscrupulous queen (Jezebel) and a weak king (Ahab) seeking Elijah's death (1 Kings 19:1–2, 10), and another unscrupulous woman (Herodias) and a weak ruler (Herod Antipas) accomplishing John's death (6:17–29). Jesus discerns a connection between Elijah and John, not only in their mission of preparing for a day of the Lord but also in what almost happened to Elijah and did happen to John.

On a human level, John's vulnerability to those in authority is a warning that Jesus is no less vulnerable. On a deeper level, the death of John the Baptist in accordance with what is **written** foreshadows the death of Jesus in accordance with what is **written:** both will have given their lives to carry out God's will, in accordance with Scripture.

For reflection: What insight into Jesus might I get from his having his suffering and death on his mind as he came down from the mount of his transfiguration?

A Call for Faith

14 When they came to the disciples, they saw a large crowd around them and scribes arguing with them. **15** Immediately on seeing him, the whole crowd was utterly amazed. They ran up to him and greeted him. **16** He asked them, "What are you arguing about with them?" **17** Someone from the crowd answered him, "Teacher, I have brought to you my son possessed by a mute spirit. **18** Wherever it seizes him, it throws him down; he foams at the mouth, grinds his teeth, and becomes rigid. I asked your disciples to drive it out, but they were unable to do so." **19** He said to them in reply, "O faithless generation, how long will I be with you? How long will I endure you? Bring him to me." **20** They brought the boy to him. And when he saw him, the spirit immediately threw the boy into convulsions. As he fell to the ground, he began to roll around and foam at the mouth. **21** Then he questioned his father, "How long has this been happening to him?" He replied, "Since childhood. **22** It has often thrown him into fire and into water to kill him. But if you can do anything, have compassion on us and help us." **23** Jesus said to him, "'If you can!' Everything is possible to one who has faith." **24** Then the boy's father cried out, "I do believe, help my unbelief!" **25** Jesus, on seeing a crowd rapidly gathering, rebuked the unclean spirit and said to it, "Mute and deaf spirit, I command you: come out of him and never enter him again!" **26** Shouting and throwing the boy into convulsions, it came out. He became like a corpse, which caused many to say, "He is dead!" **27** But Jesus took him by the hand, raised him, and he stood up. **28** When he entered the house, his disciples asked him in private, "Why could we not drive it out?" **29** He said to them, "This kind can only come out through prayer."

Gospel parallels: Matt 17:14–20; Luke 9:37–43

14 **When they came to the disciples, they saw a large crowd around them and scribes arguing with them.** Once down from the Mount of Transfiguration, Jesus, Peter, James, and John find that the rest of the **disciples** are engaged in an argument with some **scribes,** surrounded

by a **large crowd** that is observing the dispute. **Scribes** have previously come from Jerusalem to monitor what Jesus was doing (3:22; 7:1).

Scribes: See page 40

15 **Immediately on seeing him, the whole crowd was utterly amazed.** Mark doesn't tell us why the crowd was so amazed, and speculations about the source of their amazement are only guesses. **They ran up to him and greeted him.** The people in the crowd obviously recognize Jesus; apparently they have come in search of him, as has happened in the past (3:7–10; 6:30–34, 53–56). When the disciples told those seeking Jesus that he was off somewhere up the mountain, they waited for him to return.

16 **He asked them, "What are you arguing about with them?"** The *thems* are a little ambiguous, but the most natural sense is that Jesus is asking his disciples what they are arguing about with the scribes. The scribes have come to confront Jesus, and in Jesus' absence they have confronted his followers.

17 No one volunteers a direct answer to Jesus' question. Rather, there might have been an awkward silence as Jesus waited for one of his disciples to speak up (see also 9:33–34). Someone comes to their rescue and fills Jesus in on what happened while he was on the mountain. **Someone from the crowd answered him, "Teacher, I have brought to you my son possessed by a mute spirit."** This father in need has sought out Jesus. His **son** is **possessed by a mute spirit,** that is, by an evil spirit that prevents his son from speaking. But that is not all:

18 **Wherever it seizes him, it throws him down; he foams at the mouth, grinds his teeth, and becomes rigid.** A person with these symptoms today would be diagnosed as having a form of epilepsy. An epileptic seizure can prevent one from speaking, which may be why the father attributes his son's distress to a "mute spirit" (verse 17). **I asked your disciples to drive it out, but they were unable to do so.** Since Jesus was off somewhere with a few of his disciples, this father asked the disciples who had remained behind to free his son. It was a reasonable

225

request: Jesus had given the Twelve authority over unclean spirits (6:7), and with this authority they had driven out many demons and healed many who were sick (6:13). The disciples probably responded to the father's request by saying, "We will be happy to free your son of his affliction"—but then they were unable to do so. The reason they were unable to do so is not immediately evident.

The father's account provides some background for the dispute between the disciples and the scribes, and it may hint that the disciples were reluctant to answer Jesus' question out of shame over their failure (verse 16), but the father does not spell out what the disciples and the scribes were arguing about. We can suspect that the dispute was over casting out demons—or the failure to do so—and that it was a continuation of a previous dispute between some scribes and Jesus about his power over evil spirits (3:22–30). Whatever the exact nature of the dispute, the significant fact that emerges from the father's account is that Jesus' disciples found themselves unable to carry out his work in his absence.

COMMENT: DEMONS AND SICKNESS It was taken for granted in the world of Jesus that the influence of demons could be experienced in everyday life. Evil spirits were sometimes understood as the cause of physical and mental illnesses (perhaps epilepsy and schizophrenia); hence the cure of these illnesses required the expulsion of such spirits. In the Gospels of Matthew, Mark, and Luke, Jesus' casting out of demons is sometimes associated with healings, such as the healing of a woman with curvature of the spine (Luke 13:11–16). The line between healings and exorcisms in the Gospels is not always clear. How should we understand Jesus' actions? Some points to keep in mind: First, the Catholic Church teaches that Satan exists and can cause spiritual harm—and even, indirectly, physical harm (*Catechism of the Catholic Church*, #395), but the Church urges care in distinguishing between demonic activity and physical or mental illness (*Catechism*, #1673). Second, although we understand more about the natural causes of sickness than people did in the first century, this does not change the effect that Jesus had on the sick people who came to him. They were healed. Jesus remains a healer. And even if we understand the effects of Satan differently from how they were understood in the first century, Jesus is the stronger one who overcomes him (Mark 3:27). Third, Jesus' exorcisms and healings were not merely done out of compassion for afflicted individuals but were also assaults on the forces of evil. Evil is still manifestly present in the world, and Jesus' overcoming of evil is no less a part of establishing God's reign today than it was in the first century.

For reflection: Do I find a lesson in the disciples' inability to carry out Jesus' work in his absence?

19 The dispute between the scribes and the disciples fades into the background; Jesus turns his attention to the disciples' inability to free the boy of his affliction. With some exasperation **he said to them in reply, "O faithless generation."** Jesus previously characterized the people he lived among as a "faithless and sinful generation" (8:38). Now Jesus extends this stinging term to his disciples as he addresses their failure to free the boy of the demon. They failed because they were **faithless;** they had not truly put their trust in him and in his power working through them. **How long will I be with you? How long will I endure you?** Jesus' words have an ominous undertone, for Jesus knows that he will not be with them for long: his own death is much on his mind. Time is running out for his disciples to grasp who he is and what following him means. Hence Jesus' exasperation: will his disciples get it before it is too late?

For reflection: Do I give Jesus any cause to be exasperated with me?

But other needs must be attended to. Jesus tells his disciples to **bring** the afflicted boy to him.

20 **They brought the boy to him. And when he saw him, the spirit immediately threw the boy into convulsions.** Unlike Jesus' disciples, evil spirits have no difficulty recognizing who Jesus really is (1:23–24; 3:11; 5:6–7). But unlike previous evil spirits, this spirit says nothing about Jesus' identity (perhaps another reason why it was characterized as a mute spirit: verse 17). It expresses its resistance to Jesus by throwing the boy **into convulsions. As he fell to the ground, he began to roll around and foam at the mouth.** Jesus can see for himself the symptoms the father described (verse 18).

21 Jesus seems to ignore the afflicted lad writhing around at his feet: his symptoms are alarming but not fatal. Jesus turns his attention to the father, questioning him: **How long has this been happening to him?** Why Jesus wants—or needs—to know this is unclear. The father replies, **Since childhood.** The boy's affliction is long-standing.

22 **It has often thrown him into fire and into water to kill him.** An epileptic seizure can strike in any location, whether one is near a cooking fire or a lake. The boy has had some seizures that have **thrown him into fire and into water,** and the father has interpreted them as evidence that the demon is trying **to kill** his son. Jesus' disciples were unable to cast out the demon, and the father now appeals to Jesus: **But if you can do anything, have compassion on us and help us.** He asks Jesus to have compassion **on us,** on him and his son, and to do whatever he can to **help us.**

> *For reflection: How am I, and those I love, most in need of Jesus' compassion?*

23 The father has turned to Jesus for help but with less-than-complete confidence that Jesus will be able to do anything. **Jesus said to him, "'If you can!'"** Jesus notes the father's uncertain faith. Jesus solemnly pronounces that **everything is possible to one who has faith.** But who is the **one** to whom Jesus is referring? We might understand Jesus to be speaking of himself, proclaiming that **everything is possible** for him, Jesus, because he, Jesus, has faith; hence he is able to free the boy of his affliction. If Jesus is speaking of himself as **one who has faith,** it is the only instance in any of the Gospels that Jesus' faith is referred to and presented as the source of his power to exorcise and heal. However, we can also understand Jesus to be speaking of the father as the **one** for whom everything is possible if he has faith—that is, if he trusts that Jesus is able and willing to free his son. A third possible interpretation is that Jesus' disciples would have been able to free the son of his affliction if they had had sufficient faith. The most likely interpretation is that Jesus is calling the father to go beyond his **if you can** attitude and have faith. The issue is not whether Jesus has the power to overcome evil; the issue is our reliance on that power. Jesus proclaims that **everything is possible** by and for **one who has faith.**

> *For reflection: Do I take Jesus' pronouncement that everything is possible for the one who has faith as an exaggeration? Or does it provide an index of faith for me?*

24 The father understands Jesus' words as a call for him to have faith and acknowledges that his faith is limited. **Then the boy's father cried out, "I do believe, help my unbelief!"** I want my son to be well; I want to believe that you can free my son of his affliction; help me overcome my doubts that you can! This father's heartfelt cry is the cry of all those of wavering faith, all who struggle to believe. Mark writes for those who wrestle with doubts. He knows that faith is not easy in the midst of trials and persecution, but he nonetheless wants his readers to trust Jesus completely and entrust their lives to him. Mark presents the father's cry as a prayer for all those who waver: **I believe; help my unbelief!**

For reflection: What do I believe? What do I struggle to believe?

25 **Jesus, on seeing a crowd rapidly gathering, rebuked the unclean spirit:** a crowd was already present (verses 14–15), but Mark writes as if it was now just forming around Jesus and the afflicted boy. This might indicate that Mark combined several traditions about what happened that day, leaving some rough edges. Jesus previously tried to avoid making public spectacles of his healings (5:37–40; 7:33; 8:23), and now he does so once again, acting quickly before the crowd builds up. Jesus **rebuked the unclean spirit and said to it, "Mute and deaf spirit, I command you: come out of him and never enter him again!"** Jesus addresses the spirit as a **mute and deaf spirit,** presumably because the boy can neither speak nor respond to what is said to him while he is having a seizure. Jesus' rebuke and command are similar to his treatment of an unclean spirit in a man in the synagogue of Capernaum (1:25). This time, however, in addition to commanding the unclean spirit to **come out of him,** Jesus adds, **And never enter him again.** The boy's seizures are not constant but periodic, and Jesus does not simply want to end this particular seizure but also to ensure that they never occur again.

26 **Shouting and throwing the boy into convulsions, it came out.** The **shouting** may be an incoherent cry, indicating that the mute spirit's hold is being broken. Like the spirit coming out of the man in the Capernaum synagogue (1:26), this spirit throws the boy **into convulsions.** Yet then

the boy is at peace—so much so that **he became like a corpse, which caused many to say, "He is dead!"**

27 **But Jesus took him by the hand, raised him, and he stood up.** Jesus takes **him by the hand** and raises him, just as Jesus took Peter's mother-in-law and the daughter of Jairus by the hand to raise them up, one from sickness and one from death (1:31; 5:41). The boy **stood up,** freed of his affliction. Even if this boy had been dead and not simply unconscious, Jesus could still have raised him up. Mark may intend for his readers to detect a connection between Jesus' raising the boy from apparent death and Jesus' raising his followers from real death.

28 **When he entered the house, his disciples asked him in private, "Why could we not drive it out?"** The reference to **the house** does not mean that Jesus and his disciples are back in Capernaum (see 9:33) but that they have been received into someone's house as guests. Jesus relied on the hospitality of others during his travels and taught his disciples to do the same (6:10). Jesus and the disciples are together in private, and the disciples often use such occasions to ask Jesus about things that puzzle them (4:10; 7:17). They are baffled by their inability to free the boy of an unclean spirit, given their earlier successes (6:13). They want to know **why** they **could not drive it out.**

29 **He said to them, "This kind can only come out through prayer."** Jesus views **this kind** of evil spirit as more difficult to deal with than other evil spirits but does not explain why. By **prayer,** Jesus does not mean a prescribed set of words that are required to perform an exorcism but **prayer** as an expression of faith and reliance on the power of God. Our prayer is an admission that we are not in control. The Twelve have been given authority over unclean spirits (6:7), but it is not an authority that can be exercised mechanically, as if it is an ability they possess. Spiritual gifts are manifestations of God working through a person; hence they can be exercised only in reliance on the power of God. **Prayer** expresses our dependence on God and our trust in God. Perhaps the disciples' earlier successes (6:13) made them overconfident

of their abilities and less reliant on God, resulting in shipwreck when the father asked them to free his son of his affliction.

For reflection: What forms do my prayers most characteristically take? What is the relationship between my prayer and my faith?

ORIENTATION: *Jesus sets out on a journey to Jerusalem, knowing that death and rising await him there. Mark provides only a few geographical markers along the way. Jesus' journey will take him from the Mount of Transfiguration to the rock of Golgotha.*

Jesus Teaches about His Dying and Rising

³⁰ They left from there and began a journey through Galilee, but he did not wish anyone to know about it. ³¹ He was teaching his disciples and telling them, "The Son of Man is to be handed over to men and they will kill him, and three days after his death he will rise." ³² But they did not understand the saying, and they were afraid to question him.

Gospel parallels: Matt 17:22–23; Luke 9:44–45
OT: Isaiah 53:6, 12
NT: Mark 8:31; 10:33–34; Rom 4:25; 8:32

30 **They left from there and began a journey through Galilee:** their point of departure is somewhere near the site of Jesus' transfiguration (9:9, 14, 28). As Jesus and his disciples travel **through Galilee,** Jesus does **not wish anyone to know about it.** Jesus knows that he will not be with his disciples for long (9:19), and he wants to instruct them in private, away from the demanding crowds. Jesus' public ministry in Galilee is over; his attention is on preparing his followers for what lies ahead.

31 **He was teaching his disciples and telling them:** the connotation is that Jesus is repeatedly **teaching** his disciples, **telling them** about something. In the forefront of Jesus' mind is his coming death and rising: he is **telling them, "The Son of Man is to be handed over to men and**

they will kill him, and three days after his death he will rise." Jesus' fate is to be **handed over;** the Greek word can be understood in several ways. It can mean be betrayed, as when it is used to characterize Judas as the one who betrayed Jesus (3:19). It can also mean be arrested, as when it is used to describe the arrest of John the Baptist (1:14). Jesus tells his disciples that he will be **handed over** to those who will **kill him.** Jesus does not describe the manner in which he will be killed but simply states that it will happen.

Son of Man: See page 41

There is another dimension of meaning in **handed over:** Mark's words imply that Jesus will be **handed over** *by* God to be killed. Mark's first readers might already have been familiar with this understanding of Jesus' death, for Paul had written of it in his letter to Rome. Paul spoke of Jesus being "handed over for our transgressions" (Rom 4:25) and of God as one "who did not spare his own Son but handed him over for us all" (Rom 8:32). Judas might be the human who betrays Jesus, but Jesus' death is a part of God's saving plan, which is why Jesus earlier said that he "must" suffer and die (8:31). Why God chose the death of his Son as the means for us to receive eternal life is a mystery we must ponder.

Some of Mark's first readers might also have been familiar with the Greek translation of Isaiah and recalled its use of the term **handed over.** Isaiah says of an unnamed servant of God that "the Lord handed him over for our sins," and "on account of their sins he was handed over" (Isaiah 53:6, 12, in the Greek version). The early Church turned to Isaiah 52:13–53:12 in an effort to understand the meaning of Jesus' death.

For reflection: What does it mean for my life that Jesus was handed over by his Father to death?

Jesus' death will not be the end. Jesus goes on to promise his disciples that **three days after his death he will rise.** Jesus will triumph over death, and some of his disciples have been given a foreshadowing of his triumph (9:2–7). The expression **three days after** is an echo of words used in Hosea 6:2, but that prophecy does not specifically speak of a messiah (or a messianic figure) rising from the dead. The Old Testament provides clues, not a blueprint, for understanding the death and rising of

Jesus. Jesus says that **he will rise:** the last time he spoke of his rising from the dead, Peter, James, and John were puzzled by his words (9:10).

32 They, along with the rest of the disciples, are still puzzled. **But they did not understand the saying:** they do not understand Jesus' statement that he will be handed over and killed but will rise (verse 31). Their perplexity is perplexing. This is not the first time that Jesus has warned them of what lies ahead (8:31; 9:9, 12); he has been speaking of it repeatedly (verse 31). What don't they understand? Why don't they understand it? Are their hearts still hardened (6:52)? Are they capable of thinking only on a very human level (8:33)? **And they were afraid to question him.** The disciples are **afraid** to face the prospect of Jesus' death and its consequences for them, despite his assurance that his death will lead to his rising. They avoid questioning him lest he confirm that his words mean exactly what they seem to mean. They don't want to talk about it. Jesus invited them to deny themselves (8:34), but they are in denial.

When Mark makes evident the failures of the first followers of Jesus, he does so not to throw mud on them but to challenge any self-assured readers and to reassure any despairing readers. To the self-assured, Mark's account says, "You think you would have done better than the first disciples if you had been one of them? Think again. Do you fully accept the implications of following a Jesus who was handed over to be crucified? Are you living out a discipleship that requires walking in his footsteps?" To those buffeted by discouragement, Mark's account says, "You see how much the first followers of Jesus disappointed him? Well, you are no worse than they were. Just as Jesus stuck with them, so he will stick with you. Take courage, despite your failures."

*For reflection: What lesson can I take away from the obtuseness of Jesus'
first followers?*

The Way to Greatness

³³ They came to Capernaum and, once inside the house, he began to ask them, "What were you arguing about on the way?" ³⁴ But they remained silent. They had been discussing among themselves on the way who was the greatest. ³⁵ Then he sat down, called the

Twelve, and said to them, "If anyone wishes to be first, he shall be the last of all and the servant of all." **36** Taking a child he placed it in their midst, and putting his arms around it he said to them, **37** "Whoever receives one child such as this in my name, receives me; and whoever receives me, receives not me but the One who sent me."

Gospel parallels: Matt 18:1–5; Luke 9:46–48
NT: Mark 8:34–37; 10:43–44

33 Jesus has been traveling through Galilee with his disciples, instructing them in private (9:30–31), and now they come **to Capernaum,** on the northwest shore of the Sea of Galilee. Jesus used **Capernaum** as his base of operations during his public ministry in Galilee, staying in Peter's house (1:29; 2:1). Jesus and his disciples have apparently returned to this house, which is the most natural place for them to stay in Capernaum, **and, once inside the house, he began to ask them, "What were you arguing about on the way?"** Jesus would not have needed supernatural knowledge to notice that something was brewing among his disciples as they walked: first-century Jewish country folk did not air their disputes with the restraint of British diplomats. Their gestures and the expressions on their faces would have given them away, along with the tone of any words Jesus might have overheard. Their argument arose while they were **on the way** with Jesus, on the road that he knew would lead to his death.

Capernaum: See page 37

34 **But they remained silent,** just as they had when Jesus previously asked them a question they were too embarrassed to answer (9:16–17). They understand enough of Jesus' teachings to know that he would not be pleased that they were **discussing among themselves on the way who was the greatest.** The disciples were jockeying for position, seeking the highest status and honor. It was a natural thing to do in a society that considered honor very important. Yet the disciples' jockeying for the highest status indicates that they had not yet embraced the way of Jesus, who had told them how they were to behave as his followers (8:34–37). They do not understand the implications of his suffering and dying (8:31–33; 9:31–32). Mark again notes that they were **on the way**

that would lead to Jesus' death: their argument was as out of place there as it would have been at the foot of the cross.

For reflection: What status or honors or prerogatives do I demand for myself? Am I willing to model myself on a Jesus who followed the way of the cross?

35 **Then he sat down:** today lecturers and teachers stand, but in the world of Jesus, teachers sat while teaching (see 4:1–2). Jesus calls **the Twelve** to him. He is in the company of his followers, so this apparently indicates that he singled out the Twelve, as if what he was going to say was very important for them as his specially chosen (3:13–14). They, more than other disciples, may be tempted to consider themselves the greatest. Jesus says **to them, "If anyone wishes to be first, he shall be the last of all and the servant of all."** Rulers, aristocrats, and those with influence were hailed as the "firsts" of society (in 6:21, the "leading men of Galilee" are literally "the firsts of Galilee"). To be the absolute **first** was to be on top. Jesus turns conventional thinking upside down and teaches that the **first,** the greatest, in the reign of God will be the person at the bottom. The one who will be at the head of the pecking order will not be the person who is greatest but rather the person who is at the end, **last of all.** This is a matter not merely of where one stands but also of what one does: the person who wants to be **first** must be **the servant of all.** Peter's mother-in-law "waited on" (literally, served) Jesus and his disciples (1:31); Jesus pronounces her and those like her to be the real firsts among his followers. But it is not enough to simply be a **servant:** one could serve only those one liked or those who made service pleasant and rewarding, but Jesus calls his followers to be servants **of all.**

36 To drive home his message, Jesus performs a parable-in-action, a symbolic gesture. **Taking a child he placed it in their midst.** Children had no status in the world of Jesus; they were considered nobodies. Being kind to children was not a way to get ahead. **And putting his arms around it he said to them:** Jesus' gesture is a display of genuine affection but is also meant to convey a message to his followers. He explains what his message is:

37 **Whoever receives one child such as this in my name, receives me.** To "receive" means to warmly welcome and serve. To receive one **such as** a **child** means to accept and serve those who count for nothing in the eyes of the world, those who are the neediest, who cannot repay what is done for them. That is what it means to be the servant "of all" (verse 35). To carry out such service in Jesus' **name** means, in this context, to do so for the sake of Jesus. Jesus says that in receiving and serving the nobodies, one **receives** him. Jesus identifies himself with the unimportant people of this world. Thus what we do for them we do for Jesus. If we want to hug Jesus, we can hug someone held in no esteem by others, as Jesus hugged this child. Jesus adds that **whoever receives me, receives not me but the One who sent me.** Jesus is God's agent, and in serving Jesus through serving the insignificant we serve God. In addressing the disciples' dispute, Jesus teaches that the way to true greatness lies in service. By serving nobodies we become somebody in the eyes of God, for in serving them we serve God.

For reflection: What do Jesus' words and acted-out parable mean for me? Whom does he ask me to serve?

Jesus speaks of God as **the One who sent me.** Just as Jesus chose the Twelve so that he could send them out on mission (3:14; 6:7), so he was chosen and sent on a mission by God. This provides a glimpse of who Jesus is and of his relationship with God. The implications of Jesus being **sent** by God on a mission that will culminate in Jesus being "handed over" to those who will kill him (9:31) are staggering. Jesus turns human logic on its head by pronouncing that the way to greatness lies in humble service, but this surprising notion pales in comparison with the mystery of God sending his Son to his death.

A Lesson in Acceptance

38 **John said to him, "Teacher, we saw someone driving out demons in your name, and we tried to prevent him because he does not follow us."** 39 **Jesus replied, "Do not prevent him. There is no one who performs a mighty deed in my name who can at the same time speak ill of me.** 40 **For whoever is not against us is for us.** 41 **Anyone**

who gives you a cup of water to drink because you belong to
Christ, amen, I say to you, will surely not lose his reward."

Gospel parallels: Matt 10:42; Luke 9:49–50
NT: Acts 19:13–16

38 **John said to him, "Teacher, we saw someone driving out demons
in your name":** although **John** was one of the first disciples called by
Jesus (Mark 1:16–20) and one of Jesus' closest associates (5:37; 9:2), this
is the only instance in Mark's Gospel in which **John** speaks up on his
own. He addresses Jesus as **teacher:** Jesus is sitting and teaching his
followers about service (9:35–37). John tells Jesus, **We** (the disciples)
saw someone driving out demons in your name. Exorcisms were
not uncommon in the first century, and Jesus was not the only one who
drove out demons. Exorcists might invoke the name of a powerful figure
as a way of asserting authority over a demon; Jewish exorcists sometimes
invoked the name of Solomon, who in popular tradition was thought
to have had the wisdom to expel demons. The person who was **driving
out demons** recognized Jesus' authority over demons and tried to draw
on it by invoking Jesus' name, apparently with success. (Luke reports
an unsuccessful attempt made some years later: Acts 19:13–16.) Jesus'
disciples were irked by this exorcist: John tells Jesus that **we tried to
prevent him** from using your name to drive out demons **because he
does not follow us.** The disciples thought he had no business using
Jesus' name if he was not one of them; Jesus' power should be restricted
to Jesus' authorized agents (6:7). Jesus gave John and his brother James
the nickname "sons of thunder" (3:17), which seems appropriate in light
of John's behavior toward this exorcist. The disciples might also have
been chagrined that this exorcist was successfully driving out demons,
while they had recently failed (9:18, 28).

39 **Jesus replied, "Do not prevent him."** Jesus rebukes his disciples' nar-
rowness, telling them to leave the exorcist alone. If the disciples are to
be last of all and servant of all (9:35), there is no room for jealousy or
party spirit. Jesus says that **there is no one who performs a mighty
deed in my name who can at the same time speak ill of me.** Even
if this exorcist is not a follower of Jesus, neither is he an opponent if
he is relying on the name of Jesus to perform mighty deeds. Jesus has

in mind his coming time of crisis, when he will be rejected and put to death. It is enough for Jesus that this exorcist does not line up with Jesus' opponents.

40 Jesus adds, **For whoever is not against us is for us.** Jesus expresses his stance with what may have been a popular proverb (the Roman author Cicero had written similar words in the previous century). It is a sweeping principle that calls upon the disciples to be tolerant toward the neutral and the lukewarm. The followers of Jesus should not build a fence around themselves, shutting out those who are not within.

> *For reflection: What fences have I erected that separate me from others? Do I demand that others prove they are for me before I accept them?*

41 If others are to be accepted even in their neutrality, they are to be that much more valued when they do something positive. Even a small act of compassion toward followers of Jesus will be rewarded by God: **Anyone who gives you a cup of water to drink because you belong to Christ, amen, I say to you, will surely not lose his reward.** The **anyone** in this context means anyone who is not a disciple of Jesus but who nonetheless is kind to disciples of Jesus: they will be rewarded by God. God's love is not limited to those who follow Jesus.

This saying of Jesus is an instance where Mark might have adapted Jesus' words to current usage. Scholars suspect that Jesus more likely spoke of his followers being given a drink of water "because you belong to me" rather than "because you belong to Christ." Jesus was reticent to speak of himself as the Messiah, or Christ, during his public ministry (8:29–30). By the time Mark wrote his Gospel, however, Paul had frequently referred to Christians as belonging to Christ (Rom 8:9; 1 Cor 1:12; 3:22–23; 2 Cor 10:7; Gal 3:29), and Mark may have adopted this expression. This does not change the meaning of Jesus' teaching.

In trying to stop an exorcist who was not one of them, the disciples have again failed to understand the implications of Jesus' coming death and rising (9:31–32). Jesus will give up his life for all (10:45; 14:24), not for a small elite. Jesus will leave behind an open door to God (15:38), and he doesn't want his disciples slamming it shut.

For reflection: Have I been treated kindly by those who respect my faith even though they do not share it? What do Jesus' words about them mean for me?

Choose Life

42 "**Whoever causes one of these little ones who believe [in me] to sin, it would be better for him if a great millstone were put around his neck and he were thrown into the sea. 43 If your hand causes you to sin, cut it off. It is better for you to enter into life maimed than with two hands to go into Gehenna, into the unquenchable fire. [44] 45 And if your foot causes you to sin, cut it off. It is better for you to enter into life crippled than with two feet to be thrown into Gehenna. [46] 47 And if your eye causes you to sin, pluck it out. Better for you to enter into the kingdom of God with one eye than with two eyes to be thrown into Gehenna, 48 where 'their worm does not die, and the fire is not quenched.'"**

Gospel parallels: Matt 18:6–9; Luke 17:1–2
OT: Deut 30:19–20; 2 Macc 7; Isaiah 66:24
NT: Rom 14:1–15:6

42 Jesus has taken a child in his arms (9:36), providing a link for his next teaching. **Whoever causes one of these little ones who believe [in me] to sin:** children would naturally qualify as **little ones.** But Mark's first readers would likely have understood **little ones who believe [in me]** to include the weaker members of the Christian community, those with a tender conscience or uncertain faith. Paul in his letter to Rome had written at some length about the special consideration that should be given to weak Christians so as not to scandalize them (Rom 14:1–15:6). Paul could have based his instructions on this teaching of Jesus, for Jesus warns against causing any of the little ones **to sin:** the Greek word translated as **to sin** means to stumble, to be scandalized. Woe to anyone who makes children or weaker Christians stumble, leading them to sin, for **it would be better for him if a great millstone were put around his neck and he were thrown into the sea.** Grain was milled between two stones; a **great millstone** is literally a "donkey millstone," an upper grinding stone so large that it took a donkey to turn it. Such a stone might have been the heaviest object that rural Galileans were familiar with. A **great millstone** around one's neck would ensure a speedy and permanent descent to the bottom of the sea. Jesus uses this vivid image of death by drowning to indicate the seriousness of leading the vulnerable into sin.

For reflection: How do I look upon those with a weak or troubled faith? Do I do anything that might cause them to stumble?

43 The followers of Jesus not only have to worry about causing others to stumble, but they also have to be concerned with stumbling themselves. **If your hand causes you to sin** (literally, causes you to stumble), **cut it off.** Strictly speaking, a **hand** can be an instrument of sin but not its cause: no judge would accept a pickpocket's argument "Your honor, I didn't steal the man's wallet; my hand did." Nor is self-mutilation much of a safeguard against sin. Jesus is using vivid imagery to convey a lesson, just as he did when he spoke of a great millstone (verse 42). **It is better for you to enter into life maimed than with two hands to go into Gehenna, into the unquenchable fire.** Jesus does not speak of preserving life but says **enter into life,** meaning life in the age to come. This is clear from the alternative, which is **to go into Gehenna.** The valley of **Gehenna,** adjacent to Jerusalem, was a refuse dump, and its maggot-infested and smoldering garbage was used in Jewish tradition as an image for punishment by **unquenchable fire** in the age to come. Loss of a hand pales in comparison with consignment to **Gehenna.**

44 (Some manuscripts of Mark's Gospel insert the words found in verse 48 here, but the most reliable manuscripts do not. The New American Bible omits this verse.)

45 **And if your foot causes you to sin, cut it off. It is better for you to enter into life crippled than with two feet to be thrown into Gehenna.** Jesus continues to stress the ultimate consequences of our behavior. His mention of a hand and now a foot being cut off might have reminded his listeners of the martyrdom of seven brothers during a religious persecution two centuries earlier. The brothers preferred being

dismembered to disobeying God's laws, confident that their bodies would be restored in the resurrection of the dead (2 Macc 7). Jesus now contrasts entering **into life** with being **thrown into Gehenna:** the implied meaning is **thrown** *by* God **into Gehenna.** We face a judgment that will decide our eternal destiny.

For reflection: What causes me to sin? What stumbling blocks have I put on my path to God?

46 (Again, some manuscripts of Mark's Gospel insert the words found in verse 48 here, but the most reliable manuscripts do not. The New American Bible omits this verse.)

47 **And if your eye causes you to sin, pluck it out. Better for you to enter into the kingdom of God with one eye than with two eyes to**

BACKGROUND: JUDGMENT AND GEHENNA For much of the Old Testament era, Israelites did not expect a meaningful life after death but only a shadowy existence in the netherworld for good and bad alike. As expectations arose that there would be life after death, so also arose the expectation that God would judge individuals after death, rewarding those who had led good lives and punishing those who had done evil. God's judgment is implicit in the book of Daniel, written about 164 BC: "Many of those who sleep / in the dust of the earth shall awake; / Some shall live forever, / others shall be an everlasting horror and disgrace" (Dan 12:2). The book of Judith, written after Daniel, speaks of judgment: "The LORD Almighty will requite them; / in the day of judgment he will punish them: / He will send fire and worms into their flesh, / and they shall burn and suffer forever" (Judith 16:17). Some nonbiblical writings portray Gehenna as the place of fiery punishment. *Gehenna* is a transliteration of the Hebrew for Hinnom Valley, a steep ravine on the western and southern sides of Jerusalem. In Old Testament times the Hinnom Valley was the setting for idolatrous worship (Jer 7:31; 19:1–6), which took place at sites that might have been considered entrances to the underworld. The Hinnom Valley was also used for burials and as a refuse dump. As the ideas of judgment after death and fiery punishment developed, the Hinnom Valley became a symbol of such punishment—perhaps because of its smoldering refuse and associations with death and idolatry. When Jesus spoke of Gehenna as a place of everlasting punishment, he was using imagery familiar to his listeners. *Related topic: Life after death (page 257), Nonbiblical writings (page 243).*

be thrown into Gehenna. What was called entering into "life" in the preceding verses is now identified with entering **into the kingdom of God.** Jesus announced that the kingdom of God was at hand (1:15) and spoke of some of his listeners living long enough to "see that the kingdom of God has come in power" (9:1). Jesus now speaks of the **kingdom of God** as God's reign in the age to come and contrasts those who **enter into** this reign with those who are **thrown** (by God) **into Gehenna.** The reign of God was being established on earth by Jesus, but God would not reign completely until the end of this age, when a final judgment would sort out good and evil.

Kingdom of God: See page 96

48 Jesus adds a final note about Gehenna: it is **where "their worm does not die, and the fire is not quenched."** Jesus borrows words from the last verse of the book of Isaiah to describe the torments of Gehenna. Gehenna was not a place for a family picnic. Nor would one want to spend the age to come in the midst of maggots and fire.

> They shall go out and see the corpses
>   of the men who rebelled against me;
> Their worm shall not die,
>   nor their fire be extinguished;
>   and they shall be abhorrent to all mankind.
>
> Isaiah 66:24

Several aspects of Jesus' teachings demand examination. First, how should we understand his injunctions to cut off a hand or a foot or pluck out an eye if they cause us to sin? Clearly Jesus did not intend his words to be taken as an instruction to mutilate oneself, any more than his words about losing one's life for his sake (8:35) were to be taken as an invitation to suicide. Rather, Jesus used vivid comparisons or parables to talk about the seriousness of our actions in light of their long-term consequences. Just as it is better to sacrifice a body part than to lose one's entire body, so it is better to make any sacrifice, no matter how costly, than to lose eternal life. Trying to connect hands, feet, and eyes to specific sins is futile and misses Jesus' point. Jesus was dramatizing the implications of his earlier question "What could one give in exchange for his life?" (8:37).

Second, how literally should we understand Jesus' words about Gehenna as a place of maggots and unquenchable fire? Again, Jesus provided a vivid image to indicate the eternal consequences of our actions. Jesus' imagery is the basis of the common imagining of hell as a place of everlasting fire (the maggots somehow disappeared). The Catholic Church, however, does not endorse such a literal understanding of hell and teaches that hell is not so much a place of punishment as a state of eternal separation from God. Fire might be an image for the suffering of being eternally separated from God, but it is only an image.

The final aspect to be noted in this teaching of Jesus is that the accent is on the positive. Jesus is exhorting his listeners to choose life, no matter the cost. He is reaffirming the final exhortation of Moses in the book of Deuteronomy: "I have set before you life and death, the blessing and the curse. Choose life, then, that you and your descendants

---

BACKGROUND: NONBIBLICAL WRITINGS Other religious writings besides the books of the Old Testament were in circulation among Jews at the time of Jesus. Many of these texts had been written in the previous two centuries. Two of these writings, *1 Enoch* and *The Assumption of Moses,* are quoted in the letter of Jude (Jude 6, 9, 14–15). Other writings included *Jubilees, Psalms of Solomon,* and some of *The Testaments of the Twelve Patriarchs,* as well as writings found among the Dead Sea Scrolls. Some of these writings claim to be revelations of how God will act to overcome evil and begin a new age. They differ considerably over what lies ahead. Various ideas about messianic figures, angels, the present age and the age to come, judgment, the resurrection of the dead, and life in the age to come are found in these writings, in more developed forms than they are found in the books of the Old Testament. It is uncertain how popular each of these writings was at the time of Jesus and how familiar the average Jew was with them. Yet at least some of their ideas and imagery, such as of Gehenna as a place of fiery punishment, were sufficiently familiar to first-century Jews for Jesus to invoke them in his teachings without having to explain them as if his listeners were hearing of them for the first time. These writings form part of the background for the Gospels and help bridge the Old and the New Testaments, even though they are not part of inspired Scripture. *Related topics: Dead Sea Scrolls (page 245), Psalms of Solomon (page 207), Revelations of the end (page 342).*

---

may live, by loving the LORD, your God, heeding his voice, and holding fast to him. For that will mean life for you, a long life for you" (Deut 30:19–20).

For reflection: How often do I think of my eternal destiny? Am I more motivated by a desire to be with God or by fear of punishment?

ORIENTATION: *The sayings of Jesus in the last part of chapter 9 are linked together by certain recurring words rather than by logic. Mention of the fire of Gehenna in verse 48 leads to another saying about fire in verse 49, and mention of salt in verse 49 leads to two more sayings about salt in verse 50. Jesus is at his most cryptic, giving his listeners something to think about.*

Fire and Salt

⁴⁹ Everyone will be salted with fire. ⁵⁰ Salt is good, but if salt becomes insipid, with what will you restore its flavor? Keep salt in yourselves and you will have peace with one another.

Gospel parallels: Matt 5:13; Luke 14:34–35

49 **Everyone will be salted with fire:** Jesus' words can apply to **everyone,** but he is speaking to his disciples. What does it mean for them to **be salted with fire?** It is hard to pin down one specific meaning for this mixed metaphor (scholars have come up with more than a dozen suggestions), so perhaps Jesus did not want to limit his words to a single meaning. Salt not only flavors food but also preserves it. In one Old Testament incident salt was used for purification (2 Kings 2:19–22). **Fire** can consume and destroy (as in the refuse dump of Gehenna: 9:43–48), but it can also refine and purify metals (Mal 3:2–3). Perhaps being **salted with fire** primarily means being purified, whether by suffering persecution as a disciple of Jesus or through the self-denial it takes to be his disciple. Some of Mark's first readers might have felt that **salted with fire** was a good metaphor for the persecution they endured.

For reflection: What meaning or meanings do I find in these words of Jesus?

50 In the first saying (verse 49), salt stood for something affecting the disciples, but in the next saying, **salt** stands for the disciples themselves. **Salt is good,** useful for preserving and seasoning; Jesus' disciples have their usefulness too, their share in the work of Jesus. **But if salt becomes insipid, with what will you restore its flavor?** The word **insipid** is literally "unsalty": if all your salt loses its saltiness, with what can you salt it? We don't have to turn to chemistry to know that it is impossible for salt to be anything other than salt; Jesus could just as well have posed his question in terms of fire losing its burning. Jesus' point is that when the essential characteristic of something is lost, the thing itself is lost. If Jesus is comparing his disciples to salt, then his words warn them against losing their discipleness by losing their usefulness. Disciples who do nothing for Jesus are disciples in name only, just as salt that does not season is not salt.

In the last saying, **salt** stands for yet a third thing: it is used as a metaphor for some characteristic or activity of the disciples. **Keep salt in yourselves and you will have peace with one another.** There

---

BACKGROUND: DEAD SEA SCROLLS In 1947, a Bedouin shepherd boy came across some clay jars in a cave overlooking the Dead Sea. The jars contained seven ancient scrolls, including the book of Isaiah. Over the next nine years more scrolls were found in ten other caves in the area. Almost nine hundred different scrolls have been discovered, virtually all of them incomplete and decayed, in more than one hundred thousand fragments. The process of assembling and translating the fragments has taken scholars many years. The scrolls were copied between roughly 200 BC and AD 68 and represent an entire library. About two hundred of the scrolls were copies of books of the Old Testament, including thirty-six copies of the Psalms. Also discovered were copies of nonbiblical religious writings, including about ten copies of *1 Enoch* and fifteen copies of *Jubilees,* as well as scrolls of religious writings that had been previously unknown. Along with these works, which had been in general circulation among Jews at the time of Jesus, were a number of works that pertained to the religious community that owned the library. Some of these scrolls were community rules, hymns used in the community, and commentaries on books of the Old Testament written from the community's perspective. The community that owned this library is commonly identified as the Essenes, a sect headquartered at Qumran, on the shore of the Dead Sea, where the scrolls were found. *Related topics: Essenes (page 297), Nonbiblical writings (page 243).*

---

are many suggestions for what the **salt** that the disciples were to keep in themselves might be. Love? Self-denial? Willingness to face death for Jesus? Service of one another? The only immediate clue is that such **salt** enables the disciples to **have peace with one another.** Jesus' instructions to his disciples in the house in Capernaum began in response to the disciples' dispute over who was greatest (9:33–35), and his instructions draw to a close with a saying about how the disciples will be able to avoid such disputes and **have peace with one another.** Jesus taught that they were to consider themselves last of all and servants of all (9:35), and this could be the **salt** that will enable them to get along. But so could their willingness to face death together for Jesus (8:34–38). Jesus' enigmatic words give his disciples something they must think about.

For reflection: What is my saltiness—my usefulness—for Jesus? How do I achieve peace in my relations with others?

CHAPTER 10

ORIENTATION: *Jesus leaves Galilee and journeys toward Jerusalem. He attracts and teaches crowds along the way but continues to instruct his disciples in private.*

God's View of Marriage

¹ He set out from there and went into the district of Judea [and] across the Jordan. Again crowds gathered around him and, as was his custom, he again taught them. ² The Pharisees approached and asked, "Is it lawful for a husband to divorce his wife?" They were testing him. ³ He said to them in reply, "What did Moses command you?" ⁴ They replied, "Moses permitted him to write a bill of divorce and dismiss her." ⁵ But Jesus told them, "Because of the hardness of your hearts he wrote you this commandment. ⁶ But from the beginning of creation, 'God made them male and female. ⁷ For this reason a man shall leave his father and mother [and be joined to his wife], ⁸ and the two shall become one flesh.' So they are no longer two but one flesh. ⁹ Therefore what God has joined together, no human being must separate." ¹⁰ In the house the disciples again questioned him about this. ¹¹ He said to them, "Whoever divorces his wife and marries another commits adultery against her; ¹² and if she divorces her husband and marries another, she commits adultery."

Gospel parallels: Matt 19:1–12; Luke 16:18
OT: Gen 1:27; 2:24; Deut 24:1–4

1 **He set out from there:** after teaching his disciples in a house in Capernaum (9:33–35), Jesus sets out **from there** for Jerusalem. He and his disciples **went into the district of Judea [and] across the Jordan.** Although Mark mentions **the district of Judea** first, he likely means that Jesus traveled south along the eastern side of the Jordan River (**across the Jordan**), a route that Jews traveling from Galilee to **Judea** took to avoid going through Samaria (Samaritans could be hostile to Jewish pilgrims on their way to Jerusalem: Luke 9:51–53). After traveling south **across the Jordan,** Jesus will turn west, recross the Jordan, and pass by Jericho (10:46) on his way to Jerusalem.

Again crowds gathered around him and, as was his custom, he again taught them. Although Jesus recently avoided notice in Galilee (9:30), he now welcomes those who come to him and spends time teaching them, as he did earlier in his public ministry in Galilee (6:34). This is the first time Mark's Gospel describes Jesus traveling through the southern part of the region east of the Jordan River. It was a territory ruled by Herod Antipas (who also ruled Galilee), and it had a mixed Jewish and Gentile population. Jesus' reputation has spread to this region (3:8), so crowds gather around him as he walks, and he teaches them. Mark does not indicate the content of Jesus' teaching.

2 **The Pharisees approached and asked, "Is it lawful for a husband to divorce his wife?"** For Jews, **divorce** meant a husband dismissing his wife; a Jewish wife did not have the right to dismiss her husband. In the ancient world, **divorce** usually implied remarriage, not simply separation from one's spouse. Jews accepted the practice of **divorce,** but there might have been some debate over what constituted sufficient grounds for dismissing a wife. Some **Pharisees** ask Jesus' view of divorce because they are **testing him.** They want to put him on the spot, much as someone today might try to pin down an American politician by asking, "Where do you stand on abortion?"

Pharisees: See page 163

3 **He said to them in reply, "What did Moses command you?"** Jesus asks his questioners what the law of Moses says about divorce, knowing that it says very little. Only one passage in the first five books of the Bible explicitly addresses the question of divorce (Deut 24:1–4); it presumes that men can dismiss their wives but regulates the practice.

4 If the Pharisees are to respond in terms of what Scripture says, they have no choice but to refer to the single passage that deals with

---

BACKGROUND: JUDEA was the region of Palestine around and to the south of Jerusalem. It was originally the territory of the tribe of Judah, which gave it its name. Israelites from this region who had been in exile in Babylon returned to Judea after 538 BC. Thereafter they began to be called Judeans, which passed through Greek and Latin into English as the word *Jews.*

---

divorce. **They replied, "Moses permitted him to write a bill of divorce and dismiss her."** The Greek word translated **divorce** means relinquishment of a legal right. A **bill of divorce** provided some legal protection for a woman: her husband was relinquishing his right to her, and another man could thus be free to marry her—and she had it in writing.

> When a man, after marrying a woman and having relations with her, is later displeased with her because he finds in her something indecent, and therefore he writes out a bill of divorce and hands it to her, thus dismissing her from his house: if on leaving his house she goes and becomes the wife of another man . . .
>
> Deut 24:1–2

5 **But Jesus told them, "Because of the hardness of your hearts he wrote you this commandment."** The law of Moses took into account men dismissing their wives because of their hardness of heart and gave wives some legal protection when it happened. This was hardly a ringing endorsement of divorce! The law had rather made provision for humans not living up to what God wanted. We might compare this with what Deuteronomy says regarding the poor. On the one hand, God gave his people a land that would produce more than enough crops for everyone: "Since the Lord, your God, will bless you abundantly in the land he will give you to occupy as your heritage, there should be no one of you in need" (Deut 15:4). That was God's plan in giving the land. But on the other hand, no society ever achieves perfect sharing of land and resources, and the law realistically faced this by requiring help for those in need. Even though there should be no one in need, "the needy will never be lacking in the land; that is why I command you to open your hand to your poor and needy kinsman in your country" (Deut 15:11). Just as the law's provision for the needy was not a justification for people living in poverty, so the law's provision for a wife who had been sent away was not a justification for divorce.

For reflection: How has God taken my hard-heartedness into account in his dealings with me?

6 Having put what the law says in perspective, Jesus goes on to lay out God's intentions for husband and wife in marriage. Jesus invokes not the law God gave to Moses but what God did much earlier. **But from the beginning of creation, "God made them male and female."** Just as Jesus turned to God's purpose in creating the Sabbath in order to declare what could be done on the Sabbath (2:27), so he turns to God's purpose in creating men and women in order to teach about marriage and divorce. Jesus quotes the book of Genesis: **God made them male and female** (see Gen 1:27). God created the human race to be made up of males and females, who by their nature would be attracted to each other.

> God created man in his image;
>> in the divine image he created him;
>> male and female he created them.
>
> Gen 1:27

7 **For this reason,** because of their sexual differentiation and mutual attraction, **a man shall leave his father and mother [and be joined to his wife]**—another quotation from Genesis (see Gen 2:24). Not all manuscripts of Mark's Gospel contain the words **and be joined to his wife,** but they are part of the Genesis passage that Jesus is quoting. A man and a woman marry out of attraction to each other, and this is part of God's purpose in creating the human race as male and female.

> That is why a man leaves his father and mother and clings
> to his wife, and the two of them become one body.
>
> Gen 2:24

8 The quotation from Genesis concludes **and the two shall become one flesh** (the New American Bible translation of Gen 2:24 reads "become one body," translating the Hebrew word for flesh as body). Marriage is a man and a woman not merely living together but also becoming **one flesh.** The Hebrew notion of **flesh** encompassed not simply the soft tissues of the body but also the entire person as enfleshed, the whole person as a physical being. Becoming **one flesh** means that a woman and a man are so intimately and completely joined together in marriage that they have

become one person, as it were; two lives have entered into a common life. Jesus emphasizes their union: **So they are no longer two but one flesh.** Jesus proclaims that the union of a woman and a man in marriage is part of God's purpose in creating the human race the way he did.

For reflection: If I am married, how does my experience of marriage match up with Jesus' words?

9 **Therefore what God has joined together, no human being must separate.** If God's intention is that a woman and a man become one in marriage, and if God has **joined** them **together** to be one, then **no human being** should divide the one into two. Specifically, husbands are not to dismiss their wives. Jesus proclaims that divorce is contrary to God's intention in creating the human race the way he did. There undoubtedly were husbands in Jesus' audience who did not want to hear this, for they took it for granted that they had the right to divorce their wives. There probably were wives in Jesus' audience who welcomed his words, for Jesus taught that their husbands did not have the right to trade them in for new wives.

10 **In the house the disciples again questioned him about this.** Jesus is in a **house** with his disciples, again indicating that he relied on the hospitality of others as he traveled. As has happened a number of times before (4:10; 7:17; 9:28), Jesus' disciples are puzzled and question him when they are alone with him. Their questioning indicates that they assumed Jewish men were allowed to divorce their wives, and they want to make sure that Jesus said what they think he said.

11 Jesus responds by stating his teaching in even stronger terms. **He said to them, "Whoever divorces his wife and marries another commits adultery against her,"** that is, commits adultery against his wife. Jesus' speaking of **adultery** as an offense against a wife introduces a new element into the understanding of adultery, which was considered to be an offense that could be committed only against a husband. A married woman committed adultery against her husband by having sexual relations with another man, but a husband did not

251

commit adultery against his wife by having intercourse with another woman. This understanding of adultery reflected the view that a wife was in some sense the property of her husband (see Exod 20:17); to have intercourse with another man's wife violated his right to her. Jesus does not accept the view that a wife is the property of her husband. If a man and a woman become one in marriage, then what is adultery for one is adultery for the other. Jesus implicitly teaches that there is a basic equality between women and men in marriage.

12 A man who dismisses his wife in favor of another woman commits adultery against his wife, and the reverse is true as well: **and if she divorces her husband and marries another, she commits adultery.** Since Jewish women were not able to divorce their husbands, but Roman women were, many scholars suggest that Mark added these words to apply Jesus' teaching to the situation of those for whom he was writing (see 7:19 for another example of Mark drawing out the implications of Jesus' teaching). Other scholars note that Herodias abandoned her first husband to marry Herod Antipas (6:17–19) and that Jesus' words might have been a barb against her. Certainly, however, the principles behind Jesus' teaching on marriage and divorce apply equally to women and to men.

Jesus' teaching on the permanence of marriage runs counter to the practices of both ancient and modern societies. Applying and living up to Jesus' teaching about marriage is a challenge for individuals and for the Church today. Jesus' words call husbands and wives to cultivate the selfless love that is necessary for them to be one, and to maintain the unconditional commitment to each other that is necessary for their marriage to endure. It is perhaps no accident that Jesus' teaching on marriage and divorce occurs in Mark's Gospel after Jesus has spoken of the cost of discipleship (9:35, 42–48). Jesus does not propose that the permanent commitment entailed in marriage is easy, only that it is what God wants.

For reflection: What does Jesus' teaching about marriage mean to me in my situation?

The Embrace of Jesus

13 And people were bringing children to him that he might touch them, but the disciples rebuked them. 14 When Jesus saw this he became indignant and said to them, "Let the children come to me; do not prevent them, for the kingdom of God belongs to such as these. 15 Amen, I say to you, whoever does not accept the kingdom of God like a child will not enter it." 16 Then he embraced them and blessed them, placing his hands on them.

Gospel parallels: Matt 18:3; 19:13–15; Luke 18:15–17

OT: Gen 48:14–16

NT: Mark 9:36–37

13 The setting may shift from the house in which Jesus was teaching his disciples (10:10–12) to a more public place, for now people are **bringing children to him that he might touch them.** The word translated **children** covers those up to twelve years old. Jairus sought Jesus' healing touch for his daughter (5:22–23), but those who are **bringing children** to Jesus want him to **touch them** to impart a blessing. Laying hands on someone's head while blessing them was an ancient practice (Gen 48:14–16). The **people** who are bringing children to Jesus for a blessing recognize Jesus as a man of God, someone whose blessing might carry special weight.

Those bringing children to Jesus ran into an obstacle: **but the disciples rebuked them** and tried to keep them away from Jesus. The disciples' rebuking them indicates that the disciples think that these people are out of place in bringing children to Jesus and deserve a reprimand. Do the disciples think that Jesus has more important things to do than be bothered with children? Is this another example of the disciples' exclusionist tendencies? The disciples should know Jesus' attitude toward children from his hugging a child and telling them that whoever receives a child in his name receives him (9:36–37). Once again, the disciples fail to understand Jesus and to act on what he has taught them.

For reflection: Are there instances in my life where I know what Jesus teaches but do not act in accord with it?

14 **When Jesus saw this he became indignant:** this is the only place in the Gospels where Jesus is said to become **indignant,** although he has been quite unhappy with his disciples' behavior on other occasions (8:17–21; 9:19). The Greek word translated **indignant** has the connotation of a strong emotional reaction, of being very upset and angry. Jesus reacts strongly when he sees that his disciples are trying to turn away those who are bringing children to him for a blessing. He **said to them, "Let the children come to me; do not prevent them."** Jesus pairs a positive command with a negative command to make sure that his disciples get the point: Let them come; don't stop them. Jesus then adds a comment that might have startled the disciples: **For the kingdom of God belongs to such as these.** God's sovereign rule in all its fullness **belongs** to children and **to such as** them. Children had no status in the culture of the time; they were powerless. Jesus proclaims that the **kingdom of God belongs** not to the powerful and important but to the nobodies, the weak, the overlooked, the little ones, those who are "last of all" (9:35). A startling pronouncement!

Kingdom of God: See page 96

For reflection: In my world, who are the "such as these" to whom the kingdom of God belongs? Might Jesus be indignant over my attitude toward any of them?

There is a subtle but real connection between Jesus saying, "Let the children **come to me**" and his proclaiming that **the kingdom of God** belonged to such as them. The kingdom of God was being established through Jesus; to enter into relationship with him was to enter into God's reign. Jesus welcomed sinners, outcasts, and those with no status (2:15–17); to such as them the kingdom of God belonged, not because of their own worthiness (they had none) but because of their relationship with Jesus.

15 Jesus draws out the implication of his pronouncement that the kingdom of God belongs to children and nobodies. He prefaces it with **Amen, I say to you** to indicate the seriousness and importance of what he is about to say. He declares that **whoever does not accept the kingdom of God like a child will not enter it.** Whoever does not receive the kingdom of God as a child receives it does not receive it at

all. Jesus is not speaking about the cuteness or the supposed innocence of children; he is referring to their powerlessness and their dependence on others. A three-year-old child cannot hold down a job but must accept the necessities of life from parents or others. Likewise, the kingdom of God must be accepted as a gift: entrance into God's kingdom is not something that can be earned. Children are role models for receiving because they have no choice but to receive what they need. Jesus proclaims, **Amen, I say to you,** if you do not receive the **kingdom of God** as a sheer gift, you **will not enter it.**

> *For reflection: Do I think of God's relationship to me as a relationship of gift giver to gift receiver?*

16 Those who brought children to Jesus hoped that he would lay his hands on them, but Jesus does more. **Then he embraced them,** wrapping his arms around them, hugging them as he had previously hugged another child (9:36). We may long for Jesus to simply touch us, but he wants to wrap his arms around us and hug us. Jesus' embracing these children is an image for what God does for us through Jesus, and these children's receiving his embrace is an image for receiving the kingdom of God. Jesus goes on to fulfill the wishes of those who brought these children to him: he **blessed them, placing his hands on them,** just as Jacob called down God's blessing on his grandsons Ephraim and Manasseh (Gen 48:14–16).

> *For reflection: Does Jesus' hugging the children provide me with an image of the relationship he wants to have with me?*

A Man Whom Jesus Loves

17 As he was setting out on a journey, a man ran up, knelt down before him, and asked him, "Good teacher, what must I do to inherit eternal life?" 18 Jesus answered him, "Why do you call me good? No one is good but God alone. 19 You know the commandments: 'You shall not kill; you shall not commit adultery; you shall not steal; you shall not bear false witness; you shall not defraud; honor your father and your mother.'" 20 He replied and said to him, "Teacher, all of these I have observed from my

youth." **²¹ Jesus, looking at him, loved him and said to him, "You are lacking in one thing. Go, sell what you have, and give to [the] poor and you will have treasure in heaven; then come, follow me." ²² At that statement his face fell, and he went away sad, for he had many possessions.**

Gospel parallels: Matt 19:16–22; Luke 18:18–23

OT: Exod 20:12–17; Deut 5:16–21; Tobit 4:7–11; 2 Macc 7:9; Sirach 29:8–12; Dan 12:2

17   **As he was setting out on a journey:** Jesus is continuing his **journey** to Jerusalem (10:1, 32). **A man ran up** and **knelt down before him:** Mark describes this person only as a man, and we will best appreciate Mark's account if we allow his identity and character to be revealed in the course of his encounter with Jesus. This **man ran up** to Jesus and **knelt down before him.** The fact that he **ran up** to Jesus indicates that there is something he urgently wants from Jesus. He **knelt down before** Jesus to show his respect, recognizing that Jesus could meet his need. The only other man whom Mark has described as kneeling before Jesus was a leper in need of cleansing (1:40); this man has apparently come to Jesus with his own urgent need.

For reflection: What do I most urgently need from Jesus?

Addressing Jesus, the man asks, **Good teacher, what must I do to inherit eternal life?** We now learn why he has come to Jesus: he wants nothing less than **eternal life.** He recognizes Jesus as someone who can teach him about eternal life; hence he addresses Jesus as **Teacher.** In line with his respectfully kneeling before Jesus, he addresses him as **good teacher.** There is no reason to think that he is insincere or trying to flatter Jesus; we can presume that he has genuine admiration for Jesus. His quest is for **eternal life:** this is the first explicit mention of **eternal life** in Mark's Gospel. It is an expression that occurs in some late Old Testament writings (Dan 12:2 literally speaks of awakening to "eternal life"; see also 2 Macc 7:9) and in nonbiblical writings of the time. **Eternal life** is a life of happiness in the age to come. The idea that a person could be raised after death to have **eternal life** was a relatively recent development in Jewish thinking, and thus it is understandable that this man wanted to know more about it, particularly what he had to **do to inherit** it. He asks not how to earn eternal life but how to **inherit** it, as something that will be given to him. This is the right question to ask, in light of Jesus' equating entering into (eternal) life with entering into the kingdom of God (9:43–47) and Jesus' teaching that entrance into the kingdom of God must be received as a gift (10:15). Surely Jesus will approve of his asking what he must **do** to receive this gift.

> Many of those who sleep
> > in the dust of the earth shall awake;
> Some shall live forever,
> > others shall be an everlasting horror and disgrace.
>
> Dan 12:2

18 Jesus' response is puzzling: **Jesus answered him, "Why do you call me good?"** Mark's Greek construction puts emphasis on the word **me**: Why do you call *me* good? **No one is good but God alone.** While the

---

BACKGROUND: LIFE AFTER DEATH Most scholars agree that there was no belief in an afterlife worth living during most of the Old Testament era. For the Israelites, a human being was living flesh, and meaningful life apart from the flesh was inconceivable. There was no belief in an immortal soul; the Hebrew word that is sometimes translated as soul can mean the livingness of a body but not something that can enjoy existence apart from a body. What survived death was at best a shadow or a ghost of one's former self, consigned to a netherworld beneath the surface of the earth (Num 16:31–33). The netherworld was a place of darkness and silence; those in the netherworld were cut off from the living and from God (Job 14:20–21; Sirach 17:22–23). Good and bad alike languished in the netherworld, sharing the same fate. It was only near the end of the Old Testament era that hopes arose that there would be meaningful life after death. These hopes were often expressed in terms of bodily resurrection from the dead (2 Macc 7; Dan 12:2). However, the book of Wisdom, written in Egypt around the time of Jesus, drew on Greek thinking and taught that after death, "the souls of the just are in the hand of God" (Wisd 3:1). Greek philosophers thought of souls as immortal and as temporarily imprisoned in bodies; death meant the release of the soul from this imprisonment. Some nonbiblical writings presumed that there would be life in the age to come but were vague about its nature. *Related topics: The age to come (page 267), Judgment and Gehenna (page 241), Nonbiblical writings (page 243), Resurrection (page 320).*

Old Testament calls God good, it does so relatively few times; many things other than God are also called good, beginning with the world God created (Gen 1:4–31). Scholars have made various proposals for what Jesus meant by his words, ranging from the improbable suggestion that Jesus was acknowledging that he was a sinner, to the equally improbable suggestion that Jesus was claiming to be divine. My suggestion is that Jesus wanted to direct attention away from himself and to God. He had been sent by God (9:37) with the mission of announcing and inaugurating the kingdom of God; Jesus preached the kingdom, not himself (1:14–15). Jesus thought that the focus should be on the goodness of God and the coming of God's kingdom, not on himself as God's agent. This is consistent with Jesus downplaying the spectacular in his healings: Jesus was not out to win personal acclaim.

19 Jesus then addresses the man's question, telling him, **You know the commandments:** obeying God's commands is necessary for inheriting eternal life. The commandments Jesus recounts are **you shall not kill; you shall not commit adultery; you shall not steal; you shall not bear false witness; you shall not defraud; honor your father and your mother.** These commands are (with one exception) part of the Ten Commandments (Exod 20:1–17; Deut 5:6–21), but with a few twists. Jesus does not quote the commands having to do with our relationship with God but only the commands covering our relationships with one another; it is unclear why Jesus quotes only these commandments. Jesus omits the command against coveting (Exod 20:17; Deut 5:21) but includes a command against defrauding; it is unclear why Jesus shifts the prohibition from what one desires to what one does. Finally, Jesus moves the first command having to do with relationships with others ("Honor your father and your mother") to the last place on his list. Perhaps Jesus does so because this command contains a promise: "Honor your father and your mother, that you may have a long life in the land which the Lord, your God, is giving you" (Exod 20:12; see also Deut 5:16). The "long life" the man is seeking is eternal life.

For reflection: What significance might I see in Jesus highlighting the commandments that deal with human relationships?

20 **He replied and said to him, "Teacher, all of these I have observed from my youth."** The man drops mention of "good" and simply addresses Jesus as **teacher.** His claim, **All of these I have observed from my youth,** can be taken not as a vain boast but as a simple statement of fact. He has not killed anyone; he has not committed adultery or stolen or borne false witness or defrauded; he has honored his parents. There is no indication in Mark's Gospel that God's commands are impossible to obey. A scribe named Ben Sira had taught, "If you choose you can keep the commandments" (Sirach 15:15), and Paul will boast that he was "blameless" in observing the law (Phil 3:6). This man states, in less-boastful terms than Paul, that he has obeyed God's basic commands ever since he was old enough to do so—**from my youth.** His expression implies that he is no longer a youth.

21 Jesus accepts his claim as an honest one: Jesus does not tell him that he is deluding himself and is really a terrible sinner. Rather, **Jesus, looking at him, loved him.** Jesus gazes on him intently and affectionately. This man is the only person that the Gospel of Mark says Jesus **loved.** This does not mean that Jesus did not love others; it does mean that Jesus was filled with a special love for this man. Jesus sees him as a man who has obeyed God's commands all his life and has come to him in search of eternal life, and Jesus loves him.

> *For reflection: Does Jesus look upon me with love? What does he see in me that is lovable?*

Jesus says to him, **You are lacking in one thing. Go, sell what you have, and give to [the] poor and you will have treasure in heaven; then come, follow me.** Jesus tells the man that he is **lacking in one thing:** what the man is missing is that he is not a disciple of Jesus. Jesus wants to remedy the man's lack: Jesus invites him to **follow me**—the same call that Jesus issued to the first disciples (1:17, 20; 2:14). This man whom Jesus loves can enjoy the same relationship with Jesus that Peter and Andrew, James and John, Levi and the rest of the disciples enjoy, and through this relationship he can inherit eternal life.

But being a disciple of Jesus has its requirements. The first disciples accompanied Jesus as he went from village to village proclaiming the kingdom of God. Traveling with Jesus meant leaving boats and families and jobs behind (1:18, 20; 2:14). It can be no different with this man whom Jesus loves: Jesus is on his way to Jerusalem, and the man will have to travel light if he wishes to accompany him. Jesus tells him to **go, sell what you have:** go back to your home and sell everything. Use the proceeds to help those in need: **Give to [the] poor.** This will make the man dependent on the care of God and the generosity of others for what he needs; he will become like a child (10:15). But, Jesus tells him, you will be making a good bargain, for by using your possessions to help the poor, **you will have treasure in heaven.** Some late Old Testament writings taught that in helping the needy, one stored up **treasure** in the sight of God (Tobit 4:7–11; Sirach 29:8–12), and Jesus agrees. Once the man has disposed of his property, he will be free to answer Jesus' call, **Follow me.**

22 **At that statement his face fell,** for he was shocked, even appalled, by what Jesus asked of him. He had come to Jesus with high hopes, but he **went away sad, for he had many possessions.** The word **possessions** has the connotation of land: the man owns large estates. Jesus has asked him to sell his estates and presumably his fine house, give the proceeds to the poor, and then accompany Jesus as a destitute man dependent on the hospitality of others. That is a lot to ask of him—more than he is prepared to do. He **went away sad** because he could not bring himself to give up his wealth in order to become a disciple of Jesus. It is a somber and sobering outcome to what started out as a beautiful story about a man whom Jesus loved.

Did Jesus know how much he was asking of this man whom he loved? Since clothing indicated social status, Jesus probably knew that the man was a member of the upper class by the way he dressed. But Jesus' call to him was no different from his call to every disciple. It doesn't matter whether one owns a single boat or an entire fleet, whether one has a tiny garden or vast estates: the call to discipleship is a call to leave behind whatever cannot be taken along on one's journey with Jesus.

Clothing: See page 117

Jesus does not ask every disciple of every age to embrace absolute poverty. Jesus does ask those he loves to get rid of whatever is an obstacle to responding to his particular call to them—and Jesus asks this knowing that it will require self-denial and taking up one's cross (8:34).

For reflection: What must I do to inherit eternal life? Has Jesus asked me to give up anything that I am unwilling or unable to relinquish?

Squeezing through the Eye of a Needle

²³ Jesus looked around and said to his disciples, "How hard it is for those who have wealth to enter the kingdom of God!" ²⁴ The disciples were amazed at his words. So Jesus again said to them in reply, "Children, how hard it is to enter the kingdom of God! ²⁵ It is easier for a camel to pass through [the] eye of [a] needle than for one who is rich to enter the kingdom of God." ²⁶ They were exceedingly astonished and said among themselves, "Then who can be saved?" ²⁷ Jesus looked at them and said, "For human beings it is impossible, but not for God. All things are possible for God."

Gospel parallels: Matt 19:23–26; Luke 18:24–27

23 A man whom Jesus loved went away sad because he was unwilling to give up his wealth to become a disciple (10:22), and Jesus is sad as well. **Jesus looked around,** turning his gaze from the departing man to his disciples, **and said to his disciples, "How hard it is for those who have wealth to enter the kingdom of God!"** Jesus' words are not merely an observation but also a lament. **How hard it is for those who have wealth** to let go of their wealth. **Wealth** provides comfort, security, social status, and the ability to do what one enjoys.

But having wealth can also lead to selfish individualism, arrogance, hedonism, and injustice. To **enter the kingdom of God** means to come under the reign of God, to rely on God rather than on oneself, to give God first place, to serve God rather than one's pleasures, to be just and compassionate toward others. It is hard to have wealth without succumbing to its lures and placing being wealthy above submission to God.

Kingdom of God: See page 96

For reflection: What is my attitude toward wealth? Do my possessions possess me?

24 **The disciples were amazed at his words.** A Jewish tradition, based on a number of Scripture passages, viewed wealth as a sign of God's favor (Deut 28:1–14; Job 1:9–10; 42:10; Sirach 11:21–22). How could it be hard for those who enjoy God's favor to enter the kingdom of God? Shouldn't it be easiest for them? The disciples are puzzled. **So Jesus again said to them in reply, "Children, how hard it is to enter the kingdom of God!"** Jesus addresses them as **children,** an affectionate term, for he knows that what he is telling them is a hard saying. Jesus reaffirms but broadens his first pronouncement: **How hard it is to enter the kingdom of God**—hard for everyone, not simply for those who have wealth.

25 If it is hard for everyone to enter the kingdom of God, it is especially difficult for those who have wealth: **it is easier for a camel to pass through [the] eye of [a] needle than for one who is rich to enter the kingdom of God.** Jesus loved to use comparisons, and this is one of his most striking. The **camel** was the largest animal in the region, and the **eye of [a] needle** was the tiniest opening that his listeners would have been familiar with. (If Jesus had lived in India, he might have spoken of an elephant.) Can a camel squeeze through the eye of a needle? Impossible to the point of being absurd! Yet that would be less of a squeeze than a rich person making it through the entrance to the kingdom of God. (Some try to tame Jesus' comparison by claiming that he was talking about a rope, not a camel, or that there was a small gate in the wall of Jerusalem called

the Eye of the Needle. Such suggestions are baseless and miss the point: Jesus intended his comparison to be outlandishly impossible.)

For reflection: Am I clinging to anything that won't fit through the needle-eye entrance to the kingdom of God?

26 The disciples are more bewildered than ever. **They were exceedingly astonished and said among themselves, "Then who can be saved?"** If it is hard for everyone to enter the kingdom of God, and seemingly impossible for some whom they thought were specially favored by God, then where does that leave them? Their question, **Then who can be saved?** introduces the word **saved** into the discussion. A man came to Jesus seeking eternal life (10:17), which Jesus had spoken of in terms of entering the kingdom of God (verses 23–25); now the disciples speak of the same reality as being **saved.** Being saved can mean being saved from sickness (5:28, 34) or from death (5:23), but here being **saved** means being given life after death. This is what Jesus meant when he promised, "Whoever loses his life for my sake and that of the gospel will *save* it" (8:35; emphasis added). Salvation is not rescue from this or that evil or affliction but rescue from eternal death and inheritance of eternal life. Yet who can be saved if it is hard for everyone to enter the kingdom of God?

27 **Jesus looked at them,** gazing at them as he had gazed at the man seeking eternal life (10:21), **and said, "For human beings it is impossible."** It is not merely hard for humans to enter the eternal kingdom of God; it is downright **impossible.** Eternal life is not this life continued indefinitely after death but a whole new form of existence. Receiving eternal life means being transformed, and it is beyond human capability to effect this transformation. But it is not beyond God's capability: what is **impossible** for human beings is not impossible **for God. All things are possible for God,** including granting salvation (verse 26) and eternal life (10:17) in God's kingdom (10:24). The words **all things are possible for God** echo the words of an angel in Genesis who told Sarah that she would become pregnant at the age of ninety, because nothing

was too marvelous for God to do (Gen 17:17; 18:14). Jesus has taught that "everything is possible to one who has faith" (9:23): faith is trust in God doing the impossible. But the primary accent belongs on God, who does for us what we cannot do for ourselves: God pulls us through the needle eye of death and gives us eternal life.

For reflection: What impossible hopes does Jesus offer me?

Mark began his Gospel by telling us that he was bringing us good news (1:1). Jesus' assurance that God can do the impossible for us and give us eternal life is very good news indeed!

The Rewards of Discipleship

²⁸ Peter began to say to him, "We have given up everything and followed you." ²⁹ Jesus said, "Amen, I say to you, there is no one who has given up house or brothers or sisters or mother or father or children or lands for my sake and for the sake of the gospel ³⁰ who will not receive a hundred times more now in this present age: houses and brothers and sisters and mothers and children and lands, with persecutions, and eternal life in the age to come. ³¹ But many that are first will be last, and [the] last will be first."

Gospel parallels: Matt 19:27–30; Luke 18:28–30
NT: Matt 20:16; Mark 1:14–20; 2:14; 3:31–35; 8:34–38; 9:35; Luke 13:30

28 The man who could not give up his estates to follow Jesus (10:21–22) is apparently still on Peter's mind. **Peter began to say to** Jesus, **We have given up everything and followed you.** Peter's words can be read as a statement of fact: Jesus' disciples have responded to his call, leaving behind boats and families and jobs (1:18, 20; 2:14). But Peter's words can also be taken as a boast: We have done better than that rich man; we **have given up everything** for you! Peter's claim has an element of self-delusion. It is not completely true that the disciples have given up **everything.** For example, they have not put aside all their self-seeking, as is evident by their debating among themselves who is the greatest (9:34). Giving ourselves to Jesus is like peeling an onion: we may give him all that we are able to give at any particular time and think that

we are giving all, but we may be unaware of deeper layers that we are holding back. Just as an onion is peeled one layer at a time, so we give up our selfishness and pride layer by layer.

For reflection: Have I given up everything for Jesus? What is the next layer of my onion?

29 Jesus neither affirms nor denies Peter's claim to have given up everything. Jesus says, **Amen, I say to you:** Jesus is about to make a solemn pronouncement to his disciples. **There is no one who has given up:** Jesus' statement is not limited to his present disciples but is directed to all who will make sacrifices in order to follow him. Some will have to sacrifice possessions, such as a **house** or **lands**—the sacrifice that the man whom Jesus loved was unwilling to make (10:21–22). (In later times some followers of Jesus will put their property at the disposal of the Church—Acts 2:44–45; 4:32–37.) Some of Jesus' followers will also have to leave behind **brothers or sisters or mother or father or children,** as James and John did (1:19–20). Some (which will include some of Mark's first readers) will be rejected by their families because they have become Christians. This was a painful breach in ancient societies, for one's family provided one's identity and security, but it was a pain that Mark's Gospel presents Jesus experiencing first (3:21, 31–35). While Jesus lists **brothers or sisters or mother or father or children** as those who may be left behind, he does not mention husbands or wives, perhaps because of his previous teaching on the permanence of marriage (10:6–12).

Jesus does not ask his followers to renounce possessions or family as if such renunciations were good in themselves but because such renunciations may be necessary **for my sake and for the sake of the gospel.** His words again have meaning both for his first disciples and for all later disciples. The first disciples gave up many things in order to follow him as he proclaimed "the gospel of God," the good news that the kingdom of God was at hand (1:14–15). In later times men and women will also leave behind their ordinary lives in order to accept "the gospel of Jesus Christ" (1:1) and become his followers.

For reflection: Have I had to give up anything "for the sake of the gospel"?

30 Jesus promised that those who lost their lives "for my sake and that of the gospel" would save their lives (8:35), and now he amplifies his promise. There is no one who has given up family ties or possessions for Jesus and the gospel **who will not receive a hundred times more now in this present age: houses and brothers and sisters and mothers and children and lands, with persecutions, and eternal life in the age to come.** Jesus' amplified promise has three elements. The first is that those who have left family and possessions behind for Jesus will **receive a hundred times more** in return **now in this present age.** Their seed of sacrifice will yield a hundredfold harvest (4:8): **houses and brothers and sisters and mothers and children and lands.** Disciples who traveled with Jesus shared in the hospitality he received from others; the early Church in Jerusalem so generously shared its resources that "there was no needy person among them" (Acts 4:34). Those who became disciples of Jesus and did the will of God became the new family of Jesus (3:33–35), **brothers and sisters and mothers and children** of one another. Jesus does not include fathers in his list of new relations, perhaps a hint that his disciples have a Father in heaven (see 11:25).

Jesus' promise of a new family that will provide identity and security is a consolation to all who have given up possessions and relationships for him. His promise is also a challenge for the Church to be a welcoming family, to care for the needs of its members, to be all that Jesus promised it would be. This is a challenge for each member of the Church and not simply for its leadership.

> *For reflection: How has Jesus' promise of a new family been fulfilled in my life? Have I been able to be family for others?*

The second element in Jesus' promise is that **now in this present age** his followers will experience **persecutions.** In his explanation of the parable of the seed, he mentioned those who would fall away when "persecution comes because of the word" (4:17); now Jesus assures his followers that there will indeed be persecutions. Many of Mark's first readers had firsthand experience of persecutions and knew that taking up one's cross (8:34) was not merely a metaphor: many Christians were crucified in Rome during Nero's persecution. Jesus promises his followers a bountiful life despite hardships, a rewarding life but not a life free of sacrifice.

Nero's persecution: See A Roman view of Christians, page 347

For reflection: Have I experienced anything that would qualify as persecution for the sake of Jesus and the gospel?

The third element that Jesus promises is **eternal life in the age to come.** The expectation that there would be an **age to come** arose late in the Old Testament era, but Jesus' listeners would have been familiar with the idea. **Eternal life in the age to come** meant survival after death and entrance into a life of happiness, but popular expectations were vague about the details. Jesus does not spell out the nature of **eternal life,** but he does assure his listeners that a great prospect is in store for those who place discipleship above all else: **eternal life in the age to come.** This is the second (see 10:17) and last time the term **eternal**

BACKGROUND: THE AGE TO COME In the early books of the Old Testament, God's dealings with his people are limited to this world. There was no expectation of meaningful life after death in early Old Testament times; if God was to reward good and punish evil it had to be in this life. Most of the prophecies of the Old Testament share this perspective: God will rescue or punish his people through the events of history. Late in the Old Testament era a new perspective developed that is expressed in a first-century Jewish writing: "The Most High has made not one age but two" (*4 Ezra* 7:50—a book not in the Bible). God would bring an end to the present age and inaugurate a new age. The age to come was conceived of differently in different writings; there was general agreement that God would bring human history (with all its evils) to an end and reward good and punish evil at a judgment. This was often associated with God fully establishing his reign over his people and all peoples, but there were different expectations for how this would happen. Jesus spoke of the present age and the age to come (Mark 10:30) and proclaimed that the kingdom of God was at hand (Mark 1:15), which meant that the present age was drawing to an end (Matt 13:39–40, 49; 24:3; 28:20). Paul speaks of Christians as living in the present age (Rom 8:18; 11:5; 12:2) and yet having been rescued from it (2 Cor 5:17; Gal 1:4): Jesus began establishing the reign of God, but we still await its fullness. *Related topics: Judgment and Gehenna (page 241), Kingdom of God (page 96), Life after death (page 257), Nonbiblical writings (page 243).*

---

life is used in the Gospel of Mark; Jesus usually speaks of its reality in terms of entering into or inheriting or receiving the kingdom of God, which will be established in its fullness in the age to come. God doing the impossible (10:27) and giving us **eternal life** is indeed good news (1:1), far outweighing any sacrifices and persecutions that might be entailed in discipleship.

For reflection: What does Jesus' promise of eternal life mean to me?

31 Jesus concludes with a proverb he apparently invoked on various occasions; it has different meanings in different contexts (see Matt 20:16; Luke 13:30). **But many that are first will be last, and [the] last will be first** in this context means that those who are **first** in this age (those with wealth and power) will be **last** in the age to come, while those who are **last** in this age (those without status or power, such as children—10:14) will be **first** in the age to come. This forecast of reversals is both a promise and a warning. Those who obey Jesus' injunction to make themselves "last of all and the servant of all" will be **first** in the kingdom of God (9:35); those who have given up family and possessions for Jesus will receive eternal life. But those who strive for places of honor (9:34), those who cling to what they have (10:22), those who are complacent because they think they have done enough (perhaps Peter is in this category—verse 28) will end up **last,** having made a very poor bargain (8:36–37).

For reflection: What promise do Jesus' words have for me? What warning do they bear for me?

Jesus Again Speaks of His Death and Rising

32 They were on the way, going up to Jerusalem, and Jesus went ahead of them. They were amazed, and those who followed were afraid. Taking the Twelve aside again, he began to tell them what was going to happen to him. 33 "Behold, we are going up to Jerusalem, and the Son of Man will be handed over to the chief priests and the scribes, and they will condemn him to death and hand him over to the Gentiles 34 who will mock him, spit upon

him, scourge him, and put him to death, but after three days he will rise."
Gospel parallels: Matt 20:17–19; Luke 18:31–34
NT: Mark 2:20; 8:31; 9:9, 12, 31

32 **They were on the way, going up to Jerusalem:** Jesus and his disciples continue on their journey. **On the way** is an expression that means on the road; in Mark's Gospel it also has connotations of the **way** of discipleship. They are **going up to Jerusalem:** Jerusalem lies twenty-five hundred feet above sea level, so traveling to Jerusalem was spoken of as **going up** (2 Sam 19:35; Psalm 122:1–4; John 2:13; 5:1; Acts 11:2; 25:1). Along the way **Jesus went ahead of them.** Jesus leads the way, and his followers follow: that is the **way** of discipleship. Jesus resolutely proceeds to Jerusalem, although he knows what awaits him there.

Jerusalem: See page 290

They were amazed, and those who followed were afraid: the identity of **they** and **those** is not completely clear, nor are the reasons for their being **amazed** and **afraid.** One explanation is that **they** refers to Jesus' followers in general (Mark will later mention women who accompanied Jesus to Jerusalem: 15:40–41), and their amazement may be over what Jesus has been teaching (10:1–31; see 1:22, 27; 6:2). **Those who followed** could refer more narrowly to the Twelve, whom Jesus has privately instructed about his coming suffering and death (8:31; 9:30–31). They are **afraid** because his words have begun to sink in, and they realize that Jesus has powerful opponents in Jerusalem (see 3:22; 7:1, 5). Jesus is putting himself in danger by **going up to Jerusalem**—and he is putting the disciples in danger as well. But they follow after him, despite their fears.

For reflection: Am I beset by any fears as a follower of Jesus?

Taking the Twelve aside again, he began to tell them what was going to happen to him. Jesus has instructed his disciples in private (4:34; 7:17–23; 9:28–29), and he does so **again, taking the Twelve aside.** Jesus responds to the fears of the Twelve by laying out **what was**

going to happen to him. Jesus does not sugarcoat his destiny in order to allay their fears, for fear cannot be banished by wishful thinking.

33 **Behold, we are going up to Jerusalem, and the Son of Man will be handed over to the chief priests and the scribes:** Jesus has previously spoken of being rejected by the elders and **the chief priests and the scribes** (8:31) who formed the Sanhedrin (the Jewish ruling council) and wielded whatever power was in Jewish hands in Jerusalem. That Jesus will be **handed over** to them means that he will be betrayed into their hands and arrested, but in this context the expression also has the connotation of handed over *by* God (see also 9:31). One of the Twelve, Judas, will betray Jesus (3:19), but Jesus' suffering and death are an integral part of the mission he has received from God. Why this is God's will for Jesus is not yet apparent, but Mark's Gospel will address it shortly.

High priest, chief priests: See page 403
Scribes: See page 40

Once Jesus is in the power of religious leaders in Jerusalem, **they will condemn him to death and hand him over to the Gentiles.** The Sanhedrin apparently lacked the authority to have anyone executed, because the Roman governor reserved such authority for himself (John 18:31). The **Gentiles** to whom Jesus would be handed over could only be the Romans, who had ruled directly or indirectly over Palestine for the last century.

34 Jesus has spoken explicitly and implicitly of his death a number of times (2:20; 8:31; 9:9, 12, 31) and now adds more details. Gentiles (Romans) **will mock him, spit upon him, scourge him, and put him to death.** Jesus does not mention death by crucifixion, but this was the way Rome normally executed those who threatened its rule. It would not be out of the ordinary for mocking, spitting, and scourging to accompany crucifixion as part of the pageantry of pain and humiliation.

Jesus' death will not be the end of him: **after three days he will rise.** This is the answer to the disciples' fears: God will hand Jesus over to death, but Jesus **will rise.** If Jesus' followers are to experience persecution on their way to eternal life (10:30), Jesus will have first endured such persecution himself on his way to risen life. Jesus does not describe what his risen life will be like; he simply assures his followers that **after three days he will rise.**

It is worth noting that Jesus' three most explicit predictions of his suffering, death, and rising occur while he is on the road with his disciples (8:27, 31; 9:30–31; 10:32–34). This highlights that the way of discipleship is the way of suffering, dying, and rising—following Jesus, who has gone ahead of us.

For reflection: What is my experience of the way of discipleship?

The Ambition of James and John

35 Then James and John, the sons of Zebedee, came to him and said to him, "Teacher, we want you to do for us whatever we ask of you." 36 He replied, "What do you wish [me] to do for you?" 37 They answered him, "Grant that in your glory we may sit one at your right and the other at your left." 38 Jesus said to them, "You do not know what you are asking. Can you drink the cup that I drink or be baptized with the baptism with which I am baptized?" 39 They said to him, "We can." Jesus said to them, "The cup that I drink, you will drink, and with the baptism with which I am baptized, you will be baptized; 40 but to sit at my right or at my left is not mine to give but is for those for whom it has been prepared."

Gospel parallels: Matt 20:20–23

NT: Mark 1:19–20; 3:13–17; 5:37; 9:2, 38; Luke 12:50; Acts 12:2

35 **Then James and John, the sons of Zebedee, came to him:** James and John were among the first four disciples Jesus called (1:19–20) and, with Peter, were the disciples Jesus chose to be with him when he raised the daughter of Jairus (5:37) and was transfigured (9:2). Since Jesus has just finished telling his disciples of the suffering, death, and rising that await him in Jerusalem (10:33–34), we might expect James and John to make some kind of acknowledgment of Jesus' words. They do so, but in a strange way: they **said to him, "Teacher, we want you to do for us whatever we ask of you."** They address Jesus as **teacher,** as John did previously (9:38). They tell Jesus, **We want you to do for us whatever we ask of you:** they want a blank check from Jesus, his promise to do

whatever they ask, no matter what it is (in Mark's Gospel, a promise of doing **whatever** was asked led to the beheading of John the Baptist: 6:22–23). James and John seem to presume they have the right to make such a sweeping request, perhaps because of their status as members of the Twelve and of Jesus' inner circle.

> *For reflection: Do I approach Jesus as if I have a right to ask of him whatever I want?*

36 Jesus ignores the presumption of these "sons of thunder" (3:17) in making such a demand of him and simply asks what they have in mind: **he replied, "What do you wish [me] to do for you?"**

37 **They answered him, "Grant that in your glory we may sit one at your right and the other at your left."** The seats on the **right** and the **left** of a king were positions of power (see 1 Kings 2:19; Psalm 110:1); the seats on either side of a banquet host were the places of honor. James and John are asking for the top two positions of power and honor under Jesus when he comes into his **glory.** How do James and John conceive of Jesus' **glory?** Since Jesus has proclaimed that the kingdom of God is at hand (1:15), they might expect that Jesus as the Messiah (8:29) will set up some kind of kingdom on earth (this would be in line with what is written of the Messiah in the nonbiblical *Psalms of Solomon:* see page 207). When God's kingdom comes in power (9:1), James and John want to be numbers one and two under Jesus.

There is another possibility for what James and John envision, based on the fact that they refer to Jesus coming into his **glory.** Jesus spoke of his coming in his Father's glory at a time of judgment (8:38). James and John saw Jesus transfigured atop a mountain (9:2–3), and Jesus told them not to talk about it until he had risen from the dead (9:9), which suggested that his transfiguration was a glimpse of his risen glory. And Jesus has just spoken of his being put to death in Jerusalem but rising from the dead (10:33–34). James and John may be thinking of Jesus' rising as his coming into his **glory,** and they want to have the largest shares in it.

We cannot know exactly what was on the minds of James and John or whether they foresaw an earthly or heavenly triumph for Jesus. They probably did not foresee it very clearly themselves. Their spiritual sight was like the eyesight of the man half-healed of his blindness, to whom people appeared as walking trees (8:24). But we do know that they wanted the best shares in whatever happened to Jesus for themselves.

38 James and John skipped over the suffering and death of Jesus and seized only on his rising and receiving glory. But Jesus cannot skip over what he—and his followers—must endure on the way to risen life. **Jesus said to them, "You do not know what you are asking."** You haven't grasped that glory comes only after suffering and death; you do not yet understand that you must lose your lives to save your lives (8:35). Those who want to share my glory must also share my sufferings. Are you able to do that? **Can you drink the cup that I drink or be baptized with the baptism with which I am baptized?** In the Old Testament, a **cup** is used as a symbol for what God bestows on someone, whether pleasant (Psalm 23:5) or unpleasant (Psalm 75:9). Prophets spoke of the **cup** of God's wrath (Isaiah 51:17; Jer 25:15–28; 49:12; 51:7; Ezek 23:31–34). Jesus could be evoking such allusions here. However, there is no Old Testament use of **baptism** as a comparable symbol; being **baptized** simply means being immersed in water. Jesus may therefore merely be using the expressions **drink the cup that I drink** and **be baptized with the baptism with which I am baptized** as comparisons for his acceptance of suffering and death as God's will for him. To **drink** a **cup** is to take liquid into oneself; to be **baptized** is to be immersed in a liquid. The two comparisons taken together indicate that Jesus will be filled with and plunged into suffering. He asks James and John if they are willing to join him in his sufferings as the necessary step to sharing in his glory.

Baptism: See page 7

39 **They said to him, "We can."** Just as they did not realize what they were asking of Jesus (verse 38), so now they do not realize what they are promising. Because they have no real grasp of what lies ahead for Jesus, they can be naively confident that they can endure it themselves. But despite their overconfidence, they will in fact follow the path of Jesus: **Jesus said to them, "The cup that I drink, you will drink, and with the baptism with which I am baptized, you will be baptized."** As his followers, they will share in his sufferings. The New Testament does

not describe what they went on to suffer for Jesus, except to record that James was martyred about a dozen years later (Acts 12:2).

What was true for James and John is true for every follower of Jesus. The first letter of Peter warns, "Beloved, do not be surprised that a trial by fire is occurring among you, as if something strange were happening to you. But rejoice to the extent that you share in the sufferings of Christ, so that when his glory is revealed you may also rejoice exultantly" (1 Pet 4:12–13).

For reflection: Have I ever felt filled with and overwhelmed by suffering? What impact did this have on my faith?

40 Jesus now turns to the request that James and John made. He tells them, **But to sit at my right or at my left is not mine to give but is for those for whom it has been prepared.** The words **has been prepared** imply "has been prepared *by God*." It is up to God, not Jesus, to assign honors and rewards in the kingdom. Jesus once again puts the spotlight on God and deflects attention from himself (see 10:18). Jesus will teach that he is a servant (10:45), and as a servant he defers to the one whom he serves.

Jesus' Death as a Ransom

⁴¹ When the ten heard this, they became indignant at James and John. ⁴² Jesus summoned them and said to them, "You know that those who are recognized as rulers over the Gentiles lord it over them, and their great ones make their authority over them felt. ⁴³ But it shall not be so among you. Rather, whoever wishes to be great among you will be your servant; ⁴⁴ whoever wishes to be first among you will be the slave of all. ⁴⁵ For the Son of Man did not come to be served but to serve and to give his life as a ransom for many."

Gospel parallels: Matt 20:24–28; Luke 22:24–27
OT: Isaiah 52:13–53:12
NT: Mark 9:33–35; 14:23–24

41 James and John's attempt to secure the top positions for themselves (10:35–40) does not go unnoticed by the other disciples. **When the ten**

heard this, they became indignant at James and John. The ten could be **indignant** that James and John want to outrank them. More likely, the ten are **indignant** because each of them wants a top spot for himself, and James and John have beat them off the starting blocks. Our self-righteous indignation is often over our own faults mirrored in others.

42 **Jesus summoned** his disciples **and said to them, "You know that those who are recognized as rulers over the Gentiles lord it over them."** First-century Jews knew what it was like to be ruled by Roman governors or Rome's client kings, and Jesus appeals to his disciples' experience: **You know** the Roman style of rule. Those with authority **lord it over** those they govern. The Greek word translated as **lord it over** has connotations of governing for one's own advantage, to the disadvantage of others. **Their great ones make their authority over them felt:** greatness is proved by throwing one's weight around. That is how the world operated at the time of Jesus, and it is how much of the world still operates today.

43 **But it shall not be so among you.** Jesus issues a stark command: his disciples must not operate as the world operates. They must not equate greatness with the power to exploit others. The disciples should know this, for Jesus has taught them that if they wish to be first, they have to be "last of all and the servant of all" (9:35). It is utterly against Jesus' teaching for James and John and the other ten to lust after positions of power and prestige. But the disciples have not gotten the message yet, and Jesus must try to get it across again: **Rather, whoever wishes to be great among you will be your servant.** A servant serves the desires of others, not his or her own desires, in contrast to those who lord it over others for their own advantage. True greatness lies in putting the interests of others above one's own interests, not in having power over others. Jesus' disciples must relate to one another as servants, a radical demand for Jesus' first disciples—and for us.

For reflection: How do I live out Jesus' call to be a servant?

We can note that Jesus has spoken explicitly of his death three times, and each time his followers have demonstrated that they have not accepted its implications for them (8:31–33; 9:31–40; 10:32–41). Mark recounts their repeated failures in order to prod his readers to examine themselves. Those who consider themselves followers of Christ must face up to his crucifixion and his call for his disciples to deny themselves and take up their cross (8:34). This call is exceedingly difficult to live out and, consequently, all too easy to ignore.

44 Jesus repeats his instruction about service in even stronger terms: **Whoever wishes to be first among you will be the slave of all.** Here the prize is not merely being great (verse 43) but being the greatest, the **first among** Jesus' followers. But the price of being **first** is also higher: the one who wishes to be first must be **the slave of all.** Slaves, like servants, served others, but slaves, unlike servants, were owned by masters and were completely at their disposal. The disciples must become slaves **of all**—of everyone—for the sake of Jesus and the gospel. Paul will write, "Although I am free in regard to all, I have made myself a slave to all so as to win over as many as possible" (1 Cor 9:19).

Jesus turns the way of the world on its head. Greatness is found in service, not in power; the one who is first is not the Roman emperor but the one who is the slave of all. Jesus demands a complete reversal of our desire to be on top, of our wanting to be admired and served, of our putting ourselves ahead of others.

For reflection: What values and motives shape my behavior? What values does Jesus ask me to adopt?

45 **For the Son of Man did not come to be served but to serve.** Here the word **for** means because: Jesus' disciples are to be servants and slaves because Jesus has come as a servant and a slave, and they are to imitate his example. Jesus speaks of himself as **the Son of Man,** as he did when he spoke of his coming death (8:31; 9:31; 10:33–34). Jesus explains the reason he has **come,** filling out his earlier statements about his having come (1:38; 2:17) as one sent by God (9:37). He has not come **to be served but to serve.** Jesus' words do not simply mean that he carries out humble acts on behalf of others. While the word **serve** is sometimes used for waiting on someone at table (as Peter's mother-in-law did—1:31), its most basic meaning is act as a go-between, perform a task for someone,

act on someone's behalf. A servant is someone who comes and goes on behalf of another (as a waiter comes and goes with food). Jesus has **not come to be served** and waited on; he has come **to serve.** Whom does Jesus serve? Jesus serves God: Jesus has come as God's agent, to carry out an undertaking for God. But Jesus has also come **to serve** women and men, to free them from sickness and evil, to draw them into the reign of God, for that is what God has sent Jesus to do.

Son of Man: See page 41

Jesus then states the heart of his mission from God, what he has been sent to do: Jesus has come **to give his life as a ransom for many.** Jesus told his disciples that he was going to suffer and die in fulfillment of God's will for him (8:31), in accordance with what was written in Scripture (9:12). Jesus' assertion that he will **give his life as a ransom for many** is the first time in Mark's Gospel that Jesus speaks of what his death will accomplish (Jesus will speak of it only once again in this Gospel: 14:23–24).

BACKGROUND: SERVANT, SLAVE Both servants and slaves did the bidding of others, and may even have done identical work, but with a major difference: servants were hired, and slaves were owned. A servant was free to decide whom to work for and could quit; a slave had no choice but to work for his or her owner. At the time of Jesus, one became a slave by being born to a woman slave, or by being taken as a prisoner of war, or by incurring a debt one could not pay off, or by voluntarily becoming a slave. Slaves made up around a fifth of the population in the Roman Empire. There are important differences between slavery in the first-century Roman Empire and slavery in the Americas in the seventeenth to nineteenth centuries. In the world of Jesus, slavery was not based on race: the slaves referred to in Jesus' parables are Jews owned by other Jews. Owners could treat slaves badly, but slaves could own property (including other slaves!) and hold important positions; some slaves were better educated than their owners. Slaves served as managers, doctors, and bankers as well as farm workers and domestic servants. Some freely chose slavery because it offered them guaranteed employment: slaves were often better off than day laborers. Slaves could be freed after a certain period of service; a slave of a Roman citizen was generally given citizenship upon being freed. There are different Greek words for servant and slave, but the New American Bible sometimes translates the Greek word for slave as servant (e.g., Mark 12:2, 4; 13:34; 14:47), apparently to avoid confusing the ancient practice of slavery with slavery in the American experience.

Jesus will give his life as a ransom for **many**—an expression meaning a great number of people. The key to Jesus' explanation of the significance of his death is the word **ransom.** One Old Testament use of the word **ransom** is for the price paid to buy freedom for a slave (Lev 25:51). If Jesus is speaking of giving his life as a literal **ransom,** then we might ask who owns those whom Jesus is ransoming: to whom is Jesus' life as a ransom being paid? There is no satisfactory answer to this question, which may indicate that it is the wrong question to ask.

The Old Testament also uses the idea of **ransom** as a comparison or a metaphor for what God did in freeing the Israelites from Egypt (Deut 7:8; 9:26; 13:6; 15:15; 21:8; 24:18). God gave up nothing to free his people: the Egyptians received no payment or ransom. When Jesus speaks of giving himself as a **ransom,** he is using the word as a metaphor for what giving his life will accomplish: it will free others. Asking to whom the ransom of Jesus' life is being paid is a misreading of the metaphor.

If Jesus gives his life as a ransom to set others free, we can ask, Free from what? Many scholars believe that Jesus' words should be understood in light of Isaiah's prophecy of a servant of God who "gives his life as an offering for sin" (Isaiah 53:10). Because this servant "surrendered himself to death / . . . he shall take away the sins of many, / and win pardon for their offenses" (Isaiah 53:12). Jesus understood his death as a fulfillment of Scripture (9:12), and this passage is the most appropriate Scripture that can be cited. Yet Jesus does not quote Isaiah's prophecy; Jesus speaks of giving his life as a **ransom,** a word not used by Isaiah. Perhaps Jesus uses this term because what he will do will go beyond all that is written in the Old Testament, even if it is in fulfillment of it.

> *If he gives his life as an offering for sin,*
>> *he shall see his descendants in a long life,*
>> *and the will of the LORD shall be accomplished through*
>>> *him. . . .*
> *Through his suffering, my servant shall justify many,*
>> *and their guilt he shall bear. . . .*
> *Because he surrendered himself to death*
>> *and was counted among the wicked;*

And he shall take away the sins of many,
and win pardon for their offenses.

Isaiah 53:10–12

One other word that Jesus uses deserves examination: Jesus says he will give his life as a ransom **for** many. Here **for** can mean on behalf of, and it can also mean in place of or instead of. Jesus will die in place of those he ransoms so that they may be freed and may live. We cannot give anything in exchange for our lives (8:37), but Jesus can: he can give himself.

For reflection: What is the meaning for me of Jesus' giving himself as a ransom?

By the time Mark composed his Gospel, Paul had written of Jesus giving up his life as a ransom from sin, making explicit what is only implicit in the words of Jesus. Paul speaks of Christians as having been "purchased at a price" (1 Cor 6:20; 7:23), an allusion to having been ransomed. Paul quotes an early Christian tradition that "Christ died for our sins in accordance with the scriptures" (1 Cor 15:3). He writes, "They are justified freely by his grace through the redemption in Christ Jesus" (Rom 3:24; in Greek, the word for redemption is related to the word for ransom).

ORIENTATION: *Jesus passes through Jericho on the last leg of his journey to Jerusalem.*

Bartimaeus Receives Sight

46 They came to Jericho. And as he was leaving Jericho with his disciples and a sizable crowd, Bartimaeus, a blind man, the son of Timaeus, sat by the roadside begging. 47 On hearing that it was Jesus of Nazareth, he began to cry out and say, "Jesus, son of David, have pity on me." 48 And many rebuked him, telling him to be silent. But he kept calling out all the more, "Son of David, have pity on me." 49 Jesus stopped and said, "Call him." So they called the blind man, saying to him, "Take courage; get up, he is calling you." 50 He threw aside his cloak, sprang up, and came to Jesus.

⁵¹ **Jesus said to him in reply, "What do you want me to do for you?" The blind man replied to him, "Master, I want to see."** ⁵² **Jesus told him, "Go your way; your faith has saved you." Immediately he received his sight and followed him on the way.**

Gospel parallels: Matt 20:29–34; Luke 18:35–43
NT: Matt 9:27–31

46 **They came to Jericho,** fifteen miles northeast of Jerusalem. Jericho lies in the Jordan Valley; from there one would begin the ascent to Jerusalem (10:32–33). **And as he was leaving Jericho with his disciples and a sizable crowd:** Jesus is going to Jerusalem before Passover (14:1), a springtime feast that was celebrated by making pilgrimage to Jerusalem. Some came early to be ritually purified so that they could enter the inner courts of the Temple. The **sizable crowd** is made up of pilgrims as well as those accompanying Jesus. **Bartimaeus, a blind man, the son of Timaeus, sat by the roadside begging.** The road to Jerusalem was heavily traveled before pilgrimage feasts and was a good place for a blind beggar to appeal for alms. Of the many people whom Jesus healed, Mark's Gospel tells us the name of only one of them: **Bartimaeus.**

The Feast of Passover and Unleavened Bread: See page 363

BACKGROUND: JERICHO can lay claim to being both the lowest and the oldest city on earth. Jericho lies in the Jordan Valley, ten miles from where the Jordan River empties into the Dead Sea. Jericho is about 850 feet below sea level (for comparison, Death Valley in the United States is about 280 feet below sea level). Jericho was built at the site of a powerful spring that flows to this day. In ancient Jericho archaeologists have discovered a thirty-foot-high tower and city walls dating from around 8000 BC—almost seven thousand years before Joshua came along. At the time of Jesus, the tower and the wall had long been buried in a pile of rubble. Jericho lay along one of the most commonly used routes for travel between Galilee and Jerusalem. The road from Jericho to Jerusalem went by a palace that Herod the Great had built to enjoy Jericho's warm winter weather; Jerusalem, only fifteen miles away but twenty-five hundred feet above sea level, is cold and damp in the winter.

---

47 **On hearing that it was Jesus of Nazareth:** Jesus was notable enough to draw comments like "There's Jesus of Nazareth!" He was called **Jesus of Nazareth** to distinguish him from all other men named **Jesus,** which as an Aramaic form of the name Joshua was a popular name for Jewish men. When Bartimaeus hears that Jesus is passing by, he begins **to cry out and say, "Jesus, son of David, have pity on me."** His plea, **Have pity on me,** echoes a cry for God's mercy found in various psalms (Psalms 6:3; 41:5, 11; 51:3). As a beggar, Bartimaeus knows what it means to be dependent on the mercy of others. He addresses his cry for mercy to **Jesus;** Bartimaeus is the only person in Mark's Gospel to call Jesus by name in seeking a healing from him. Bartimaeus also calls him **son of David,** but it is not certain what he had in mind when he did so. **Son of David** could be a way of labeling Jesus as a descendant of David. The words could also be used as a title for the Messiah, as they were in the nonbiblical *Psalms of Solomon* (see page 207). Or they could be a reference to David's son Solomon, whom Jewish tradition revered as skilled in healing: Bartimaeus might have been acknowledging Jesus to be as great a healer as Solomon. By the time Mark wrote his Gospel, Christians would have understood the title **son of David** as applied to Jesus to mean that he was the particular descendant of David through whom God's promises to David were fulfilled.

BACKGROUND: SON OF DAVID Broadly speaking, any descendant of David could be called a son of David (as Joseph is: Matt 1:20). As applied to Jesus in the Gospels, the title Son of David is usually taken to mean that Jesus is the specific descendant of David through whom God's promise of everlasting reign for the house of David will be fulfilled (2 Sam 7:12–16; Psalm 89:3–5, 29–38; Luke 1:32–33; Rom 1:3–4). The title Son of David does not occur in the Old Testament as a title for the Messiah but does have this meaning in one of the *Psalms of Solomon*, a nonbiblical writing from around 50 BC. It has also been suggested that popular Jewish tradition looked upon Solomon, a son of David, as an exorcist and a healer and that Jesus was hailed as the Son of David because he too exorcised and healed. Save for the cry of the crowd in Matthew's Gospel during Jesus' entry into Jerusalem (Matt 21:9), Jesus is hailed as the Son of David during his ministry only in conjunction with healing. *Related topics: Nonbiblical writings (page 243), Psalms of Solomon (page 207).*

---

48 **And many rebuked him, telling him to be silent.** Mark doesn't indicate whether the **many** who tried to silence Bartimaeus were Jesus' disciples or pilgrims or bystanders. Whoever they are, they may think that Jesus is too important a person to be bothered by beggars, and this beggar is making a noisy nuisance of himself. The disciples should have remembered what happened when they tried to prevent children from being brought to Jesus for his blessing: Jesus welcomed the children and told the disciples that the kingdom of God belonged to children and nobodies (10:13–16)—and a blind beggar certainly counts as a nobody. Bartimaeus is not about to shut up: he is determined that Jesus hear his appeal for mercy. **But he kept calling out all the more, "Son of David, have pity on me."** Bartimaeus's **calling out all the more** may remind us of the Syrophoenician woman who wanted Jesus to free her daughter of an unclean spirit and would not take no for an answer (7:24–30). Fervent prayer springs from having great needs and great faith in Jesus' ability to meet those needs.

For reflection: What are my greatest needs? How strong is my faith that Jesus can meet them?

49 **Jesus stopped and said, "Call him."** Jesus hears Bartimaeus's cries for pity and stops. Even though Jesus is on the most important journey of his life, answering a plea for pity from a nobody takes precedence. Jesus does not call Bartimaeus to himself but asks others (presumably his disciples) to do so. **So they called the blind man, saying to him, "Take courage; get up, he is calling you."** This is a snapshot of the message that disciples bear: they call others with the call of Jesus. They tell the blind man to **take courage,** even though he has already demonstrated courage in crying out to Jesus despite others trying to shush him up. Mark's first readers would have understood why a disciple would tell someone he was bringing to Jesus to **take courage:** it took considerable courage to become a Christian in the midst of persecution, when accepting baptism could be a death warrant. The disciples tell the blind man to **get up** and go to Jesus because Jesus **is calling you.** Coming to Jesus is a response to his call, and his call gives one the courage to respond.

50 Bartimaeus responds immediately. **He threw aside his cloak, sprang up, and came to Jesus.** Jericho, lying far below sea level, is very hot at Passover time, and Bartimaeus would not have needed to wear an outer cloak during the day. He might have laid it on the ground to receive the coins given him as alms. As a beggar, he might not have owned much more than his clothes, and his casting **aside his cloak** is a sign of his abandoning everything to go to Jesus. He **sprang up** with eagerness **and came to Jesus.** Mark doesn't describe him needing the assistance of others; he might have simply been guided by the sound of Jesus' voice.

Cloak: See Clothing, page 117

51 **Jesus said to him in reply** to his plea for mercy, **What do you want me to do for you?** Jesus could presume that Bartimaeus wasn't asking for alms but wanted to be healed of his blindness, but Jesus leaves it up to Bartimaeus to tell him what he wants. Jesus' question, **What do you want me to do for you?** is the same response he made to James and John after they asked him to do for them whatever they asked of him (10:36). They wanted power and prestige, but this **blind man replied to him, "Master, I want to see."** The word translated as **master** is *rabbouni* (it occurs also in John 20:16), a form of the word *rabbi* that was used as a respectful form of address. Bartimaeus comes to Jesus not only with faith but also with reverence and asks to be able **to see.**

> *For reflection: How would I answer Jesus if he asked me, "What do you want me to do for you?"*

52 **Jesus told him, "Go your way; your faith has saved you."** Instead of performing an elaborate healing, as he previously did for a blind man (8:22–26), Jesus simply tells Bartimaeus to get on with his life, for his **faith has saved** him. His **faith** was his confidence that Jesus could and would heal him. The Greek word translated **saved** covers both physical healing and the far greater healing of receiving eternal life (see 5:23, 28, 34; 8:35; 10:26). **Immediately he received his sight and followed him on the way.** Bartimaeus instantly has not only sight so that he can see Jesus but also insight into who Jesus is, for when Jesus continues

his journey to Jerusalem, Bartimaeus goes with him. He **followed** Jesus, joining with the others who followed him (1:18, 20; 2:14). He follows Jesus **on the way,** an expression that means on the road leading up to Jerusalem but also means on the way of discipleship, the way of suffering, death, and rising. Bartimaeus is a model not only of faith but also of discipleship.

For reflection: What lesson does Bartimaeus offer me?

CHAPTER 11

ORIENTATION: *Jesus makes his first and only visit to Jerusalem recounted in Mark's Gospel. The events that take place here could be compressed into little more than a week.*

Jesus Comes to Jerusalem

¹ **When they drew near to Jerusalem, to Bethphage and Bethany at the Mount of Olives, he sent two of his disciples ² and said to them, "Go into the village opposite you, and immediately on entering it, you will find a colt tethered on which no one has ever sat. Untie it and bring it here. ³ If anyone should say to you, 'Why are you doing this?' reply, 'The Master has need of it and will send it back here at once.'" ⁴ So they went off and found a colt tethered at a gate outside on the street, and they untied it. ⁵ Some of the bystanders said to them, "What are you doing, untying the colt?" ⁶ They answered them just as Jesus had told them to, and they permitted them to do it. ⁷ So they brought the colt to Jesus and put their cloaks over it. And he sat on it. ⁸ Many people spread their cloaks on the road, and others spread leafy branches that they had cut from the fields. ⁹ Those preceding him as well as those following kept crying out:**

> **"Hosanna!**
> **Blessed is he who comes in the name of the Lord!**
> **¹⁰ Blessed is the kingdom of our father David that**
> **is to come!**
> **Hosanna in the highest!"**

¹¹ **He entered Jerusalem and went into the temple area. He looked around at everything and, since it was already late, went out to Bethany with the Twelve.**

Gospel parallels: Matt 21:1–11; Luke 19:28–40; John 12:12–16
OT: Psalm 118:25–26; Zech 9:9

1 **When they drew near to Jerusalem, to Bethphage and Bethany at the Mount of Olives:** Jesus' destination is **Jerusalem,** which may be

why Mark mentions it first. In coming from Jericho, Jesus would have passed by the village of **Bethany,** less than two miles east of Jerusalem, and then the village of **Bethphage,** somewhere between Bethany and Jerusalem. The **Mount of Olives** was a ridge just east of Jerusalem; the Kidron Valley separated the Mount of Olives from the Temple. Bethany lay on a southeastern slope of the Mount of Olives. When Jesus is at or near Bethany, **he sent two of his disciples** to carry out a task, as he earlier sent out the Twelve two by two to heal and exorcise (6:7).

2 Jesus **said to them, "Go into the village opposite you"**—in this context, most likely Bethphage—**"and immediately on entering it, you will find a colt tethered on which no one has ever sat."** Entering a village and finding a **colt** (a young donkey) tied to a post or a tree would not be out of the ordinary. Jesus' command would be like saying today, "Go downtown, and you will find a car parked on the street." But how does Jesus know that his disciples will find a colt **on which no one has ever sat**? We will return to this question shortly. Jesus instructs the two disciples to **untie it and bring it here.**

3 Jesus adds, **If anyone should say to you, "Why are you doing this?" reply, "The Master has need of it and will send it back here at once."** Key to understanding the meaning of Jesus' instructions is the Greek word for **Master,** a word that is usually translated as Lord but has a range of meanings. It can mean a person with some kind of authority, such as the authority the owner of a donkey has over his donkey. The word *Lord* can be used as a title for God (as it is in verse 9). When Jesus speaks of the **Master** having need of the colt, is he referring to himself and associating himself with the lordship of God? This would be the only time in the Gospel of Mark that Jesus explicitly calls himself Lord. Jesus' speaking of himself as **Master** (Lord) would fit in with his having some kind of divine foreknowledge of the colt.

Lord: See page 332

Another interpretation is that the person whom Jesus refers to as **the Master** is the owner of the colt that the disciples are being sent to fetch. Presumably this man is with Jesus and has volunteered the use of his donkey, but with the warning that it has never been ridden and is unbroken. Mark's account does not tell us enough to settle whether Jesus had divine foreknowledge of the colt or whether there was a more mundane explanation for Jesus' knowledge.

For reflection: Which explanation of Jesus' knowledge of the colt makes more sense to me?

4 **So they went off and found a colt tethered at a gate outside on the street, and they untied it.** Whatever the source of Jesus' knowledge, it was accurate, and everything unfolds as Jesus said it would.

5 **Some of the bystanders said to them, "What are you doing, untying the colt?"** Note that it is not the owner of the colt who questions what the disciples are doing but simply **some bystanders;** the owner never appears on the scene. The **bystanders** know who owns the colt: everyone living in a small village recognized its donkeys and knew their owners. The bystanders wonder who these two men are who are taking the colt and challenge them, much as we might challenge a stranger poking around in our neighbor's car.

6 **They answered them just as Jesus had told them to:** the disciples tell the bystanders that "the Master has need of it" (verse 3) and will send it back once he is finished with it. Do the bystanders understand "the Master" to be the owner of the colt or Jesus? In any case, the disciples' reply satisfied them, **and they permitted them to do it.**

7 **So they brought the colt to Jesus and put their cloaks over it** as makeshift blankets for Jesus to sit on. **And he sat on it** and began riding toward Jerusalem.

At this point we must wonder why Jesus chose to ride a colt for the final mile or so of his journey to Jerusalem. This is the only time Mark's Gospel recounts Jesus riding an animal. It is strange for him to ride an animal now, since pilgrims normally entered Jerusalem on foot. Adding to the strangeness are the rather elaborate preparations, which take up seven of the eleven verses in Mark's account.

The most likely explanation is that Jesus, who was familiar with the prophecies of Zechariah (14:27), chose to ride a colt into Jerusalem in order to act out Zechariah's prophecy of a king meekly riding a colt into Jerusalem (Zech 9:9). Jesus did so to help define the kind of Messiah he was: not a warrior king, riding a stallion or in a chariot, but a savior king on a much humbler mount. Kings did ride donkeys or mules (1 Kings 1:32–34) but not into battle. Jesus was not the warrior Messiah that many Jews expected.

> *Rejoice heartily, O daughter Zion,*
> *shout for joy, O daughter Jerusalem!*
> *See, your king shall come to you;*
> *a just savior is he,*
> *Meek, and riding on an ass,*
> *on a colt, the foal of an ass.*
>
> Zech 9:9

8 **Many people spread their cloaks on the road:** Jesus again draws a crowd of **many people.** They **spread their cloaks on the road,** a gesture of respect for a king (2 Kings 9:13), like rolling out the red carpet. **Others spread leafy branches that they had cut from the fields,** apparently also as a gesture of homage.

9 **Those preceding him as well as those following kept crying out:** those coming to Jerusalem with Jesus have formed a procession on the road, with some **preceding** Jesus and others **following** him. This stream of people around Jesus cry out **Hosanna!** as they walk. We use this word as a shout of praise or joy, but **hosanna** is a Hebrew word that means please save or please help. Psalm 118 uses this word to ask God to "grant salvation" (Psalm 118:25). Those accompanying Jesus are echoing Psalm 118's cry of **hosanna,** for they go on to cry out, **Blessed is he who comes in the name of the Lord!** (see Psalm 118:26). Psalm 118 was prayed at Passover, and its words were used to greet and bless pilgrims. In the context of this psalm, **blessed is he who comes in the name of the Lord** means blessed in the name of the Lord is he who comes to Jerusalem on pilgrimage. Jesus is greeted as a pilgrim coming into Jerusalem—but as a very special pilgrim. There is irony in the crowd proclaiming Jesus' blessedness—or happiness—in his coming to Jerusalem, for he has come to die.

> LORD, *grant salvation!*
>> LORD, *grant good fortune!*
>
> *Blessed is he*
>> *who comes in the name of the* LORD.
> *We bless you from the* LORD's *house.*
>>>> Psalm 118:25–26

Mark may want his readers to understand **blessed is he who comes in the name of the Lord** in a fuller sense: blessed is he who has come as God's agent; blessed is he who comes as Son of God to carry out God's will.

10 The crowd's next cry is not from Scripture: **Blessed is the kingdom of our father David that is to come!** These words extol the **kingdom** of David and proclaim that it **is to come;** the crowd's exuberance may indicate that they expected it to come soon. Many thought that reestablishing the kingdom of David meant throwing off Roman rule. Jesus proclaimed that the kingdom of God was at hand (1:15); those hailing Jesus' entry into Jerusalem might have interpreted his words as an announcement that Rome's rule was about to end. They cry out, **Hosanna in the highest,** asking God in the highest heaven to help or save. Are they asking God to help Jesus deliver them from foreign domination? Or are they simply asking to be saved from foreign domination?

The crowd did not explicitly proclaim Jesus to be the Messiah, but their shouts nonetheless seem to indicate that they saw him as someone who might bring an end to Roman rule. They missed the significance of Jesus riding a colt as a sign that he was not a warrior Messiah, perhaps because a man riding a donkey was a common sight, and they made no connection between Jesus' action and Zechariah's prophecy.

Mark does not tell us whether any Roman authorities or informers noticed Jesus coming over the Mount of Olives surrounded by a crowd of people hailing the kingdom of David. If Roman authorities did get wind of it, they would not have taken it lightly. The Roman governor Pontius Pilate came to Jerusalem with troops of soldiers at Passover to deal with any threats to Roman rule. Popular uprisings were a danger when large crowds of pilgrims gathered in Jerusalem to observe Passover, a celebration of Israel's liberation from Egypt. Crowds of enthusiasts with their minds on liberation and **the kingdom of our father David that is to come** would have made Roman authorities nervous. Jesus would have known that the more the crowd acclaimed him, the more his life was endangered. He knew that he would be "handed over . . . to the Gentiles," to Roman authorities who would put him to death (10:33–34), but that this would happen as God's will for him (8:31).

For reflection: What insight into Jesus do I find in his entering Jerusalem at the risk of his life?

11   The celebration around Jesus apparently ended as quickly as it began, with pilgrims dispersing to find lodgings in and around Jerusalem. There was no commotion as Jesus **entered Jerusalem and went into the temple area.** The Temple lay on the eastern edge of Jerusalem and thus could be the first stop of pilgrims coming by way of Bethany and Bethphage. **He looked around at everything** in the Temple area, sizing things up. Jesus takes no action on the basis of what he sees; rather, **since it was already late** in the day, Jesus **went out to Bethany with the Twelve.** At Passover, Jerusalem was swollen with pilgrims, many more than could

---

BACKGROUND: JERUSALEM lies in the rocky hills of Judea, about twenty-five hundred feet above sea level; hence the Bible speaks of "going up" to Jerusalem and "going down" from Jerusalem. Jerusalem's importance was political and religious rather than geographic or economic. It did not lie on any trade routes, nor is the region a lush agricultural area: the eastern outskirts of Jerusalem border on the Judean wilderness. However, David had chosen Jerusalem to be his capital, and Solomon had built the first Israelite Temple in Jerusalem. Jerusalem remained the religious center even after Israelite political independence was lost. Jerusalem's population at the time of Jesus is estimated to be around forty thousand. Well over one hundred thousand more people would crowd into the city during pilgrimage feasts (Passover, Weeks, Booths). The Temple was the mainstay of Jerusalem's economy, accounting for 20 percent of the city's income, by one estimate. The massive revamping of the Temple complex that Herod the Great began in 20 BC continued almost until the time of the Jewish revolt in AD 66—a major public-works project. Offerings brought to the Temple and the sale of animals for sacrifice brought income to Jerusalem and to those who controlled the Temple. Jerusalem was a company town, and that company was the Temple. *Related topic: Temple (page 294).*

stay within the city itself. Jesus stays at nearby Bethany, which will serve as his base of operations while he is in Jerusalem, just as Capernaum did while he was in Galilee.

Temple: See page 294

Jesus and a Fruitless Fig Tree

¹² The next day as they were leaving Bethany he was hungry. ¹³ Seeing from a distance a fig tree in leaf, he went over to see if he could find anything on it. When he reached it he found nothing but leaves; it was not the time for figs. ¹⁴ And he said to it in reply, "May no one ever eat of your fruit again!" And his disciples heard it.

Gospel parallels: Matt 21:18–19

12 **The next day as they were leaving Bethany he was hungry.** After spending the night in **Bethany** (11:11), Jesus and the Twelve begin walking back to Jerusalem. Strange things happen along the way. It is a little odd that Jesus is **hungry** as he sets out from Bethany (the only mention of his being hungry in Mark's Gospel). There is nothing strange about Jesus getting hungry, as every human being gets hungry. But hospitality was such a great social obligation that a host would never allow a guest to go hungry (Gen 18:1–8; Luke 11:5–8). Were Jesus and his disciples camping out in Bethany rather than staying in someone's house?

13 **Seeing from a distance a fig tree in leaf, he went over to see if he could find anything on it.** Fig trees were common in Palestine, and figs a favorite fruit. Fig trees leafed out in early April, so the sight of a **fig tree in leaf** at Passover was normal. What is strange is that Jesus went **over to see if he could find anything on it,** for figs did not become ripe or edible before June, and the full crop not until August—and every Palestinian Jew would have known this. We have to wonder what Jesus was thinking. **When he reached it he found nothing but leaves,** which should have been no surprise, for **it was not the time for figs.** Mark might have included **it was not the time for figs** for his Roman readers, who might not have known when fig trees yielded edible fruit in Palestine.

14 When Jesus finds nothing but leaves on the tree, **he said to it in reply, "May no one ever eat of your fruit again!"** Jesus' reaction is, on first reading, very puzzling. Was Jesus in a bad mood that morning? Why would he blame a fig tree for not having fruit when it was not the time of year for figs to be ripe? Why did Jesus say, **May no one ever eat of your fruit again?** Mark notes that **his disciples heard** what Jesus said: how did they understand Jesus' words?

For reflection: How do I understand Jesus' reaction to the fig tree?

Just as real-estate values depend on location, location, location, biblical meanings depend on context, context, context. The remote context for Jesus' words is found in the prophets of the Old Testament, who performed symbolic actions in order to convey a message. Jeremiah wore an animal yoke (Jer 27:2), Isaiah walked around naked (Isaiah 20:1–4), and Ezekiel did even stranger things (Ezek 4:1–15). The strangeness of Jesus' reaction to the fig tree is a signal that he was performing a symbolic act. Isaiah's going about naked does not mean that he was an exhibitionist, and likewise Jesus' reaction to the fig tree does not mean that he was spiteful.

Another context for Jesus' words: the previous day Jesus rode over the Mount of Olives on a colt, not because he was tired of walking but as a symbolic act meant to evoke a prophecy of Zechariah (Zech 9:9–10). Jesus was performing symbolic acts during the last days of his life.

The final bit of context for understanding Jesus' reaction to the fruitless fig tree lies in what happens next. We can't really understand the significance of Jesus' words to the fig tree at this point; we have to read on and then return to this incident.

Jesus Disrupts Commerce in the Temple Area
15 They came to Jerusalem, and on entering the temple area he began to drive out those selling and buying there. He overturned the tables of the money changers and the seats of those who were selling doves. 16 He did not permit anyone to carry anything through the temple area. 17 Then he taught them saying, "Is it not written:

'My house shall be called a house of prayer for all peoples'?
But you have made it a den of thieves."

18 The chief priests and the scribes came to hear of it and were seeking a way to put him to death, yet they feared him because the whole crowd was astonished at his teaching. 19 When evening came, they went out of the city.

Gospel parallels: Matt 21:12–17; Luke 19:45–48; John 2:13–17
OT: Isaiah 56:1–8; Jer 7:1–15

15 **They came to Jerusalem, and on entering the temple area he began to drive out those selling and buying there.** When Jesus went to the Temple the previous evening to look around (11:11), he apparently didn't like what he saw. He took no action then, for Temple activities were shutting down for the night. Now, the next morning, Jesus enters the **temple area** again and begins to **drive out those selling and buying there.** It was more convenient for pilgrims to buy unblemished animals to offer as sacrifices once they reached Jerusalem rather than drag along their own animals from home and hope they passed inspection. There were markets for sacrificial animals on the Mount of Olives, but the high priest, Caiaphas, had recently opened a market in the Temple area itself, in the vast courtyard that Gentiles could enter. Jesus disrupted this commercial activity and **overturned the tables of the money changers.** Every Jewish man over nineteen years old paid an annual tax (equivalent to two days' wages for an ordinary worker) toward the upkeep of the Temple. As a convenience for the pilgrims, **money changers** exchanged the various currencies in circulation for coins acceptable for payment of the tax. Jesus also overturned **the seats of those who were selling doves.** Doves were offered for ritual purifications (Lev 15:14, 29), including those of women after childbirth and those of people healed of leprosy who could not afford to offer lambs (Lev 12:8; 14:21–22; Luke 2:22–24). Jesus disrupts the selling of doves along with the other commercial activities taking place in the Court of the Gentiles.

16 **He did not permit anyone to carry anything through the temple area:** the significance of Jesus' action is unclear. Was this simply part of Jesus' disruption of commercial activities? Was Jesus interfering with

priests carrying out their normal duties? Was Jesus shutting down a shortcut between Jerusalem and the Mount of Olives? While such suggestions have been made, it is probably best to admit that we do not understand exactly why Jesus **did not permit anyone to carry anything through the temple area** or why Mark included mention of it in his Gospel. (Nowhere is it guaranteed that we can understand every verse of Scripture.)

We can note that Jesus is not described as being angry when he disrupts activities going on in the Temple precincts, even though this incident is sometimes used as a justification for righteous anger by those who wish to consider their anger righteous.

17 Jesus explains why he has disrupted commercial activities in the Temple area. **Then he taught them saying, "Is it not written: / 'My house shall be called a house of prayer for all peoples'? / But you have**

BACKGROUND: TEMPLE In the ancient Near East, a temple was thought of as the "house" or "palace" of God. Solomon (ruled from about 970 to 931 BC) built the first Israelite Temple in Jerusalem. From the time of King Josiah (ruled from about 640 to 609 BC), the Jerusalem Temple was the only site where Jews could offer animal sacrifices. Solomon's Temple was destroyed by the Babylonians in 587 BC. A second Temple was built after the Exile and dedicated in 515 BC. Herod the Great rebuilt and refurbished this second Temple, plating its exterior with gold, and enlarged the surrounding courtyard to more than thirty-five acres. Around the perimeter of the courtyard, Herod erected magnificent colonnaded halls similar to structures found around pagan temples in the Greek and Roman world. The Temple itself was a rather small building (perhaps about 165 by 85 feet); worshipers gathered outside the Temple rather than within it. An altar for offering burnt sacrifices stood in a courtyard reserved for priests that was in front of—east of—the Temple. East of the Court of Priests was a small Court of Israel, which ritually clean Jewish men could enter, and to its east was a Court of the Women for ritually clean Jews of any age or sex. The remaining, and by far the largest, portion of the Temple area was a Court of the Gentiles, available to both Jews and non-Jews. The open spaces and colonnaded halls in the Court of the Gentiles provided places for meetings, instruction, the selling of animals for sacrifice, and the changing of coins for Temple taxes and offerings. The Temple also served as a national religious treasury and depository for savings. Rome destroyed the Temple in AD 70 while putting down a Jewish revolt. It was never rebuilt.

---

made it a den of thieves." Jesus first quotes a prophecy in which Isaiah speaks of a time to come when God will welcome the sacrificial offerings of foreigners (non-Jews) who observe the Sabbath and God's laws and come to the Temple: **My house shall be called a house of prayer for all peoples** (see Isaiah 56:7). What point is Jesus trying to make when he invokes this prophecy as an explanation for his disruption of commercial activities? Jesus cannot mean that this commerce is preventing Gentiles from praying in their part of the Temple, for the Court of the Gentiles was vast enough to allow many activities to take place without interfering with one another. Compared with the crowds of Jews, relatively few Gentiles came to the Temple; most of the people who prayed in the Court of the Gentiles were Jews who could not be accommodated in the much smaller courtyards adjacent the Temple.

> And the foreigners who join themselves to the LORD,
>   ministering to him,
> Loving the name of the LORD,
>   and becoming his servants—
> All who keep the sabbath free from profanation
>   and hold to my covenant,
> Them I will bring to my holy mountain
>   and make joyful in my house of prayer;
> Their holocausts and sacrifices
>   will be acceptable on my altar,
> For my house shall be called
>   a house of prayer for all peoples.
>
> Isaiah 56:6–7

I suggest that Jesus invoked Isaiah's prophecy because it spoke of a time to come when God would receive worship from his people and all peoples—or, in terms of Jesus' message, when God's kingdom would be established on earth. The Temple was the place of God's special presence on earth, and what went on there should manifest God's reign. I suspect that Jesus might have had in mind not only the particular words of Isaiah that he quoted but also passages toward the end of Isaiah that spoke of a time to come when Jerusalem would be exalted and God's reign established (Isaiah 60–62; 65:17–25; 66). That was what God wanted.

The reality Jesus found in the Temple area was quite different from what God wanted. Herod had transformed a simple Temple into a grand architectural showcase meant to demonstrate his greatness as a builder. Herod's enlarged Temple courtyard was the largest temple precinct in the Roman Empire; the Temple building itself was plated with gold so that it shone in the sun. The high-priestly families who controlled the Temple also controlled the commerce that took place in the Temple area, and they were in charge of taxes and donations received by the Temple. Being in control of the Temple made them wealthy (the remains of palatial houses belonging to the religious aristocracy have been excavated in Jerusalem). Ancient writings describe these high-priestly families as corrupt, exploitative, and self-enriching—the opposite of what characterizes those under God's reign (10:42–45). One Jewish group, the Essenes, rejected the legitimacy of the high priests altogether. Jesus addresses those in charge of the Temple and says that, in contrast to what God wants his Temple to be, **you have made it a den of thieves**—words Jesus borrows from a prophecy of Jeremiah (Jer 7:11). A **den of thieves** is where thieves take refuge and store what they have stolen.

> *Are you to steal and murder, commit adultery and perjury, burn incense to Baal, go after strange gods that you know not, and yet come to stand before me in this house which bears my name, and say: "We are safe; we can commit all these abominations again"? Has this house which bears my name become in your eyes a den of thieves? . . . You may go to Shiloh, which I made the dwelling place of my name in the beginning. See what I did to it because of the wickedness of my people Israel. . . . I will do to this house named after me, in which you trust, and to this place which I gave to you and your fathers, just as I did to Shiloh.*
>
> Jer 7:9–12, 14

Jeremiah condemned those who thought they could commit sins and then use the Temple as a refuge, reasoning that they were safe there because God would protect his Temple. Jeremiah reminded them that God had allowed a shrine at Shiloh to be destroyed and warned them that the same fate awaited the Temple in Jerusalem unless his people changed their ways.

How do these two prophecies that Jesus invoked make sense of his disruption of commerce in the Temple area? Jesus' act was symbolic and aimed at those who ran the Temple. His disruption of their sources of income was a symbol of a far greater disruption that lay ahead unless they changed their ways. Jesus was not striking at the Temple itself or at sacrificial worship in itself; Jesus accepted these as legitimate. But what they had become—a gaudy display and a source of wealth—endangered the existence of the Temple, just as the sins of God's people had endangered the Temple at the time of Jeremiah. Babylon destroyed the Temple about twenty-two years after Jeremiah delivered his prophecy.

Jesus' action in the Temple area was symbolic rather than practical: he could not have single-handedly shut down all the commerce taking

---

BACKGROUND: ESSENES are not mentioned in the Bible. Ancient writers described them as a sect of Jews. Pliny the Elder (a Roman who lived from AD 23 to 79) wrote, "On the west side of the Dead Sea is the solitary tribe of the Essenes, which is remarkable beyond all the other tribes in the whole world, as it has no women and has renounced all sexual desire, has no money, and has only palm trees for company" (*Natural History* 5:73). The Jewish historian Josephus described the Essenes as celibate men who lived at the Dead Sea and owned everything in common; he added that there were also other Essenes, some married, who lived throughout the land. Josephus numbered the Essenes at four thousand, several hundred of whom lived at their headquarters by the Dead Sea (in all likelihood at the site known today as Qumran). Most scholars identify the Essenes as the group who collected or wrote the Dead Sea Scrolls. Some scrolls show that the Essenes rejected the current high priests in Jerusalem as illegitimate and Temple worship as corrupt. Essenes determined religious feasts by a calendar different from the one used by the Temple. They expected God to act soon to vindicate them in a cosmic battle that would bring the end of this age; God would send two messiahs, one priestly and one royal. The Essenes carefully studied and rigorously observed the law of Moses and made daily ritual washings and communal meals part of their life. The Gospels describe no encounters between Jesus and the Essenes, but Jesus was likely aware of them. Jesus and the Essenes would have agreed that God was about to act but would have differed over how. Rome destroyed Qumran in AD 68, and the Essenes disappeared from history. *Related topics: Dead Sea Scrolls (page 245), Jewish religious diversity at the time of Jesus (page 164).*

---

place there. Had his disruption lasted very long, the Temple police would have stepped in. Given the size of the Temple area—about the size of thirty American football fields—and the thousands of people who crowded into it around Passover, Jesus' actions might have gone largely unnoticed.

> *For reflection: How do I understand Jesus' actions and words in the Temple area? What implications do they have for me?*

18 **The chief priests and the scribes came to hear of it:** they did not witness what Jesus did, but reports reached them. As a result, they **were seeking a way to put him to death.** Not only is Jesus a threat to the religious authority of those who run the Temple, but Jesus' disruption of Temple commerce was also a threat to their income and luxurious life-style. In a few days Jesus will be taken into custody and brought before **chief priests, scribes,** and elders, and they will confirm their decision that he must die (14:53–65). For the moment they do nothing, for **they feared him because the whole crowd was astonished at his teaching.** Jesus apparently taught the crowd at some length, for the following verse indicates that he did not leave until evening. Mark does not tell his readers what the crowd found astonishing about Jesus' teaching, but Jesus' teachings have astonished people from the beginning of his public ministry (1:22).

High priest, chief priests: See page 403
Scribes: See page 40

19 **When evening came, they went out of the city:** Jesus and his disciples return to Bethany for the night.

The Fig Tree and Prayer

20 Early in the morning, as they were walking along, they saw the fig tree withered to its roots. 21 Peter remembered and said to him, "Rabbi, look! The fig tree that you cursed has withered." 22 Jesus said to them in reply, "Have faith in God. 23 Amen, I say to you, whoever says to this mountain, 'Be lifted up and thrown into the sea,' and does not doubt in his heart but believes that what he says

will happen, it shall be done for him. ²⁴ Therefore I tell you, all that you ask for in prayer, believe that you will receive it and it shall be yours. ²⁵ When you stand to pray, forgive anyone against whom you have a grievance, so that your heavenly Father may in turn forgive you your transgressions. [26]"

Gospel parallels: Matt 21:20–22
NT: Matt 6:14–15; 17:20; Mark 9:23; 10:27; 11:12–14; Luke 17:5–6

20 **Early in the morning, as they were walking along:** after spending the night in Bethany, Jesus and his disciples return to Jerusalem, following the route they walked the previous day (11:12). **They saw the fig tree withered to its roots.** The day before, Jesus pronounced that no one would ever again eat fruit from this tree (11:14), and it has become not merely perpetually fruitless but completely dead, **withered to its roots.** During its withering, Jesus was disrupting commerce in the Temple precincts (11:15–17). Mark, by weaving together his accounts of the fig tree and the Temple, indicates that the two incidents are to be understood in light of each other. In both cases Jesus went somewhere with a hunger or an expectation: to the fig tree with physical hunger (11:12) and to the Temple with spiritual hunger for the establishment of God's reign. In both cases Jesus knew that his expectations would be disappointed. He realized that he would not find any edible figs on the tree, despite its leaves, for it was not the season for figs to be ripe (11:13). He knew that he would not find God's reign properly manifested in the Temple, despite its magnificent trappings, for he had previously gone to the Temple and seen what was happening there (11:11). Jesus pronounced the end of a fig tree as a sign of the end of a Temple that had become a profit center and an architectural showcase. It wasn't the fig tree's fault that it was fruitless (any more than there was fault in the clay flask that Jeremiah broke as a sign: Jer 19:1–2, 10–11), but those who controlled the Temple were responsible for what they had done with it.

21 **Peter remembered and said to him, "Rabbi, look! The fig tree that you cursed has withered."** Peter seems amazed that Jesus' words have had an effect, despite his having witnessed Jesus calm a storm at sea and raise a girl to life by his words (4:37–39; 5:41–42). It is almost as if Peter needs a daily reminder of who Jesus is and what he is able to

do. Peter speaks of the fig tree that Jesus **cursed,** but Jesus' words are better understood as a prophetic pronouncement, just as his words in the Temple prophetically pronounced God's judgment on what the Temple had become.

For reflection: How often do I need to be reminded of who Jesus is and of what he has done and is able to do?

22 **Jesus said to them in reply, "Have faith in God."** As is indicated by what Jesus will go on to teach, the words **have faith in God** are an introduction to teachings on prayer. We might wonder why we find these teachings here. One possibility: Jesus spoke of the Temple as a "house of prayer" (11:17) and now teaches about prayer.

Jesus tells his disciples to **have faith in God,** that is, to trust God, rely on God, have confidence in God. Everything else that Jesus will teach about prayer will be based on this trust and reliance and confidence. Prayer is not a matter of words but an expression of our fundamental relationship with God.

For reflection: How absolute is my dependence on God? My trust in God?

23 **Amen, I say to you, whoever says to this mountain, "Be lifted up and thrown into the sea":** by **this mountain** Jesus might mean the Mount of Olives, on which they are standing; **the sea** could be the Dead Sea, visible from some places on the Mount of Olives. But Jesus probably intends his words as a hyperbole, a deliberate exaggeration to emphasize a point. Moving a mountain is an image for an extremely difficult task (we speak of a mountain of paperwork). Commanding a mountain to **be lifted up and thrown into the sea** is commanding something beyond our control. Yet whoever gives such a command **and does not doubt in his heart but believes that what he says will happen, it shall be done for him.** Having **doubt** is the opposite of having faith in God (verse 22). Faith is reliance on God to do what we cannot do, even the impossible, and confidence that he can do it (10:27). Jesus is not saying, "If you have the right state of mind, you can rearrange stones without having to bend over." Jesus is saying, "Have an unshakable trust in God, no matter how big an obstacle you face."

24 **Therefore I tell you, all that you ask for in prayer, believe that you will receive it and it shall be yours.** Jesus taught, "Everything is possible to one who has faith" (9:23). Now Jesus seems to promise that **all that you ask for** in prayer **shall be yours,** provided that you **believe that you will receive it.** Are we to take his words literally, as a promise that God will give us everything we ask for if we believe that he will? Experience suggests otherwise. Good Christians have prayed fervently for things they have dearly wanted, such as the healing of a loved one, and have believed that God would answer their prayers, but have not received what they asked for. Were their prayers defective? Or did they understand Jesus' promise too literally, as a blank check from God that they could fill in as they wished? There is a mystery in prayer, in human longing and words moving the Creator of the universe, and this mystery cannot be reduced to a set of rules. I believe that Jesus is using hyperbole here, as he did in speaking of moving a mountain, in order to exhort his followers to trust God, rely on God, have confidence in God. To pray with our minds focused on our certainty that God will answer our prayer shifts our focus away from God. Jesus invites us to grow in faith, even if we must cry out, "I do believe, help my unbelief" (9:24).

The first letter of John seems to echo this teaching of Jesus on prayer but includes a qualification: "We have this confidence in him, that if we ask anything *according to his will,* he hears us. And if we know that he hears us in regard to whatever we ask, we know that what we have asked him for is ours" (1 John 5:14–15; emphasis added).

For reflection: Do I pray expecting God to hear and answer my prayer? What has been my experience of praying for something I wanted dearly?

25 **When you stand to pray, forgive anyone against whom you have a grievance.** The usual Jewish practice was to **stand** in prayer (1 Kings 8:22; Psalm 134:1), although one might also kneel (1 Kings 8:54; Dan 6:11). This is the only time in Mark's Gospel that Jesus speaks of the necessity of forgiving others, and he makes it a requirement for our receiving forgiveness from God: **so that your heavenly Father may in turn forgive you your transgressions.** Jesus speaks of God as the **heavenly Father** of his disciples—the only time in Mark's Gospel that he does so. (Jesus will pray to God as his Father: 14:36.) We can have

complete confidence in God because God as our **Father** loves us and cares for us as parents care for their children. God does not forgive us because we forgive others, as if our granting forgiveness earns God's forgiveness. Rather, we must forgive others because our failure to do so blocks God's forgiveness of us. Our failure to forgive is likewise an obstacle to prayer: how can we speak to God as our **Father** if our hearts are closed to God's other children?

> For reflection: Have I experienced a connection between my forgiving others and my being able to turn to God in prayer? Is anyone in need of my forgiveness?

26 (Some manuscripts of Mark's Gospel include at this point the verse "But if you do not forgive, neither will your heavenly Father forgive your trespasses." These words are not found in the most reliable manuscripts and were probably added by a scribe who copied them from Matt 6:15, since Matt 6:14 is similar to verse 25 of Mark. The New American Bible omits this verse.)

ORIENTATION: *Jesus taught in synagogues while in Galilee, and now in Jerusalem he teaches in the Temple courtyard—an easy place to draw a crowd. Some people approach Jesus to confront and challenge him.*

The Authority of Jesus Is Questioned

27 They returned once more to Jerusalem. As he was walking in the temple area, the chief priests, the scribes, and the elders approached him 28 and said to him, "By what authority are you doing these things? Or who gave you this authority to do them?" 29 Jesus said to them, "I shall ask you one question. Answer me, and I will tell you by what authority I do these things. 30 Was John's baptism of heavenly or of human origin? Answer me." 31 They discussed this among themselves and said, "If we say, 'Of heavenly origin,' he will say, '[Then] why did you not believe him?' 32 But shall we say, 'Of human origin'?"—they feared the crowd, for they all thought John really was a prophet. 33 So they said to Jesus in

reply, "We do not know." Then Jesus said to them, "Neither shall I tell you by what authority I do these things."

Gospel parallels: Matt 21:23–27; Luke 20:1–8

27 After passing by the fig tree near Bethany (11:20), Jesus and his disciples **returned once more to Jerusalem.** It is the day after Jesus disrupted commerce in the Temple (11:15–17). **As he was walking in the temple area,** in an open space or through a colonnaded hall in the Court of the Gentiles, **the chief priests, the scribes, and the elders approached him.** The Sanhedrin (the Jewish ruling council) was made up of **chief priests, scribes,** and **elders** (15:1); the group that now approaches Jesus is a delegation from this ruling council. Jesus foretold that he would be rejected and handed over to death by **chief priests, scribes,** and **elders** (8:31; see also 10:33), and they reacted to his disruption of commerce in the Temple by seeking his death (11:18). They have come to Jesus to confront him.

High priest, chief priests: See page 403

Scribes: See page 40

For reflection: What glimpse of Jesus am I given by his returning to the Temple despite knowing that those in charge of it were seeking his death?

28 The delegation of chief priests, scribes, and elders **said to him, "By what authority are you doing these things? Or who gave you this authority to do them?"** By **these things** they mean Jesus' disruption of buying and selling and money changing in the Temple area (11:15–17). The high priest was in charge of the Temple, and he certainly had not authorized

---

BACKGROUND: ELDERS The word *elder* (*presbyteros* in Greek) literally means someone who is older (see Luke 15:25), and it was used to refer to someone with authority within a family or a clan or within a group such as a synagogue (Luke 7:3). Religious scholars of the past could also be called elders (Mark 7:3). In the Gospels, the word *elders* usually refers to influential Jewish laymen, particularly those who are part of the Sanhedrin in Jerusalem (Mark 15:1). In the early Church, the word *elders* (or *presbyters*) was used for leaders of a local church (Acts 14:23), and the Greek word came through Latin into English as the word *priest*. Related topic: Sanhedrin (page 400).

Jesus to interfere with commercial activities that operated under his authority. So what **authority** did Jesus have for his actions? **Who gave Jesus authority** to do what he did? If Jesus says that his **authority** came from God, then he can be charged with falsely claiming divine authorization or with blaspheming (as he in fact will be charged: 14:61–64). If Jesus claims no divine authority, then he will have to admit that he was acting on his own and infringing on the high priest's authority.

Mark's readers know the answer to the question **Who gave you this authority?** Jesus' authority comes from God. Jesus is the Son of God (1:1, 11; 9:7) filled with the Holy Spirit (1:10). Jesus has been sent by God (9:37) to announce and inaugurate the kingdom of God (1:15). Jesus will give his life as a ransom (10:45) in accordance with God's will (8:31; 9:12). The question **Who gave you this authority?** goes to the heart of Jesus' identity and mission. Jesus poses a far greater threat to the status quo than those questioning him realize: they are trying to preserve their power and wealth; Jesus is establishing the reign of God on earth.

29 **Jesus said to them, "I shall ask you one question. Answer me, and I will tell you by what authority I do these things."** Responding to a question with a question was a common debating tactic of the time, and Jesus made use of it (10:2–3). Jesus refuses to answer the question put to him until his questioners first answer a question.

30 **Was John's baptism of heavenly or of human origin? Answer me.** John was not authorized by the religious authorities in Jerusalem to administer a baptism of repentance for the forgiveness of sins (1:4); these authorities maintained that offering sacrifice in the Temple was necessary for the forgiveness of sins. This means that John either was authorized by God (and **John's baptism** was **of heavenly origin**) or was operating on his own (and his **baptism** was of purely **human origin**). The parallel with Jesus' own situation is unmistakable. Both Jesus and John operated outside the recognized structures, and they either were authorized by God or had no authorization at all. By asking whether **John's baptism** was **of heavenly or of human origin,** Jesus is presenting those who are challenging him with a dilemma. He is also intimating that his authority is from God, just as John's was. Jesus puts his question to them as a demand: **Answer me.**

31 **They discussed this among themselves and said, "If we say, 'Of heavenly origin,' he will say, '[Then] why did you not believe him?'"** To acknowledge that John was authorized by God would mean that the religious authorities should have accepted his baptism of repentance and his message that a mightier one was coming (1:7–8). The authorities in Jerusalem had accepted neither.

32 **"But shall we say, 'Of human origin'?"—they feared the crowd, for they all thought John really was a prophet.** While those challenging Jesus were the acknowledged religious authorities, they were not the most popular people around. John had attracted a large following (1:5) who accepted him as a **prophet.** Jesus' own popularity was likewise a check on those in authority: those who sought Jesus' death after he disrupted commerce in the Temple area "feared him because the whole crowd was astonished at his teaching" (11:18). Now the religious authorities hesitate to say anything against John that will upset the many people who revere him as a prophet.

33 **So they said to Jesus in reply, "We do not know."** Their reply is disingenuous: they lack not knowledge but honesty and courage. They refuse to answer Jesus' question because any answer they can offer will put them in a bad light. **Then Jesus said to them, "Neither shall I tell you by what authority I do these things."** Jesus uses their refusal to answer his question as a justification for his refusal to answer theirs. It is not yet the time for Jesus to speak directly of the source of his authority. Instead, Jesus will tell a parable that will reveal his identity and authority to those who have ears to hear.

For reflection: Do I avoid facing up to questions that I would be uncomfortable answering?

CHAPTER 12

ORIENTATION: *Although Bibles introduce a chapter break at this point, Jesus'*
words in the beginning of chapter 12 continue his confronta-
tion with religious leaders begun in chapter 11.

The Beloved Son and the Defiant Tenants
¹ He began to speak to them in parables. "A man planted a vineyard, put a hedge around it, dug a wine press, and built a tower.
Then he leased it to tenant farmers and left on a journey. ² At the
proper time he sent a servant to the tenants to obtain from them
some of the produce of the vineyard. ³ But they seized him, beat
him, and sent him away empty-handed. ⁴ Again he sent them
another servant. And that one they beat over the head and treated
shamefully. ⁵ He sent yet another whom they killed. So, too, many
others; some they beat, others they killed. ⁶ He had one other to
send, a beloved son. He sent him to them last of all, thinking,
'They will respect my son.' ⁷ But those tenants said to one another,
'This is the heir. Come, let us kill him, and the inheritance will
be ours.' ⁸ So they seized him and killed him, and threw him out
of the vineyard. ⁹ What [then] will the owner of the vineyard do?
He will come, put the tenants to death, and give the vineyard to
others. ¹⁰ Have you not read this scripture passage:

'The stone that the builders rejected
has become the cornerstone;
¹¹ by the Lord has this been done,
and it is wonderful in our eyes'?"

¹² They were seeking to arrest him, but they feared the crowd, for
they realized that he had addressed the parable to them. So they
left him and went away.

Gospel parallels: Matt 21:33–46; Luke 20:9–19
OT: Psalms 80:9–12; 118:22–23; Isaiah 5:1–7

1 **He began to speak to them in parables:** Jesus is still in the Temple
precincts (11:27), and he addresses the delegation of chief priests, scribes,

and elders who challenged his authority to disrupt Temple commerce (11:27–28). Jesus speaks to them **in parables:** Jesus will tell a story and follow it with a comparison.

Parables: See page 79

A man planted a vineyard, put a hedge around it, dug a wine press, and built a tower. Jesus describes a scene that would have been familiar to his listeners. Someone established a **vineyard,** planting grapevines, probably on a terraced hillside. He surrounded it with a **hedge,** perhaps of thornbush or thistle, to keep out animals and thieves. He **dug a wine press** in an outcropping of limestone bedrock, hewing an upper basin for pressing grapes, with a channel to a lower basin for collecting the juice (an ancient winepress of this design has been found on a hillside in Nazareth). He **built a tower** of fieldstones, ten or so feet high, so that a watchman could keep guard over the ripened grapes until they were harvested.

Jesus' description of the vineyard probably triggered an association for his listeners, since his words echoed a prophecy of Isaiah that compared Israel to a vineyard (Isaiah 5:1–7). Some of Jesus' listeners likely thought, "Jesus is not simply speaking about a vineyard; he is retelling Isaiah's parable. He intends for us to understand that the man who constructed the vineyard represents God, and the vineyard is God's people."

> Let me now sing of my friend,
>   my friend's song concerning his vineyard.
> My friend had a vineyard
>   on a fertile hillside;
> He spaded it, cleared it of stones,
>   and planted the choicest vines;
> Within it he built a watchtower,
>   and hewed out a wine press.
> Then he looked for the crop of grapes,
>   but what it yielded was wild grapes. . . .
>
> The vineyard of the LORD of hosts is the house of Israel,
>   and the men of Judah are his cherished plant.
>
> Isaiah 5:1–2, 7

As Jesus continues his parable, however, he departs from Isaiah. In Jesus' version, the vineyard owner did not manage the vineyard himself (as in Isaiah) but **leased it to tenant farmers.** Leasing a vineyard to **tenant farmers** was not out of the ordinary: a good deal of farmland in Judea and Galilee was owned by absentee landlords who rented it to farmers for an agreed-upon portion of the harvest. In Jesus' parable, after leasing his vineyard the owner **left on a journey;** the implication is that he would be absent for an extended time. Some in Jesus' audience would have noted that Jesus was no longer following Isaiah's story and might have pondered who the **tenant farmers** represented. If God was the vineyard owner, and the vineyard was God's people, then the tenant farmers apparently represented those whom God had put in charge of his people.

2 **At the proper time he sent a servant to the tenants to obtain from them some of the produce of the vineyard.** Rent for leased farmland was collected at harvesttime, when the crop would be divided between owner and tenants or, more commonly, when the crop would be sold and the proceeds divided. Grapes were grown for their juice, which by natural fermentation became wine. The owner sent a **servant** (literally, a slave) to collect the proceeds from the sale of his share of the wine.

Servant, slave: See page 277

For reflection: What is the vineyard that God has entrusted to my management? What share of the produce do I give him?

3 **But they seized him, beat him, and sent him away empty-handed.** Jesus' story takes a twist. Absentee landlords were sometimes resented by their tenants, but tenant farmers normally paid what they had agreed to pay. To withhold the owner's share of the proceeds of the harvest would inevitably invite eviction. These vineyard tenants seem loutish and shortsighted.

4 **Again he sent them another servant. And that one they beat over the head and treated shamefully.** The owner did what any owner would do and tried again to collect the share of the harvest due him. The second **servant** (slave) that he sent received even worse treatment

308

than the first; this servant was not only beaten but also treated **shame-fully.** Being shamed could be as painful as being physically assaulted in a culture that placed a high value on honor. Jesus does not describe the nature of the shameful treatment (for an Old Testament example of emissaries being treated shamefully, see 2 Sam 10:4–5). The owner's sending of first one servant and then another probably reminded some of Jesus' listeners of God's sending prophets to his people, for prophets were called the servants of God and were often given a poor reception (2 Kings 17:13–14; Jer 7:25–26; 25:4).

5 **He sent yet another whom they killed.** The tenants' violence escalated: they murdered a servant sent by the owner to collect his due. But the owner was exorbitantly persistent and kept sending servants to his vineyard: **so, too, many others; some they beat, others they killed.** In the real world, the kind of defiance and violence that these tenants displayed would be considered extreme. Yet the story is a realistic comparison for God's relationship with his people: prophets sent by God were rejected and even killed (1 Kings 19:10; 2 Chron 36:15–16; Neh 9:26)—the most recent being John the Baptist.

For reflection: Who are the messengers God has sent to me? How did I receive them and their message?

6 **He had one other to send, a beloved son.** The owner had sent many to collect from the tenants; now he had **one other to send,** and that was his **beloved son.** The word **beloved** has the connotation of only; the owner had a single son whom he could send as his emissary, a son who was very dear to him. **He sent him to them last of all:** this was the final attempt of the owner to obtain what was due him. He could send no one who would carry greater authority than his son. Yet why would he risk his **beloved son** on such a dangerous mission after his previous emissaries had met with physical harm and death? He sent his son **thinking, "They will respect my son."** The owner didn't want to believe that the tenants were so evil that they would harm even his son. He wanted to give them one last chance by sending his own son to them.

Mark's readers know that Jesus is the **beloved son** of God, for God has twice proclaimed him such (1:11; 9:7). Did those listening to Jesus realize that he was implicitly identifying himself as the **beloved son** of God? Did the disciples grasp the significance of what Jesus was saying? It will soon be evident that the delegation of religious leaders understood that Jesus was portraying them as murderous tenant farmers (verse 12), and the high priest will ultimately ask Jesus if he is the Son of God (14:61). Jesus' words were not completely lost on his audience.

7 **But those tenants said to one another, "This is the heir. Come, let us kill him, and the inheritance will be ours."** Their reaction makes the most sense if they assumed that the son's showing up indicated that the owner had died and the son had come to take possession of his inheritance. They referred to the son as **the heir,** apparently aware that the owner had only one son. Their reasoning, **Come, let us kill him, and the inheritance will be ours,** is logical (although ruthless and immoral) in light of the laws of the time. If a property became ownerless (such as by its owner dying without an heir), then tenants occupying the property had first claim to it.

8 **So they seized him and killed him, and threw him out of the vineyard.** They treated the son even worse than they had treated the previous emissaries sent by the owner. After they **killed him** they threw his corpse outside the vineyard, where it would be carrion for wild animals. To go unburied was a great disgrace (see 1 Sam 31:6–13). If it was possible to compound the crime of murder, the tenants did so by their treatment of the slain son's body.

9 **What [then] will the owner of the vineyard do?** The Greek word translated as **owner** is in other contexts translated as lord—one more hint that the vineyard owner in the parable represents the Lord God in relation to his people. Jesus asks a question whose answer is fairly obvious. No father would ignore the murder of his son; no **owner** would acquiesce in what amounted to the theft of his vineyard. Jesus does not wait for someone to reply to his question but answers it himself. The vineyard owner **will come, put the tenants to death, and give the vineyard to others.** Putting **the tenants to death** can mean executing blood vengeance or involving civil authorities who will impose a death

sentence for multiple murders. To **give the vineyard to others** means to put it under new management, who will give the owner his proper return. Jesus should not be interpreted as saying that Gentiles will replace Jews as God's people. Rather, Jesus is saying that God will provide new leadership for his people, as foreshadowed by Jesus' selection of the Twelve (3:14).

Jesus' parable is an implicit answer to the religious leaders who questioned his authority (11:28): his authority comes from God, for he is the beloved Son of God whom God has sent as his agent. Jesus' parable is also a warning to these leaders. Jesus knows that those to whom he is speaking—chief priests, scribes, and elders—will arrange his death (8:31; 10:33). If these religious leaders persist in their deadly course of action, they will not go unpunished. They need to have ears to hear what Jesus is saying to them and to stop plotting his death.

10 Jesus continues, **Have you not read this scripture passage: / The stone that the builders rejected / has become the cornerstone:** Jesus quotes Psalm 118—the same psalm that provided the words for the crowd's acclamation as he entered Jerusalem (11:9; Psalm 118:22–23, 25–26). Jesus will be rejected by elders, chief priests, and scribes despite the warning he has just given them, and he compares himself to a stone that is **rejected** by builders. Despite being rejected, this stone becomes **the cornerstone** of a new building. A **cornerstone** is a foundation block linking two walls at a corner. The Hebrew of Psalm 118 calls it the "head" of the corner, with connotations of it being the chief or first stone. Jesus, by speaking of himself becoming a **cornerstone,** indicates that just as the rejected stone in Psalm 118 became the cornerstone, so he too, after he has been rejected and put to death, will become the cornerstone of a new building. Jesus does not explicitly predict his resurrection, but he does indicate that he will play a uniquely important role in a new edifice.

> The stone the builders rejected
> has become the cornerstone.
> By the LORD has this been done;
> it is wonderful in our eyes.
>
> Psalm 118:22–23

11 Jesus continues to quote from Psalm 118: **by the Lord has this been done, / and it is wonderful in our eyes.** Jesus' vindication will come from God; God is the builder who will make Jesus the cornerstone of a new edifice. Mark's first readers would probably have understood this new edifice as the Church, the new people of God, the new Temple where God is present on earth. What God will do through Jesus is **wonderful,** a cause for marvel and amazement.

> *For reflection: Do I marvel in amazement that God sent his beloved Son to give up his life?*

By quoting Psalm 118, Jesus reinforces his warning to the religious leaders: the one whose death they are plotting will be vindicated by God.

12 **They were seeking to arrest him:** Jesus' warning is ignored. Chief priests and scribes sought Jesus' death after he disrupted commerce in the Temple (11:18); this is the first mention of their intent **to arrest** Jesus as a step toward his death. They hold back, as before (11:18), because **they feared the crowd:** Jesus has a substantial popular following among those present in Jerusalem for Passover, as was clear from the acclaim of the crowds as he came into the city (11:8–10). The last thing the religious leaders want is a riot when Jerusalem is crowded with pilgrims. The Roman governor Pontius Pilate held the Jewish religious leaders responsible for keeping order.

If Jesus' disruption of Temple commerce upset these leaders, they are now even more enraged at him, **for they realized that he had addressed the parable to them.** They know that his parable characterized them as vicious, murderous tenants who were not giving their Lord his due, and they probably realize that Jesus identifies himself as the beloved son in the parable. For Jesus to hint that he sees himself as the beloved Son of God challenges their authority, just as Jesus challenged their authority by disrupting their commercial arrangements in the Temple (11:15–17). But for the moment, there is nothing they can do: to arrest Jesus in public, surrounded by his supporters, would invite outcry and unrest. **So they left him and went away.** This is an ironic twist: those who are in charge of the Temple beat a retreat while Jesus the outsider remains in the Temple area, a challenge to their authority.

Jesus' story is usually labeled the parable of the wicked tenants, and the parable does indeed focus on these tenants. But the most striking feature of the parable is Jesus' implicit identification of himself as the vineyard owner's beloved son. Jesus did not announce directly, "I am the Son of God," just as he had refused to tell the religious leaders the source of his authority (11:33). Yet it is clear that his parable portrays him as God's beloved Son, sent "last of all" (verse 6)—last of all because this age is drawing to an end with the kingdom of God at hand. God's persistence in sending prophets and now his Son is an index of God's great patience and love. Jesus has come not only as the agent and the servant of God but also as the beloved Son of God who will give his life as a ransom (10:45).

Son of God: See page 64

For reflection: What insight into Jesus' identity and mission does this parable give me?

A Taxing Question

13 They sent some Pharisees and Herodians to him to ensnare him in his speech. 14 They came and said to him, "Teacher, we know that you are a truthful man and that you are not concerned with anyone's opinion. You do not regard a person's status but teach the way of God in accordance with the truth. Is it lawful to pay the census tax to Caesar or not? Should we pay or should we not pay?" 15 Knowing their hypocrisy he said to them, "Why are you testing me? Bring me a denarius to look at." 16 They brought one to him and he said to them, "Whose image and inscription is this?" They replied to him, "Caesar's." 17 So Jesus said to them, "Repay to Caesar what belongs to Caesar and to God what belongs to God." They were utterly amazed at him.

Gospel parallels: Matt 22:15–22; Luke 20:20–26
OT: Gen 1:26–27
NT: Mark 3:6; Acts 5:37; Rom 13:1–7

13 **They sent some Pharisees and Herodians to him to ensnare him in his speech:** the context indicates that **they** refers to the chief priests, scribes, and elders who challenged Jesus' authority (11:27–28) and were

portrayed by Jesus as bad managers of God's vineyard (12:1–12). These religious leaders want to arrest Jesus but are intimidated by his popular support (11:18; 12:12). So **they sent some Pharisees and Herodians to** Jesus **to ensnare him.** The religious leaders apparently want either to have Jesus arrested by Roman authorities or to destroy Jesus' popular support so that they can arrest him themselves. They send **some Pharisees and Herodians** to accomplish one or the other objective. **Pharisees** (members of a religious party) enjoyed more popular support than did the religious elite of chief priests, scribes, and elders and consequently were in a better position to sway the crowds. **Herodians** (supporters of Herod Antipas, who ruled on behalf of Rome) would be credible in any accusations they might bring against Jesus to the Roman authorities. Pharisees and Herodians earlier conspired to seek Jesus' death (3:6), which also might be why the religious leaders make use of them. Now the Pharisees and Herodians will try to **ensnare** Jesus **in his speech:** the word translated **ensnare** is a hunting term used for the trapping of animals. The Pharisees and Herodians come to Jesus with a trap.

Pharisees: See page 163

Herodians: See page 59

14 To lure Jesus into their snare, the Pharisees and Herodians begin with flattery. **They came and said to him, "Teacher, we know that you are a truthful man":** all that they say is correct, but on their lips the words are empty. Jesus is a **teacher,** but they do not accept his teachings. He is a **truthful man,** but they do not acknowledge the truth of what he says. **You are not concerned with anyone's opinion:** Jesus does not compromise himself to win acclaim—but then why do they try to flatter him? **You do not regard a person's status:** Jesus treats everyone the same, whether a Herodian or a housewife. They tell Jesus that he teaches **the way of God,** the way that God wants his people to follow, yet they do not accept that Jesus can declare what God wants. They say that Jesus teaches **in accordance with the truth:** they are beginning to repeat themselves.

After their smooth words comes the trap: **Is it lawful to pay the census tax to Caesar or not?** Asking **Is it lawful?** is a way of asking if it is in accordance with God's laws. The **census tax** was a Roman tax collected in areas under the rule of Roman governors. Rome imposed a governor on Judea in AD 6, and a census was taken to establish a list of those who had to pay this tax (hence it is called a **census tax**). Some Jews refused to pay taxes to Rome and rebelled at the time of this census (the rebellion is referred to in Acts 5:37). At the time of Jesus, the many Jews who thought God's people should not be ruled by foreigners resented paying taxes to Rome; Pharisees generally fell into this category. The minority who supported Roman rule naturally supported payment of Roman taxes; this minority included the Herodians.

The question put to Jesus is loaded and designed to ensnare him: **Is it lawful to pay the census tax to Caesar or not?** If Jesus opposes payment of taxes, the Herodians can report him to Roman authorities as a troublemaker trying to stir up another tax rebellion. Jesus may be arrested; the leader of a previous tax revolt apparently was executed by the Romans (Acts 5:37). If Jesus advocates payment of taxes to Rome, the Pharisees can portray him to the crowds as a lackey of Rome. Many of those who cried out, "Blessed is the kingdom of our father David that is to come!" as Jesus entered Jerusalem (11:10) probably hope that Jesus will deliver them from Roman rule, and they would be quite disappointed to hear that Jesus upholds Rome's right to tax. With his popular support undercut, Jesus would be vulnerable to the chief priests, scribes, and elders (11:18; 12:12).

BACKGROUND: ROMAN EMPIRE At the time of Jesus, the Roman Empire included all the lands bordering on the Mediterranean Sea and extended through western Europe as far as Britain. The Roman general Pompey had intervened in a Jewish civil war in 63 BC, conquering Jerusalem and pushing aside the ruling Jewish Hasmonean dynasty, thus bringing Palestine under Roman domination. This was a time of transition within the Roman government, as power became consolidated in an emperor and conquered lands gradually came under direct Roman rule. In this transitional period, Rome sometimes ruled through client kings, such as Herod the Great and his sons. The Roman government was content to have the Herods rule on its behalf as long as they did so competently, were loyal to Rome, and paid tribute (taxes). Some regions were ruled as Roman provinces by governors sent from Rome. Judea became a Roman province in AD 6 after Rome deposed Herod's son Archelaus for incompetence. During Jesus' public ministry, Pontius Pilate was the Roman governor of the province of Judea. In AD 66, many Jews rebelled against Roman rule, with disastrous consequences. Rome put down the revolt, destroying Jerusalem in AD 70. *Related topics: Herod Antipas (page 138), Pontius Pilate (page 415).*

Jesus does not seem to have any wiggle room: taxes are either paid or not paid. The Pharisees and Herodians restate their snare: **Should we pay or should we not pay?**

15 **Knowing their hypocrisy he said to them, "Why are you testing me?"** Their question was not a genuine question, asked to learn God's will, but a trap. They asked out of **hypocrisy,** making their question appear other than what it was. Jesus challenges their motives in putting their question to him: **Why are you testing me?** He does not wait for their response; they are hardly going to admit that their aim was to get him into trouble. Instead, Jesus demands, **Bring me a denarius to look at.** A **denarius** was a widely circulated Roman silver coin equivalent to a day's wages for an ordinary worker (the New American Bible translates *denarius* as "the usual daily wage" in Matt 20:2, 9–10). Jesus' asking them to bring him a denarius implies that he is not carrying one himself (Jesus might have carried no coins at all, for he instructed his disciples not to carry money when on mission: 6:8). Jesus wants **to look at** a denarius: what one sees on the coin has significance.

16 **They brought one to him:** his questioners have no trouble producing a denarius. Jesus **said to them, "Whose image and inscription is this?"** Coins were often stamped with the image of the ruler who issued them, along with an inscription identifying him. The Roman denarius bore the image of the Roman emperor, so **they replied to him, "Caesar's."** The current Roman emperor, or Caesar, was Tiberius, who ruled from AD 14 to 37. He had been adopted by the previous emperor, Augustus, and Tiberius's denarius bore the inscription "Tiberius Caesar Augustus, Son of the Divine Augustus." Hailing the emperor as divine was part of a growing cult of the emperor within Roman civil religion. On the other side of Tiberius's denarius was the inscription "Supreme Pontiff," a claim that Tiberius was the highest priest mediating between people and the gods. Such coins with their images and religious inscriptions were not acceptable for paying the Temple tax, which is why money changers were necessary (11:15).

17 **So Jesus said to them, "Repay to Caesar what belongs to Caesar."** Roman taxes had to be paid in Roman coins such as the denarius, so

Jesus may be understood as saying, "If you are going to use Roman coins, despite their pagan images and inscriptions, then you are taking on the obligation to pay Roman taxes as well." But Jesus means more than this. He tells his listeners to **repay** to the emperor what belongs to the emperor. Coins were thought of as in some sense the property of the one who minted them. The emperor's image on his coin was like a property seal, similar to the imprint of a signet ring on a blob of wax. Jesus is saying, "Give back to the emperor what belongs to him."

But that is not all that Jesus says. He adds, **And** repay **to God what belongs to God.** What belongs to God? In a real sense, everything: God created the universe (Psalm 24:1–2). However, we can find more specific meaning in Jesus' words. If the denarius belongs to the emperor because it bears the emperor's image, what belongs to God because it bears God's image? The answer: men and women. "Then God said: 'Let us make man in our image, after our likeness. . . . / God created man in his image; / in the divine image he created him; / male and female he created them" (Gen 1:26–27). We owe God our very selves. The emperor might have had a claim to the coins he minted, but God has a far greater claim to us.

> *For reflection: What does Jesus' reply mean to me? What do I owe government and society? What do I owe God?*

Jesus escapes the trap set for him. No one can argue against giving the emperor what belongs to him, and no one can argue against giving God what belongs to God. Those trying to ensnare Jesus are dumbfounded that he has escaped their snare: **they were utterly amazed at him.** Those who overheard the exchange are probably amazed as well.

Jesus' answer does not settle all questions regarding the relationship between Church and state: that would be asking too much of a saying that Jesus uttered to escape a snare. Jesus' answer does imply that God's claims have priority over all other claims. Mark's first readers probably understood Jesus' answer as a justification for paying taxes, even to a Roman government that promoted idolatrous practices. Paul had told the Christians of Rome to pay their taxes (Rom 13:1–7).

> *For reflection: Are there any situations in my life in which I must choose between what society expects of me and what God expects of me?*

Resurrection as Transformation

18 Some Sadducees, who say there is no resurrection, came to him and put this question to him, **19** saying, "Teacher, Moses wrote for us, 'If someone's brother dies, leaving a wife but no child, his brother must take the wife and raise up descendants for his brother.' **20** Now there were seven brothers. The first married a woman and died, leaving no descendants. **21** So the second married her and died, leaving no descendants, and the third likewise. **22** And the seven left no descendants. Last of all the woman also died. **23** At the resurrection [when they arise] whose wife will she be? For all seven had been married to her." **24** Jesus said to them, "Are you not misled because you do not know the scriptures or the power of God? **25** When they rise from the dead, they neither marry nor are given in marriage, but they are like the angels in heaven. **26** As for the dead being raised, have you not read in the Book of Moses, in the passage about the bush, how God told him, 'I am the God of Abraham, [the] God of Isaac, and [the] God of Jacob'? **27** He is not God of the dead but of the living. You are greatly misled."

Gospel parallels: Matt 22:23–33; Luke 20:27–40

OT: Exod 3:1–6; Deut 25:5–6; 2 Macc 7:20–29

NT: Acts 23:6–10; 1 Cor 15:35–58

18 **Some Sadducees, who say there is no resurrection, came to him:** this is the only appearance of **Sadducees** by name in the Gospel of Mark, although some of the chief priests, scribes, and elders who challenged

---

BACKGROUND: SADDUCEES were an aristocratic group or party centered in Jerusalem and largely made up of high-priestly families and members of the upper class. They were an elite and hence a rather small group within Jewish society. Sadducees were religiously conservative, upholding their own interpretation of the law of Moses and rejecting traditions developed by Pharisees. The Sadducees also rejected beliefs in a resurrection of the dead and new beliefs about angels that had arisen in the second century BC (see Acts 23:6–10). Sadducees cooperated with Roman rule in order to maintain their privileged status. Sadducees would have been uneasy about a rural carpenter coming to Jerusalem and preaching a message that threatened the status quo. Sadducees as an identifiable group did not survive the Roman destruction of Jerusalem in AD 70.

Jesus (11:27–28) might have belonged to the Sadducee party. **Sadducees** were a conservative elite who held to the written law and rejected new developments in Jewish thinking, including belief in an afterlife (Acts 23:8): they **say there is no resurrection.** Some Sadducees come to Jesus, who is still in the Temple precincts, **and put this question to him.** Jesus will again be asked a question that is not simply a question: the Sadducees likely already know Jesus' view on the resurrection and will raise the issue to dispute with him.

19 They say, **Teacher, Moses wrote for us, "If someone's brother dies, leaving a wife but no child, his brother must take the wife and raise up descendants for his brother."** They address Jesus as **teacher,** as one who can be held accountable for his views. They cite a law requiring a man to marry his brother's widow in order to perpetuate the name of his brother and keep property in the family, as well as provide for the care of his widow (Deut 25:5–6). It is doubtful whether this practice was followed at the time of Jesus, but since it was in the law of Moses, it provided a basis for the Sadducees' argument.

> *When brothers live together and one of them dies without a son, the widow of the deceased shall not marry anyone outside the family; but her husband's brother shall go to her and perform the duty of a brother-in-law by marrying her. The first-born son she bears shall continue the line of the deceased brother, that his name may not be blotted out from Israel.*
>
> Deut 25:5–6

20 **Now there were seven brothers. The first married a woman and died, leaving no descendants.** The Sadducees propose a test case involving **seven brothers:** the number **seven** has no special significance here other than to make this an extreme case involving multiple brothers. **Leaving no descendants** means leaving no male descendants, who could carry on the family name.

21 **So the second married her and died, leaving no descendants, and the third likewise.** By now it is becoming evident where the Sadducees' story is going.

22 The Sadducees jump ahead to the conclusion: **And the seven left no descendants. Last of all the woman also died.** Such a scenario is improbable to the point of absurdity, but the Sadducees' aim is to show the absurdity of belief in the resurrection.

23 The Sadducees ask Jesus, **At the resurrection [when they arise] whose wife will she be? For all seven had been married to her.** Their question is based on two premises. First, since a wife was in some sense the property of her husband, she could belong to only one man, even though a man might have more than one wife (Solomon was credited with seven hundred wives: 1 Kings 11:3). Second, the Sadducees assumed that resurrection, as their opponents pictured it, would return the dead to their previous state of life. Thus risen life would be like this life, so what was impossible in this life—a woman being married to more than one husband—would also be impossible in the next.

BACKGROUND: RESURRECTION While there was apparently no belief in an afterlife worth living during most of the Old Testament era, various hopes for the resurrection of the dead arose in the two centuries before Jesus. These hopes arose in conjunction with expectations that God would act to transform the world, ending the present age and inaugurating an age to come. One of the first hopes was that martyrs who had given up their lives for their faith would be raised to new life so that they could be part of God's new creation (2 Macc 6–7). The book of Daniel went a step further: not only would the righteous be raised to be part of God's reign, but the wicked would be raised as well, to be punished (Dan 12:2). How Jews of the time conceived of resurrected bodies depended on how they conceived of God's reign in the age to come. If the age to come was thought to be like the present age except that God would be in charge, then a person's body in the age to come would be like that person's present body (2 Macc 14:46). Some conceived of the age to come in less-earthly terms and thought that resurrected bodies would be heavenly bodies, making humans like angels. At the time of Jesus, some Jews, including Pharisees, believed in the resurrection of the dead, but other Jews, including Sadducees, did not (Acts 23:7–8). There was no uniform understanding of what the resurrection of the dead would be like. Rather, just as there were different views of how God would establish his reign and inaugurate an age to come, so there were different expectations of how those who had died would participate in his reign. *Related topics: The age to come (page 267), Jewish expectations at the time of Jesus (page 339), Judgment and Gehenna (page 241), Life after death (page 257).*

---

24 **Jesus said to them, "Are you not misled because you do not know the scriptures or the power of God?"** The Sadducees are **misled** in their thinking about resurrected life. They miss the mark because they understand neither **the scriptures,** that is, the collection of God's written word, nor **the power of God,** that is, what God is able to do. Jesus first speaks about what God is able to do:

25 **When they rise from the dead, they neither marry nor are given in marriage, but they are like the angels in heaven.** Resurrection from the dead does not mean a return to this present mode of life but entry into a transformed mode of life. Jesus compares this new mode of life to the life of **angels.** Jesus does not say that humans become angels through resurrection but that they become **like the angels.** In their risen state of life, men will not **marry** (take wives), nor will women be **given in marriage** (given by their fathers to husbands), for there will be no need to beget new

---

BACKGROUND: ANGELS The Hebrew and Greek words translated as angel also mean messenger, and angels appear in early Old Testament writings as messengers of God. These messengers are not always clearly distinguished from manifestations of God himself (Gen 16:7–13; Exod 3:2–6). Some Scripture passages speak of members of God's heavenly court, sometimes calling them sons of God, meaning heavenly beings (Job 1:6), or calling them the host (army) of heaven (1 Kings 22:19–22), an expression that can also refer to stars (Deut 4:19). Cherubim are heavenly beings too (Gen 3:24; Ezek 1:5–11; 10:18–20). Thus the Old Testament speaks of a variety of heavenly beings without relating them to one another, without calling all of them angels, and without defining their nature. Individual angels are not named until late Old Testament writings; Raphael (Tobit 5:4; 12:15), Gabriel (Dan 8:16), and Michael (Dan 10:13) are the only three angels named in the Old Testament. Michael, the prince (or guardian angel) of God's people (Dan 12:1), contends with other heavenly beings who are the guardians of other nations (Dan 10:13, 20–21). Speculations about angels multiplied late in the Old Testament era and are reflected in Jewish writings that did not become part of Scripture. The perplexing account in Genesis of "the sons of heaven" who had intercourse with women (Gen 6:1–4) developed into a story of the fall of some angels who led humans into sin. The chief of the fallen angels was given various names, including Satan. At the time of Jesus, angels were generally thought of as human in form (Dan 8:15–16) but with heavenly rather than earthly bodies, not needing to eat or drink (Tobit 12:19). *Related topics: Nonbiblical writings (page 243), Satan (page 71).*

generations to replace older generations as they die. Jesus' words may be interpreted to mean that there will be no new marriages in heaven, not that existing marriages will be dissolved. However, Jesus' basic point is that the next life will be different from this life, and human relationships will be transformed, so the Sadducees' problem will not arise.

We might wish that Jesus had said more about what resurrected life will be like: we would like to know what awaits us. Perhaps, however, the reality of the next life is not something that can be captured in words. Paul had to struggle to find comparisons for what we would be like after we had been raised from the dead (1 Cor 15:35–58).

For reflection: How do I conceive of life after death? Am I able to imagine what I will be like after God raises me?

Hope for resurrected life does not depend on knowing what it will be like; our hope is based on our confidence in the power of God (verse 24). One expression of confidence in God's power to raise the dead is found in a story in Second Maccabees, a book whose beliefs were accepted by some Jews at the time of Jesus. A mother had seven sons who were being martyred for remaining faithful to the Jewish law. She encouraged them in their hope that God would raise them to life after they were martyred, reminding them that God had made the heavens and the earth and the human race out of nothing (2 Macc 7:28) and had mysteriously formed her sons and given them life in her womb (2 Macc 7:22). "Therefore, since it is the Creator of the universe who shapes each man's beginning, as he brings about the origin of everything, he, in his mercy, will give you back both breath and life" in the resurrection (2 Macc 7:23). If God had the power to bring this vast universe into being out of nothing and to create the marvel of human life, then God likewise has the power to raise us from the dead and give us transformed life. Jesus might never have read Second Maccabees (it was written in Greek), but he would have commended this mother's insightful faith in the power of God.

For reflection: Am I confident that it is within God's power to raise me from the dead?

26 Jesus turns from what God in his power is able to do to what is written in the Scriptures. **As for the dead being raised, have you not read in the Book of Moses, in the passage about the bush:** Jesus cannot cite chapter and verse because the books of Scripture had not yet been divided into chapters and verses. Jesus instead directs the Sadducees' attention to the **Book of Moses,** that is, to what we read as the first five books of the Old Testament, which are books that the Sadducees accepted as authoritative. Jesus refers them to **the passage about the bush,** that is, to what we read as Exod 3:1–6. Jesus reminds the Sadducees of **how God,** speaking from the burning bush, **told** Moses, **I am the God of Abraham, [the] God of Isaac, and [the] God of Jacob.** Abraham, Isaac, and Jacob died centuries before the time of Moses. Yet God does not say that he used to be their God when they were alive; God says that he is their God.

> God said, "Come no nearer! Remove the sandals from
> your feet, for the place where you stand is holy ground.
> I am the God of your father," he continued, "the God of
> Abraham, the God of Isaac, the God of Jacob."
>
> Exod 3:5–6

27 Jesus proclaims, **He is not God of the dead but of the living.** From God's words in this passage Jesus draws the conclusion that Abraham, Isaac, and Jacob must still have life, even though they have died, because God speaks of himself as being their God, as if they are still alive. Jesus does not say how they have life after death; Jesus says only that Abraham, Isaac, and Jacob are among the living because God speaks of them that way in Scripture.

Even though the text from Exodus says nothing explicit about the resurrection, it does bear an implicit message. Through the resurrection of the dead we will continue in the next life the relationship with God that we have begun in this life. If God is our God now, God will continue to be our God after death. He will raise us so that we can continue our relationship with him and will transform us so that we can enter into it more fully.

For reflection: How does God need to transform me so that I can be united with him? What aspects of this transformation can take place in this life?

Jesus' concluding words to the Sadducees are **You are greatly misled.** If you think there is no foreshadowing of the resurrection of the dead in Scripture, you do not understand Scripture. If you think rising from the dead is impossible, you have no inkling of the power of God, who can do the impossible (10:27).

The Greatest Commandment

28 One of the scribes, when he came forward and heard them disputing and saw how well he had answered them, asked him, "Which is the first of all the commandments?" 29 Jesus replied, "The first is this: 'Hear, O Israel! The Lord our God is Lord alone! 30 You shall love the Lord your God with all your heart, with all your soul, with all your mind, and with all your strength.' 31 The second is this: 'You shall love your neighbor as yourself.' There is no other commandment greater than these." 32 The scribe said to him, "Well said, teacher. You are right in saying, 'He is One and there is no other than he.' 33 And 'to love him with all your heart, with all your understanding, with all your strength, and to love your neighbor as yourself' is worth more than all burnt offerings and sacrifices." 34 And when Jesus saw that [he] answered with understanding, he said to him, "You are not far from the kingdom of God." And no one dared to ask him any more questions.

Gospel parallels: Matt 22:34–40; Luke 10:25–28

OT: Lev 19:18; Deut 6:4–5

NT: 1 John 4:20–21

28 **One of the scribes, when he came forward and heard them disputing and saw how well he had answered them:** one of the **scribes** (a religious scholar and a teacher of the law of Moses) overheard Jesus' response to the Sadducees who had questioned him about the resurrection of the dead (12:18–27) and was impressed by **how well he had answered them.** Scribes have often criticized Jesus (2:6–7, 16; 3:22; 7:1–5); this particular scribe, however, seems to have professional

admiration for Jesus' knowledge of Scripture and ability to deal with a difficult matter. This scribe asks Jesus, as one scholar might seek the opinion of a fellow scholar on a debated issue, **Which is the first of all the commandments?** There are many commands in the law of Moses (613, by one count), and all of them have to be kept, but some are surely more important than others. Which commandment is the most fundamental?

Scribes: See page 40

29 **Jesus replied, "The first is this: 'Hear, O Israel! The Lord our God is Lord alone!'"** Jesus responds by quoting from Deuteronomy (Deut 6:4). These words form the beginning of a prayer that devout Jews recited twice daily, a prayer the scribe would have known well. This prayer (called the Shema, which is Hebrew for Hear!) begins with a profession of faith in the God of Israel as the only God. The call to **hear** is not simply a call to listen but also an exhortation to respond. If the God of Israel is truly God, the only God, the one who created the universe, then we must respond accordingly.

> *Hear, O Israel! The LORD is our God, the LORD*
> *alone! Therefore, you shall love the LORD, your God,*
> *with all your heart, and with all your soul, and with*
> *all your strength.*
>
> Deut 6:4–5

For reflection: What are the implications for me of there being a God? Do I treat God as God?

30 Jesus continues to cite the words of Deuteronomy (and the Jewish daily prayer): **You shall love the Lord your God with all your heart, with all your soul, with all your mind, and with all your strength** (see Deut 6:5). What God commands of us is a response to who God is. If God is God, if God brought us into existence and holds us in being, then his claim to us is total, and our response to him must be total. The "first of all the commandments" (verse 28) calls for this total response—for our repaying to God what belongs to God (12:17). **You shall love the Lord your God with all your heart:** the **heart**

was considered the core of a person, the source of one's intentions and actions. To **love** God with all our **heart** does not simply mean to have affection for God but also to love God wholeheartedly, from the depths of our being. **Love** is putting another person first, seeking another's good rather than our own, serving the one we love. To **love the Lord your God with all your heart** means to make God absolutely first, completely subordinating yourself to him.

The Hebrew word translated **soul** means the whole person as a living being; to love God **with all your soul** means to give yourself totally to God, putting God first in every area of your life. Jesus expands the text of Deuteronomy by adding that we are to love God with all our **mind,** with all our thoughts and understanding. We must be single-minded in our love of God, carefully considering how we can better love him. Finally, we are commanded to love God with all our **strength,** with all we have, with every ounce of our energy.

Jesus' speaking of **heart, soul, mind,** and **strength** is not a systematic listing of human faculties but a way of saying that we are to throw our whole being into loving God. We are to love God completely, totally, absolutely, with nothing held back. The first commandment is breathtaking in what it demands of us. But if God is God, how else can we properly respond to him?

For reflection: How do I love God? How much do I love God? What does this first commandment ask of me?

31 The scribe asked Jesus which was the "first of all the commandments" (verse 28), but Jesus immediately adds a second commandment, as if his answer would be incomplete without it. **The second is this: "You shall love your neighbor as yourself."** This is also a commandment found in the law of Moses, in the book of Leviticus (Lev 19:18). It is sometimes interpreted as saying that we ought to have a proper love for ourselves. We probably should, but that is not the intent of this law or the reason Jesus held it up as the second of all the commandments. Rather, the presumption is that we know how to take care of ourselves and put ourselves ahead of others. God, however, requires us to be as concerned for others as we are for ourselves, to care for others as we care for ourselves, to treat

others as our equals instead of as our inferiors, to **love** them as much as we instinctively love ourselves.

> Take no revenge and cherish no grudge against your fellow countrymen. You shall love your neighbor as yourself.
>
> Lev 19:18

For reflection: Whom has God entrusted to my love? What do I do out of love for them?

By joining this second command to the first, Jesus links love of neighbor with love of God and treats them as inseparable. If they are inseparable, then love of God is not only incomplete but also impossible without love of fellow human beings. The first letter of John will state it quite bluntly: "If anyone says, 'I love God,' but hates his brother, he is a liar; for whoever does not love a brother whom he has seen cannot love God whom he has not seen. This is the commandment we have from him: whoever loves God must also love his brother" (1 John 4:20–21).

For reflection: How do I understand the linkage between love of God and love of neighbor? How do I experience this linkage in my life?

The second commandment is phrased in terms of loving one's **neighbor.** In the context of Leviticus, one's neighbor was one's countryman, a fellow Israelite. When Jesus joins the second commandment to the first, prefaced by the statement that "the Lord our God is Lord alone," he provides grounds for enlarging the definition of **neighbor.** If there is only one God, then God is the God of all (whether they recognize God or not). If there is only one God, then every human being, having been created by God, is our neighbor. We do not worship a God who is God only of our own tribe or country; we worship the God who is Lord of all and who asks for our love to be as broad as his.

For reflection: What are the boundaries of my love?

Jesus concludes his answer to the scribe by saying, **There is no other commandment greater than these.** Nothing else is more urgent than loving God with all our heart, soul, mind, and strength and loving our neighbor as we love ourselves. God makes no greater demand of us, and nothing is more important for us to do.

32 **The scribe said to him, "Well said, teacher. You are right in saying, 'He is One and there is no other than he.'"** By addressing Jesus as **teacher** and saying **You are right,** the scribe recognizes Jesus' mastery of the Mosaic law and acknowledges Jesus' right to instruct him. The scribe then repeats in his own words what he has learned from Jesus—a sign that he has really understood. **He is One and there is no other than he:** the scribe adds the phrase **there is no other than he,** an expression used in the Old Testament to affirm that there is only one God (Deut 4:35, 39; 1 Kings 8:60; Isaiah 45:5–6, 18, 21–22).

33 The scribe continues, **And "to love him with all your heart, with all your understanding, with all your strength, and to love your neighbor as yourself" is worth more than all burnt offerings and sacrifices:** the scribe echoes Jesus' words as if they formed a single commandment. The scribe then adds that obeying this command **is worth more than all burnt offerings and sacrifices.** The term **burnt offerings** refers to sacrifices where the offering is completely consumed in the sacrificial fire; the term translated **sacrifices** means sacrifices where some of the offering is not burned up and is eaten by worshipers. **Burnt offerings and sacrifices** were the most important forms of worship in the Temple, yet this scribe says that loving God and neighbor **is worth more than** they. While there is ample basis in the Old Testament for saying this (1 Sam 15:22; Psalms 40:7–9; 51:18–19; Isaiah 1:11–17; Jer 7:21–23; Hosea 6:6; Amos 5:21–25; Micah 6:6–8), it would still take a bit of boldness to do so in the Temple precincts, where the scribe is conversing with Jesus.

34 **And when Jesus saw that [he] answered with understanding:** the scribe has grasped the point of Jesus' teaching and realizes that love of God and neighbor outweighs all sacrificial rituals. Jesus in turn **said to him, "You are not far from the kingdom of God."** Jesus was God's

agent in establishing the reign of God on earth. After announcing that the kingdom of God was at hand (1:15), Jesus began to call men and women to be his disciples (1:16–20). Those who became the new family of Jesus (3:34–35) were coming into the reign of God. This scribe was **not far from the kingdom of God:** he is not a disciple of Jesus, but he grasps what is at the heart of living under the reign of God. Jesus' new family is made up of those who do the will of God (3:35); this scribe understands what God expects.

Kingdom of God: See page 96

Mark does not tell us what became of this scribe. Did he simply continue on with his life? Did he take the next step and become a disciple of Jesus? Mark, in his brief account of the good news of Jesus, leaves some loose ends.

Mark's account ends with **and no one dared to ask him any more questions.** Jesus has been challenged and questioned by various parties but has met the challenges and answered the questions (11:27–12:31). His opponents have been reduced to silence but have hardly been eliminated as opponents.

In the context of Jesus' ministry, his singling out love of God and love of neighbor as the most important commandments meant that all the other commandments were based on them and spelled out how one was to love God and neighbor. Mark's first readers would have found an additional meaning in Jesus' exchange with the scribe. Love of God and love of neighbor were more important than sacrificial offerings, and such offerings would come to an end when the Temple was destroyed, as Jesus will shortly foretell (13:1–2). Christians would not be bound by all the prescriptions of the Mosaic law, particularly those having to do with ritual and sacrifice; Christians would be bound by what was at the heart of the law: love of God and love of others.

David's Son and Lord

35 As Jesus was teaching in the temple area he said, "How do the scribes claim that the Messiah is the son of David? 36 David himself, inspired by the holy Spirit, said:

329

> 'The Lord said to my lord,
> "Sit at my right hand
>   until I place your enemies under your feet."'

37 David himself calls him 'lord'; so how is he his son?" [The] great crowd heard this with delight.

Gospel parallels: Matt 22:41–46; Luke 20:41–44

OT: 2 Sam 7:11–16; Psalms 89:20–38; 110:1; Isaiah 9:5–6; 11:1–9;
    Jer 23:5–6; 33:14–17; Ezek 34:23–24; 37:24–28

NT: Matt 1:6–23; Mark 10:47–48; Luke 1:30–33; 3:23–31; John 7:42;
    Rom 1:3–4

35 **As Jesus was teaching in the temple area:** the setting continues to be the Temple precincts. Jesus has so skillfully answered the questions put to him that no one dares ask him any more questions (12:34). Jesus now asks a question of his own. Bartimaeus hailed Jesus as "son of David" (10:47–48). What does it mean to call Jesus "son of David"? Jesus raises the issue by asking, **How do the scribes claim that the Messiah is the son of David?** Jesus' question implies that it somehow misses the mark to think of **the Messiah** as **the son of David.** Those listening to Jesus probably wondered what was wrong with this view. Certain prophecies spoke of a descendant of David reigning (Isaiah 9:5–6; 11:1–9; Jer 23:5–6; 33:14–17; Ezek 34:23–24; 37:24–27) in fulfillment of God's promises to David (2 Sam 7:11–16; Psalm 89:20–38). Many Jews referred to this descendant of David as **the Messiah.** The *Psalms of Solomon*, a nonbiblical writing from the century before Jesus, called the Messiah **the son of David.** Jesus is certainly aware of these prophecies and messianic expectations; why is he questioning **how** the **Messiah** can be the **son of David**?

Messiah, Christ: See page 204

Son of David: See page 281

Psalms of Solomon: See page 207

36 Jesus says that **David himself, inspired by the holy Spirit, said: / "The Lord said to my lord, / 'Sit at my right hand / until I place your enemies under your feet.'"** Jesus follows the Jewish tradition of ascribing Psalm 110 to David and quotes the first verse of this psalm.

Jesus characterizes David's words in Psalm 110 as **inspired by the holy Spirit**—and, by extension, characterizes all of Scripture as **inspired.**

> *A psalm of David.*
>
> *The* LORD *says to you, my lord:*
> *"Take your throne at my right hand,*
> *while I make your enemies your footstool."*
>
> Psalm 110:1

The Lord said to my lord: the first **Lord** is God. Psalm 110 uses the Hebrew word *YHWH* as the personal name for God; out of reverence, Jews did not speak this name but pronounced a form of the Hebrew word for **Lord** when they came to it in their reading of Scripture. Jesus interprets the second **lord** to be the Messiah. Jesus understands Psalm 110 as David saying, **The Lord** God **said to my lord** the Messiah, **"Sit at my right hand / until I place your enemies under your feet."** God invites the Messiah to sit at his right hand, the position of power and honor (10:37), until God defeats the Messiah's enemies and places them under the Messiah's feet.

37 Jesus continues, **David himself calls him "lord"; so how is he his son?** If David refers to the Messiah as his **lord,** then how can the Messiah be

---

BACKGROUND: GOD'S NAME The word *God* is the generic name for the Supreme Being. In addition to the generic Hebrew word for God, the Old Testament also uses the personal name for God, which in Hebrew is written with letters that correspond to the English letters *YHWH*. Biblical Hebrew was written without vowels, and thus it is impossible to be certain how this name was pronounced; it may have been pronounced "Yahweh." The Old Testament presents God revealing his name, *YHWH*, to Moses at the burning bush (Exod 3:15). Out of reverence, Jews in the time of Jesus (as still today) avoided saying the name of God; when they read Scripture aloud and came to the name *YHWH* they substituted a form of the Hebrew for "Lord." When the Hebrew Scriptures were translated into Greek some two hundred years before the time of Jesus, the translators used the Greek word for Lord to translate *YHWH*. The Old Testament of the New American Bible uses the word LORD (printed with a capital and small capitals) to stand for the Hebrew *YHWH*.

---

the son of David? A father does not call his son his **lord** but the other way around (the son who addresses his father as "sir" in Matt 21:30 literally addresses him as "lord" in the Greek text). If the Messiah is David's **lord,** then it is inadequate to think of the Messiah as being merely a descendant of David. **[The] great crowd heard this with delight:** they grasp the point that Jesus is making and delight in his perceptive reasoning. The fact that a **great crowd** has admiration for Jesus is a deterrent, for the moment, to those who seek his death (11:18; 12:12).

When Peter hailed Jesus as the Messiah (8:29), Jesus did not reject the title, although he redefined what it meant for him to be the Messiah (8:30–33). Likewise, when Bartimaeus hailed Jesus as the "son of David" (10:47–48), Jesus did not deny that he was the descendant of David who had come in fulfillment of prophecies. Nor did Jesus rebuke the crowd who welcomed him to Jerusalem with the shout "Blessed is the kingdom of our father David that is to come" (11:10). But Jesus is more than a warrior son of David, and the kingdom that Jesus proclaims is not a reestablishment of David's empire. It is inadequate to think of Jesus as merely David's son; Jesus is someone whom David could call his lord and whom God will seat at his right hand.

As the time of his dying and rising draws near, Jesus begins to unveil his identity. He implies that he is God's beloved Son (12:6). He is a stone that will be rejected, but God will make him the cornerstone of a new edifice (12:10–11). He hints that he is the Messiah, the son of David yet

---

BACKGROUND: LORD The Greek word for lord is *kyrios,* familiar to many in the form in which it occurs in the petition *Kyrie, eleison* (Lord, have mercy)—Greek words used in a Latin liturgy. A *kyrios,* or lord, is someone who has power and authority; thus the word has wide application. The owner of a property could be called its *kyrios* (the "owner of the vineyard" in Mark 12:9 is literally the "lord of the vineyard"). A master would be addressed as lord by his servants, but anyone could also use *lord* as a polite form of address to another, much as the English word *sir* is used (see John 12:21). At the other extreme, Scripture uses the word *Lord* as a title for God (Psalm 114:7; Luke 1:32; Rev 1:8). Because of this range of usage, when Jesus is called *kyrios* by someone in the Gospels, it can simply be a respectful form of address (translated as "sir" in John 4:19) or an acknowledgment that he is someone with authority (the meaning of "lord" in Matt 8:21 and Luke 7:6) or a declaration that he can be called Lord as God is called Lord (the meaning of "Lord" in John 20:28 and Phil 2:11).

also David's lord; risen from the dead he will be seated at the right hand of God as God completes the establishment of his kingdom.

For reflection: Who is Jesus? Who is Jesus for me?

Jesus' use of Psalm 110 may provide insight into Jesus' humanity. Jesus accepted the Jewish tradition that Psalm 110 was written by David. This tradition is reflected in the heading "A psalm of David," which has been added to Psalm 110 but is generally not considered part of the inspired text. Scripture scholars believe that Psalm 110 was written after the time of David to celebrate the enthronement of a king. If this is correct, then Jesus was relying on a historically inaccurate tradition when he ascribed this psalm to David. Jesus' knowledge reflected views held at the time in which he lived. It would appear that Jesus, like us in every way except for sin, was not omniscient, even if he did have prophetic foresight into such matters as his death and rising.

For reflection: Except for Jesus' sinlessness, do I place any limits on Jesus' fully sharing my human condition?

The Dangers of Honors

38 In the course of his teaching he said, "Beware of the scribes, who like to go around in long robes and accept greetings in the marketplaces, 39 seats of honor in synagogues, and places of honor at banquets. 40 They devour the houses of widows and, as a pretext, recite lengthy prayers. They will receive a very severe condemnation."

Gospel parallels: Luke 20:45–47
NT: Matt 23:5–7; Mark 9:33–37; 10:42–45

38 Jesus is still in the Temple precincts, and **in the course of his teaching he said, "Beware of the scribes."** Jesus' admonition to **beware** of **scribes** (scholars and teachers of the Mosaic law) means to be wary of and discerning about them. Although Jesus has just commended one scribe (12:34), some scribes **like to go around in long robes and accept greetings in the marketplaces.** The exact design of these **long**

robes is uncertain (everyone normally wore a long outer garment), but there was something distinctive about these robes that indicated that those who wore them were scribes. That seems to have been the point of wearing such robes: to be recognized as a scribe and given public honors, such as **greetings in the marketplaces.**

Scribes: See page 40
Clothing: See page 117

39 These scribes take **seats of honor in synagogues**—literally, the first seats. Synagogues commonly had a bench along the front wall, in front of the cabinet containing the scrolls of Scripture; those seated on the bench faced the congregation. The scribes Jesus is speaking of also take **places of honor at banquets,** near the host. Jesus teaches, Be wary of those who relish honors and behave in a way that invites honors. Be wary as well of wanting honors for yourself. The greatest among you is the one who is last of all and servant of all (9:35); the first among you is the one who is slave of all (10:44). Servants and slaves hardly sat in **places of honor at banquets:** they were the ones serving the food.

Synagogue: See page 57

Is Jesus being unfair to those whose roles call for them to sit in places of honor and wear distinctive garments? Perhaps Jesus is pointing out occupational hazards. Some of us will find ourselves in positions of leadership or prominence, whether in the Church or in other spheres of life. We must carry out our duties without letting our status go to our heads. We must be especially wary of using our status to gain the deference and praise of others.

For reflection: What warning do I hear in Jesus' words?

40 Jesus' next charge against the scribes is more serious: **They devour the houses of widows and, as a pretext, recite lengthy prayers.** Because men were the breadwinners in Israelite society, the law of Moses commanded special care of **widows** (Deut 14:28–29; 24:17, 21; 26:12–13). Prophets denounced those who defrauded helpless people such as widows (Isaiah 10:1–4; Mal 3:5). It is not clear what the scribes did to **devour the houses of widows.** One possibility: some scribes embezzled from widows'

estates that they managed. Another possibility: some scribes used religion to browbeat poor widows into giving them money. The second possibility makes sense in light of the **pretext** of reciting **lengthy prayers.** The length of one's prayers is not necessarily an index of the quality of one's prayers, or even their sincerity. Jesus criticized scribes who used their status as a way of getting honors (verses 38–39); now he deals with a more serious corruption: the scribes' using their status to exploit the weak for financial gain. Enjoying honors can lead to a sense of entitlement and to taking advantage of others in order to maintain one's status and comforts. Jesus warns that those who do this **will receive a very severe condemnation.** Jesus is referring to the day of judgment, when God will deal with each person.

Judgment and Gehenna: See page 241

For reflection: Do I in any way take advantage of those who are weak and vulnerable?

A Woman Who Gives Everything

⁴¹ He sat down opposite the treasury and observed how the crowd put money into the treasury. Many rich people put in large sums. ⁴² A poor widow also came and put in two small coins worth a few cents. ⁴³ Calling his disciples to himself, he said to them, "Amen, I say to you, this poor widow put in more than all the other contributors to the treasury. ⁴⁴ For they have all contributed from their surplus wealth, but she, from her poverty, has contributed all she had, her whole livelihood."

Gospel parallels: Luke 21:1–4

41 Jesus **sat down opposite the treasury** of the Temple: the Temple functioned as a Jewish national bank, with savings as well as donations kept in its **treasury** (see 2 Macc 3:1–22). Jesus **observed how the crowd put money into the treasury.** According to a later Jewish writing, there were thirteen boxes for donations around the edge of the Court of the Women. Jesus **observed** people putting **money** in these boxes—and probably heard it as well: the word translated **money** means metal coins, which would clank when thrown

into the receptacles. **Many rich people put in large sums:** did they do so ostentatiously, with much clanking?

42 **A poor widow also came and put in two small coins worth a few cents.** The word here translated **coins** denotes the smallest coin in circulation in Palestine at the time; the widow has two of them and donates both to the Temple. To explain to his Roman readers the value of her donation, Mark adds that her coins were **worth a few cents,** using the name of the smallest coin circulated in Rome—an insignificant amount.

43 Jesus does not view her donation as insignificant. He wants his followers to see the meaning of her act, so **calling his disciples to himself, he said to them, "Amen, I say to you, this poor widow put in more than all the other contributors to the treasury."** His disciples may wonder, *How can that be true? Her little coins barely made a clink, while the donations of others raised a racket. How could she have* **put in more than all the other contributors?**

44 Jesus explains his reasoning: **They have all contributed from their surplus wealth, but she, from her poverty, has contributed all she had, her whole livelihood.** God measures donations by what is kept rather than by what is given. It is fine to give from one's **surplus,** from what one does not need to live on. But giving from **wealth** cannot compare to giving from **poverty,** giving away what one needs to survive. This woman **contributed all she had,** giving away **her whole livelihood.** She could have kept one coin for herself, but she didn't. The Greek word translated **livelihood** is also the word for life: in giving her **whole livelihood,** this widow gave her life, entrusting herself to God.

For reflection: What does the example of this woman mean to me?

Jesus' words about the widow admit of more than one interpretation. If we focus only on this scene, Jesus seems to be praising the generosity of the woman. However, if we consider the background of this scene, we might interpret Jesus' words not as praise but as a lament. Why was this widow poor in the first place? God's intention for his people was that "there should be no one of you in need" (Deut 15:4), and the law of

Moses commanded help for poor people such as widows (Deut 14:28–29; 24:17, 21; 26:12–13). Was her being down to her last two cents a symptom of a religious leadership and a society that were callous to the poor? Was she a widow who had been victimized by those who devoured the houses of widows (12:40)? Had she been encouraged to donate her livelihood to the Temple out of a sense of religious obligation? Jesus consistently placed human needs above religiosity (2:23–28; 3:1–5; 7:9–13). Were not this woman's needs of greater weight than the Temple's? Jesus will shortly teach that the Temple in all its magnificence will become rubble (13:1–2); did Jesus lament this woman giving the little she had to a lost cause? Sermons sometimes make this widow a poster child for stewardship and tithing, but this passage is an example of Scripture being a two-edged sword (Heb 4:12), able to cut in more than one direction.

Still, there is great meaning in this woman's giving of all she had. This widow did what she could to repay to God all that belonged to God (12:17): she gave her **whole livelihood,** her whole life. Loving God with all one's strength (12:30) means with all one's resources, including possessions, and she gave **all she had.** Jesus will give his life to carry out God's will (8:31; 10:45); in her own way, this widow also surrendered her life to God. Jesus might have lamented a religious system that took the last two coins of a poor woman for the upkeep of an extravagant Temple, but Jesus could have had only praise for this woman.

For reflection: What are the lessons of this incident for me?

CHAPTER 13

The End of the Temple
¹ As he was making his way out of the temple area one of his disciples said to him, "Look, teacher, what stones and what buildings!" ² Jesus said to him, "Do you see these great buildings? There will not be one stone left upon another that will not be thrown down."

³ As he was sitting on the Mount of Olives opposite the temple area, Peter, James, John, and Andrew asked him privately, ⁴ "Tell us, when will this happen, and what sign will there be when all these things are about to come to an end?"

Gospel parallels: Matt 24:1–3; Luke 21:5–7

1 **As he was making his way out of the temple area:** Jesus had been in the Temple precincts since early morning (11:20, 27). **One of his disciples said to him, "Look, teacher, what stones and what buildings!"** The thirty-five-acre Temple complex that Herod the Great built was truly impressive. Some of the limestone blocks in the retaining walls around the Temple platform weigh more than one hundred tons. (The blocks used to build the pyramids in Egypt generally weigh around two and a half tons.) **What stones** indeed! The colonnaded hall along the south end of the Temple mount had four rows of forty columns, each fifty feet high. The Temple building itself was faced with marble and gold, virtually blinding those who gazed at it in the sun. **What buildings** indeed! It would have been quite a sight for Galilean fishermen who lived in rather simple houses.

Temple: See page 294

2 Jesus does not seem to have been impressed with the grandeur of the Temple complex. He may have judged that Herod had built it not to glorify God but to glorify Herod, to display his wealth and testify to his building skills (why else use such huge stones?). **Jesus said to him, "Do you see these great buildings? There will not be one stone left upon another that will not be thrown down."** All these **great buildings** will **be thrown down** and become rubble! But these buildings were not

simply Herod's monument to himself. In the center of the complex stood the Temple of God, the place of God's special presence on earth. If **not one stone** of it will be left standing, then there will no longer be a building that is the place of God's special presence. The destruction of the Temple will mean a change in God's relationship with his people.

Jesus does not spell out the implications of the Temple being destroyed. Nor does he say how it will happen or why it will happen. He simply states that it will happen.

3 After leaving the Temple complex, Jesus and his disciples go east across the Kidron Valley and climb the Mount of Olives on their way back to Bethany, where they have been staying at night (11:11–12; 14:3). They stop at or near the top of the Mount of Olives, which provides a bird's-eye view of the Temple and Jerusalem. The disciples want to know more about the destruction of the Temple. **As he was sitting on the**

BACKGROUND: JEWISH EXPECTATIONS AT THE TIME OF JESUS Jews were ruled by Rome or by Rome's client kings, and their taxes were burdensome. The high priest served at the pleasure of Roman authority. Devout Jews revered the Temple, but many had low regard for those who controlled it. The situation Jews found themselves in fell far short of what God had seemingly promised his people through prophecy: rule by a descendant of David, an era of peace and prosperity, God manifestly dwelling in his Temple in Jerusalem, Gentiles either turning to the God of Israel or being subject to the rule of Israel, and God's spirit being poured out. Any Jew who took these prophecies seriously had to be struck by the disparity between how things were and how prophecies promised they would be. Hopes and expectations were fanned by various nonbiblical writings in the two centuries before Jesus. These writings spoke of God acting soon to set things right. Different Jewish groups envisioned different scenarios for what God would do. Some expected God to act directly; some expected God to act through one or more messiahs. Some foresaw the conversion of Gentiles to allegiance to the God of Israel; others foresaw their destruction. Some thought the end of the present age was near and that God's final triumph over evil was not far off. While there was no agreement over how God would bring an end to the unsatisfactory situation in which God's people found themselves, many shared the expectation that God would do something about it. *Related topics: The age to come (page 267), Kingdom of God (page 96), Messiah, Christ (page 204), Nonbiblical writings (page 243).*

Mount of Olives opposite the temple area, Peter, James, John, and Andrew asked him privately: they were the first four disciples Jesus called (1:16–20), and **Peter, James,** and **John** form the inner circle of Jesus' followers (5:37; 9:2). Jesus has often instructed his disciples and answered their questions **privately** (4:10, 34; 7:17; 9:28; 10:10), and the four disciples want him to do so again.

4 They ask, **Tell us, when will this happen, and what sign will there be when all these things are about to come to an end?** They do not ask why the Temple will be destroyed or how it will happen but when it will happen. They ask, **When will this happen?**—literally, when will *these things* be?—as if the destruction of the Temple will not be an isolated incident, like an asteroid hitting the Temple, but part of a larger series of events. The disciples want to know **when** these events will happen and **what sign will there be when all these things are about to come to an end.** The expression **these things** again refers to the destruction of the Temple and the events associated with it. **Come to an end** can mean be accomplished, completed, fulfilled. Are the disciples asking what **sign** there will be that the present age is **about to come to an end,** as if the destruction of the Temple will mean the beginning of the age to come? Jesus will address broader concerns than the destruction of the Temple in his response.

For reflection: What are my questions—or anxieties—about the future?

ORIENTATION: *The disciples have asked for the sign that things are coming to an end. Jesus tells them that they must be discerning: events that are taken as signs of the end are in fact not.*

The End Is Not at Hand
⁵ **Jesus began to say to them, "See that no one deceives you. ⁶ Many will come in my name saying, 'I am he,' and they will deceive many. ⁷ When you hear of wars and reports of wars do not be alarmed; such things must happen, but it will not yet be the end. ⁸ Nation will rise against nation and kingdom against kingdom.**

There will be earthquakes from place to place and there will be famines. These are the beginnings of the labor pains."

Gospel parallels: Matt 24:4–8; Luke 21:8–11

5 **Jesus began to say to them:** the Greek could also be translated *but* **Jesus began to say to them.** Jesus has been asked, "What sign will there be when all these things are about to come to an end?" (13:4), but instead of identifying such a sign Jesus warns his disciples, **See that no one deceives you.** This injunction to "see" or "watch out" is the keynote of Jesus' long discourse in chapter 13 (the same Greek expression is used in verses 5, 9, 23, and 33), just as his injunction to "hear" was the keynote in his "Sermon on the Sea" (4:1–9). To **see** or be watchful means to be perceptive and wary, to be on one's guard against being led astray. The disciples are looking for signs, but Jesus tells them, **See that no one deceives you.**

6 For there will be deceivers. **Many will come in my name saying, "I am he," and they will deceive many.** Those who **come in** the **name** of Jesus but **deceive** could be false prophets who claim that the end is at hand. Their **saying, "I am he"** is harder to understand; Jesus might be saying that they will make some sort of messianic claim. The message for the disciples—and for Mark's readers—is to be wary of those who claim to be heralds of the end.

7 Jesus now turns to events that might be interpreted as signs that the end is at hand. **When you hear of wars and reports of wars do not be alarmed; such things must happen, but it will not yet be the end.** There will be wars, but they are not signs that this age is ending: **it will not yet be the end.** Jews in Palestine revolted against Roman rule in AD 66; Mark's first readers may have wondered whether this doomed revolt was a signal of the end. Jesus' words should have assured them that it was not. Jesus says that wars **must happen,** an expression that indicates that future events are in the hands of God.

8 **Nation will rise against nation and kingdom against kingdom,** but such conflicts are not signs of the end. Neither are other calamities: **there will be earthquakes from place to place and there will be famines.**

The city of Pompeii was partially destroyed by an earthquake in AD 62; famine hit Palestine in AD 46–48 (Acts 11:28), and there was unrest in Rome over food shortages at the end of Nero's reign (AD 68). Wars, earthquakes, and famines cause great suffering, but they do not mean that the end is at hand, for they are only **the beginnings of the labor pains.** That they are **beginnings** means that more pains will follow.

Some nonbiblical writings in circulation at the time of Jesus claimed to be revelations of what would happen at the end of this age and used images of wars, earthquakes, and famines. Jesus warns his disciples to be wary in interpreting calamities as signs of the end, even if these calamities are spoken of in writings that purport to be revelations of the end.

Jesus characterizes wars, earthquakes, and famines as **labor pains** and thus introduces a note of hope. Jesus' words in John's Gospel are relevant: "When a woman is in labor, she is in anguish because her hour has arrived; but when she has given birth to a child, she no longer remembers the pain because of her joy that a child has been born into the world" (John 16:21). The pains of the present will come to an end

---

BACKGROUND: REVELATIONS OF THE END A number of books written in the centuries around the time of Jesus employed a distinctive type of writing to convey a vision of God triumphing over evil. Two of these books are Daniel in the Old Testament and Revelation in the New Testament; there were similar writings that were not accepted as inspired Scripture. The book of Revelation's Greek title is *Apokalypsis,* a word that means an uncovering or a revelation. These writings, often called apocalyptic, unveil what is hidden, characteristically employing symbols and imagery to do so. This type of writing grew out of Old Testament prophecies that described a future that would be quite different from the present (Isaiah 24–27, 34–35, 56–66; Ezek 38–39; Joel 3–4; Zech 9–14; Mal 3). Apocalyptic writings often contain an account of a revelation given to a human being by an angel, telling what is going to happen in the future by means of symbolic accounts of events on earth and in heaven. This type of writing flowered in difficult times, when evil seemed to be winning out and the only hope was for God's intervention. Different books described different futures, but they commonly spoke of God judging and destroying the wicked, transforming this world and beginning a new age. Those who remained faithful to God would be rewarded in an afterlife. *Related topics: The age to come (page 267), Judgment and Gehenna (page 241), Nonbiblical writings (page 243), Resurrection (page 320).*

---

with the birth of something new—something that will more than make up for the pain. We are perplexed by wars, natural disasters, and famines: if a loving God is in charge of the universe, why is there such great human misery? Why did tens of millions die in twentieth-century wars, why do earthquakes and hurricanes leave thousands homeless, why do famines frequently ravage African countries? Jesus does not answer our questions in this discourse, but he does characterize human suffering as a labor pain, a prelude to new life.

For reflection: How do I understand—or how am I baffled by—human suffering?

ORIENTATION: *While wars and natural disasters affect everyone, disciples will also suffer because of their allegiance to Jesus. These sufferings are no more signs of the end than are natural disasters.*

The Cost of Discipleship

9 "Watch out for yourselves. They will hand you over to the courts. You will be beaten in synagogues. You will be arraigned before governors and kings because of me, as a witness before them. 10 But the gospel must first be preached to all nations. 11 When they lead you away and hand you over, do not worry beforehand about what you are to say. But say whatever will be given to you at that hour. For it will not be you who are speaking but the holy Spirit. 12 Brother will hand over brother to death, and the father his child; children will rise up against parents and have them put to death. 13 You will be hated by all because of my name. But the one who perseveres to the end will be saved."

Gospel parallels: Matt 10:17–22; 24:9–14; Luke 12:11–12; 21:12–19

9 **Watch out for yourselves:** Jesus again warns his disciples to be discerning and take care (13:5), but now regarding what will happen to them because they are his disciples. **They will hand you over to the courts. You will be beaten in synagogues.** Jesus has told his disciples that he will be handed over to religious authorities who will hand him

over to civil authorities who will put him to death (10:33–34). Just as Jesus will be taken into custody, so too will his disciples: **they will hand you over to the courts.** The Greek word translated **courts** can refer to either civil or religious courts; here it means local Jewish councils that will pass sentence on Jewish Christians, who will then **be beaten in synagogues.** The law of Moses allowed an offender to be whipped but limited the whipping to forty lashes (Deut 25:1–3); Jewish practice reduced this to thirty-nine lashes to allow a margin for error. Before his conversion Paul hunted down Jewish Christians: "Many times, in synagogue after synagogue, I punished them in an attempt to force them to blaspheme" (Acts 26:11; *blaspheme* here means renounce Christ). After his conversion Paul was punished himself: "Five times at the hands of the Jews I received forty lashes minus one" (2 Cor 11:24).

Synagogue: See page 57

Jesus' disciples will suffer at the hands of civil as well as religious authorities: **You will be arraigned before governors and kings because of me, as a witness before them.** The words **because of me** might also be translated "on my account": the sufferings Jesus' followers will endure will be because of their fidelity to him. The **governors** could be Roman provincial administrators, such as Felix (Acts 23:23–35) and his successor, Festus (Acts 24:27); **kings** could be client kings ruling on behalf of Rome, such as Herod Agrippa (Acts 12:1–4; 25:13–27). More broadly, **governors and kings** represent civil authorities throughout the world. Jesus' disciples will be **arraigned before** them, charged with being his followers. This will provide an occasion for his disciples to bear **witness before them,** as Paul will do (Acts 26). Being arrested should be viewed as an opportunity to give witness rather than as a misfortune.

For reflection: Has opposition to my beliefs given me opportunities to bear witness?

10 The disciples asked Jesus what sign would signal that things were coming to an end (13:4), and they might have wondered whether persecution would be such a sign. It is not: **the gospel must first be preached** to all nations before the end. The **gospel** encompasses both the good news

about Jesus Christ (1:1) and the good news proclaimed by Jesus, that the reign of God is at hand (1:14–15). **Must** indicates divine necessity: the gospel reaching every nation is part of God's plan. **All nations** means all peoples, Gentiles as well as Jews. Although Jesus carried out his mission largely among Jews, he did travel and minister in pagan areas (5:1–20; 7:24–8:10), and he spoke of the Temple as a place of prayer for all peoples (11:17), foreshadowing the mission of the Church to Gentiles. Jesus did not spell out how Gentiles were to be incorporated into the body of his followers; this was left for the Church to work out, with the guidance of the Holy Spirit (Acts 15:1–35). Jesus' main point is that the gospel **must first** be preached to all nations before the present age will come to an end. Neither natural disasters nor persecutions signal that the end is at hand; they are merely the beginnings of the labor pains (13:8).

Gospel: See page 4

11 After an aside about the gospel being preached to all nations before the end, Jesus continues to address the situation of his followers standing before governors and kings (verse 9). **When they lead you away and hand you over:** the disciples are again told that they will be handed over, just as Jesus will be handed over (9:31; 10:33). When that happens, Jesus tells them, **do not worry beforehand about what you are to say.** Jesus' first disciples lacked status and education (Acts 4:13), so being arrested would have been a source of anxiety: How will I defend myself? What will happen to me? But Jesus tells his followers, **Do not worry beforehand about what you are to say. But say whatever will be given to you at that hour.** The implication of **will be given** is will be given by God. The right words will be provided **at that hour** when they are needed, not necessarily beforehand; Jesus' followers must **not worry** but trust that they will receive help when it is needed. For **it will not be you who are speaking but the holy Spirit.** This is the only mention in Mark's Gospel of the role of the Holy Spirit in the lives of Jesus' disciples. The Spirit will speak through them as they bear witness; therefore they do not need to worry about what they will say.

The Spirit: See page 12

For reflection: How have I experienced inspirations of the Spirit helping me in tight spots?

12 Disciples of Jesus bear no distinctive marks that will identify them to the authorities, but some will be arrested because of informants. **Brother will hand over brother to death:** the words **hand over** again echo what will happen to Jesus and here have the nuance of "betray." A man will betray his brother to the authorities, who will put him to death because of his allegiance to Jesus. The word **brother** means male relative, and for Mark's first readers it would also have had the connotation of brother Christian. Jesus warned that some who accepted God's word would fall away "when tribulation or persecution comes because of the word" (4:17). During Nero's persecution of Christians in Rome in the 60s, some Christians succumbed to fear and torture and betrayed the names of other Christians, leading to their arrest and death.

Betrayal will tear families apart, because **brother will hand over brother to death, and the father his child; children will rise up against parents and have them put to death.** In a culture that placed a high value on family relationships, the prospect of being handed over to death by one's immediate family would have been particularly chilling. Mark's Gospel has presented Jesus as being estranged from his family during his public ministry (3:20–21, 31–35). Suffering for the sake of Jesus entails enduring what he endured.

13 Jesus tells his followers that they will not only be denounced by those closest to them but will also **be hated by all because of my name.** Is Jesus exaggerating? Tacitus, a late first-century Roman historian, portrayed Christians as easy targets for persecution because they were so widely despised. To become a Christian in Rome in the 60s took considerable courage, for it meant joining a scorned and vulnerable group. Jesus warned that those who wanted to be his disciples had to take up their cross and follow him on the way to death and resurrection (8:34). Christians might experience severe sufferings, but these should not come as a surprise to readers of Mark's Gospel.

Despite telling of the suffering that comes with following Jesus, Mark's Gospel is still good news (1:1). Jesus speaks of the cost of discipleship but never without also speaking of what those who pay the price will receive. **But the one who perseveres to the end will be saved.**

The meaning of **to the end** is completely, fully, to the end of one's life. The one who endures to the end **will be saved:** here **saved** does not mean rescued from suffering or death but given eternal life. Jesus promised, "Whoever loses his life for my sake and that of the gospel will save it" (8:35); he promised that those who gave up everything for him and endured persecution would receive "eternal life in the age to come" (10:30). These promises give his followers the strength and hope to persevere **to the end.**

For reflection: Have I suffered because I am a Christian? What hopes sustain me?

BACKGROUND: A ROMAN VIEW OF CHRISTIANS The Roman senator and historian Tacitus (lived about AD 56 to 118) described a great fire that swept Rome in AD 64, a fire that was rumored to have been started by the emperor Nero. Nero shifted blame to Christians because they were already widely despised. Tacitus writes, "To put an end to the rumor, Nero substituted as culprits those who were commonly called Christians—a group detested for their disgraceful behavior—and inflicted extraordinary punishments on them. Christ, the founder after whom they were named, had been put to death by the procurator Pontius Pilate during the reign of Tiberius. But, while the destructive superstition was checked for a while, it had broken out again, not only in Judea, where the evil had originated, but also in the city of Rome, into which all the dreadful and abominable things in the world gather together and become popular. At first, only those who acknowledged themselves as members of the group were rounded up. Then, on their information, an enormous number of people were convicted, not so much for the crime of arson as for their hatred of the human race" (*Annals* 15.44). Tacitus reflects popular views of the time when he characterizes Christianity as an evil superstition involving shameful practices and when he portrays Christians as hated for their supposed crimes. Christians who survived Nero's persecution still faced widespread hostility. Luke writes that when Paul arrived in Rome (about AD 61), some Jewish leaders wanted to hear his views as a Christian, "for we know that this sect is denounced everywhere" (Acts 28:22).

ORIENTATION: *Jesus spoke to Peter, James, John, and Andrew about events that lay in their future, but these events were already taking place when Mark wrote his Gospel. Now Jesus begins to speak of events that lie in the future for both Jesus' first disciples and Mark's first readers.*

The Birth Pains Intensify

[14] "**When you see the desolating abomination standing where he should not (let the reader understand), then those in Judea must flee to the mountains,** [15] **[and] a person on a housetop must not go down or enter to get anything out of his house,** [16] **and a person in a field must not return to get his cloak.** [17] **Woe to pregnant women and nursing mothers in those days.** [18] **Pray that this does not happen in winter.** [19] **For those times will have tribulation such as has not been since the beginning of God's creation until now, nor ever will be.** [20] **If the Lord had not shortened those days, no one would be saved; but for the sake of the elect whom he chose, he did shorten the days.** [21] **If anyone says to you then, 'Look, here is the Messiah! Look, there he is!' do not believe it.** [22] **False messiahs and false prophets will arise and will perform signs and wonders in order to mislead, if that were possible, the elect.** [23] **Be watchful! I have told it all to you beforehand.**"

Gospel parallels: Matt 24:15–26; Luke 17:23; 21:20–24
OT: 1 Macc 1:54–59; 6:7; Dan 9:27; 11:31; 12:1, 11

14 Jesus told his disciples that the Temple would be destroyed, and they asked when it would happen (13:2–4). Jesus has not answered their question, but now he warns them about a calamity that will befall the Temple. **When you see the desolating abomination standing where he should not:** the Greek could also be translated "standing where *it* should not" and refer to a thing rather than a person. The term **desolating abomination** echoes an expression used in the book of Daniel for a pagan altar built in 168/167 BC over the Temple's altar of sacrifice by the Syrian ruler Antiochus IV Epiphanes (Dan 9:27; 11:31; 12:11; see 1 Macc 1:54–59; 6:7). Jesus employs this term as a metaphor or a comparison for something that will ravage the Temple in the future, leaving it

desolate. This something could be someone, **standing where he should not** within the Temple. Jesus does not say what or who this **desolating abomination** is or when it or he will arrive. But something is going to happen that will be as devastating to the Temple as its desecration by Antiochus IV Epiphanes.

> Armed forces shall move at his command and defile the sanctuary stronghold, abolishing the daily sacrifice and setting up the horrible abomination.
>
> Dan 11:31

> On the fifteenth day of the month Chislev, in the year one hundred and forty-five, the king erected the horrible abomination upon the altar of holocausts.
>
> 1 Macc 1:54

Mark sometimes adds parenthetical comments to explain matters his readers might not understand or to draw out an implication from Jesus' words (see 7:11, 19). Jesus did not spell out what the **desolating abomination** would be, and Mark probably would have liked to explain it to his readers—but he might not have been sure himself what form this abomination would take. Perhaps the best that Mark was able to do was interject **Let the reader understand,** which could mean "Something awful is going to happen to the Temple, and when it does, the reader should understand that this is what Jesus was talking about."

Jesus says that **when** this **desolating abomination** appears, **then those in Judea must flee to the mountains.** Some Jews did literally **flee to the mountains** during the religious persecution launched by Antiochus IV Epiphanes (1 Macc 2:28), but Jesus may use these words simply as an idiom for getting out of harm's way (just as we might say, "Head for the hills"). Jesus is saying to his disciples, When the **desolating abomination** arrives, don't hang around to gawk at it.

15 **[And] a person on a housetop must not go down or enter to get anything out of his house.** The flat roofs of houses could be used for drying crops (Joshua 2:6), sleeping (1 Sam 9:25–26), and praying (Acts 10:9). An outside stairway or ladder led to the roof. Jesus says to

his disciples, If you are up on a roof when the desolating abomination happens, get away as quickly as you can; don't even go into the house to pick up belongings.

16 **And a person in a field must not return to get his cloak:** a farmer would not wear a heavy cloak while working his fields but might wear it at night for warmth (see Exod 22:25–26). Jesus says, If you are out working in a field when the desolating abomination occurs, flee right away; don't even go back to your house to pick up a cloak. Escaping will be that urgent!

Clothing: See page 117

17 **Woe to pregnant women and nursing mothers in those days,** for they will not be able to flee swiftly. Jesus could have added, "Woe to the arthritic and the infirm when the crisis happens." If it will be urgent to get away as quickly as possible, those who move slowly will be in a difficult position.

18 **Pray that this does not happen in winter.** In Judea, **winter** was the rainy season and a bad time to travel. Footpaths became muddy; normally dry ravines filled with rushing streams that were dangerous to cross. When Jesus tells his disciples to **pray** that the desolating abomination does not **happen in winter,** is he implying that he does not know what time of year it will happen? Jesus indicates that the timing is in God's hands, and prayer might persuade God to allow the abomination to occur at a time when escape will be easier.

How were Jesus' words borne out in historical events? To suppress a Jewish revolt, a Roman army besieged and conquered Jerusalem in AD 70, burning down the Temple in the process. Several ancient accounts speak of Christians fleeing Jerusalem before the siege. These events are usually seen as fulfillments of Jesus' declarations that a desolating abomination would happen in the Temple, and his followers should flee. Jesus' words did not provide a precise blueprint, however, for what took place in Jerusalem in AD 70. Jesus seems to have had assurance that something cataclysmic was going to happen to Jerusalem, which would include the destruction of the Temple, but no foreknowledge of the details—or even of the time of year when it would occur. Jesus used the "desolating abomination" spoken of in Daniel as a metaphor for what would happen.

19 **For those times will have tribulation such as has not been since the beginning of God's creation until now, nor ever will be.** Jesus again draws on the book of Daniel, echoing words that characterized the persecution Jews suffered under Antiochus IV Epiphanes (Dan 12:1). Jesus once more uses something out of the past as a comparison for something in the future: just as there was great suffering at the time of Antiochus IV Epiphanes, so there will be great suffering during coming **times** of **tribulation.** But when will **those times** occur? There are several possibilities. Jesus may still be speaking of the crisis that will befall the Temple and Judea (verse 14) and may be saying that it will be the greatest tribulation ever. Or Jesus could be speaking of a later time, after the desolating abomination, when the greatest tribulation to ever take place will occur; Jewish speculations associated great tribulations with the end of the present age. Or perhaps Jesus is not sure of the relationship between the desolating abomination and the tribulations at the end of the age: he knows both will happen, but he does not know how soon one will follow the other.

> It shall be a time unsurpassed in distress
> since nations began until that time.
>
> Dan 12:1

20 **If the Lord had not shortened those days, no one would be saved:** the future, including all of its tribulations, is in the hands of the **Lord** God. **No one** is literally no flesh; to say that no one would be **saved** does not mean that no person would be given eternal salvation but that no one would be left alive on this earth at the end of the tribulations if God had not shortened their time. It is already in God's plan that these days be shortened: **but for the sake of the elect whom he chose, he did shorten the days.** The reference to the **elect** evokes Old Testament references to God's chosen people (Psalm 105:6;

351

Isaiah 43:20; 65:9). Jesus' followers are the new **elect** chosen by God; for their sake God has limited the birth pains of tribulation.

For reflection: What does it mean for me that I have been chosen by God?

21 Tribulation will bring in its wake wild claims and speculations, and Jesus' followers are to be wary of them. **If anyone says to you then, "Look, here is the Messiah! Look, there he is!" do not believe it.** Jesus will go on to speak of his coming (13:26), but first he warns his disciples to be on their guard against premature reports of his coming. They are to discount all purported Messiah sightings.

22 In addition to premature claims of Jesus' coming, there will also be impostors: **false messiahs and false prophets will arise and will perform signs and wonders in order to mislead, if that were possible, the elect.** Jesus has already warned his disciples that "many will come in my name saying, 'I am he,' and they will deceive many" (13:6). **Signs and wonders** are not identifying marks of the Messiah: Jesus downplayed the spectacular in his healings (5:37–43) and refused to provide signs upon demand (8:11–13). Those who claim to be prophets because they **perform signs and wonders** may be false prophets (see Deut 13:2–6). When confronted with those who use **signs and wonders** as credentials for their claims, Jesus' followers should be wary, lest they be misled.

23 Jesus once again tells his disciples to **be watchful!** (13:5, 9). As the birth pains continue, as speculations about what is happening increase, as false claims multiply, they must **be watchful,** be wary, not get carried away. Jesus has prepared the disciples for what lies ahead: **I have told it all to you beforehand.** Jesus does not seem to have told his disciples **all** the details of what would happen. We might best interpret him to mean "I have told you all that you need to know. You have been warned that difficult times are coming, when you will need to be discerning and on your guard."

For reflection: What might Christians need to be watchful about today?

The Coming of the Son of Man

24 "But in those days after that tribulation

the sun will be darkened,
and the moon will not give its light,
25 and the stars will be falling from the sky,
and the powers in the heavens will be shaken.

26 And then they will see 'the Son of Man coming in the clouds'
with great power and glory, 27 and then he will send out the angels
and gather [his] elect from the four winds, from the end of the
earth to the end of the sky."

Gospel parallels: Matt 24:29–31; Luke 21:25–28
OT: Isaiah 13:9–10; Dan 7:13–14; Joel 3
NT: Mark 8:38

24 **But in those days after that tribulation:** Jesus has not told his disciples when the time of tribulation will occur or how long it will last (save that God has shortened it: 13:19–20). Jesus now speaks of what will happen **after that tribulation** but does not say whether it will be immediately after or sometime after. He speaks of this time as **in those days,** which echoes the way the Old Testament speaks of a "day of the LORD," when God will vanquish evil (see, for example, Joel 3). Jesus invokes the imagery of some of these "day of the LORD" prophecies, such as Isaiah 13:9–10: **the sun will be darkened, / and the moon will not give its light.** These images signify that something momentous is taking place but are not to be taken literally as a prediction that the sun will burn out. Since the heavens are the dwelling place of God in the biblical view of the world, what happens in the heavens is due to God's activity. Heavenly upheavals mean that something of cosmic importance is happening.

> Lo, the day of the LORD comes,
> cruel, with wrath and burning anger;
> To lay waste the land
> and destroy the sinners within it!

> The stars and constellations of the heavens
>   send forth no light;
> The sun is dark when it rises,
>   and the light of the moon does not shine.
>
>   Isaiah 13:9–10

25 Jesus continues to invoke cosmic imagery to underline the great significance of what will happen: **and the stars will be falling from the sky, / and the powers in the heavens will be shaken.** The **powers in the heavens** can mean the stars of heaven or the angels that were popularly thought to control stars (just as the expression *the host of heaven* can mean the stars or the angelic army of God). There will be a heavenly earthquake, as it were, that will shake up the stars and send them hurtling to earth. Today we know that the stars are vastly larger than the earth and cannot literally fall to earth, but in the time of Jesus stars and meteorites could be confused. Jesus is not trying to give his disciples a

---

BACKGROUND: THE DAY OF THE LORD Old Testament prophecy is filled with expectations that God will act to vanquish evil. Some expectations are expressed in terms of "the day of the LORD" or "that day" or "the day when" God will act, or similar expressions. Originally "the day of the LORD" meant a time when God would vindicate his people by defeating their enemies, but Amos proclaimed that it would be a time when God would judge his own sinful people (Amos 5:18, 20). Other prophets issued similar warnings, sometimes with the promise that God would restore his people after punishing them. Some prophecies use cosmic imagery to convey how momentous "the day of the LORD" will be (Isaiah 13:9–10; Joel 2:10–11; 3:3–4). Isaiah prophesied that that day would have worldwide consequences, not only restoring Israel but bringing a reign of justice to all nations (Isaiah 2:2–4; 19:18–25; 25:6–9). Most prophecies envision "the day of the LORD" as a time when God will act directly; a few prophecies portray God raising up a descendant of David to rule God's people (Isaiah 11:10; Jer 23:5–6; 30:7–9; 33:14–17; Zech 3:8–10). "The day of the LORD" thus carries a range of meanings in the Old Testament, some of which influenced expectations of the Messiah and the establishment of the kingdom of God (although "the day of the LORD" prophecies do not use these terms). In the letters of the New Testament, "the day of the LORD" takes on the meaning of "the day of the Lord Jesus Christ," when he will judge the human race and establish the final reign of God (see 1 Cor 1:8; Phil 1:6, 10; 2:16). *Related topics: Cosmic signs (page 355), Jewish expectations at the time of Jesus (page 339), Judgment and Gehenna (page 241).*

---

lesson in astronomy but is using traditional imagery to convey that what is going to happen will be of such great importance that it will be as if the universe has been turned upside down.

26 The event whose significance is so great that it can be conveyed only with images of cosmic upheaval is the coming of the Son of Man: **and then they will see "the Son of Man coming in the clouds" with great power and glory.** It is a little unclear who **they** are who **will see** the Son of Man's coming. **They** presumably includes those chosen by God—referred to as the elect in verses 20 and 27—but could include everyone alive on earth at the time. They will see **"the Son of Man coming in the clouds" with great power and glory:** Jesus again draws on the book of Daniel (Dan 7:13–14; see also Mark 13:14, 19). Daniel speaks of a heavenly figure who is "like a son of man," that is, like a human being. This heavenly figure comes on the clouds of heaven into the presence of God and is given everlasting dominion and glory. Jesus has often spoken of himself as the Son of Man, and now he applies the words of Daniel to himself: he is **the Son of Man** who will come **"in the clouds" with great power and glory,** and this will be an event of such significance that the whole universe will be shaken (verses 24–25).

BACKGROUND: COSMIC SIGNS For us, the sun turning dark and stars colliding with the earth would mean the end of our world. These cosmic events had a different significance at the time of Jesus. The world was thought of as the earth and the dome of the sky above it (Gen 1:6–8), with sun, moon, and stars affixed to this dome (Gen 1:14–18). God's dwelling was in the uppermost part of the sky (the Hebrew and Greek words for sky also mean heaven). Stars looked small—small enough to fall from the sky as meteorites. There were accounts of eclipses of the sun that had darkened it. Eclipses of the moon can give it a deep red or copper hue (due to light refracted by the earth's atmosphere); Joel spoke of the sun being "turned to darkness, / and the moon to blood" (Joel 3:4). Since these events happened in God's heavenly domain, they were taken as signs of God's action. When the prophets announced that God was going to act, as on a "day of the LORD," they sometimes invoked cosmic events as signs of God's acting (Isaiah 13:9–10; Joel 2:10–11; 3:3–4). By the time of Jesus, these cosmic signs had become a standard way of indicating that God was acting in some very significant way but did not mean that the physical universe was coming to an end. *Related topic: The day of the Lord (page 354).*

In the book of Daniel, the one like a son of man comes on the clouds into the presence of God. When Jesus applies these words to himself, however, he seems to refer to his coming from God and being made manifest on earth (see 8:38).

Son of Man: See page 41

As the visions during the night continued, I saw

One like a son of man coming,
on the clouds of heaven;
When he reached the Ancient One
and was presented before him,
He received dominion, glory, and kingship;
nations and peoples of every language serve him.
His dominion is an everlasting dominion
that shall not be taken away,
his kingship shall not be destroyed.

Dan 7:13–14

27 **And then he will send out the angels:** in the Old Testament, angels are messengers and agents of God. Thus Jesus associates himself closely with God by speaking of himself as the glorified Son of Man having the power to command angels and send them on mission. The mission he will give them is to **gather [his] elect from the four winds, from the end of the earth to the end of the sky.** The Old Testament speaks of God gathering his people in from exile (Deut 30:3–4; Isaiah 43:6; Jer 32:37; Ezek 34:13; 36:24); Jesus in his power and glory will send angels to **gather [his] elect,** his new family, and bring them to him and into the presence of God. They will be gathered **from the four winds,** an expression meaning from north, south, east, and west. They will be gathered **from the end of the earth to the end of the sky,** which means from absolutely everywhere.

Angels: See page 321

Jesus previously told his disciples, "Whoever is ashamed of me and of my words in this faithless and sinful generation, the Son of Man will be ashamed of when he comes in his Father's glory with the holy

356

angels" (8:38). Now Jesus speaks of those who are not ashamed of him: his **elect.** They will be brought into the presence of God.

As Jesus' life on earth draws to an end, he speaks of another end: the fulfillment of life on this earth. Jesus does not do so in parables but invokes images from Scripture, drawing particularly on passages that deal with the final establishment of God's reign. These passages provide Jesus with a vocabulary he can use to speak about the future, and by invoking these passages he indicates that he will fulfill what they promise. Jesus does not answer his disciples' question about when the Temple will be destroyed but speaks of greater matters: not of what will become rubble but of what will last forever. The culmination of this world, after all the labor pains, will be Jesus bringing his followers to God.

For reflection: What hopes do Jesus' words give me?

ORIENTATION: *Jesus continues to speak of the future to his four disciples but now with a parable. Some of his words are enigmatic.*

The Parable of the Fig Tree

28 "**Learn a lesson from the fig tree. When its branch becomes tender and sprouts leaves, you know that summer is near. 29 In the same way, when you see these things happening, know that he is near, at the gates. 30 Amen, I say to you, this generation will not pass away until all these things have taken place. 31 Heaven and earth will pass away, but my words will not pass away.**

32 "**But of that day or hour, no one knows, neither the angels in heaven, nor the Son, but only the Father.**"

Gospel parallels: Matt 24:32–36; Luke 21:29–33

NT: Mark 8:38; 9:1

28 **Learn a lesson from the fig tree:** the Greek is literally translated Learn the *parable* from the fig tree. Jesus teaches by means of a comparison that should have a lesson for his followers. **Fig** trees were common in Judea, and Jesus could well have gestured to one on the Mount of Olives as he taught. **When its branch becomes tender and sprouts**

leaves, you know that summer is near. A fig tree drops its leaves during winter, but in the spring the sap rises and **its branch becomes tender and sprouts leaves.** Jesus and his followers are in Jerusalem for the springtime Feast of Passover (14:1), and fig trees are in leaf (11:13). Jesus' disciples know that fig trees in leaf mean that summer is not far off: **you know that summer is near.** Jesus used the everyday experiences of his listeners as the basis for comparisons.

Parables: See page 79

29 The comparison Jesus wishes to make, however, is obscure. **In the same way, when you see these things happening, know that he is near, at the gates.** What are **these things** that will happen as a sign that something else will soon happen? Is Jesus referring to events that will accompany his coming (13:24–27), or to earlier events such as tribulations and a catastrophe that will befall Jerusalem (13:5–23)?

Jesus' warning to **know that he is near, at the gates,** is enigmatic. The Greek could also be translated "know that *it* is near." Who or what is **near, at the gates**? Is Jesus speaking of his coming or of the "desolating abomination standing where he should not" (13:14)?

30 **Amen, I say to you, this generation will not pass away until all these things have taken place.** With the words **Amen, I say to you,** Jesus assures his disciples that what he is saying is important. **This generation** means Jesus' contemporaries (see 8:12, 38; 9:19). But what are **all these things** that will **have taken place** before **this generation** is dead? The catastrophe to befall Jerusalem? The times of tribulation? The coming of Jesus in power and glory? We as readers of Mark's Gospel are still not sure what Jesus is referring to here.

One way to interpret Jesus' words would be to understand that when Jesus told his followers that they would "see these things happening" (verse 29) and that **these things** would happen within the lifetime of **this generation,** he was referring to the catastrophe that befell Jerusalem, which occurred forty years after Jesus spoke.

Yet Jesus' words can also be interpreted as referring to his coming. Jesus previously alluded to his coming in glory (8:38) and then gave his followers the solemn assurance, "Amen, I say to you, there are some standing here who will not taste death until they see that the kingdom of

God has come in power" (9:1). Jesus does not seem to be simply talking about the fall of Jerusalem when he speaks of **all these things** happening; Jesus seems to be referring to something far more momentous that is imminent. We will defer further consideration until we address Jesus' words in verse 32.

31 **Heaven and earth will pass away, but my words will not pass away.** A prophecy of Isaiah raised the possibility that the universe would fade away (Isaiah 51:6), while another prophecy proclaimed that "the word of our God stands forever" (Isaiah 40:8). Jesus tells his followers, **My words will not pass away,** attributing to his words the permanence that Isaiah attributed to God's words. The universe **will pass away,** but Jesus' words will not. When Jesus speaks of **my words,** it is unclear whether he is referring only to the words he has just uttered to his disciples or to all his teachings.

32 **But of that day or hour, no one knows, neither the angels in heaven, nor the Son, but only the Father.** By **that day or hour** Jesus means "the day of the Lord," the hour of judgment when Jesus will come with great power and glory (13:26–27). Jesus tells his disciples that he does not know when it will happen! He tells them that **no one knows,** meaning no human being; nor do **the angels in heaven** know, or even **the Son.** Jesus is referring to himself when he speaks of **the Son,** and by speaking of God as **the Father,** Jesus conveys that he is **the Son** of God. By speaking first of **no one,** then no **angels,** and then **the Son,** Jesus implicitly places himself not only above humans but also above angels. Yet even as **the Son,** nearest to God, Jesus does not know the timetable of **the Father.** It is God's prerogative to determine times (13:20), just as it is God's right to assign places in his kingdom (10:40).

The day of the Lord: See page 354

Son of God: See page 64

Jesus gives his followers a glimpse of his relationship with God: he is the Son of God, as God himself has proclaimed (1:11; 9:7). But Jesus says that he does not know when God will wrap things up with his coming in glory. This confessed ignorance on the part of Jesus must be taken into account in interpreting his statements that "all these things" will happen within a generation (verse 30), with some still alive to "see that the kingdom of God has come in power" (9:1). Jesus proclaimed that the kingdom of God was at hand (1:15), he foretold a catastrophe befalling Jerusalem, and he spoke of his coming in glory. Yet Jesus seems not entirely clear about the timetable for these things because he does not know God's complete timetable.

Many New Testament writings reflect a belief that Jesus will come rather soon (Rom 13:11–12; 1 Cor 1:7–8; 4:5; 7:29, 31; 10:11; Phil 1:6, 10; 4:5; Heb 10:25; James 5:8–9; 1 Pet 4:7; 1 John 2:18; Rev 22:10, 12, 20); Paul apparently expected that it would be within his lifetime (1 Thess 4:15). Some New Testament writings try to correct such expectations (John 21:20–23; 2 Pet 3:3–10). It is easiest to understand the early Church's expectation that Jesus would return soon if Jesus had made statements that could be interpreted to mean that he would come soon, even though he also said that he did not know when it would happen.

For reflection: If Jesus did not know when he would come in glory, is it likely that anyone will ever be able to calculate it?

Watch!

33 "**Be watchful! Be alert! You do not know when the time will come. 34 It is like a man traveling abroad. He leaves home and places his servants in charge, each with his work, and orders the gatekeeper to be on the watch. 35 Watch, therefore; you do not know when the lord of the house is coming, whether in the evening, or at midnight, or at cockcrow, or in the morning. 36 May he not come suddenly and find you sleeping. 37 What I say to you, I say to all: 'Watch!'** "

Gospel parallels: Matt 24:42–51; Luke 12:35–40; 21:34–36

33 **Be watchful! Be alert!** For the fourth time, Jesus tells his disciples to **be watchful** (see 13:5, 9, 23), to be discerning and wary. This time Jesus adds a second exhortation: **Be alert!** The words **Be alert** have the connotation of Stay awake, Be attentive. Jesus tells the disciples that the reason they need to be **watchful** and **alert** is that they **do not know when the time will come,** that is, the **time** of Jesus' coming. No one knows that day or hour, not even Jesus himself (13:32). Nor will there be clear signs

that it is about to happen; Jesus has told his disciples not to be misled by supposed signs or false prophecies (13:5–13, 19–23). Not knowing when it will happen means that Jesus' followers have to be prepared for it to happen at any time—they have to be constantly **watchful** and **alert.**

34 Jesus provides a comparison. **It is like a man traveling abroad. He leaves home and places his servants in charge:** a more literal translation of the last clause would be "gives his slaves authority". Even though Jesus has not finished telling this parable, it should already trigger some associations for the disciples. Jesus told his disciples that they were to be as servants and slaves (10:43–44), and he shared his authority with them (3:15; 6:7). Now Jesus is implicitly speaking of his going away, when his disciples will have to continue to exercise his authority, **each with his work.** Each follower of Jesus has his or her share in his work, some form of service. In Jesus' parable, as the man leaves on his journey he **orders the gatekeeper to be on the watch.** Being **on the watch** is the particular function of **the gatekeeper** in the household, but it is a function with symbolic significance for the other servants: they too are to **watch,** to remain alert, to be attentive to their work.

Servant, slave: See page 277

For reflection: What work, what service has Jesus given me?

35 Jesus' disciples must also imitate the watchfulness of the gatekeeper: **Watch, therefore; you do not know when the lord of the house is coming.** The "man traveling abroad" is now called **the lord of the house,** which means the owner of the house and the master of the slaves. But after his departure Jesus will also be called Lord, just as God is called Lord. Jesus' disciples must **watch** because they do not know when the Lord Jesus **is coming.** Being watchful does not mean staring at the sky but faithfully carrying out one's service. The man's servants do not know when he will come, **whether in the evening, or at midnight, or at cockcrow, or in the morning.** These were the four watches of the night according to Roman reckoning. The time when the lord of the house will return cannot be predicted, nor will there be warning signs of his coming; hence constant vigilance is necessary.

Lord: See page 332

36 **May he not come suddenly and find you sleeping.** It is the gate-keeper's responsibility to be alert for thieves who might try to break in under cover of night; for a gatekeeper to fall asleep on the job would be dereliction of duty. All of Jesus' disciples have their duties as well, and woe to them if Jesus comes **suddenly** and finds them **sleeping** when they should be working. If there will be no warning sign of Jesus' coming, then his coming will seem sudden to us.

37 Jesus ends his instruction with a final exhortation to be watchful and alert. He addresses his words not only to the four disciples with him on the Mount of Olives (13:3) but also to all of his disciples: **What I say to you, I say to all: "Watch!"** The time of Jesus' coming is unknowable; therefore every disciple of every time must constantly be on **watch** for him, diligently carrying out his or her work.

Peter, James, John, and Andrew asked Jesus when the Temple would be destroyed and "what sign" there would be "when all things are about to come to an end" (13:3–4). Jesus has not given them a sign of the end: the "desolating abomination" (13:14) will not be a sign that all things are coming to an end, and the signs in the heavens will accompany the coming of the Son of Man rather than provide an advance warning of it (13:24–26). Instead of giving the disciples the sign they asked for, Jesus has emphasized the need for them to be watchful and alert (13:5, 9, 23, 33, 35, 37), for they cannot know when the end will be (13:32). They must not be misled by false claims or purported signs of the end. They must be attentive to their responsibilities, diligently working as if Jesus could come at any moment and demand an accounting.

Now, two thousand years later, it is hard for us to have a sense of urgency about Jesus' coming. We profess that "Christ will come again," but we generally assume that it will be in the distant rather than immediate future. Perhaps the sense of urgency we can have is about serving Jesus—watching our hands rather than the clouds.

For reflection: In practical terms, what does it mean for me to be watchful and alert?

CHAPTER 14

The Plot to Kill Jesus
¹ The Passover and the Feast of Unleavened Bread were to take place in two days' time. So the chief priests and the scribes were seeking a way to arrest him by treachery and put him to death. ² They said, "Not during the festival, for fear that there may be a riot among the people."

Gospel parallels: Matt 26:1–5; Luke 22:1–2
NT: Mark 8:31; 10:33; 11:18; 12:12

1 **The Passover and the Feast of Unleavened Bread were to take place in two days' time.** The Feast of **Passover** commemorated Israel's deliverance from Egypt (Exod 12). It was celebrated on the fifteenth day of the Jewish month of Nisan. The Jewish calendar was based on lunar months, with a new moon marking the beginning of a new month; this meant that there was normally a full moon on the fifteenth. Sheep were slaughtered in the Temple on the afternoon of the fourteenth of Nisan,

---

BACKGROUND: THE FEAST OF PASSOVER AND UNLEAVENED BREAD Passover commemorated God's freeing the Israelites from captivity in Egypt; a description of the Passover meal and the command to celebrate it are found in chapter 12 of Exodus. The Feast of Passover incorporated several ancient elements. One element was the annual sacrifice of a young lamb as an offering for the fertility and safety of the flock; shepherds made the offering in the spring before moving to new pastures. Another ancient element was a "feast of Unleavened Bread" (Exod 23:15–16; Lev 23:6), an agricultural festival celebrating the beginning of the grain harvest. In Palestine during biblical times, grain crops grew during the winter, which is the only rainy season. Barley was the first grain to ripen in the spring. To celebrate the barley harvest, bread made from only newly harvested grain was eaten for seven days. This bread was unleavened because leaven was kept in the form of starter dough, and no grain or starter dough from previous harvests could be used during this feast (Exod 12:18–20). Passover thus incorporated traditions of nomadic shepherds and settled farmers but gave them greater meaning as part of a celebration of liberation from Egypt. Originally Passover was celebrated in one's home, wherever one lived; after sacrificial worship was restricted to the Temple in Jerusalem by King Josiah in 622 BC, Passover became a pilgrimage feast celebrated in Jerusalem, since the sacrificing of lambs could then be done only at the Temple.

---

and then, after sunset (the beginning of the next day by Jewish reckoning), they were consumed in a Passover meal. The fifteenth of Nisan also marked the beginning of a weeklong **Feast of Unleavened Bread,** during which only unleavened bread was eaten. Mark writes that the festival was **to take place in two days' time,** apparently indicating that it was the thirteenth of Nisan, which would be a Wednesday by our calendar. **So the chief priests and the scribes were seeking a way to arrest him by treachery and put him to death.** Jesus has told his disciples that he will be "handed over to the chief priests and the scribes," who will condemn him to death (10:33; see also 8:31). **Chief priests** and **scribes** have been seeking a way to put Jesus to death but have been deterred by Jesus' popularity with the crowds (11:18; 12:12). These religious leaders had power but were generally not very popular with the people, and they did not want a confrontation with Jesus' supporters. Hence they are **seeking a way to arrest him by treachery,** to seize him stealthily, when he is isolated from others. Their aim is to **put him to death** before his supporters can rally.

High priest, chief priests: See page 403

Scribes: See page 40

2 **They said, "Not during the festival, for fear that there may be a riot among the people."** The pilgrims who crowded into Jerusalem for Passover more than quadrupled its population. Since Passover celebrated Israelite liberation, nationalistic fervor could run high (see 11:9–10). Trying to seize Jesus at this time would be like playing with matches in a fireworks factory; it would be better to deal with him after the crowds of pilgrims had dispersed. But Jesus will in fact be seized and put to death during the Passover festival. Before telling us how this came about, Mark has another story to recount (14:3–9).

A Woman Anoints Jesus

³ **When he was in Bethany reclining at table in the house of Simon the leper, a woman came with an alabaster jar of perfumed oil, costly genuine spikenard. She broke the alabaster jar and poured it on his head. ⁴ There were some who were indignant. "Why has there been this waste of perfumed oil? ⁵ It could have been sold for**

more than three hundred days' wages and the money given to the poor." They were infuriated with her. **⁶** Jesus said, "Let her alone. Why do you make trouble for her? She has done a good thing for me. **⁷** The poor you will always have with you, and whenever you wish you can do good to them, but you will not always have me. **⁸** She has done what she could. She has anticipated anointing my body for burial. **⁹** Amen, I say to you, wherever the gospel is proclaimed to the whole world, what she has done will be told in memory of her."

Gospel parallels: Matt 26:6–13; John 12:1–8
OT: Deut 15:1–11

3 **When he was in Bethany reclining at table in the house of Simon the leper.** While in Jerusalem for Passover, Jesus has been staying overnight in **Bethany,** a village on a southeastern slope of the Mount of Olives (11:1, 11–12, 19–20). If **Simon the leper** had an active case of leprosy, he would have been shunned and unable to host a meal. Perhaps Jesus healed him, and he is throwing a banquet for Jesus in gratitude. Or perhaps his leprosy has gone away naturally, as some skin conditions labeled leprosy in the Bible could do. That Jesus is **reclining at table** indicates that it is a rather formal meal, for the custom at banquets was to recline rather than sit.

Leprosy: See page 32
Banquets: See page 142

A woman came with an alabaster jar of perfumed oil. Banquets were normally men-only affairs. If all of Simon's guests are men, then it would take some boldness on this woman's part to burst into their midst. She carries **an alabaster jar of perfumed oil:** small **alabaster** flasks were used for expensive perfumes and oils. Her flask contains **costly genuine spikenard,** an aromatic oil (also called nard) made from the root of a plant that grew in India. Was she a wealthy woman who could afford luxuries like nard, or was she an ordinary woman for whom a **costly** flask of nard was a huge expenditure? Mark does not tell us.

She broke the alabaster jar and poured the oil **on his head.** Breaking the neck off an alabaster flask ruined it and meant that none of its contents could be saved. But this woman does not want to save her aromatic oil for a later time; she wants to use all of it for Jesus in an extravagant gesture. She **poured it on his head,** an act that has several levels of meaning. Being anointed with oil was refreshing. Banquet hosts sometimes anointed the heads of their guests, as a welcome and a refreshment (Luke 7:46); one of the blessings proclaimed in Psalm 23 is "You anoint my head with oil" (Psalm 23:5). This woman is performing a caring act by anointing the head of Jesus.

For reflection: What is the most extravagant thing I have ever done for Jesus?

A second level of meaning arises from Israelite kings having their heads anointed with oil as a sign that God had chosen them (1 Sam 10:1; 16:13; 1 Kings 1:39; 2 Kings 9:6). Hopes that God would send a descendant of David to restore his people were expressed as hopes for a messiah—literally, an anointed one. In the first verse of his Gospel, Mark proclaimed Jesus to be the "Christ," using the Greek word for anointed. Even if the woman did not see this significance in her act, some of Mark's first readers probably noticed it—and might have noted that Jesus the Messiah was anointed by a woman.

Messiah, Christ: See page 204

4 **There were some who were indignant.** Mark does not identify those who **were indignant;** did they include some of the disciples? They grumble, **Why has there been this waste of perfumed oil?** They think that the woman's anointing Jesus' head is a **waste** of the perfumed oil, despite the fact that this is how aromatic oils were used.

5 Their reasoning becomes clearer: **it could have been sold for more than three hundred days' wages and the money given to the poor.** The flask of oil cost as much as an ordinary worker earned in a year (three hundred **days' wages** is literally three hundred denarii: see 6:37; 12:15). Those who are grumbling think that the woman's gesture was extravagant and that she should have used her resources to help the poor rather than anoint Jesus. **They were infuriated with her:** the word **infuriated** has the connotation that they were berating her.

6 **Jesus said:** a more literal translation would be *"but* **Jesus said."** Jesus interrupts their scolding of the woman and tells them to **let her alone.** For a similar indignant reaction of Jesus, see 10:13–14. Jesus asks, **Why do you make trouble for her?** Who authorized you to sit in judgment of this woman? Jesus defends her action: **She has done a good thing for me.** A better translation would be "she has done a *beautiful* thing for me." Jesus has accepted her anointing as a beautiful expression of her love, a fine thing for her to have done. Jesus has done good things for a lot of people, but there are few instances in Mark's Gospel where someone does something really nice for Jesus. Jesus appreciates what this woman has done for him.

> *For reflection: What might be something beautiful that I could do for Jesus?*

7 Jesus has addressed those who were berating this woman, but what about their argument that even though it is good to do nice things for Jesus, it is even better to help the poor—in this case, to use a year's earnings to feed a destitute family for a year rather than blow it all on one luxurious head anointing? Jesus responds, **The poor you will always have with you, and whenever you wish you can do good to them.** His response is sometimes taken as a justification for letting people live in poverty, but his intention was just the opposite. **The poor you will always have with you** is an allusion to the words of Deuteronomy: "The needy will never be lacking in the land" (Deut 15:11). Deuteronomy views poverty as an aberration, for God's plan in giving a land to his people was that "there should be no one of you in need" (Deut 15:4). The presence of people in need is a call for God's people to do something about it: "I command you to open your hand to your poor and needy kinsman" (Deut 15:11). Hence Jesus says, **Whenever you wish you can**—and must—**do good** for the poor. Helping those in need will always be an imperative, until God's plan is realized and no one is in need.

> *Since the LORD, your God, will bless you abundantly in the land he will give you to occupy as your heritage, there should be no one of you in need.*
>
> Deut 15:4

> The needy will never be lacking in the land; that is why I command you to open your hand to your poor and needy kinsman in your country.
>
> Deut 15:11

For reflection: How am I able to do good for those in need?

Jesus says that while there will unfortunately be plenty of opportunities to help the poor, the opportunities to do something nice for him are coming to an end: **But you will not always have me.** Jesus' death is on his mind; he knows that his days on earth are very few. The bridegroom is about to be taken away, and the time for enjoying his presence is almost over (2:19–20).

8 The woman who did something beautiful for Jesus made use of the dwindling opportunities to do so; Jesus says that **she has done what she could.** She has done all that is within her power. Her expensive gesture mirrors that of the poor widow who donated her two small coins (12:42–44): each woman, in her own way, gave all she could. Jesus knows that the woman who anointed him could not prevent or postpone his suffering and death. All she could do was comfort him, and that she did. Jesus sees more meaning in her gesture than she probably saw herself: he says that **she has anticipated anointing my body for burial.** Corpses were anointed with oils or perfumes before being laid in the tomb. Jesus' death is so imminent that he sees an anointing he has received as akin to the anointing of a corpse; traces of her oil might linger on his body after his death. (The body of Jesus will be placed in a tomb without the customary anointing—15:46–16:1—but there is no evidence that Jesus foresaw this detail.)

Burial practices: See page 446

9 This woman has been extravagant toward Jesus, and Jesus is in turn extravagant toward her: he declares, **Amen, I say to you, wherever the gospel is proclaimed to the whole world, what she has done will be told in memory of her.** The **gospel** is the good news that Jesus has proclaimed (1:14–15) and the good news about Jesus (1:1). Jesus implies that

there will be time for this good news to be **proclaimed to the whole world** before the present age comes to an end (see 13:10). **What she has done** will indeed be remembered—and included in Mark's Gospel. But although **what she has done will be told in memory of her,** her name will be forgotten: she will be identified only in terms of what she did. Mark's Gospel generally does not tell us the names of those who interacted with Jesus, beyond the circle of Jesus' disciples, but it seems that this woman should have been one of those who were named. Jesus praised her deed more highly than he praised any other deed; she alone was the subject of a solemn pledge that what she did would be remembered. Yet her name was not remembered.

Gospel: See page 4

For reflection: Am I willing to serve Jesus even if my deeds and my name are soon forgotten?

One of the Twelve Turns against Jesus
¹⁰ Then Judas Iscariot, one of the Twelve, went off to the chief priests to hand him over to them. ¹¹ When they heard him they were pleased and promised to pay him money. Then he looked for an opportunity to hand him over.

Gospel parallels: Matt 26:14–16; Luke 22:3–6
NT: Mark 3:13–19; 9:31; 10:33; 14:1–2

10 **Then Judas Iscariot, one of the Twelve, went off to the chief priests to hand him over to them.** This is one of the most chilling verses in Mark's Gospel. Jesus has invited men and women into an intimate relationship with him as his disciples, as members of his new family (3:33–35). Jesus has specially chosen twelve of them to share in his authority and carry on his work (3:14–15). **One of the Twelve is Judas Iscariot** (3:19), yet Judas **went off to the chief priests to hand him over to them.** Judas takes the initiative: he is not recruited by the chief priests. Judas has been present during Jesus' confrontations with **chief priests** (11:15–18; 12:1–12), and Judas realizes that they want Jesus dead. But they are stalemated: arresting Jesus may start a riot (11:18; 12:12;

14:2). Judas tells them that he might be able to put Jesus in their hands when there is not a crowd around. Judas knows that he would be handing Jesus over to death, as Jesus foretold he would be (9:31; 10:33).

The Twelve: See Apostle, page 146

High priest, chief priests: See page 403

11 **When they heard him they were pleased:** some of the chief priests have been "seeking a way to arrest him {Jesus} by treachery and put him to death" (14:1), and they are **pleased** that Judas is willing to provide a way. Because of Jesus' popular support, they had decided not to do anything until after the Passover pilgrims had gone home (14:2), but Judas's offer is too good to pass up: Judas is in a privileged position to know when Jesus could be arrested quietly. They **promised to pay him money:** Mark presents this as their offer rather than Judas's demand. **Then he looked for an opportunity to hand him over.** Judas looks for a chance to betray Jesus: Judas does not yet know where and when it could be done. The word for **opportunity** could also be translated "good time": Judas is on the watch for the right moment when Jesus could be seized.

Mark provides no explanation for why Judas turned against Jesus. Even if Judas welcomed the payment he was to receive, this does not satisfactorily explain his betrayal. How did Judas, one of the Twelve, go from willing disciple to deadly betrayer? Perhaps nothing Mark could have said would have really explained it. Evil is ultimately a darkness that our minds cannot fathom.

Judas stands in sharp contrast to the woman who anointed the head of Jesus (14:3–9). She did all she could for Jesus, preparing his body for burial (14:8); Judas spurns all that Jesus has done for him and betrays him into the hands of those who will put him to death. The woman's name has been forgotten; the name of Judas Iscariot unfortunately cannot be.

Mark's first readers also suffered betrayal by those closest to them. When persecution came, some Christians renounced their faith and betrayed the names of fellow Christians, bringing about their torture and death. In some cases brother handed over brother, and the father his child (13:12). As the anguish of Christian betraying Christian racked the early Church, Mark's readers could reflect on the fact that Jesus knew what it was like to be handed over to suffering and death by someone you loved and trusted.

For reflection: Have I ever betrayed someone who trusted me? Why did I do it? Did I make amends?

Preparations for Passover

12 On the first day of the Feast of Unleavened Bread, when they sacrificed the Passover lamb, his disciples said to him, "Where do you want us to go and prepare for you to eat the Passover?" 13 He sent two of his disciples and said to them, "Go into the city and a man will meet you, carrying a jar of water. Follow him. 14 Wherever he enters, say to the master of the house, 'The Teacher says, "Where is my guest room where I may eat the Passover with my disciples?"' 15 Then he will show you a large upper room furnished and ready. Make the preparations for us there." 16 The disciples then went off, entered the city, and found it just as he had told them; and they prepared the Passover.

Gospel parallels: Matt 26:17–19; Luke 22:7–13
NT: Mark 11:1–6

2 On the first day of the Feast of Unleavened Bread, when they sacrificed the Passover lamb: since days ran from sunset to sunset by Jewish reckoning, the Feast of Passover began with a late-evening Passover meal. In preparation for it, lambs were slaughtered at the Temple during the afternoon. Mark calls this the **first day of the Feast of Unleavened Bread,** perhaps because preparations for this feast (such as baking the unleavened bread) were also being made. By our calendar, it would be a Thursday afternoon. **When they sacrificed the Passover lamb, his disciples said to him:** while **they** could mean everyone who is slaughtering lambs, **they** could also refer specifically to Jesus' **disciples,** and this seems to be Mark's meaning. Jesus and his disciples have come to the Temple with a lamb; Jesus or one of his disciples has slit the lamb's throat, and a priest has taken some of the blood and sprinkled it at the base of the altar. The lamb's carcass can now be prepared and roasted for the Passover meal. After the lamb was slaughtered, **his disciples said to him, "Where do you want us to go and prepare for you to eat the Passover?"** Jesus and his disciples are staying in Bethany (11:11, 19; 14:3), but Jewish law called for the Passover meal to be eaten within the city of Jerusalem (Deut 16:7). The disciples want to know where in Jerusalem Jesus intends to have his Passover meal so that they can **go** there with the lamb, roast it, and make other preparations.

The Feast of Passover and Unleavened Bread: See page 363

13 **He sent two of his disciples,** just as he has sent his followers by twos on missions on previous occasions (6:7; 11:1). Jesus does not tell the two disciples where he plans to eat the Passover meal but instead instructs them, **Go into the city and a man will meet you, carrying a jar of water. Follow him.** A man carrying a water jar would have been an unusual sight, since water jars were normally carried by women. How did Jesus know that his disciples would encounter a man carrying a jar of water? One explanation is that this is an instance of Jesus having knowledge of future or remote events. Another explanation is that Jesus had already made some arrangements for his Passover meal but wanted as few people as possible to know where he would eat it. As will be evident shortly, Jesus knows that one of the Twelve is looking for an opportunity when Jesus could be seized. Jesus tells the two disciples that once they have left the Temple area and are in the city, **a man will meet** them. Jesus speaks as if he has arranged for a man to be looking for the two disciples, and this man will be **carrying a jar of water** to identify himself to the disciples. The disciples do not need to say anything to him but are to **follow him:** the whole arrangement seems quite surreptitious.

14 **Wherever he enters, say to the master of the house**—the home-owner—**"The Teacher says, 'Where is my guest room where I may eat the Passover with my disciples?'"** Those living in Jerusalem put their extra rooms at the disposal of pilgrims who needed a place within the city where they could eat the Passover meal. The homeowner presumably will know that **the Teacher** is Jesus and will

cooperate with the two disciples. Jesus speaks of **my guest room** as if he has already made arrangements to use it. Jesus sent two disciples to carry out detailed instructions on a previous occasion, and that incident also unfolded as if Jesus had contacts in the Jerusalem area (11:1–6).

15 Jesus continues his instructions: **Then he will show you a large upper room furnished and ready.** An **upper room** could be a top-floor room or a rooftop enclosure. The word translated **furnished** has connotations of couches with fabric coverings, upon which those dining could recline. It is a **large** room, large enough for a fair number of people to share the Passover meal with Jesus. Passover meals were family affairs that included women and children. Did Jesus want to gather his entire new family of disciples for a last meal with them? Mark will write only of the Twelve joining Jesus for the Passover meal (14:17), but **a large upper room** could have accommodated more. Jesus tells his disciples, **Make the preparations for us there:** roast the lamb and prepare the other foods customarily eaten at a Passover meal.

16 **The disciples then went off, entered the city, and found it just as he had told them; and they prepared the Passover.** Mark does not record any surprise on the part of the disciples that Jesus knew what would happen when they went into the city. Rather, they seem to accept that they are carrying out their part of the preparations, which fit in with other arrangements that Jesus has made. Mark does not tell us that Jesus wanted to keep the location of his Passover meal a secret, but Mark's account makes sense if that was Jesus' intent.

For reflection: Have I ever had a sense of what Jesus wanted me to do but without knowing how my efforts would fit into the larger picture?

ORIENTATION: *Mark provides few details of the Passover meal as such. Instead he focuses on Jesus giving his body and blood to his disciples. Jesus' gift is preceded and followed by somber words about betrayal and denial.*

Betrayal

¹⁷ When it was evening, he came with the Twelve. ¹⁸ And as they reclined at table and were eating, Jesus said, "Amen, I say to you, one of you will betray me, one who is eating with me." ¹⁹ They began to be distressed and to say to him, one by one, "Surely it is not I?" ²⁰ He said to them, "One of the Twelve, the one who dips with me into the dish. ²¹ For the Son of Man indeed goes, as it is written of him, but woe to that man by whom the Son of Man is betrayed. It would be better for that man if he had never been born."

Gospel parallels: Matt 26:20–25; Luke 22:21–23; John 13:21–30

OT: Psalm 41:10

NT: Mark 10:33; 14:10–11

17 **When it was evening, he came with the Twelve:** Passover meals were eaten after sunset. When the time for the meal arrives, Jesus comes to the place where the two disciples have prepared the meal (14:13–16), bringing **the Twelve** with him. Jesus has presumably spent the day in public, protected from arrest by the crowds (14:1–2). Now he enters a private house, where he is less safe but whose location he has kept rather secret (the apparent point of his convoluted instructions in 14:13–15).

18 **And as they reclined at table and were eating:** the Passover meal may originally have been eaten while standing (see Exod 12:11), but Jews adopted the Greek custom of reclining on one elbow at banquets. Reclining was interpreted as a sign of liberation from slavery in Egypt, since slaves did not recline while eating.

Banquets: See page 142

Jesus said, "Amen, I say to you, one of you will betray me, one who is eating with me." Jesus' words are shocking, but the shock has been softened for Mark's readers: Mark has identified Judas Iscariot as the one who will betray Jesus (3:19) and has told of Judas going to the chief priests with an offer of betrayal (14:10–11). The disciples have heard Jesus' warning that he will be "handed over to the chief priests and the scribes, and they will condemn him to death" (10:33), but Jesus has not told them who will hand him over. Now he tells them that it will be one of them, one who is sharing the meal with him. Jesus' pronouncement is solemn: **Amen, I say to you, one of you will betray me,** one whom I called to be my disciple and share my life. Jesus will be handed over to death by a member of his new family (3:33–35), by someone **who is eating with** him. Meals were an expression of intimacy; to be betrayed by someone with whom one had shared a meal heightened the betrayal (see Psalm 41:10). Some of Mark's first readers had experienced such betrayal when fellow Christians, and even family members, had withered under the pressure of persecution and betrayed them to the authorities (13:9–13).

19 **They began to be distressed.** The disciples' distress is not over Jesus being betrayed and what that will mean for him but over what Jesus' words say about them. The disciples are **distressed** that Jesus thinks that one of them will betray him. Except for Judas (14:10–11), they are all convinced that they will not let Jesus down (see 14:31); how could Jesus have any doubts about them? They begin **to say to him, one by one, "Surely it is not I?"** They phrase the question in a way that invites and almost demands a reassuring response from Jesus: "No, of course it's not you." They want Jesus' personal vote of confidence.

For reflection: Surely I would never betray Jesus?

20 Jesus does not give them the reassurance they are seeking. Instead he narrows his focus: his betrayer will be **one of the Twelve, the one who dips with me into the dish.** It will not simply be a disciple present at this meal who will hand Jesus over to his enemies but **one of the Twelve,** one of those commissioned by Jesus for a special role (3:13–19; 6:7–13).

Some of those eating the Passover meal are reclining so close to Jesus that they are eating food from the same dish. The betrayer will be **the one who dips with me into the dish.** Sometimes pieces of bread were used as edible spoons to scoop up vegetable sauce (Ruth 2:14);

375

during a Passover meal, bitter herbs (Exod 12:8) were dipped into a sauce. That Jesus and his betrayer are sharing from the same dish indicates the intimacy that the betrayer enjoys with Jesus, but it does not identify him: more than one of **the Twelve,** perhaps even all of them, could be dipping into the same dish as Jesus.

21 **For the Son of Man indeed goes, as it is written of him:** Jesus speaks of himself as the **Son of Man,** as he has on other occasions, including when he has spoken of his coming suffering and death (8:31; 9:12, 31; 10:33–34). He says that the Son of Man **goes,** which means goes to his death but may also hint at his going to God as the outcome of his death. The Son of Man goes **as it is written of him:** Jesus again speaks of his coming suffering and death being in accordance with what is written in Scripture (9:12), perhaps having in mind Isaiah 52:13–53:12. Jesus' suffering and death are in accordance with the will of God (see 8:31), which Jesus freely accepts.

Son of Man: See page 41

But even if Jesus being handed over to death is in accordance with God's will, the one who will hand him over will still be responsible for his actions: **but woe to that man by whom the Son of Man is betrayed.** Jesus' **woe** is a cry of sorrow. Jesus still does not name his betrayer but speaks of him as **that man.** That man's betrayal of Jesus will result in the death of Jesus, but his betrayal will mean a fate worse than death for himself: **it would be better for that man if he had never been born.** Jesus does not spell out how the betrayer will be punished; Jesus only indicates that never having existed will seem preferable. Jesus' words are not merely a statement of fact but also a warning: he is giving the betrayer the chance to abandon his plan to tell the authorities when Jesus could be quietly seized. If the betrayer will not remain faithful to Jesus out of love, perhaps he will do so out of fear: what could be scarier than a fate worse than nonexistence? Jesus has let the betrayer know that he is on to him but without revealing the betrayer's identity to the others; this way the betrayer can back down without anyone ever learning who he is. Yet Jesus also knows that he will go ahead with his betrayal once he has the opportunity to do so. This meal will be Jesus' last supper.

For reflection: How has Jesus given me opportunities to change my course? Am I faithful to him more out of love or out of fear?

Jesus Gives His Body and Blood

22 **While they were eating, he took bread, said the blessing, broke it, and gave it to them, and said, "Take it; this is my body." 23 Then he took a cup, gave thanks, and gave it to them, and they all drank from it. 24 He said to them, "This is my blood of the covenant, which will be shed for many. 25 Amen, I say to you, I shall not drink again the fruit of the vine until the day when I drink it new in the kingdom of God."**

Gospel parallels: Matt 26:26–29; Luke 22:15–20

OT: Exod 24:3–8; Lev 17:11; Isaiah 53:11–12

NT: Mark 6:41; 8:6; John 6:51–58; 13:1–17; 1 Cor 11:23–27

22 Jesus has just told his disciples that he will be betrayed by one of the Twelve—by one who is sharing this meal with him (14:18–21). **While they were eating, he took bread, said the blessing, broke it, and gave it to them.** The host at a Passover meal or other formal Jewish meal would offer a **blessing** for a loaf of bread, thanking God for providing food for his people. One formulation of such a blessing is "Blessed are you, O Lord our God, King of the universe, who brings forth bread from the earth." The host would then break the bread into portions and distribute it among those eating together as a sign of the fellowship they were enjoying. Jesus does this, giving bread **to them,** to those with whom he is eating. In Mark's account this apparently includes Judas, for Mark has made no mention of him leaving. Jesus' disciples would not have been surprised by his blessing, breaking, and sharing bread; he had done so at previous meals (6:41; 8:6). But they would have been surprised by what Jesus said: **Take it; this is my body.** To the Hebrew way of thinking, the **body** was not just one's flesh but one's whole person as a physical being. Jesus gives bread to his disciples and says, **Take it,** which in the context of the meal means eat it. He says that the bread they are eating is his **body,** his person, his self. The meaning of this is something that the disciples need to ponder—and that we need to ponder as well.

Jesus' giving bread as his body to his followers has many dimensions of significance. Jesus has repeatedly spoken of his coming death: his body will be broken just as this bread is broken. Jesus' giving of broken bread signifies his giving of his life (10:45). If Jesus' surrendering of his life for the sake of others is a sacrificial offering, then this meal is a sacrificial banquet, that is, a meal in which a portion of what has been offered to God is eaten. Jesus will no longer be bodily present to his followers, but he will continue to be present through bread that is his body. Bread is life-sustaining nourishment; the bread that is Jesus' body gives life, eternal life. Bread shared at a meal creates fellowship; the bread Jesus shares with his followers unites them to him and to one another.

For reflection: How do I understand Jesus' statement "This is my body"?

23 **Then he took a cup, gave thanks, and gave it to them, and they all drank from it.** Wine was drunk on festive occasions, such as the Passover meal and other formal meals. Later Jewish practice called for four cups of wine to be drunk during a Passover meal, but it is uncertain whether this was the custom in the time of Jesus. Just as Jesus said a blessing for the bread (verse 22), he **gave thanks** to God for the wine: the Greek word translated **gave thanks** gives us the word *Eucharist*. One Jewish formulation of a thanksgiving for wine is "Blessed are you, O Lord our God, King of the universe, creator of the fruit of the vine." Jesus **took a cup** of wine and, after giving thanks for it, **gave it** to his disciples, **and they all drank from it.** Just as sharing a loaf of bread is a sign of fellowship, so is drinking from the same cup.

24 The disciples would not have been surprised that Jesus as the host had thanked God for the wine and shared it with them, but his words of explanation would again have been surprising. **He said to them, "This is my blood of the covenant, which will be shed for many."** Wine was commonly red at the time of Jesus and might have reminded one of blood, but Jews had a great abhorrence for drinking blood. The Hebrew notion of **blood** was that it was the life of a human or an animal and was never to be consumed (Gen 9:4; Deut 12:16, 23). When an animal was

sacrificed, its blood was offered to God as an intrinsic part of offering the life of the animal (Lev 17:11).

> Since the life of a living body is in its blood, I have made you put it on the altar, so that atonement may thereby be made for your own lives, because it is the blood, as the seat of life, that makes atonement.
>
> Lev 17:11

In speaking of **my blood, which will be shed for many,** Jesus refers to his coming death: pouring out one's blood means pouring out one's life. Jesus' words invoke the Old Testament understanding of blood being poured out as a sacrificial offering to God; it has been only a few hours since Passover lambs were slaughtered in the Temple and their blood sprinkled on the altar. Jesus has one particular blood offering in mind. The phrase **blood of the covenant** echoes the words Moses uttered at Mount Sinai as he mediated the covenant that established a relationship between God and the people of Israel. Moses read the terms of the covenant to the people, and they agreed to them: "All that the Lord has said, we will heed and do" (Exod 24:7). Bulls were offered in sacrifice to God, and their blood was divided into two portions. One portion was poured on the altar as an offering to God, and Moses sprinkled the other portion on the people as "the blood of the covenant" (Exod 24:8)—the blood that sealed their participation in the covenant relationship that God was establishing with them.

> Then he took the blood and sprinkled it on the people, saying, "This is the blood of the covenant which the Lord has made with you in accordance with all these words of his."
>
> Exod 24:8

The blood that Jesus will shed will be **blood of the covenant:** in pouring out his lifeblood **for many,** Jesus will establish a covenant relationship between them and God. **Many** has the Hebrew sense of all, as opposed to a few. The expression **for many** echoes a prophecy of Isaiah that speaks of a servant of God who takes upon himself the sins and sufferings of many and dies on their behalf (Isaiah 53:11–12).

> Through his suffering, my servant shall justify many,
>> and their guilt he shall bear.
> Therefore I will give him his portion among the great,
>> and he shall divide the spoils with the mighty,
> Because he surrendered himself to death
>> and was counted among the wicked;
> And he shall take away the sins of many,
>> and win pardon for their offenses.
>
> Isaiah 53:11–12

Just as the bread that is the body of Jesus has multiple dimensions of significance, so does the cup of wine that is his blood. Jesus' death will be his offering his life to God, and that offering will create a covenant relationship between God and the disciples of Jesus. In sharing a cup of wine as his blood, Jesus shares his life with his followers. By drinking from the same cup, they enter into a union with Jesus and with one another. Jesus told James and John that they would drink from his cup of suffering (10:38–39); drinking from the cup of wine that is the blood of Jesus signifies one's willingness to share his suffering and death.

For reflection: What is the significance for me of Jesus' giving a cup of wine as his blood?

25 **Amen, I say to you, I shall not drink again the fruit of the vine until the day when I drink it new in the kingdom of God.** The phrase **fruit of the vine** means wine. Jesus solemnly assures his disciples that he will not drink wine again until he drinks it **new in the kingdom of God.** Jesus announced that the **kingdom of God** was at hand (1:15), and he began to establish God's reign through his healings, exorcisms, teachings, and gathering of disciples. But God's reign is not yet fully established on earth: that will happen only at the end of the present age. At the time of Jesus, one image for God's reign was

a banquet (Isaiah 25:6), and Jesus implicitly invokes that image when he speaks of drinking wine in the kingdom of God. Jesus knows that he is about to die, but his dying will mean entering into the fullness of God's reign. Jesus proclaimed the resurrection of the dead (12:18–27), and he goes to his death with the confidence that he will rise (8:31; 9:31; 10:34).

Jesus' words and actions during his last meal with his disciples anticipate and interpret his death. He will give his life for the sake of others; his death will bring him to God. He will no longer be bodily present to his followers but will be present in bread and wine that have become his body and blood. Who is Jesus? He is the one who gives his life as a ransom for many (10:45) and thereby establishes a covenant relationship between them and God. He is the one who gives us his body and blood to nourish us on our way to the eternal banquet of the kingdom of God.

Kingdom of God: See page 96

For reflection: How is my understanding of Jesus shaped by what he did and said at the Last Supper?

COMMENT: THE EUCHARIST Mark's first readers would have known about Jesus' final meal with his followers before they read Mark's Gospel. Proclaiming what Jesus did and said on the night before he died was part of the gospel message, as Paul makes clear (1 Cor 11:23–26). The Church from its earliest days celebrated "the breaking of the bread" (Acts 2:42), or "the Lord's supper" (1 Cor 11:20). Mark's audience would have understood Mark's account of what Jesus did during the Last Supper in light of their own celebration of the Eucharist. The same is true for us today: we do not read the Gospel of Mark in a vacuum. Our understanding of what Jesus did and said during the Last Supper is shaped by a number of factors, above all by our own participation in the celebration of the Eucharist. Our understanding of the Eucharist rests not only on what we read in Mark but also on what we read in the other Gospels and writings of the New Testament. We are also the heirs of two millennia of theological reflection on the meaning of the Eucharist. St. Thomas Aquinas in the thirteenth century employed concepts from the Greek philosopher Aristotle in characterizing bread and wine becoming the body and blood of Christ as "transubstantiation"—a change of their underlying reality. The Roman Catholic Church embraces this term even as it acknowledges that bread and wine being the body and blood of Christ surpasses our understanding.

Denial

26 Then, after singing a hymn, they went out to the Mount of Olives.

27 Then Jesus said to them, "All of you will have your faith shaken, for it is written:

> **'I will strike the shepherd,**
> **and the sheep will be dispersed.'**

28 But after I have been raised up, I shall go before you to Galilee." 29 Peter said to him, "Even though all should have their faith shaken, mine will not be." 30 Then Jesus said to him, "Amen, I say to you, this very night before the cock crows twice you will deny me three times." 31 But he vehemently replied, "Even though I should have to die with you, I will not deny you." And they all spoke similarly.

Gospel parallels: Matt 26:30–35; Luke 22:31–34; John 13:36–38
OT: Zech 13:7

26 **Then, after singing a hymn, they went out to the Mount of Olives.** The Greek for **singing a hymn** could also be translated "singing *hymns*." Later Jewish writings called for singing Psalms 114 or 115 through 118 at the conclusion of a Passover meal; this may have been the custom at the time of Jesus. From the upper room in Jerusalem (14:13–17), Jesus and his disciples **went out to the Mount of Olives.** Jesus and the disciples have been spending their nights in Bethany, on a southeastern slope of the Mount of Olives (11:1, 11–12, 19–20; 14:3). The law requiring the Passover meal to be eaten in Jerusalem (Deut 16:7) was interpreted to mean that the entire night should be spent in Jerusalem. As a way of accommodating the pilgrims who flooded Jerusalem, the western slope of the **Mount of Olives,** which faces Jerusalem, was considered within the city limits. This may account for Jesus stopping on the Mount of Olives instead of going on to Bethany.

27 **Then Jesus said to them, "All of you will have your faith shaken":** the disciples will come to an obstacle that will trip them up, and **all** will fall away. Jesus earlier spoke of those who embraced his words with joy

but would fall away when faced with trials and persecution (4:16–17). The disciples have left everything behind to follow Jesus (10:28), but they have chronically misunderstood him (6:52; 8:17–21; 9:34–35; 10:13–14, 37), especially when he has spoken of his coming suffering and death (8:33; 9:32). They are like shallow-rooted plants that will quickly wither when the sun comes out (4:5–6); they will not be able to cope with Jesus being handed over to death.

Jesus turns to a prophecy of Zechariah to throw light on what will happen. **For it is written: "I will strike the shepherd, / and the sheep will be dispersed."** Jesus implicitly identifies himself as the shepherd (Jesus has cared for those who were like sheep without a shepherd—6:34). But Jesus makes an adjustment in Zechariah's prophecy. Zechariah's prophecy begins "Strike the shepherd" (Zech 13:7), but in Jesus' version God says that he will strike down the shepherd: **I will strike the shepherd.** Jesus' death is in accordance with God's will (see 8:31; 9:12; 12:10–11; 14:21). When Jesus the shepherd is struck down, **the sheep will be dispersed.** The disciples will abandon Jesus out of weakness and fear, yet this will be a fulfillment of Zechariah's prophecy, and their failure has been incorporated into God's plans. Even so, the disciples being **dispersed** is a reversal of what is at the heart of discipleship: being with Jesus (3:14).

> Strike the shepherd
> > that the sheep may be dispersed.
>
> Zech 13:7

Some analyses of Mark's Gospel highlight three predictions that Jesus makes of his death (8:31; 9:31; 10:33–34), which might give the impression that Jesus spoke about his death only three times. However, Jesus has referred to his death many times, from the allusion of the bridegroom who is taken away (2:20) to the allusion of the shepherd who is struck down. Jesus has his death on his mind throughout the Gospel of Mark; his dying is integral to his mission.

28 Jesus characteristically does not speak of his dying without also speaking of his rising: **But after I have been raised up, I shall go before you to Galilee.** Neither the death of Jesus nor the scattering of his disciples

will be the end. Jesus will be **raised up:** the expression implies that he will be raised up *by* God. As a result of his being raised up, his scattered flock will be gathered together around him again. He tells his disciples, **I shall go before you to Galilee.** His words might mean that the disciples will return to Galilee after Passover to find the risen Jesus already there, but his words also have a fuller meaning. Just as Jesus walked at the head of his disciples as he led them to Jerusalem (10:32), so he will again **go before** them and lead them after his resurrection as a shepherd leads his flock. Their failure will not be final; they will get a second chance at discipleship. The disciples lived in Galilee; by speaking of leading his disciples in **Galilee,** Jesus indicates that he will be present in their everyday lives. **Galilee** can therefore serve as a symbol for our everyday lives as well. Jesus promised to be with his followers after he was raised up, and his promise extends to us.

For reflection: How is the risen Jesus present to me?

29 Peter hears only half of what Jesus has said. **Peter said to him, "Even though all should have their faith shaken, mine will not be."** Peter seizes upon Jesus' prediction that all of them will fall away (verse 27) and ignores Jesus' promise to gather them together after he has been raised (verse 28). Peter is ready to believe that **all** the other disciples will fail Jesus, but Peter refuses to accept that his own **faith** will be **shaken** and that he will be tripped up. Peter takes Jesus' prediction as a slur on his loyalty and contradicts Jesus, as he has done before (8:31–32).

30 Jesus knows that Peter will do worse than desert him. **Then Jesus said to him, "Amen, I say to you, this very night before the cock crows twice you will deny me three times."** Jesus' pronouncement is solemn: **Amen, I say to you.** Before sunrise, **before the cock crows twice,** Peter will **deny** Jesus, not just once but **three times.** Jesus has said that anyone who wants to be his disciple has to deny himself or herself (8:34), but Peter will do the opposite: he will deny Jesus. To **deny** Jesus means to repudiate him, to be ashamed of him. Jesus earlier warned of the danger of being "ashamed of me and of my words in this faithless and sinful generation" (8:38).

31 **But he vehemently replied, "Even though I should have to die with you, I will not deny you."** Peter again contradicts Jesus, doing so **vehemently.** Peter declares that he is determined to give up his life for Jesus rather than **deny,** or disown, Jesus. But in denying that he will deny Jesus, Peter is in denial: his vehemence is the bluster of self-deception. **And they all spoke similarly:** all of Jesus' disciples indicate that they are willing to die with Jesus rather than deny him, but they are also in denial about their weakness.

For reflection: Am I able to face up to my own weaknesses and sins?

Even though Peter will not live up to his words, they express the right response to Jesus. Jesus called his followers to lose their lives for his sake (8:35), imitating his example of serving others and giving his life for their sake (10:43–45). If only Peter could follow through on what he professed he would do!

For reflection: How am I at following through on what I want to do for Jesus?

The forecasts Jesus has made of the disciples' scattering and Peter's denials will be fulfilled (14:50, 66–72), but Mark's audience knows that Jesus' promise to rise and restore his disciples' relationship with him (verse 28) was also fulfilled. Peter will fulfill his pledge to die for Jesus; he will be martyred in Rome a few years before the Gospel of Mark is written. Mark's Gospel contains consolation for those who are persecuted for the sake of Jesus (10:29–30), including those who are betrayed by fellow Christians (13:13). Mark's Gospel also has a message for those who crumble under persecution or betray other Christians. Peter will deny Jesus three times, and it will become Roman practice to give Christians three opportunities to deny Jesus in order to escape martyrdom. Jesus' original disciples will desert him, and Peter will deny him, but the risen Jesus will gather them to him again. In the same way, all later Christians who desert Jesus or deny him under persecution may be forgiven and restored to the family of Jesus.

In Mark's Gospel, Jesus' giving of bread and wine as his body and blood is preceded by his warning that one of the Twelve will hand him over to death (14:17–21) and is followed by his warnings that all of his disciples will desert him and one will deny him (14:27–31). Jesus will shed his blood for the sake of many (14:24), including those who repudiate him. Jesus taught that "those who are well do not need a physician, but the sick do. I did not come to call the righteous but sinners" (2:17). Jesus demonstrated what this meant on the night before he died.

For reflection: What are the implications for me of Jesus giving his body and blood to those who would betray, desert, and deny him?

Jesus Prays and Waits in Gethsemane

³² Then they came to a place named Gethsemane, and he said to his disciples, "Sit here while I pray." ³³ He took with him Peter, James, and John, and began to be troubled and distressed. ³⁴ Then he said to them, "My soul is sorrowful even to death. Remain here and keep watch." ³⁵ He advanced a little and fell to the ground and prayed that if it were possible the hour might pass by him; ³⁶ he said, "Abba, Father, all things are possible to you. Take this cup away from me, but not what I will but what you will." ³⁷ When he returned he found them asleep. He said to Peter, "Simon, are you asleep? Could you not keep watch for one hour? ³⁸ Watch and pray that you may not undergo the test. The spirit is willing but the flesh is weak." ³⁹ Withdrawing again, he prayed, saying the same thing. ⁴⁰ Then he returned once more and found them asleep, for they could not keep their eyes open and did not know what to answer him. ⁴¹ He returned a third time and said to them, "Are you still sleeping and taking your rest? It is enough. The hour has come. Behold, the Son of Man is to be handed over to sinners. ⁴² Get up, let us go. See, my betrayer is at hand."

Gospel parallels: Matt 26:36–46; Luke 22:39–46
NT: John 12:27; Heb 4:15; 5:7–9

32 After the Last Supper, Jesus and his disciples went to the Mount of Olives (14:26), where **they came to a place named Gethsemane.** The name **Gethsemane** in Aramaic means oil press—a press for extracting oil from olives. The Mount of Olives was used, as its name indicates, for

growing olives. A tradition dating back to the fourth century or earlier locates **Gethsemane** near the foot of the Mount of Olives and directly across the Kidron Valley from the Temple. Jesus **said to his disciples, "Sit here while I pray."** Jesus wants to pray and selects a grove of olive trees near an olive press as a suitable site.

33 **He took with him Peter, James, and John.** Jesus previously chose **Peter, James, and John** to witness his raising of the daughter of Jairus (5:37) and his transfiguration (9:2) and to hear (along with Andrew) his teaching about the coming of the Son of Man (13:3). Jesus might have wanted their moral support as he prayed, just as we turn to our closest friends in a time of crisis. All three disciples have boasted that they can share Jesus' sufferings (10:38–39; 14:29–31). They have been given a privileged glimpse of Jesus' glory as the Son of God (9:2–7); now they will see Jesus in all his humanness.

Jesus **began to be troubled and distressed.** Noting that the Greek words for **troubled** and **distressed** are forceful words, scholars suggest that their meaning could be conveyed in English by expressions like *greatly distraught and anguished* or *seized by horror and distress.* Jesus is very troubled, but it is not immediately apparent why. Jesus knows that his death is near, but he was calm and resolved when he spoke of it earlier in the evening (14:17–28).

34 **Then he said to them, "My soul is sorrowful even to death."** Jesus' expression could be paraphrased "I am so sorrowful that I could die." The reason for Jesus' sorrow is still not clear, but the humanity of Jesus is evident: Jesus is able to feel deep distress and profound sorrow. He tells Peter, James, and John, **Remain here and keep watch.** One implication of **keep watch** is stay awake. It is nighttime, and the disciples drank wine with their late-evening meal; they might naturally be drowsy. But Jesus tells them to stay awake and **keep watch.**

For reflection: What does Jesus' being troubled, distressed, and sorrowful mean for me?

35 **He advanced a little and fell to the ground:** Jesus previously prayed in solitude (1:35; 6:46), but now he goes only a short distance away from

Peter, James, and John. Jews customarily prayed out loud; the three disciples might be close enough to overhear Jesus' words. Jesus **fell to the ground:** lying prostrate was a position of supplication (5:6, 22, 33; 7:25). Mark tells us that Jesus **prayed that if it were possible the hour might pass by him.** The **hour** means the time when Jesus will be handed over to death (see verse 41). Jesus prays that this hour might **pass by him;** he asks to be excused from death, **if it were possible.** Jesus is sure that all things are possible for God (10:27), and he asks God to rearrange his plans so that they will not require Jesus' death. Surely God can find some other way to accomplish what he wants to accomplish.

36 Mark has summarized the content of Jesus' prayer, and now he quotes it; the double presentation gives emphasis. Jesus **said, "Abba, Father, all things are possible to you. Take this cup away from me, but not what I will but what you will."** Jesus prays to God as **Abba,** an Aramaic word that Mark translates for his readers as **Father.** A child would call his or her father "Abba"; it was a familiar form of address, roughly equivalent to "Dad." There is something new and striking in Jesus addressing God as **Abba.** We have no evidence that Abba was used by any individual before the time of Jesus as a personal form of address for God. Jesus prays out of his intimate experience of God as his Father, just as God addressed Jesus as his beloved Son (1:11; see also 9:7). Jesus does not pray to an aloof God but to his loving Father. Later Christians will imitate Jesus in calling upon God as Abba (Rom 8:15; Gal 4:6).

> *For reflection: What are the implications for me of Jesus praying to God as his Father?*

Jesus tells his Father, **All things are possible to you** (see 10:27). Since everything is possible for God, then God could liberate humans without Jesus giving his life as a ransom (10:45); God could establish a covenant without the shedding of Jesus' blood (14:24). Jesus asks his Father to **take this cup away from me.** The **cup** is the cup of Jesus' suffering (10:38–39; see also 14:23–24); Jesus' asking to be relieved of drinking this cup is the same as his asking that the hour pass by (verse 35). In light of everything Jesus has said about his coming death, it is a surprising request. Jesus has spoken of his death as being God's will for him and in accordance with Scripture (8:31; 9:12; 14:21). He has repeatedly talked with his disciples about his death without showing the least sign of fear at the prospect. But now that the hour for him to drink the cup of suffering is drawing near, Jesus is greatly troubled and distressed and sorrowful (verses 33–34), and he asks God to spare him from what he knows is God's will for him.

Mark's Gospel does not explain why Jesus is now so distressed by what lies ahead that he asks God to excuse him from it. Jesus was acquainted with the horrors of crucifixion, but Jesus' reaction seems to be based on more than an aversion to a painful death. Jewish martyrs embraced torture and death as the price of faithfulness to God (2 Macc 6–7). Mark's educated readers would have known that the Greek philosopher Socrates had accepted an unjust death with calm nobility.

In my own speculations I wonder if Jesus' anguish was not simply over the prospect of suffering and death but also over suffering and death as *his Father's will for him and his followers*. It was one thing for Jesus to suffer at the hands of an enemy; it was another thing for him to suffer at the hands of an Abba who had professed his love (1:11; 9:7). It was one thing to be crucified if that might spare others from suffering. It was another thing for Jesus to embrace crucifixion not only for himself but also as a pattern for what his followers would have to endure.

Mark's first readers knew what it meant to lay down one's life for Jesus, and even literally to take up one's cross. They may have wondered why it was necessary, why God not only allowed their suffering but also seemingly demanded it as the price of eternal life. Mark's Gospel does not directly answer such questioning but it does describe Jesus in anguished prayer on the night before he died. If Jesus confronted the mystery of a loving God allowing or ordaining suffering, then his followers should not be surprised when they are plunged into this mystery themselves.

For reflection: What is my understanding of why Jesus asked his Father to spare him from what he knew was his Father's will for him?

Jesus prays, **Take this cup away from me,** but he also prays, **But not what I will but what you will.** Jesus wants his Father to accomplish his purposes in some other way, but Jesus nonetheless submits himself to his Father's will. The new family of Jesus is made up of those who do the will of God (3:35); for Jesus to refuse to do God's will would mean betraying and abandoning his mission. Jesus instead abandons himself into his Father's hands.

Jesus' prayer in Gethsemane—**Abba, Father, all things are possible to you. Take this cup away from me, but not what I will but what you will**—can be said in a few seconds, but it will soon be clear that Jesus spent an extended time in prayer. Mark gives us the substance of Jesus' prayer: in anguish he committed himself to do what his Father was asking of him but pleaded that his Father not ask it. **Not what I will but what you will** was not so much the conclusion of Jesus' prayer as a refrain that ran through it, even as he asked his Father to change his will.

For reflection: When has it been most difficult for me to pray, "Thy will be done"?

Mark has told us of God twice speaking from the heavens, proclaiming Jesus to be his beloved Son (1:11; 9:7). No voice from the heavens responds to Jesus in Gethsemane. God's silence is God's answer to Jesus' prayer.

For reflection: Has God ever spoken to me by his silence?

37 Jesus interrupts his prayer and walks the few steps back to where he left Peter, James, and John. **When he returned he found them asleep.** He asked them to keep watch (verse 34), but they have failed to do so. **He said to Peter, "Simon, are you asleep? Could you not keep watch for one hour?"** Jesus gave him the nickname **Peter** (meaning rock; see 3:16), but Jesus now addresses him as **Simon,** perhaps because Simon is not behaving very rocklike. **Could you not keep watch?** is more literally *Have you not the strength* to keep watch? Peter and the other disciples were not able to keep watch even for the **one hour** that Jesus was in prayer. If they did not even have the strength to stay awake, how will they react when faced with a greater challenge?

38 **Watch and pray that you may not undergo the test.** Jesus repeats his charge to his disciples but explains more fully what they must do

and why. To **watch** means to stay awake, but it also echoes the exhortations to watch in Jesus' parable of the gatekeeper whose master will return unexpectedly (13:33–37). To **watch** means to be vigilant and prepared for a time of crisis, and Jesus' arrest will be a crisis for his followers. They will be prepared only if they **pray,** just as Jesus has been praying as the hour draws near for him. They should **pray** that they **may not undergo the test.** Jesus may be speaking here of the testing that he will endure and may be saying to them, Pray that you will not be tested as I will be tested.

Jesus' next words, **the spirit is willing but the flesh is weak,** are usually taken as his comment on the condition of his disciples. Their **spirit** (their thoughts, their wills, their aspirations) may be set on remaining faithful to Jesus (as they have professed: 14:29, 31), but their **flesh** (their humanness in all its vulnerability and weakness) is not up to it. They should pray that they will not be tested because, despite their intentions, they will fail, as Jesus has warned (14:27).

There is another way to understand Jesus' words. When he says, **The spirit is willing but the flesh is weak,** he may also be speaking of himself. Jesus has been resolved to do his Father's will, even to the point of laying down his life. But now that the hour is at hand, he is torn by sorrow and distress and anguish. Jesus experienced the human struggle between willingness and weakness. The letter to the Hebrews says that Jesus is able to "sympathize with our weaknesses" because he has been "tested in every way" that we are tested (Heb 4:15; see also Heb 5:7–9).

For reflection: Can I accept that Jesus experienced struggles similar to my struggles with my weaknesses?

39 **Withdrawing again, he prayed, saying the same thing.** The implication of Jesus **saying the same thing** is that he continued to ask his Father to release him from drinking the cup of suffering and death but also continued to profess that he would accept that cup if his Father did not release him. It was not enough for Jesus to simply say once, "Not what I will but what you will"; Jesus' willingness of spirit is wrestling with his weakness of flesh. Mark does not tell us how long Jesus prayed this second time, but it was long enough for his disciples to fall asleep again, despite Jesus' exhortation to stay awake.

40 **Then he returned once more and found them asleep, for they could not keep their eyes open.** Their not being able to **keep their eyes open** may be due to the late time of night and their having had a full meal with wine, but Jesus expected them to stay awake nonetheless. When Jesus has to wake them again after repeated exhortations to keep watch, they **did not know what to answer him,** apparently because they were embarrassed. We can note, though, that Peter was also at a loss for words after Jesus' transfiguration (9:6); it seems as if he cannot cope with Jesus in glory or Jesus in anguish.

Although Mark will speak of Jesus returning to find his disciples asleep a third time (verse 41), Mark does not describe Jesus going off for a third period of prayer, nor does he say how long it lasted. Other factors that Mark does not make explicit can help us reconstruct the drama of Jesus in Gethsemane in Mark's Gospel. One factor is Judas's movements. Judas was looking for an opportunity when Jesus could be seized without a crowd around to protect him (14:1–2, 10–11). Mark's account of Jesus' arrest makes sense if Judas accompanied Jesus to Gethsemane after their meal together (14:17–26), saw where Jesus was praying and that there were few people around, and then went to inform the authorities of Jesus' whereabouts after the other disciples had fallen asleep.

Another factor is the geography of the Mount of Olives. Since Jesus was praying on a western slope of the Mount of Olives across the narrow Kidron Valley from the Temple, it would have taken Judas twenty minutes at most to walk from Gethsemane to where Jewish authorities were awaiting word from him. Jesus' lengthy time of prayer would have given Judas plenty of time to lead an arresting party to Jesus. The geography of the Mount of Olives would also have given Jesus ample opportunity to escape arrest. It would have taken Jesus less than twenty minutes to walk up and over the Mount of Olives, which is really a hill. If Jesus had gone northeast instead of turning southeast toward Bethany, he would have quickly come to the beginning of the Judean wilderness, a desolate region that stretches from an eastern crest of the Mount of Olives all the way to Jericho. Jesus could easily have found a hiding place there. Jews followed a lunar calendar, which meant that there was a full moon on Passover, celebrated on the fifteenth day of the month. Jesus might have been able to see an arresting party leaving an eastern gate of Jerusalem, allowing him to escape ahead of them into the Judean wilderness.

Instead of escaping, Jesus remains in Gethsemane, waiting for Judas to show up with an arresting party. The waiting prolongs Jesus' struggle between flesh and spirit, between wanting release and saying, "Your will be done." Jesus' agony in Gethsemane is his waiting in Gethsemane: waiting either for his Father to change his mind or for Judas to arrive. God is silent; Judas is on his way.

41 **He returned a third time and said to them, "Are you still sleeping and taking your rest?"** Jesus' disciples have fallen asleep a third time; while he has been praying in anguish they have been snoring. We would like to believe that we learn from our mistakes and are able to overcome our faults. The example of Jesus' first followers is a sobering warning about the weakness of flesh despite the willingness of spirit.

> *For reflection: What is the lesson for me in the disciples' repeatedly falling asleep?*

It is enough. The hour has come. Behold, the Son of Man is to be handed over to sinners. The precise meaning of the Greek word translated **it is enough** is obscure, but its sense might be that Jesus' waiting is over, for **the hour has come** for him **to be handed over** by Judas. The implication of **handed over** is "handed over *by God*": Jesus' death is part of God's mysterious purposes. Jesus has spoken of being "handed over to men" (9:31) and "handed over to the chief priests and the scribes" who will "hand him over to the Gentiles" (10:33). Now Jesus speaks of being handed over to **sinners.** Jesus will be put to death not only by sinners but also *for* sinners, in fulfillment of Isaiah's prophecy (Isaiah 52:13–53:12).

Son of Man: See page 41

42 **Get up, let us go. See, my betrayer is at hand.** Jesus might have caught sight of Judas and the arresting party before his disciples did. Jesus invites his disciples to **get up** and **go** with him to meet them. Jesus' waiting and wrestling in prayer are over; he now steps forth to embrace his Father's will, and he asks his disciples to accompany him as he goes to his death. These are the last words of Jesus to his disciples in the Gospel of Mark.

Jesus Is Handed Over

⁴³ Then, while he was still speaking, Judas, one of the Twelve, arrived, accompanied by a crowd with swords and clubs who had come from the chief priests, the scribes, and the elders. ⁴⁴ His betrayer had arranged a signal with them, saying, "The man I shall kiss is the one; arrest him and lead him away securely." ⁴⁵ He came and immediately went over to him and said, "Rabbi." And he kissed him. ⁴⁶ At this they laid hands on him and arrested him. ⁴⁷ One of the bystanders drew his sword, struck the high priest's servant, and cut off his ear. ⁴⁸ Jesus said to them in reply, "Have you come out as against a robber, with swords and clubs, to seize me? ⁴⁹ Day after day I was with you teaching in the temple area, yet you did not arrest me; but that the scriptures may be fulfilled." ⁵⁰ And they all left him and fled. ⁵¹ Now a young man followed him wearing nothing but a linen cloth about his body. They seized him, ⁵² but he left the cloth behind and ran off naked.

Gospel parallels: Matt 26:47–56; Luke 22:47–53; John 18:2–12
NT: Mark 9:31; 10:33–34; 14:18–21, 27

43 Jesus announced that his betrayer was at hand (14:42), and **while he was still speaking, Judas, one of the Twelve, arrived.** Mark's identifying Judas as **one of the Twelve** highlights Judas's being not merely a disciple of Jesus but also one whom Jesus specially chose to be with him and exercise his authority (3:13–19; 6:7). Jesus will be handed over to death by one of his closest associates. Mark's first audience may have experienced similar betrayals when persecution led some Christians to hand over other Christians, even their relatives, to death (see 13:12).

For reflection: Have I ever felt betrayed by someone I loved and trusted?

Judas came **accompanied by a crowd with swords and clubs who had come from the chief priests, the scribes, and the elders.** The armed **crowd** is a group of men hired by the religious authorities. (Josephus, a first-century Jewish historian, writes that a later high priest hired thugs to collect tithes by force.) The armed men have been sent by the chief priests, the scribes, and the elders, the three groups that make up the Jewish ruling body known as the Sanhedrin (15:1).

Sanhedrin: See page 400

44 **His betrayer had arranged a signal with them.** Mark does not refer to Judas by name but identifies him by his deed: he is the **betrayer,** the one who will hand Jesus over to those who seek his death. Judas has led an armed party to where Jesus has been praying on the Mount of Olives, and Judas has told them, **The man I shall kiss is the one; arrest him and lead him away securely.** Some in the arresting party might not be able to pick Jesus out from his disciples at night; Judas will identify Jesus with a kiss. A **kiss** on the cheek was a form of greeting, as it is in some cultures today. Judas tells those he has led to Jesus to **arrest him**—literally, to seize him—**and lead him away securely.** By telling them to make sure Jesus is held **securely,** Judas might have been implying, Don't let him escape. Judas seems to have a quick strike in mind, with the authorities spiriting Jesus away before his supporters can rally. Jesus has no intention of escaping: he has waited for the arresting party to arrive, in accordance with his Father's will for him (14:32–42).

45 **He came and immediately went over to him and said, "Rabbi."** Judas **immediately** goes to Jesus, with no hesitation, and calls him **Rabbi.** This was a respectful form of address at the time of Jesus (Peter also addressed Jesus as Rabbi: 9:5; 11:21); it later became a title for Jewish teachers and scholars. Then Judas **kissed him:** Mark uses an emphatic form of the Greek word for **kissed** to highlight the cynicism of Judas's action. A kiss was an affectionate greeting, but Judas's kiss is a kiss of death. Mark records no response or reaction of Jesus to Judas's greeting and kiss. This is the last glimpse the Gospel of Mark provides of Judas.

Rabbi: See page 217

46 **At this they laid hands on him and arrested him.** Jesus repeatedly foretold that he would be handed over to those who would kill him (9:31; 10:33–34; 14:18–21), and his words are now being fulfilled. Jesus will be in physical captivity from now until his death.

47 **One of the bystanders drew his sword, struck the high priest's servant, and cut off his ear.** Mark's account does not read as if the one wielding the sword is a disciple of Jesus: Mark uses the word **bystanders** elsewhere to refer to onlookers (14:69, 70; 15:35) but never to disciples. The Mount of Olives was likely used as a campground by Passover pilgrims who could not find lodging in Jerusalem. Mark has three times noted that Jesus' popular support deterred those who wanted to seize him (11:18; 12:12; 14:1–2). If pilgrims were camping near Gethsemane, some of them might have witnessed Jesus being seized. One of them could have carried a sword on his journey to Jerusalem for protection against highway robbers (a problem at the time of Jesus: Luke 10:30); he could have tried to prevent Jesus' arrest. If **the high priest's servant** was in charge of the arresting party, he would have made a natural target. A few individuals trying to protect Jesus would have been no match for a "crowd with swords and clubs" (verse 43), and the scuffle could have been over rather quickly, with only the high priest's servant suffering much injury. Judas had looked for an opportunity for Jesus to be seized without a crowd around to protect him but might have had to settle for Jesus being relatively alone on the Mount of Olives in the middle of the night. All of this reconstruction is conjectural but would make sense of Mark's words in this verse. In Mark's account, Jesus ignores both the sword wielder and his victim and addresses those who have seized him.

48 **Jesus said to them in reply, "Have you come out as against a robber, with swords and clubs, to seize me?"** Jesus reacts not to being arrested but to the manner of his arrest, for it misrepresents him. Jesus is not a **robber,** a violent man who has to be subdued with **swords and clubs.** Later in the first century the Greek word for **robber** was also used for violent insurrectionists. If it already had this meaning at the time of Jesus, then Jesus was denying that he was a rebel trying to overthrow Roman rule, and he was telling his captors that he did not need to be treated as such.

49 **Day after day I was with you teaching in the temple area, yet you did not arrest me.** Mark has recounted Jesus teaching in the **temple area** on only two days (11:15–13:1). Mark's account of Jesus' time in Jerusalem may be simplified, just as his account of Jesus' ministry in

Galilee is condensed. Jesus' point is that he has made no attempt to hide. On the contrary, Jesus has taught **in the temple area,** which is under the control of the religious authorities who have sent this arresting party, yet these authorities did not seize Jesus there. They held back for fear of the crowds (11:18; 12:12; 14:1–2), but Jesus proclaims that they restrained themselves so **that the scriptures may be fulfilled.** It is difficult to find any text of Scripture that concerns the place and timing of Jesus' arrest. While Isaiah 52:13–53:12 is related in a general way and Zechariah 13:7 will be fulfilled very shortly, Jesus may mean that his arrest is part of the working out of God's will, which is revealed in Scripture.

50 **And they all left him and fled.** This is one of the shortest sentences or verses in Mark's Gospel, and one of the saddest. Mark's Greek construction emphasizes that **all** of Jesus' disciples flee (another translation would be "And leaving him they fled, all of them"). Jesus is deserted by those whom he called to be with him (3:14). He has invested a lot of time in instructing and forming them, but they abandon him in his hour of crisis. Jesus is not surprised: he told them they would scatter (14:27, invoking Zech 13:7), and they do so, despite their promises that they would stand by him even at the cost of their lives (14:31). They are unable to pay the price of discipleship (8:34–38). Their failure is a warning to Mark's readers: Don't be too sure of yourselves; better disciples than you have failed. But there is also a message of hope: Jesus promised to gather his disciples to him after his resurrection, despite their forsaking him at his arrest (14:27–28).

For reflection: Have I ever let Jesus down out of fear or self-interest?

51 What happens next is enigmatic. **Now a young man followed him wearing nothing but a linen cloth about his body.** This **young man** does not seem to be one of the disciples, for they have all fled. Yet he **followed** Jesus, which indicates some sort of discipleship. His **wearing nothing but a linen cloth about his body** (more literally, over his nakedness) is strange, for spring nights in Jerusalem are usually cool, as it is on this particular night (see 14:54, 67). **Linen cloth** was expensive: was he wealthy? He seems to have tried to remain with Jesus after the disciples fled, but some in the arresting party **seized him,** apparently grabbing hold of his linen wrap.

52 **But he left the cloth behind and ran off naked.** There have been numerous speculations about this young man's identity and the meaning of this strange incident. Some suggest the man was Mark. Some see connections with Jesus' leaving behind a linen burial cloth (15:46) after he was raised and with there being a young man at the empty tomb (16:5). Others find connections with the later baptismal ritual of the person to be baptized going into the water naked and being given a new garment afterward. All these explanations seem strained. I prefer to view the incident as a vivid image, however enigmatic, of what it means to desert Jesus. The disciples left all to follow Jesus (1:18, 20; 10:28); now this follower leaves behind all—even his clothes—to desert Jesus. What better image could there be for abandoning Jesus than running off naked into the darkness?

Jesus Is Accused

⁵³ **They led Jesus away to the high priest, and all the chief priests and the elders and the scribes came together. ⁵⁴ Peter followed him at a distance into the high priest's courtyard and was seated with the guards, warming himself at the fire. ⁵⁵ The chief priests and the entire Sanhedrin kept trying to obtain testimony against Jesus in order to put him to death, but they found none. ⁵⁶ Many gave false witness against him, but their testimony did not agree. ⁵⁷ Some took the stand and testified falsely against him, alleging, ⁵⁸ "We heard him say, 'I will destroy this temple made with hands and within three days I will build another not made with hands.'" ⁵⁹ Even so their testimony did not agree.**

Gospel parallels: Matt 26:57–61; Luke 22:54–55; John 18:12–16

53 **They led Jesus away to the high priest:** Jesus is brought to the house of the high priest. Mark does not name him, but the high priest from AD 18 to 36 was Caiaphas. His long tenure as high priest was unusual and indicates that he was an effective collaborator with the Roman governor, who had the power to depose him. **And all the chief priests and the elders and the scribes came together.** Mark sometimes uses the word **all** to mean many (see 1:5). We should

probably envision a meeting of those **chief priests, elders,** and **scribes** who want Jesus dead (11:18; 12:12; 14:1, 10–11), held in the spacious house of the high priest.

High priest, chief priests: See page 403

Elders: See page 303

Scribes: See page 40

54 **Peter followed him at a distance into the high priest's courtyard.** Peter fled with the other disciples when Jesus was arrested (14:50) but did not completely run away. He watched as Jesus was taken to the high priest's house and **followed** behind, but **at a distance.** Being a disciple of Jesus requires more than following him at a safe distance; it involves denying oneself, taking up one's cross, and remaining with Jesus (8:34). Yet Peter's following at a distance is better than abandoning Jesus altogether, as the other disciples have done. Peter enters **the high priest's courtyard:** fine houses were usually built around a central courtyard. Peter **was seated with the guards, warming himself at the fire.** The **guards** are attendants or servants of the high priest and of the chief priests, the elders, and the scribes who have come to the house of the high priest. While the religious leaders deliberate inside, their servants wait for them outside. They are warming themselves at a **fire,** since spring nights in Jerusalem (at an elevation of twenty-five hundred feet) are chilly. Peter sits down with them, **warming himself at the fire.** Peter could have run some risk in doing this: some of those in the courtyard could have been members of the party that seized Jesus and could have recognized Peter as one of Jesus' companions. Following Jesus even at a distance can have its risks.

For reflection: Do I follow Jesus only at a safe distance?

55 **The chief priests and the entire Sanhedrin kept trying to obtain testimony against Jesus in order to put him to death.** The **Sanhedrin** was a council made up of chief priests, elders, and scribes (15:1) and chaired by the high priest. It was the highest Jewish authority in religious and some civic matters, under Roman governance. It is not

, known how many members the **Sanhedrin** had at the time of Jesus. Just as Mark might have been overstating things when he wrote that "all" the chief priests, elders, and scribes had gathered (verse 53), so he may also be overstating matters when he writes that the **entire Sanhedrin** was assembled. Apparently many or all of the Sanhedrin members who have sought Jesus' death have gathered, at what seems to be a hastily called middle-of-the-night meeting on the Feast of Passover. They do not give Jesus a formal trial but conduct a hearing or an inquiry, **trying to obtain testimony against Jesus in order to put him to death.** They have already decided that Jesus must die (11:18; 14:1), and they want a justification for his execution. **But they found none:** they are not able to obtain **testimony** that justifies executing Jesus.

56 The council's failure to come up with testimony that provides an excuse for executing Jesus is not for lack of trying. **Many gave false witness against him, but their testimony did not agree.** The law of Moses required evidence from at least two witnesses in judicial proceedings (Deut 19:15), particularly when the penalty was execution (Num 35:30; Deut 17:6). **Many** testify against Jesus, but their testimony is **false** and inconsistent. Mark's account gives the impression that the religious leaders assembled hastily, and there wasn't time for witnesses to be coached and rehearsed.

BACKGROUND: SANHEDRIN At the time of Jesus, it was common for cities to have some form of city council, with what we think of as legislative, judicial, and executive responsibilities. In Jerusalem this council was called the Sanhedrin (from the Greek for "sitting together"). Its members were drawn from the aristocracy of high-priestly families and wealthy or influential citizens (elders) and included some religious scholars (scribes): see Mark 15:1. The high priest presided over the council's deliberations. Since AD 6, Jerusalem had been under direct Roman rule, exercised through governors such as Pontius Pilate. Rome normally allowed subject peoples to manage their own affairs, as long as public order was maintained and taxes paid. The Sanhedrin was the chief Jewish ruling body in Jerusalem under the umbrella of Roman authority. It dealt primarily with religious matters, but since religion pervaded all of Jewish life, authority in religious matters covered a wide range of concerns. The Sanhedrin's religious authority extended beyond Jerusalem, because of its makeup and the importance of the Jerusalem Temple in Jewish life. *Related topics: Elders (page 303), High priest, chief priests (page 403), Scribes (page 40).*

> *The testimony of two or three witnesses is required for*
> *putting a person to death; no one shall be put to death*
> *on the testimony of only one witness.*
>
> Deut 17:6

57 Some took the stand and testified falsely against him, alleging:
Mark again characterizes the testimony given against Jesus as false. Mark
leaves no doubts in his readers' minds about Jesus' innocence.

58 Those who testify allege that they **heard him say, "I will destroy this
temple made with hands and within three days I will build another
not made with hands."** Mark has not recounted Jesus saying what the
witnesses allege he said; their version of Jesus' words is garbled. Jesus has
said that the Temple will be destroyed (13:2), but he has not said that he
will be the one to destroy it. Jesus has used expressions like **within three
days,** but he has done so in speaking about his rising from the dead (8:31;
9:31; 10:34). Jesus has implied that he will be the cornerstone of a new
structure erected by God (12:10–11), but Jesus has not said, **I will build**
it, any more than he has said, **I will destroy** the Temple.

The charges made against Jesus may be garbled, but Jesus has done
and said things that would threaten those who control the Temple. He
entered Jerusalem surrounded by a crowd who acclaimed him and the
coming of the kingdom of David (11:7–11); Jewish authorities might
view him as a messianic pretender out to oust them from power. Jesus
disrupted commerce in the Temple and quoted a prophecy that characterized those who controlled the Temple as thieves; when Jewish
authorities heard about it, they wanted him dead (11:15–18). They
demanded to know what authority Jesus thought he had to tamper
with what was under their jurisdiction (11:27–28). They were further
enraged when Jesus told a parable that implied that he was the beloved
Son of God and they were murderous tenants plundering God's vineyard (12:1–9, 12). If Jesus has spoken of the Temple being destroyed
(13:1–2) and God erecting some kind of new edifice (12:10–11), those
whose power and wealth depend on the Temple have to view Jesus as
a threat. The charge made against Jesus—**We heard him say, "I will
destroy this temple made with hands and within three days I will
build another not made with hands"**—indicates what these religious

leaders are worried about, even if this charge is so garbled as to be (as Mark twice notes) false.

For reflection: How do I react when Jesus' teachings pose a threat to my status or comfort?

Mark's first readers might have found truth in this false accusation against Jesus. Jesus did accomplish something **within three days:** he rose from the dead. In rising he did **build another** edifice, one **not made with** human **hands.** Jesus became the cornerstone (12:10–11) of a new place of God's presence on earth: the community of his followers, the new family of Jesus (3:34–35), gathered together again after his rising (14:28) and to be gathered to God at the end of this age (13:24–27).

59 Mark again notes that the charges made against Jesus were inconsistent: **even so their testimony did not agree** (see verse 56). The chief priests, elders, and scribes wanted to build a case against Jesus (verse 55), but they have not succeeded. The hearing seems to be stalemated.

ORIENTATION: *The Gospel of Mark reaches one of its climaxes: for the first time Jesus publicly proclaims his identity.*

Jesus Proclaims Who He Is
⁶⁰ The high priest rose before the assembly and questioned Jesus, saying, "Have you no answer? What are these men testifying against you?" ⁶¹ But he was silent and answered nothing. Again the high priest asked him and said to him, "Are you the Messiah, the son of the Blessed One?" ⁶² Then Jesus answered, "I am;

> **and 'you will see the Son of Man**
> > **seated at the right hand of the Power**
> > **and coming with the clouds of heaven.'"**

⁶³ At that the high priest tore his garments and said, "What further need have we of witnesses? ⁶⁴ You have heard the blasphemy. What do you think?" They all condemned him as deserving to die.

⁶⁵ Some began to spit on him. They blindfolded him and struck him and said to him, "Prophesy!" And the guards greeted him with blows.

> Gospel parallels: Matt 26:62–68; Luke 22:63–71; John 18:19–23
> OT: Psalm 110:1; Isaiah 50:6; 53:7; Dan 7:9–10, 13–14
> NT: Mark 8:29–31, 38; 10:33–34; 13:24–27

60 Witnesses have not been able to produce testimony that would justify executing Jesus (14:55–59), so the high priest takes matters into his own hands. **The high priest rose before the assembly and questioned Jesus, saying, "Have you no answer? What are these men testifying against you?"** Those who want to do away with Jesus previously "sent some Pharisees and Herodians to him to ensnare him in his speech" (12:13); now the **high priest** tries to get Jesus to incriminate himself. Jesus has heard the testimony against him; the high priest challenges him, **Have you no answer?** His question implies that Jesus has made no response to the testimony. The high priest asks, **What are these men testifying against you?** What about these charges? Did you say that you would destroy the Temple and in three days build another (14:58)?

BACKGROUND: HIGH PRIEST, CHIEF PRIESTS The office of high priest is traced back to Aaron in the Old Testament. Over the course of time, high priesthood became restricted to descendants of Zadok, the high priest at the time of Solomon. This succession was broken by Maccabean rulers in the second century BC when they usurped the office of high priest. Thereafter the high priest was a political appointee. Some Jews, especially the Essenes, considered these latter high priests illegitimate, since they were not descendants of Zadok. The high priest had religious functions, and only the high priest could enter the Holy of Holies of the Temple, once a year, on the Day of Atonement. The importance of the high priest extended beyond religious matters. The high priest had authority over the Temple and its income, which was the mainstay of the economy in Jerusalem. Because the high priest was the highest-ranking Jewish authority, he served as an intermediary between Rome and the Jewish people. Rome expected the high priest to help keep the nation in line and to ensure payment of tribute, or taxes, to Rome, and the high priest remained in office at the pleasure of Rome. The Gospels refer to "chief priests," a group that would have included the current high priest, former high priests, other high-ranking priests, and members of high-priestly families. The chief priests were a wealthy aristocracy within the priesthood; ordinary priests carried out their assigned duties in the Temple but had little say over how it was run.

---

61 **But he was silent and answered nothing:** Mark makes the same point twice to highlight Jesus' silence in face of the charges made against him. Jesus will not enter into the charade. Those of Mark's first readers who were familiar with the book of Isaiah might have recalled the prophecy about a servant of God who, "though he was harshly treated, . . . submitted / and opened not his mouth; / Like a lamb led to the slaughter / or a sheep before the shearers, / he was silent and opened not his mouth" (Isaiah 53:7).

Again the high priest asked him and said to him, "Are you the Messiah, the son of the Blessed One?" The high priest continues to interrogate Jesus but turns from what Jesus allegedly said he would do (destroy and rebuild the Temple) to who he is. The high priest asks, **Are you the Messiah?** The Greek of Mark's Gospel puts emphasis on the word **you.** The question is contemptuous: Do **you,** a Galilean village handyman, claim to be **the Messiah?** The question seems unconnected to the previous charges against Jesus: there was no popular expectation that **the Messiah** would either destroy or rebuild the Temple. But Jesus was hailed at his entry into Jerusalem as one who would reestablish the kingdom of David (11:9–10), which many expected the Messiah to do. Jesus spoke in the Temple area about the Messiah (12:35–37), and Peter might not have been alone in thinking that Jesus was the Messiah (8:29). If Jesus claimed to be **the Messiah,** that would be of concern to the high priest. Whatever the Messiah would do when he came, he would hardly endorse the high priest's comfortable partnership with Rome.

Messiah, Christ: See page 204

Along with asking Jesus if he is **the Messiah,** the high priest also demands to know whether Jesus thinks he is **the son of the Blessed One.** The expression **Blessed One** is a way of referring to God that, out of reverence, avoids the use of God's name. At the time of Jesus, the title Son of God was not a title for the Messiah. However, the Messiah was expected to be a descendant of David, and some Old Testament passages refer to kings in David's dynasty as sons of God (2 Sam 7:12–14; Psalms 2:2, 7; 89:27–28), so the concepts of Messiah and Son of God were linked in a way. Jesus addressed a parable to religious leaders that implicitly identified him as the beloved Son of God the vineyard owner

(12:1–9).The high priest challenges Jesus, Who do you think you are? Do you pretend to be **the son of the Blessed One**?

Son of God: See page 64

62 **Then Jesus answered, "I am."** Jesus affirms what the Gospel of Mark was written to proclaim: he is the Messiah, that is, the Christ and the Son of God (1:1). This is the only time in Mark's Gospel that Jesus publicly proclaims himself to be the Messiah and God's Son. Jesus previously silenced demons who recognized his identity (1:24–25, 34; 3:11–12), and he did not let his disciples tell anyone that he was the Messiah (8:29–30). As his death approached, Jesus hinted at his being the Son of God and the Messiah (12:1–11, 35–37). Now that his death is at hand, Jesus speaks openly about his identity. There is no danger now that he will be taken to be a Messiah who will vanquish his enemies by force; Jesus has submitted himself to the power of his enemies. There is no danger now that his status as the Son of God will be seen as an entitlement to earthly honors; Jesus is on his way to the most ignominious of deaths.

For reflection: What significance do I find in Jesus' not publicly proclaiming his identity until just before his death?

When Peter proclaimed Jesus to be the Messiah (8:29), Jesus corrected Peter's understanding of the Messiah by speaking of himself as the Son of Man who would suffer greatly, be rejected, and be killed (8:31). Jesus again speaks of himself as **the Son of Man,** telling the high priest, **I am** the Messiah, the son of the Blessed One, **and "you will see the Son of Man / seated at the right hand of the Power / and coming with the clouds of heaven."** Jesus combines two Scripture passages that he has previously invoked (12:36; 13:26). The book of Daniel portrays thrones being set up in heaven and "one like a son of man coming, / on the clouds of heaven" to receive glory and dominion (Dan 7:9, 13–14). Mark's readers know that Jesus' **coming with the clouds of heaven** means his coming in judgment (see 8:38; 13:26–27).

Thrones were set up
and the Ancient One took his throne. . . .

405

I saw

> *One like a son of man coming,*
> > *on the clouds of heaven; . . .*
> *He received dominion, glory, and kingship;*
> > *nations and peoples of every language serve him.*
> > > Dan 7:9, 13–14

Jesus also invokes Psalm 110, in which God speaks to the psalmist's Lord and tells him, "Take your throne at my right hand" (Psalm 110:1). The image of the psalmist's Lord sitting on a throne to the right of God's heavenly throne provides a link with Daniel's vision of thrones being set up in heaven (Dan 7:9).

> The LORD *says to you, my lord:*
> > *"Take your throne at my right hand,*
> > *while I make your enemies your footstool."*
> > > Psalm 110:1

Jesus combines these Scripture passages so that **the Son of Man** is first **seated at the right hand of the Power,** that is, at the right hand of God, and then is **coming with the clouds of heaven.** The Jesus who now stands before the high priest will be seated at the right side of God. The Jesus who is now being judged will come as God's judge at the end of this age. Jesus corrected Peter's understanding of him by speaking of his suffering and death; now Jesus challenges the high priest's view of him by speaking of his enthronement at the side of God and his coming on the clouds of heaven. Jesus says, **You will see** this: the **you** is plural, and Jesus is addressing all those assembled in the high priest's house. They now see a Jesus who has been arrested like a criminal and is at their mercy. They will see Jesus in his glory when they are judged by him.

Mark's Gospel proclaims a Jesus who cannot be understood apart from his suffering and his exaltation. Both are difficult for us to grasp. That God would send his Son to suffer and die is beyond our comprehension. That we will be judged at the end of this age by a carpenter from Nazareth is also hard to take in.

For reflection: Who is Jesus? What do his words to the high priest mean for me?

63 **At that the high priest tore his garments.** Tearing one's garments was a traditional expression of grief, as over the death of someone (Gen 37:29, 34; 2 Sam 1:11–12; Judith 14:19; Job 1:18–20), but it could also be done as a sign of great distress (2 Kings 18:37–19:1). The high priest tears his garments not out of grief or distress but as a theatrical gesture. He reacts as if Jesus has said something very scandalous, but he is actually delighted that Jesus has made a claim that can be used to justify his execution. The high priest says, **What further need have we of witnesses?** Witnesses did not work out, but Jesus has just ensnared himself by his words.

64 **You have heard the blasphemy:** the high priest characterizes Jesus' words as **blasphemy.** There was no prohibition in the law of Moses against claiming to be the Messiah, nor was there a law against claiming to be a son of God. If Jesus' words were to justify his execution, they had to be interpreted as violating a law whose penalty was death. **Blasphemy** did call for the death penalty (Lev 24:15–16). In a narrow sense, blasphemy is sacrilegious use of God's name, which Jesus is not guilty of. But in a broader sense, the charge of blasphemy could be leveled against anyone claiming divine prerogatives for himself or herself. Thus Jesus was previously accused of blasphemy when he pronounced a man's sins forgiven (2:5–7). Jesus' claim that he is the Messiah and the Son of God and that he will be seen seated at the right hand of God and coming on the clouds of heaven is labeled **blasphemy** by the high priest, and thus it is a justification for Jesus' execution. The high priest elicits the agreement of the rest of those who are seeking Jesus' death: **What do you think?** Not surprisingly, they agree: **they all condemned him as deserving to die.**

It is important to note that the **all** who **condemned** Jesus **as deserving to die** were not all the Jews of the time of Jesus, nor even all the Jewish religious leaders (see 15:43–46), but a certain number of Jewish leaders who felt threatened by Jesus. Christians have all too often held all Jews guilty for the death of Jesus and used the involvement of some Jews in the death of Jesus as a justification for collective contempt for and persecution of Jews, forgetting that Jesus himself and his first followers were Jews. The Second Vatican Council declared, "Even though the Jewish authorities and those who followed their lead pressed for the death of Christ (cf. John 19:6), neither all Jews indiscriminately at that time, nor Jews today, can be charged with the crimes committed during his passion" (*Declaration on the Relationship of the Church to Non-Christian Religions,* section 4).

65 **Some began to spit on him.** Mark's account reads as if the **some** who **began to spit** on Jesus were the chief priests, elders, and scribes who had assembled in seeking Jesus' death. In the ancient world, as today, spitting on a person was an act of contempt (Num 12:14; Deut 25:9; Job 30:10). **They blindfolded him and struck him and said to him, "Prophesy!"** There were children's games at the time in which a person was blindfolded and buffeted and had to guess who was delivering the blows. Jesus is subjected to such play and told to **prophesy** who is hitting him. Jesus has just foretold his enthronement at the side of God and his coming on the clouds of heaven, and he is being mocked for pretending to have prophetic powers. Mark's readers can grasp the profound irony here. Jesus has foretold his rejection and suffering (8:31; 10:33–34), and his words are fulfilled by his being struck and mocked as a false prophet. Jesus has also foretold Peter's denying him three times (14:30), and this is happening even as Jesus is being mocked as a prophet (14:54, 66–72). **And the guards greeted him with blows:** Mark's somewhat peculiar expression conveys that those who have seized Jesus and are holding him in custody are slapping him, joining in on the abuse being heaped on Jesus.

Some of Mark's first readers might have been reminded of the words of a servant of God in a prophecy of Isaiah: "I gave my back to those who beat me, / my cheeks to those who plucked my beard; / My face I did not shield / from buffets and spitting" (Isaiah 50:6).

For reflection: What does the image of Jesus being spit upon and slapped signify for me?

ORIENTATION: *Peter followed Jesus at a distance and went into the courtyard of the high priest's house (14:54). As Jesus is being interrogated inside the house, Peter faces scrutiny outside.*

Peter Denies Jesus

⁶⁶ While Peter was below in the courtyard, one of the high priest's maids came along. ⁶⁷ Seeing Peter warming himself, she looked intently at him and said, "You too were with the Nazarene, Jesus." ⁶⁸ But he denied it saying, "I neither know nor understand what you are talking about." So he went out into the outer court. [Then the cock crowed.] ⁶⁹ The maid saw him and began again to say to the bystanders, "This man is one of them." ⁷⁰ Once again he denied it. A little later the bystanders said to Peter once more, "Surely you are one of them; for you too are a Galilean." ⁷¹ He began to curse and to swear, "I do not know this man about whom you are talking." ⁷² And immediately a cock crowed a second time. Then Peter remembered the word that Jesus had said to him, "Before the cock crows twice you will deny me three times." He broke down and wept.

Gospel parallels: Matt 26:69–75; Luke 22:56–62; John 18:17–18, 25–27
NT: Mark 14:29–31, 54

66 **While Peter was below in the courtyard:** when Jesus was taken to the house of the high priest, Peter followed as far as the **courtyard,** where he joined a group of servants sitting by a fire to keep warm (14:53–54). The courtyard is **below** the room in which Jesus is being interrogated, which implies that the high priest's house has more than one story. The ruins of a palatial, several-story house built around a courtyard with a vestibule have been excavated in Jerusalem. The house was not far from the Temple and had ritual baths, which suggests that it belonged to someone in the priestly aristocracy. There is no evidence that it was the house of the high priest Caiaphas, but it provides an example of upper-class housing at the time of Jesus. As Peter is sitting by the fire, **one of the high priest's maids** comes along. Jesus is standing in front of the high priest, a person of power; Peter will be confronted by one of his **maids,** a woman with no status or authority.

67 **Seeing Peter warming himself, she looked intently at him:** she first glances at Peter, **seeing** him by the flickering light of the fire, and then looks **intently at him,** taking a closer look to see if she recognizes him. She does, and she says, **You too were with the Nazarene, Jesus.** Her words are an observation, not an accusation. She identifies **Jesus** as **the Nazarene,** the Jesus who came from Nazareth, which is how Jesus was distinguished from other men who were also named Jesus (10:47). The maid tells Peter that he was **with** Jesus. She can mean only that she saw Peter in the company of Jesus, but Mark's readers know that being **with** Jesus is at the heart of discipleship and that Jesus specifically called Peter to be **with** him as one of the Twelve (3:14). She says to Peter that he **too** was with Jesus, as if she saw him with others who were with Jesus.

68 **But he denied it saying, "I neither know nor understand what you are talking about."** Peter pretends he has no idea what she is talking about but protests a bit too much: **I neither know nor understand.** Peter's seat by the fire has become a hot seat for him, **so he went out into the outer court.** The **outer court** was a vestibule between the central courtyard and the street. Peter retreats into the shadows, away from others, edging toward the exit.

For reflection: Have I ever feigned ignorance to avoid confronting an issue?

Some ancient manuscripts of Mark's Gospel include the words **Then the cock crowed** at this point, while other manuscripts omit these words. Mark will in any case write of a second cock crow (verse 72).

69 **The maid saw him and began again to say to the bystanders, "This man is one of them."** Peter may have moved away from the fire, but the **maid** can still see him. Peter told her that he didn't know what she was talking about, but she is convinced that she has seen him with other disciples of Jesus. She tells those in the courtyard, **This man,** the one in the shadows, **is one of them,** identifying Peter as a disciple of Jesus of Nazareth.

70 The maid is now speaking to bystanders and not to Peter, but Peter can't let it rest. **Once again he denied it:** the form of the Greek word for **denied** conveys repeated denials. Peter denies that he is "one of them" (verse 69), a disciple of Jesus. Instead of denying himself so that he can be a disciple (8:34), Peter denies that he is a disciple.

A little later the bystanders said to Peter once more, "Surely you are one of them; for you too are a Galilean." The **bystanders** find the maid's identification of Peter as a disciple of Jesus convincing because Jesus and his disciples are known to be Galileans, and Peter **too** is **a Galilean.** Peter's speech probably betrayed his origins: Jewish writings as well as Matthew's Gospel (Matt 26:73) indicate that Galileans spoke Aramaic with a regional accent (see also Acts 2:7). There would have been many Galileans in Jerusalem for Passover, but it had to be more than coincidence that a **Galilean** had slipped into the high priest's courtyard while Jesus the Galilean was under interrogation inside the house, particularly since Peter's denials seem overdone. **Surely** Peter is **one of them,** one of Jesus' disciples.

71 It is uncertain how dangerous it would have been for Peter to admit that he was a disciple of Jesus. Perhaps the bystanders' interest in Peter was only idle curiosity, something to pass the time while their masters delayed inside. Peter, however, seems terrified at the prospect of being identified as a disciple of Jesus. **He began to curse and to swear, "I do not know this man about whom you are talking."** Peter cannot even bring himself to call Jesus by name; he refers to him as **this man about whom you are talking.** Peter disavows any connection to Jesus and seals his disavowal with cursing and swearing. His cursing might have been calling down God's wrath on himself if he was lying; his swearing might have been denying under oath that he knew Jesus. A more ominous possibility cannot be ruled out: Peter might have cursed Jesus as a way of demonstrating that he could not possibly be one of Jesus' followers. In later times, Roman persecutors will give Christians a choice between cursing Christ and dying. Peter has gone from feigned ignorance (verse 68) to denial (verse 70) to perjury or worse (verse 71). Jesus warned his followers about being "ashamed of me and of my words"

(8:38), and it would be hard to be more ashamed of Jesus than Peter was in his sworn rejection of him.

> *For reflection: Have I ever been ashamed or afraid to admit that I am a follower of Jesus Christ?*

Peter's lie that he does not know Jesus contains an ironic truth, for in a sense Peter does not really know Jesus. Peter rejected the idea that Jesus would have to suffer and die (8:31–32); Peter cannot accept the cross for Jesus or for himself.

I do not know this man about whom you are talking: these are the last recorded words of any of the disciples in the Gospel of Mark. Given the failures of the disciples, we may wonder whether it was a little strange for Mark to characterize what he was writing as "good news" (1:1). But Mark knew what he was doing: he wanted to proclaim that the message of Jesus is good news despite human failure.

72 **And immediately a cock crowed a second time. Then Peter remembered the word that Jesus had said to him, "Before the cock crows twice you will deny me three times."** Everything has unfolded just as Jesus said it would (14:27–30), down to the cock crows. Peter is overcome by a sudden realization of what he has done, and he is shattered: **he broke down and wept.** Mark does not explain whether these were tears of self-pity or tears of remorse or even tears brought on by a realization that Jesus knew Peter would deny him but loved him anyway. Mark simply leaves us with the image of a broken and weeping Peter.

> *For reflection: Does anything in my own experience help me understand Peter's tears?*

Mark's first audience likely found multiple facets of meaning in Peter's denials. They were a warning about their own weaknesses. No matter how resolved they might be to remain faithful to Jesus at whatever cost, Peter had been just as resolved (14:31)—and look what he did. Disciples of Jesus must "watch and pray" that they will not be put to the test, for "the spirit is willing but the flesh is weak" (14:38).

Mark's first audience also knew that Peter went on to become one of the great leaders of the early Church and gave his life as a martyr for Jesus. There was still hope for any of Mark's readers who had fallen away because of persecution (4:17): if Peter could be rehabilitated, so could they. Likewise, Christians who had remained firm in times of persecution needed to forgive those who had denied their faith but later repented. If the risen Jesus gathered Peter to himself again despite Peter's denials (14:28–30), Jesus' followers must be willing to forgive as well.

Peter's example also has multiple meanings for us as we come to grips with our own weaknesses and failings and betrayals, and those of others.

For reflection: What lessons do I find in Peter's denials?

BACKGROUND: ROMAN PERSECUTION OF CHRISTIANS The earliest Roman documents describing procedures for dealing with Christians are letters exchanged in AD 110 between Emperor Trajan and Pliny the Younger. Trajan sent Pliny to revitalize Roman rule in the province of Bithynia-Pontus, on the southern shore of the Black Sea, in present-day Turkey. Pliny wrote letters to Trajan asking how the emperor wanted various matters handled. One letter (X.96) deals with the treatment of Christians. Pliny writes, "This is the approach I have followed with those who have been brought before me on the charge of being Christians. I have asked them whether they are Christians. If they acknowledge that they are, I ask them a second and third time, with a warning of the punishment. Those who persist I command to be taken off to execution. . . . Those who deny that they are or have been Christians I lead in reciting a prayer to the gods; then, with offerings of incense and wine, they pray to your statue and, in addition, speak evil of Christ. . . . Others, who were identified by an informer, declared themselves to be Christians but then denied it. They had been Christians, they said, but had ceased to be, three or more years ago—some as long as twenty years. All of these worshiped your statue and the images of the gods and reviled Christ." Pliny mentions ordering the "torture of two slave girls, whom they called deaconesses." Trajan replied that Pliny was following the right course of action. Pliny's procedures reflected earlier Roman practice, although it is doubtful whether these procedures date back to the time of Mark. Some of Mark's later readers would have found parallels between Peter's three denials of Jesus and Christians being demanded to deny Christ three times. Some would have interpreted Peter's cursing (Mark 14:71) as cursing the name of Christ, which persecutors demanded Christians do.

CHAPTER 15

Jesus Is Handed Over to Pilate

¹ As soon as morning came, the chief priests with the elders and the scribes, that is, the whole Sanhedrin, held a council. They bound Jesus, led him away, and handed him over to Pilate. ² Pilate questioned him, "Are you the king of the Jews?" He said to him in reply, "You say so." ³ The chief priests accused him of many things. ⁴ Again Pilate questioned him, "Have you no answer? See how many things they accuse you of." ⁵ Jesus gave him no further answer, so that Pilate was amazed.

> Gospel parallels: Matt 27:1–2, 11–14; Luke 23:1–5; John 18:28–38
> NT: Mark 10:33–34

1 **As soon as morning came, the chief priests with the elders and the scribes, that is, the whole Sanhedrin, held a council.** This may read as if at daybreak there was a second meeting of the **chief priests, elders,** and **scribes** who had interrogated Jesus during the night (14:55–65), but there is another way to understand Mark's words. Mark interrupted his account of Jesus' interrogation to recount Peter's denials (14:66–72), and now Mark is simply picking up the story of Jesus where he left off. Members of the **Sanhedrin held a council,** that is, they reached the end of their deliberations, deciding that Jesus deserved to die (14:64). **As soon as morning came** they acted: **they bound Jesus, led him away, and handed him over to Pilate.** It was not unusual for Roman legal proceedings to begin at sunrise, which was the start of the Roman workday. **They bound Jesus:** this is the first mention of Jesus being **bound.** Jesus did not resist arrest or attempt escape, so there is no need for him to be bound. However, sending him **bound** to Pilate subtly conveys that Jesus is dangerous and has to be restrained. **Pilate** was the Roman governor of Judea and some adjacent areas; as governor he had the authority to act as a judge and impose penalties, including the death penalty. When Pilate was in Jerusalem, he likely stayed in a grand palace built by Herod the Great near the main western gate of Jerusalem (see 15:16). They **handed him over:** Jesus has foretold that "the Son of Man will be handed over to the chief priests and the scribes, and they will condemn

him to death and hand him over to the Gentiles who will . . . put him to death" (10:33–4). God's will (8:31; 9:12; 14:21) is unfolding step-by-step.

Sanhedrin: See page 400

2 **Pilate questioned him, "Are you the king of the Jews?"** This would be a rather surprising question for Pilate to think of on his own. It is likely that Jewish religious leaders lodged charges against Jesus when they handed him over to Pilate. These religious leaders had concluded that Jesus deserved to die because he had blasphemed (14:64), but blaspheming the God of Israel was not against Roman law. Jesus had said that he was the Messiah (14:61–62), but this title may not have had much meaning for a Roman governor. Those handing Jesus over to Pilate translated the term *Messiah* into words that Pilate could understand: they said that Jesus claimed to be **the king of the Jews.**

BACKGROUND: PONTIUS PILATE was the Roman governor of Judea and the adjacent regions of Samaria and Idumea from about AD 26 to 36. His official title was prefect (military commander), but he also carried out the duties of a procurator (civil administrator), keeping order and collecting taxes. Pilate was a member of the lower Roman nobility that Rome drew on for governors of unimportant but sometimes troublesome provinces like Judea. Pilate lived in Caesarea, on the Mediterranean coast, using a seaside palace built by Herod the Great as his headquarters, or praetorium (Paul was later held captive here: Acts 23:35). Pilate commanded about twenty-five hundred to three thousand soldiers, most of whom were stationed in Caesarea but some of whom manned the Antonia Fortress, adjacent to the Temple in Jerusalem. During Jewish pilgrimage feasts, when Jerusalem was crowded with pilgrims, Pilate and his Caesarea troops went to Jerusalem to keep order. Pilate could be quite heedless of Jewish sensitivities, and he aroused anger by bringing images of the Roman emperor into Jerusalem and taking money from the Temple treasury to pay for an aqueduct. The Gospels portray Pilate as weak and indecisive. Philo, a first-century Jewish writer living in Egypt, might have been exaggerating when he characterized Pilate as arrogant, corrupt, cruel, and given to executing people without trial. Pilate seems to have been a man who made ill-considered decisions but backed down under pressure. Pilate was removed as governor after his troops killed some Samaritans. The fact that Pilate kept Caiaphas as high priest during his whole term as governor indicates that the two men had established a working relationship.

This is the first time that the title **king of the Jews** appears in Mark's Gospel; Jesus has never used this title for himself. The first man to call himself **the king of the Jews** was a Jewish ruler who ruled about a century before the birth of Jesus; the last ruler to use this title was Herod the Great, who ruled at the time of Jesus' birth. Since then, Rome had not allowed Jewish rulers to use the title. If Jesus is now claiming this title for himself, then Jesus is setting himself up in opposition to Roman rule. Rome dealt harshly with those who challenged its rule: crucifixion was the normal penalty. Having Pilate crucify Jesus would solve a lot of problems for Jewish religious leaders. They fear Jesus' popular support (11:18; 12:12; 14:1–2), but some of this support is based on the hope that Jesus will reestablish the kingdom of David (11:9–10). The sight of Jesus crucified would dash such hopes more thoroughly than Jewish religious leaders could ever do themselves. Jesus' crucifixion would not only do away with him but dissipate his following as well.

Hence Pilate is prompted to ask Jesus, **Are you the king of the Jews?** Mark's Greek construction puts emphasis on **you** and makes Pilate's question one of surprise or contempt: Are **you**, this Galilean peasant who stands bound before me, **the king of the Jews?** Is this your claim? Jesus **said to him in reply, "You say so."** Jesus' reply has the sense of "That may be how you put it; it is not how I would describe myself." Jesus does not accept the title **king of the Jews:** Jesus' mission is not to establish his own kingdom but the kingdom of God, and Jesus repudiates how earthly kings rule (10:42–45). But Jesus does not reject the title either: **the king of the Jews** is how Pilate expresses Jesus' identity as the Messiah, and Jesus is the Messiah (14:61–62).

For reflection: What do I mean when I hail Jesus as Christ the king?

3 **The chief priests accused him of many things:** they add other charges to their claim that Jesus purported to be the king of the Jews. Mark does not tell us what these additional charges were. We can suspect that the charge that Jesus claimed to be able to destroy the Temple and rebuild it in three days may have come up, for that was on the minds of Jesus' accusers (14:58). Perhaps they also mentioned Jesus' disruptive behavior in the Temple (11:15–17). Pilate has come to Jerusalem for Passover to make sure that no religious-nationalist riots break out; tampering with

the Temple, the central symbol of Jewish religion, is playing with fire. Whatever the exact nature of the **many things** that the chief priests accuse Jesus of, the purpose of the charges is to establish that Jesus needs to be executed.

4 **Again Pilate questioned him:** the word translated **questioned** conveys that Pilate questions Jesus repeatedly. **Have you no answer?** Do you have nothing at all to say in your defense? **See how many things they accuse you of.** Jesus is not merely charged with claiming to be the king of the Jews but accused of **many** other **things** as well.

5 Just as Jesus was silent before the high priest (14:61), so Jesus has nothing more to say to Pilate: **Jesus gave him no further answer.** Pilate is **amazed** by Jesus' silence. A man would normally speak up and defend himself if his life was at stake. Roman law at the time may have presumed the guilt of those who made no defense of themselves. Jesus' silence astonishes and perplexes Pilate, and Pilate reaches no decision about Jesus. Instead Pilate turns his attention to other matters.

For reflection: How do I understand Jesus' silence in face of the charges against him?

ORIENTATION: *Pilate has other cases on his docket, and attention briefly shifts away from Jesus.*

Jesus Is Handed Over to Crucifixion

6 Now on the occasion of the feast he used to release to them one prisoner whom they requested. 7 A man called Barabbas was then in prison along with the rebels who had committed murder in a rebellion. 8 The crowd came forward and began to ask him to do for them as he was accustomed. 9 Pilate answered, "Do you want me to release to you the king of the Jews?" 10 For he knew that it was out of envy that the chief priests had handed him over. 11 But the chief priests stirred up the crowd to have him release Barabbas for them instead. 12 Pilate again said to them in reply, "Then what [do you want] me to do with [the man you call] the king

of the Jews?" ¹³ They shouted again, "Crucify him." ¹⁴ Pilate said to them, "Why? What evil has he done?" They only shouted the louder, "Crucify him." ¹⁵ So Pilate, wishing to satisfy the crowd, released Barabbas to them and, after he had Jesus scourged, handed him over to be crucified.

Gospel parallels: Matt 27:15–26; Luke 23:13–25; John 18:38–40; 19:1, 4–16

6 **Now on the occasion of the feast he used to release to them one prisoner whom they requested.** Mark tells us that on Passover, Pilate customarily pardoned **one prisoner** upon request. This particular practice is not mentioned outside the Gospels, but in the Greek and Roman world prisoners were sometimes released at festivals as a goodwill gesture and to win popular favor. Long-term imprisonment was not common in the ancient world; a **prisoner** would likely be someone awaiting trial.

7 **A man called Barabbas was then in prison,** charged with a serious enough offense to be held until Pilate could judge him. Barabbas was in custody **along with the rebels who had committed murder in a rebellion.** Crimes like **murder** and **rebellion** were tried by Roman authorities who could impose the death penalty (two criminals will be crucified with Jesus: 15:27). Mark leaves it unclear whether Barabbas committed murder himself or was merely detained along with the insurrectionists. Mark provides no information about the **rebellion** either. It may have been a very minor affair, for ancient historians did not record any armed revolts against Roman rule in Palestine during the decades preceding Jesus' death, nor did they describe any instances of Rome executing Jewish revolutionaries during this period. Jesus' ministry took place during a period of relative calm, but this does not rule out minor incidents. There apparently was a skirmish in which some people were killed; others were arrested—including **Barabbas**—and now their cases are before Pilate. The name **Barabbas** means son of Abba or son of the Father in Aramaic, but this does not seem to be of interest to Mark, for he does not explain its meaning to his readers.

8 **The crowd came forward and began to ask him to do for them as he was accustomed.** The crowd is probably in a large courtyard adjacent to Herod's palace (15:16 makes this setting more explicit). Mark

does not tell us the makeup of this **crowd.** There is no reason to believe that it was made up of the same people who hailed Jesus' entry into Jerusalem (probably mostly Galilean pilgrims; see 11:8–10). Nor was this crowd made up of those who had until now supported Jesus (11:18; 12:12; 14:2): the reason for arresting Jesus at night in Gethsemane was to cut him off from his popular support. Many of those who showed up at daybreak to see Pilate have most likely come for reasons having nothing to do with Jesus: they are there to lobby Pilate to release Barabbas or another prisoner. Others in the crowd include the religious authorities who brought Jesus to Pilate, probably accompanied by their servants (14:54).

9 The crowd asked Pilate to release a prisoner (verse 8), but which prisoner do they want released? Pilate asks, **Do you want me to release to you the king of the Jews?** It would be nice to know what Pilate's tone of voice was as he asked this question; it may well have been mocking. Pilate does not refer to Jesus by name, and some in the crowd may have no idea who Pilate means by **the king of the Jews:** that was not what Jesus called himself during his public ministry. The chief priests certainly know who Pilate means, and Pilate may be baiting them by speaking of Jesus in this manner to the crowd. Pilate's raising the possibility of Jesus being the one to be released would taunt the chief priests: they brought Jesus to Pilate to be executed, not pardoned.

10 Mark explains Pilate's thinking: **For he knew that it was out of envy that the chief priests had handed him over.** Pilate recognizes that the chief priests' motives have little to do with Jesus being guilty of a serious crime; the priests are rather acting out of **envy.** In a narrow sense, **envy** here means jealousy of Jesus' popularity, which was a threat to their influence and power. In a broader sense, the Greek word for **envy** can mean malicious intent or spite (as it does in a passage in the book of Wisdom: "By the envy of the devil, death entered the world"—Wisd 2:24). Pilate perceives that Jesus has been **handed over** to him not because Jesus deserves to die but because the chief priests want Jesus done away with.

1 If Pilate is looking for an easy out by suggesting that the crowd ask for Jesus' release, it doesn't work. **The chief priests stirred up the crowd**

to have him release Barabbas for them instead. It may have been fairly easy for the chief priests to incite the **crowd** to ask for the **release** of **Barabbas.** Some in the crowd had probably come to clamor for his release; others had no idea who "the king of the Jews" was. Everyone would have recognized the **chief priests** as people with clout; why not go along with what they asked?

12 Mark implies that the crowd did ask for Barabbas to be released. **Pilate again said to them in reply, "Then what [do you want] me to do with [the man you call] the king of the Jews?"** The words in brackets are found in some but not all ancient manuscripts of Mark's Gospel. With or without these words, Pilate's question is strange. Pardoning Barabbas does not force Pilate's hand regarding Jesus; Pilate is free to release Jesus as well as Barabbas. The crowd is hardly impaneled as a jury with a say in the matter. Pilate may again be baiting the high priests, who brought the charge against Jesus that he claimed to be **the king of the Jews.** Pilate may also be trying to shift responsibility for the fate of Jesus from himself to others.

13 **They shouted again, "Crucify him."** The Greek word translated **again** can mean in turn or thereupon, which is its sense here: the crowd responds to Pilate by crying out for Jesus' crucifixion. Rome used crucifixion to execute violent criminals and rebels. Some of those awaiting trial before Pilate have committed murder and insurrection (15:7), and crucifixion will likely be their punishment. But why does the crowd cry out for Jesus' crucifixion? Mark does not tell us that the chief priests incited the crowd to ask for Jesus' crucifixion, but even if they did, why would the crowd follow their lead? It is one thing to clamor for the release of someone (verse 11); it is quite another thing to demand the worst-possible death for someone. Yet that is what the crowd does.

Crucifixion: See page 429

Some popular interpretations of this scene identify those shouting for Jesus' crucifixion with the crowd that hailed Jesus as he came into Jerusalem (11:8–10). These interpretations take the incident as an index of human fickleness. I find this identification unlikely: Jesus had been cut off from his supporters by his middle-of-the-night arrest. I believe that the crowd crying out, **Crucify him** was for the most part made up of people who had little idea who Jesus was, with a leavening of those who were actively seeking Jesus' death. In my reading of the incident, the cry of the crowd is not an index of human fickleness but of human callousness—of indifference to the suffering of others and perhaps even delight in their suffering. Those in the crowd who didn't know Jesus didn't care what happened to him.

For reflection: Have I in any way grown callous to the sufferings of others?

14 **Pilate said to them, "Why? What evil has he done?"** Pilate argues with the crowd, asking, **Why?** Why crucify Jesus? Even if Jesus purports to be the "king of the Jews," what has he actually **done** that is **evil**? Pilate is not convinced that Jesus deserves crucifixion. Why then does the crowd want him dead? They can provide no reason, so **they only shouted the louder, "Crucify him,"** substituting frenzy for justification. Pilate is losing control of the situation. He can dismiss the chief priests in their quest for Jesus' death with a wave of his hand, but an agitated mob in Jerusalem during Passover could be the tinder for revolt. Pilate has come to town precisely to prevent this from happening.

15 Pilate takes the easiest and most expedient course of action. **So Pilate, wishing to satisfy the crowd**—in an effort to placate the crowd, lest they riot—**released Barabbas to them,** as they requested. **Barabbas** could otherwise have been on his way to execution, if Pilate judged him guilty of insurrection and murder (15:7). Jesus said that he would give his life as a ransom (10:45); **Barabbas** is, ironically, the first to be set free because of Jesus. The freeing of Barabbas, whatever his crimes, can serve as an image for our own undeserved release by Jesus from the consequences of our sins.

For reflection: Am I able to see myself as Barabbas in relation to Jesus?

Pilate also gives in to the crowd's demands that Jesus be crucified: **after he had Jesus scourged, he handed him over to be crucified.** Mark mentions that Jesus was **scourged** but provides no description of it. No details would have been necessary for Mark's first readers: they knew the horrors of Roman scourging. Romans used whips made of leather thongs braided with pieces of bone or metal; these whips flayed through flesh and muscle down to bone. Scourging was a severe punishment in itself but was also done as a prelude to crucifixion, to inflict additional pain and weaken the victim. Pilate hands Jesus **over to be crucified,** and as the first stage of this awful death he has **Jesus scourged.** Mark will later provide a hint that this scourging left Jesus severely torn and weakened (15:21).

> *For reflection: In my meditations on the passion of Jesus, do I dwell on or pass over the scourging of Jesus?*

Pilate capitulates to the crowd despite knowing that Jesus has done no evil that justifies his death and despite knowing the malicious intent of those who seek his death. Pilate is as responsible for Jesus' death as anyone else in the chain of events. Judas handed Jesus over to the chief priests, who handed him over to Pilate, who **handed him over to be crucified.** Jesus foretold that this would happen (9:31; 10:33–34; 14:18) as God's will for him (8:31; 9:12; 14:21), but this does not lessen the guilt of those involved (14:21).

Even if we can reconstruct from Mark's account the chain of events that led to Jesus' death, and even if Jesus' death was part of God's plan, there is nonetheless an element of absurdity in how Jesus came to be crucified. Some of his teachings and actions were controversial (2:5–7, 16, 23–24; 3:5–6, 22, 30; 7:5), but they do not seem to have played a role in the deliberations that led to his death (14:55–64). Jesus proclaimed that the kingdom of God was at hand (1:15), but he never claimed to be "king of the Jews." Even though this will be put forth as the charge justifying his death (15:26), Pilate doesn't seem convinced that the charge is justified. Rather, Pilate caves in to a noisy crowd of people, many of whom may have been hard put to identify Jesus but nevertheless clamored for his crucifixion. Jesus accepts death despite its injustice.

> *For reflection: From my point of view, why did Jesus die?*

Jesus Is Mocked

¹⁶ The soldiers led him away inside the palace, that is, the prae-torium, and assembled the whole cohort. ¹⁷ They clothed him in purple and, weaving a crown of thorns, placed it on him. ¹⁸ They began to salute him with, "Hail, King of the Jews!" ¹⁹ and kept striking his head with a reed and spitting upon him. They knelt before him in homage. ²⁰ And when they had mocked him, they stripped him of the purple cloak, dressed him in his own clothes, and led him out to crucify him.

²¹ They pressed into service a passer-by, Simon, a Cyrenian, who was coming in from the country, the father of Alexander and Rufus, to carry his cross.

Gospel parallels: Matt 27:27–32; Luke 23:26; John 19:2–3, 17

OT: Isaiah 50:6; 53:3–5

NT: Mark 8:34; 10:34

16 **The soldiers led him away inside the palace, that is, the praeto-rium, and assembled the whole cohort.** The word translated **palace** can mean either courtyard or palace, but Mark explains to his readers that he has **the praetorium** in mind. **Praetorium** is a Latin term for the residence of a governor. When he was in Jerusalem, Pilate very likely made use of the luxurious palace that Herod the Great had built near the western gate of Jerusalem (called the Jaffa Gate today). At the northern end of this palace complex was a fortress guarding the gate, and **soldiers** would have been stationed there. These **soldiers** would have for the most part been recruits from Syria and the Gentile regions of Palestine rather than ethnic Romans. The soldiers lead Jesus **away inside the praetorium,** which implies that Jesus' hearing before Pilate and his scourging took place in an open area outside the praetorium. The soldiers might have taken Jesus into an interior courtyard where **the whole cohort** of soldiers who were stationed there gathered. A **cohort** was normally six hundred troops, but Mark may simply mean all the soldiers who were around at the time. We might wonder why Jesus was taken into the praetorium rather than immediately led away to be crucified. One conjecture is that Pilate was still trying the cases of men whom he might sentence to death (two will be crucified with Jesus:

15:27), and the soldiers were waiting for the trials to end so that they could execute the condemned prisoners as a batch. If this is so, then the mockery that the soldiers will heap on Jesus is their way of killing time and amusing themselves at his expense.

17 **They clothed him in purple.** Those subjected to Roman scourging were normally stripped of their clothes. Mark's words can be understood to mean that after Jesus was stripped and scourged in an outer courtyard (15:15), the soldiers brought him into the praetorium and **clothed him** again, but **in purple.** The dye used to produce **purple** cloth was extremely expensive, which led royalty to adopt purple as the color for their garments. It is improbable that ordinary soldiers actually had any purple clothing at their disposal. Roman soldiers wore red or scarlet cloaks; an old, faded military cloak might have served as an approximation for royal purple clothing in the soldiers' charade. **Weaving a crown of thorns,** the soldiers **placed it on him.** Roman crowns were not the metal affairs of the Middle Ages; emperors wore wreaths or diadems woven of laurel or ivy. The soldiers braid a mock crown of **thorns,** using one of the thorny plants or bushes that grow in Palestine. The purpose is not so much to inflict pain on Jesus (he is already in horrible pain from his scourging) as to heap mockery on him.

18 **They began to salute him with, "Hail, King of the Jews!"** A customary **salute** to the Roman emperor was "Hail, Caesar!" Jesus is mockingly hailed as **King of the Jews.** This was Pilate's term for Jesus (15:2), and it will be posted on Jesus' cross as the charge against him (15:26); Pilate probably used this term for Jesus as he handed him over to the soldiers to be crucified (15:15). It gave the soldiers an idea for how they might have some sport with Jesus. There are examples of ancient games involving similar mockery, but the soldiers could easily have devised theirs on their own. As Gentile soldiers in the employ of Rome, many of them probably had little love for the native Jewish population. Now here was this wretch of a Jew, on his way to the cross, called the **King of the Jews.** What a ridiculous king!

19 The soldiers' mockery degenerates into crude abuse. They **kept striking his head with a reed:** the soldiers presumably stuck a **reed** into Jesus' hand as a play scepter but now beat him with it. They are **spitting upon him**—an expression of contempt. **They knelt before him in homage,** as was done with kings: the soldiers use a sign of respect to disrespect Jesus.

There is profound irony in the soldiers' mockery of Jesus. Jesus never aspired to be the "King of the Jews," as Pilate and the soldiers understand the term. The soldiers' mockery hence misses the mark: they mock Jesus for pretending to be someone he does not claim to be. Yet their mockery does reveal who he is. What kind of Messiah is Jesus? He is a Messiah who "must suffer greatly and be rejected" (8:31), one whom Gentiles mock, spit upon, scourge, and will put to death (10:34). Jesus crowned with thorns, bleeding from his scourging, spit upon, and mocked—that is who the Messiah is.

For reflection: What does the image of Jesus battered and scorned convey to me about who Jesus is?

20 **And when they had mocked him, they stripped him of the purple cloak, dressed him in his own clothes, and led him out to crucify him.** Those to be crucified were normally paraded naked to the place of crucifixion and whipped along the way. Jews had an extreme aversion to public nakedness, and Roman authorities may have accommodated Jewish sensibilities by allowing the condemned to be clothed as they were led out to crucifixion. Those to be crucified were made to carry the crossbeam from which they would hang; it was usually laid across their shoulders, and their arms were sometimes tied to it. Upright beams (perhaps about seven feet tall) would already be set in the ground at the site of execution. Jesus is led **out:** crucifixions took place outside the city.

Crucifixion: See page 429

21 Jesus is unable to carry the crossbeam on which he is to die, despite the soldiers' probably rough prodding. He has been so weakened and his muscles so torn by scourging that he cannot bear the load. We can reflect that as a carpenter (6:3), Jesus had likely hewn and carried many beams; he had

a body hardened by a life of manual labor. That he is no longer capable of carrying a crossbeam is an index of how severely he has been scourged. Because of Jesus' inability to carry the beam, the soldiers **pressed into service a passer-by, Simon, a Cyrenian, who was coming in from the country.** Roman soldiers had the authority to compel anyone to carry burdens for them; that was one of the perks of being an army of occupation. The expression *press into service* (which also occurs in Matt 5:41) is the technical term for the exercise of this right. Since Jesus cannot carry the crossbeam, the soldiers collar the first man who happens by and force him to do so. His name is **Simon,** and he is a **Cyrenian:** he comes from Cyrene, on the northern coast of Africa (in today's Libya). Cyrene was home to a colony of Jews (some of whom became Christians: Acts 11:19–20; 13:1; see also Acts 2:10). Simon has apparently come to Jerusalem for Passover and has been staying somewhere outside the city but has now come into town (the most likely meaning of **coming in from the country**).

Mark identifies Simon as **the father of Alexander and Rufus,** as if his readers knew them or were at least familiar with their names. This might imply that Alexander and Rufus were Christians, and Simon as well, making his chance carrying of Jesus' cross a turning point in Simon's life. Paul sent greetings to a Christian living in Rome named Rufus (Rom 16:13), but Rufus was such a common name that we cannot be sure it was the same Rufus.

Simon happens along when the soldiers need to conscript a burden bearer, and they make Simon **carry** (literally, take up) Jesus' **cross.** Jesus told his disciples that he was a Messiah who would suffer and die, and he told them that whoever wanted to be his disciple had to "take up his cross, and follow me" (8:34). Although Simon the Cyrenian did not volunteer for the honor, he was the first to follow behind Jesus bearing a cross. Simon did for Jesus what Jesus could not do himself. Jesus did not fully establish the reign of God on earth during his public ministry; being his disciple means sharing in his work and suffering as part of the coming of God's reign.

Some of us may see a bit of Simon in ourselves when we reflect on our own discipleship. We did not volunteer to carry a cross for Jesus but were given a cross to bear nonetheless. We usually think of our cross as suffering we cannot escape, such as a chronic illness. The example of Simon shows that the cross we carry can take another form. Carrying our cross can mean shouldering the crosses of others, relieving them of their burdens by taking them on ourselves. Paul will write, "Bear one another's burdens, and so you will fulfill the law of Christ" (Gal 6:2).

For reflection: What does the example of Simon mean for me?

The Crucifixion of Jesus

22 They brought him to the place of Golgotha (which is translated Place of the Skull). 23 They gave him wine drugged with myrrh, but he did not take it. 24 Then they crucified him and divided his garments by casting lots for them to see what each should take. 25 It was nine o'clock in the morning when they crucified him. 26 The inscription of the charge against him read, "The King of the Jews." 27 With him they crucified two revolutionaries, one on his right and one on his left. [28]

Gospel parallels: Matt 27:33–38; Luke 23:33–34, 38; John 19:17–24

22 **They brought him to the place of Golgotha:** the Greek word translated **brought** can also mean drove or carried, which might indicate that Jesus was so weak that he had to be pulled along. He is led to the place of **Golgotha,** an Aramaic word that means skull, as Mark explains for his readers: **which is translated Place of the Skull.** At the time of Jesus, **Golgotha** was a hump of rock just outside the western wall of Jerusalem, not far from a road leading out of the city.

BACKGROUND: GOLGOTHA During the Old Testament era, the limestone hillside west of Jerusalem was quarried for building blocks. Seams of quality limestone were dug out; poor stone was left unquarried. Eventually the good stone played out, and the quarry was abandoned. At the time of Jesus, the old quarry lay just outside the western wall of Jerusalem. A hump of unquarried rock jutted up twenty to thirty feet from the quarry floor. Romans used this mound of rock as a place to crucify criminals, since it made a public display of their deaths. The site was called Golgotha, from the Aramaic word for skull, perhaps because the unquarried hump of rock was shaped like the top of a skull. The Latin word for skull gives us the name Calvary. Today the site of Golgotha is within the Church of the Holy Sepulchre in Jerusalem. *Related topic: Tomb of Jesus (page 449).*

Crucifying criminals atop this mound was a way to make their deaths more visible to those passing by. Rome used crucifixion as a gruesome public-service announcement: Don't do what these people did, or you will end up like them.

23 **They gave him wine drugged with myrrh, but he did not take it.** There is a later Jewish custom, based on Proverbs 31:6–7, of giving a condemned person wine to drink to dull the pain of execution, but it is uncertain whether this was a custom at the time of Jesus. Mark's account probably portrays wine being offered not out of mercy but in mockery. Soldiers who hailed Jesus as "king of the Jews" (15:17–19) now try to give him **wine drugged with myrrh** (the Greek simply reads "myrrhed wine"). **Myrrh** was not a narcotic but a perfume (Psalm 45:9; Prov 7:17; Song 5:5) and was expensive enough to make a fine gift (Matt 2:11). Romans added myrrh to wine to create a scented drink enjoyed by royalty. The soldiers' giving Jesus wine with myrrh may be similar to their clothing him in purple (15:17): just as they likely had no purple clothing for their charade, so they may not have fine wine with myrrh either. They perhaps present Jesus with what-ever coarse or sour wine they have, proffering it as scented wine fit for royalty—one more bit of mockery of the "King of the Jews." **But he did not take it:** Jesus refuses to play games with them. The only cup he will drink is the cup of suffering that God has prepared for him (10:38; 14:36), and he will not mitigate his suffering by befuddling his mind with wine.

24 **Then they crucified him:** Mark tersely states the fact, omitting details. Mark's first audience in Rome needed no details: some of their fellow Christians had died on crosses, and they knew all too well what it involved.

We have been spared the horror of seeing someone die on a cross, making it easy for us to pass over the words **They crucified him** rather quickly. They are words that should shatter us, much as a phone call telling us that someone we deeply love has been killed in an automo-bile accident would shatter us, bringing to a halt whatever we were doing. The one whom God proclaimed to be his beloved Son hangs on a cross—how can that be? The one who brings God's reign ends up executed like a criminal—an absurdity!

Some of Mark's first readers might have wondered, *How can God allow Christians to be tortured, martyred, even crucified? How could they believe they were part of God's plan for establishing his reign on earth when such horrible things were happening to them?* We too may have questions. Why does a good God allow so much evil to afflict the human race? Why does a God who loves me allow me and my loved ones to suffer? Mark does not address such questions directly but confronts his readers with the fact of Jesus' crucifixion. Jesus did not abolish suffering and death in this world; he accepted them as the will of his loving Father for him and as the means by which he would ransom others. Jesus on the cross is a stark emblem and assurance of God's unfathomable love.

For reflection: What does the image of the crucified Jesus mean for me?

BACKGROUND: CRUCIFIXION was an exceedingly cruel form of execution used by a number of ancient peoples. Rome adopted crucifixion as its way of executing slaves, rebels, and lower-class violent criminals. The Romans crucified many both before and after Jesus, including thousands when Rome put down the Jewish revolt of AD 66–70. Crucifixions were done in a variety of ways using different styles of crosses. Common Roman practice was to first scourge the one to be crucified, to increase suffering. Then the condemned was forced to carry a crossbeam to the place of execution, where an upright beam would already be in place. Roman crucifixions were done at public sites, such as along a busy road, in order to make them a public display. The one to be crucified was stripped of his clothing, and his arms were tied or nailed to the crossbeam. The crossbeam was then lifted up and fixed to the upright beam at a notch cut either in its top or in its side. Sometimes the person's feet were nailed or tied to the upright beam. Romans posted a sign indicating the crime for which the person was being crucified. Despite their suffering, those who were crucified could survive for several days, tormented by pain, thirst, insects, and the shame of dying naked before others. Death usually resulted from suffocation when chest muscles gave out. A body was sometimes left on the cross until it disintegrated, eaten by rats and vultures. Crucifixion was designed to be as painful and degrading a death as possible. Rome used crucifixion not merely as a punishment but also as a warning of what would happen to those who challenged Roman authority.

After the soldiers affix Jesus to the cross, they **divided his garments by casting lots for them to see what each should take.** Roman soldiers had a right to the minor possessions, including clothing, of those they executed. Romans normally stripped their victims before crucifying them, and Mark gives no indication that Jesus was spared this humiliation. The letter to the Hebrews states that Jesus "endured the cross, despising its shame" (Heb 12:2). Some soldiers would apparently stand guard as the crucified were dying, lest friends try to rescue them. The soldiers cast **lots** for Jesus' clothing: apparently they have brought dice to pass the time until the last of the crucified die. It is a jarring image: a dice game is being played as Jesus hangs dying.

Mark's first readers who were familiar with Psalm 22 might have been reminded of its words: "They divide my garments among them; / for my clothing they cast lots" (Psalm 22:19).

25 **It was nine o'clock in the morning when they crucified him.** Mark periodically makes note of the time during his account of the twenty-four hours that began with Jesus' last supper (14:17; 15:1, 25, 33, 34, 42). By Mark's chronology, Jesus was crucified roughly twelve hours after he gave bread and wine as his body and blood in anticipation of his death.

26 **The inscription of the charge against him read, "The King of the Jews."** Romans posted a notice that gave the reason a person was being crucified, which served as a warning to others against committing the crime. The notice might be hung around the condemned person's neck or affixed to the cross. Jesus is charged with being **the King of the Jews.** If this charge is taken literally, it means that Jesus is a rival to Rome for political dominion over Jews and is being executed as a would-be insurrectionist. Jesus is hardly an insurrectionist; he is being executed because various people in power found it expedient to get rid of him. Posting the **charge** that he is **the King of the Jews** is another bit of mockery, in line with previous mockery (15:17–19). Ironically, these seem to have been the only words written about Jesus during his lifetime.

As with previous mockery, the charge supposedly justifying Jesus' execution does contain a deeper truth. Jesus is the Messiah (the title that is twisted into king of the Jews), and he accomplishes his mission as the Messiah by suffering humiliation and death on the cross.

For reflection: What do I mean when I address Jesus as Christ (Messiah)?

27 **With him they crucified two revolutionaries:** Mark literally calls them robbers, but the Greek word came to be used for violent rebels. The two crucified with Jesus could have been men who had been arrested for committing murder in a rebellion (15:7), who were awaiting judgment from Pilate as Jesus was being tried before him. The two are crucified **one on his right and one on his left.** This is another of the stark visual images presented to us by the crucifixion of Jesus, images that convey better than words who Jesus is and what it means to be his disciple. James and John asked for places of status and power on the right and left of Jesus (10:37); those who now die on the right and left of Jesus show what is involved in occupying these places—a point that Jesus tried to make to James and John (10:38). Being close to Jesus means suffering as he suffered; being his disciple means taking up one's cross (8:34).

> *For reflection: Do I accept that being a disciple of Jesus means following him to Golgotha?*

28 (Some ancient manuscripts of Mark's Gospel include at this point the verse "And the scripture was fulfilled that says, 'And he was counted among the wicked.'" These words are not found in the most reliable manuscripts and may have been added by a scribe who copied them from Luke 22:37. The New American Bible omits this verse.)

ORIENTATION: *Mark says nothing about the physical pain Jesus suffered on the cross but highlights the taunts hurled at him.*

Jesus Is Taunted

29 Those passing by reviled him, shaking their heads and saying, "Aha! You who would destroy the temple and rebuild it in three days, 30 save yourself by coming down from the cross." 31 Likewise the chief priests, with the scribes, mocked him among themselves and said, "He saved others; he cannot save himself. 32 Let the Messiah, the King of Israel, come down now from the cross that we may see and believe." Those who were crucified with him also kept abusing him.

> Gospel parallels: Matt 27:39–44; Luke 23:35–43
> OT: Psalm 22:7–9

29 Mark presents the reactions of those who witnessed the crucifixion of Jesus, beginning with **those passing by.** Romans often crucified along busy roads to make sure that people saw what happened to those who ran afoul of Roman authority. Some people are **passing by** on the road that runs past Golgotha, coming into or going out of Jerusalem. There is no indication that they were involved in any of the events leading to the crucifixion of Jesus. Yet they **reviled him, shaking their heads and saying, "Aha!"** Making fun of those being crucified was popular sport for some elements of society. **Reviled** is literally "blasphemed" but here means verbally abused. The passersby are **shaking their heads,** a gesture of scorn (2 Kings 19:21; Lam 2:15), and saying, **Aha,** a cry of derision. Some of these passersby have apparently gotten wind of the charges made against Jesus (14:58), for they mock him as **you who would destroy the temple and rebuild it in three days.**

30 If Jesus could destroy the Temple and quickly rebuild it, then he should be able to do something far easier: they challenge him to **save yourself by coming down from the cross.** If Jesus can't escape from the cross, then he was deluded in thinking he could perform greater feats.

31 **Likewise the chief priests, with the scribes, mocked him among themselves.** The **chief priests,** with the cooperation of **scribes** and

elders, are the Jewish leaders who conspired to have Jesus executed (11:18; 12:12; 14:1–2, 10–11, 43, 55–65; 15:1–11). Some of them have come to Golgotha to witness the results of their efforts. They **mocked him among themselves,** gloating to one another over their success in getting rid of Jesus. They say, **He saved others; he cannot save himself.** The Greek word for **saved** has different nuances of meaning; it sometimes means physically healed (5:23, 28; 6:56). Jesus' reputation as one who healed and saved lives has spread far and wide (3:7–8), and the **chief priests** and **scribes** have to acknowledge that Jesus **saved others.** But they turn this against Jesus as a taunt: even though he was able to save others, **he cannot save himself.** They think that Jesus does not have the power to escape death, as his hanging on a cross demonstrates in their eyes.

There is a sense in which their words are profoundly true, even though they do not realize it. Jesus submitted himself to his Father's will in Gethsemane (14:36) and continues to do so on the cross: Jesus **cannot** save himself and remain obedient to God. By not saving himself, he saves others. Jesus gives his life as a ransom (10:45), dying so that others may be freed. Jesus gives his body and pours out his blood to establish a new relationship between God and his people (14:22–24). And paradoxically, by not saving himself Jesus does save himself. Jesus taught that it is in losing our lives that we save them (8:35); Jesus' death is the prelude to Jesus' rising, as he has foretold (8:31; 9:9, 31; 10:34).

32 **Let the Messiah, the King of Israel, come down now from the cross that we may see and believe.** The high priest asked Jesus if he was **the Messiah,** and Jesus acknowledged that he was, which the high priest labeled blasphemy (14:61–64). Pilate's term for Jesus was "king of the Jews" (15:2, 26); the chief priests rephrase the title as **the King of Israel,** which is perhaps a more religious and less political title than king of the Jews. Those taunting Jesus use these titles in derision: they do not accept that Jesus is **the Messiah** or **the King of Israel.** The chief priests and scribes demand that Jesus **come down now from the cross** to prove that he is who he claims to be. The passersby also invited Jesus to come down from the cross if he could (verse 30); the chief priests and scribes demand that Jesus do it **now,** at their command. They tell Jesus to do this so **that we may see and believe.** They demand that Jesus offer

proof that he is the Messiah by coming down from the cross. Ironically, it is Jesus' remaining on the cross that is proof of who he is.

Once again the issue is the identity of Jesus. If Jesus is a Messiah who will vanquish enemies, end Roman domination, and take control here and now, then he would hardly suffer Roman crucifixion. If Jesus is a Messiah whose mission is to shed his blood for others (14:24) and lay down his life as a ransom (10:45), then the cross is an emblem of Jesus' identity. If Jesus, even though he is Lord (12:36–37), does not lord it over others but serves them as their slave (10:42–44), then it is fitting that he die in a manner in which slaves were commonly executed, by crucifixion.

For reflection: What do the taunts hurled at Jesus teach me about him?

Those who were crucified with him also kept abusing him. Jesus is taunted and abused from all quarters: ordinary passersby, religious authorities, and even the criminals who are dying with him. Jesus was handed over to death by one of his specially chosen disciples; one of Jesus' closest friends has denied he even knows Jesus, and the rest of Jesus' disciples have run away. He faces death abandoned and rejected by all.

Mark's first readers who were familiar with Psalm 22 might have again been reminded of its words. It is the cry of a person in dire straits who is mocked for his reliance on God.

> But I am a worm, hardly human,
>   scorned by everyone, despised by the people.
> All who see me mock me;
>   they curl their lips and jeer;
>   they shake their heads at me:
> "You relied on the LORD—let him deliver you;
>   if he loves you, let him rescue you."
>   Psalm 22:7–9

For Mark's first readers, the scene of Jesus being taunted on the cross was a reminder of the kind of Messiah (Christ) to whom they had given their allegiance, and a reminder as well that they should not be surprised if they also were reviled and taunted and subjected to awful deaths. The

Jesus who did not come down from the cross invited them to take up their own crosses (8:34).

For reflection: What insight or message do I take away from this scene?

Jesus Dies

³³ At noon darkness came over the whole land until three in the afternoon. ³⁴ And at three o'clock Jesus cried out in a loud voice, "Eloi, Eloi, lema sabachthani?" which is translated, "My God, my God, why have you forsaken me?" ³⁵ Some of the bystanders who heard it said, "Look, he is calling Elijah." ³⁶ One of them ran, soaked a sponge with wine, put it on a reed, and gave it to him to drink, saying, "Wait, let us see if Elijah comes to take him down." ³⁷ Jesus gave a loud cry and breathed his last. ³⁸ The veil of the sanctuary was torn in two from top to bottom. ³⁹ When the centurion who stood facing him saw how he breathed his last he said, "Truly this man was the Son of God!"

Gospel parallels: Matt 27:45–54; Luke 23:44–48; John 19:28–30
OT: Psalm 22:2–3; Amos 8:9–10

33 Jesus was crucified at nine in the morning (15:25), and it is now **noon.** Mark has described Jesus being repeatedly taunted (15:29–32) but has otherwise left Jesus' sufferings during these three hours to his readers' imaginations. **At noon darkness came over the whole land until three in the afternoon.** The Greek word that is translated **land** also means earth, so Mark's words can mean that darkness came over the whole land of Judea or over the whole earth. Those who look for natural explanations for the darkness rule out an eclipse of the sun (this cannot happen during a full moon, and Passover is celebrated during a full moon) but note that strong east winds off the Judean wilderness are sometimes filled with so much fine sand that the sun seems blotted out. Mark's interest is not in natural explanations but in the significance of the darkness. In the Old Testament, **darkness** heralds God coming in judgment on the "day of the LORD" (Isaiah 13:9–10; Joel 2:10–11; Amos 8:9–10). Those of Mark's first readers who were familiar with the book of Amos might have recalled his prophecy about a midday darkness

covering the earth and about mourning as for the death of an only son. Even if Mark's readers were not familiar with these passages, **darkness** coming over **the whole land** would have conveyed that something of cosmic consequence was taking place.

> On that day, says the Lord GOD,
> I will make the sun set at midday
> and cover the earth with darkness in broad
>   daylight. . . .
>
> I will make them mourn as for an only son,
> and bring their day to bitter end.
>
> Amos 8:9, 10

It remains dark from **noon** until **three in the afternoon:** Jesus hangs on the cross for another three hours, but now in darkness. Mark tells his readers nothing about what happened during that dark gap of time.

Mark's writing that darkness covered the whole land **until three** does not necessarily imply that it became bright again at three o'clock. The meaning rather seems to be that darkness persisted until three and that the events that took place at three occurred in darkness.

34 **And at three o'clock Jesus cried out in a loud voice, "Eloi, Eloi, lema sabachthani?" which is translated, "My God, my God, why have you forsaken me?"** The words translated **cried out in a loud voice** could also be translated "screamed with a loud cry." Mark recounts Jesus speaking only once during his six hours on the cross, and Jesus does not so much speak as scream, crying out in his native Aramaic, *Eloi, Eloi, lema sabachthani?* For his Greek-speaking audience Mark translates Jesus' words as **My God, my God, why have you forsaken me?** These are the opening words of Psalm 22, a psalm that begins as a lament but concludes with expressions of confidence in God.

> My God, my God, why have you abandoned me?
> Why so far from my call for help,
> from my cries of anguish?

436

My God, I call by day, but you do not answer;
by night, but I have no relief.

Psalm 22:2–3

How should Jesus' cry from the cross be interpreted? Some suggest that by quoting the opening words of Psalm 22, Jesus is invoking the entire psalm and expressing his ultimate confidence in God. This interpretation softens Jesus' cry of being forsaken and brings the scene more in line with how Luke and John present Jesus on the cross. This interpretation does not, however, do justice to what Mark describes. Jesus does not quote Psalm 22 in Hebrew (the language in which it was written and traditionally prayed) but cries out in his own language of Aramaic, echoing the opening lament of Psalm 22. If Jesus had wanted to pray the words of confidence found in Psalm 22, he could have done so. Instead Jesus uses the most desolate wail of the psalm to express his agony, screaming to God, **Why have you forsaken me?** Jesus asked his Father to release him from his cup of suffering but accepted suffering and death as God's will for him when God made no answer to his prayer (14:36). God continued to be silent as Jesus was scourged and abused and crucified—a silence that is now accented by the darkness, making it seem as if God has hidden his face from his Son. It is not too late for Jesus' Father to save him: God can take him down from the cross. But God does not. Jesus cries out, not addressing God as Father, as he did in Gethsemane, but nonetheless still crying out to God as his God: **My God, my God.** Jesus asks, **Why have you forsaken me?** Why have you not acted to save me?

No voice from heaven answers Jesus; no hand reaches down to free him from the cross. Jesus has been forsaken not only by his friends and followers but apparently even by his God. Mark gives us a chillingly vivid glimpse of the humanity of Jesus: weakened from scourging and from hanging on the cross for six hours, Jesus experiences utter desolation and the absence of God. Jesus does not abandon God or his mission from God, but in fulfilling his mission he feels abandoned by God.

Some Christians have found it hard to accept that the Son of God could experience such suffering and desolation. The early heresy of Docetism (from the Greek word for seem) held that Jesus only seemed to suffer. Mystics may have had the greatest insight into the desolation Jesus experienced, for they knew firsthand that one could be very near to God and yet experience God as utter absence and darkness. St. John of the Cross wrote of Jesus' experience of abandonment and his cry of desolation on the cross as the model for those who wished to enter into union with God (*Ascent of Mount Carmel* II:7:9–11).

> *For reflection: How do I understand Jesus' cry from the cross? What insight into Jesus does it give me?*

Some in Mark's audience might have uttered similarly desolate cries to God, asking God why he had abandoned Christians into the hands of torturers and executioners. Some Christians today also cry out Why? to God, trying to find a reason for suffering. Some may experience God's presence as absence, darkness, utter silence. Mark's Gospel holds up the image of Jesus, so near to God as his beloved Son and so faithful in serving him, yet feeling abandoned by God. If Jesus could experience such desolation, so may those who accept his invitation to follow him.

> *For reflection: Have I ever felt forsaken by God? What meaning does Jesus' experience of abandonment have for me?*

35 **Some of the bystanders who heard it said, "Look, he is calling Elijah."** Jesus remains misunderstood to the end. It is not easy to confuse Jesus' cry of *"Eloi, Eloi"* (verse 34) with the Hebrew or Aramaic name Elijah, but **some of the bystanders** do so. Perhaps Jesus, exhausted and near death, was not perfectly articulate as he screamed his last words. If the **bystanders** were Jewish, they may have taken the midday darkness as a sign that the "day of the LORD" was at hand, a time at which Elijah was expected to return (Mal 3:23). With Elijah on their minds they may have thought that Jesus was calling for him to come. Or this may simply be one more instance of Jesus being utterly misunderstood.

36 **One of them ran, soaked a sponge with wine, put it on a reed, and gave it to him to drink, saying, "Wait, let us see if Elijah comes to take him down."** The Greek word that is translated **wine** refers to sour wine or vinegar, which was drunk by soldiers and laborers as a cheap

thirst quencher. **One of them**—one of those watching Jesus die—might have thought that a bitter drink would revive Jesus so that he could see that **Elijah** was not coming **to take him down.** Sour wine was offered to Jesus not out of compassion but to prolong Jesus remaining conscious. Mark does not indicate that Jesus accepted the wine.

37 **Jesus gave a loud cry and breathed his last.** Mark's words do not mean that Jesus gave a loud cry and then breathed his last but rather that Jesus let out a loud cry as his final breath. This could be crudely interpreted as Jesus dying with a scream, but there is a deeper level of meaning in Mark's words. Genesis portrays God forming man out of clay and blowing "into his nostrils the breath of life . . . so man became a living being" (Gen 2:7). In expelling his last breath Jesus gives his life back to the God from whom he received it. In both Greek and Hebrew the word for breath also means spirit. Jesus hands over his spirit, his life, to God as his final act of abandoning himself to God.

Mark presents not the slightest ray of light in this darkness-shrouded scene. Jesus dies in great pain amid the jeers of others; he dies abandoned by all, apparently even by the God for whom he dies. Yet Mark has characterized his message about Jesus as "good news" (1:1), forcing his readers to ponder how his portrait of Jesus' death can be good news.

For reflection: What does the death of Jesus mean for me? What implications does the manner of Jesus' death have for me?

38 Mark turns to the consequences of Jesus' death. The first is that **the veil of the sanctuary was torn in two from top to bottom.** The expression **was torn** implies that it was torn *by* God. Although the Temple apparently had more than one veil, **the veil of the sanctuary** most likely refers to the veil covering the doorway of the innermost room of the Temple, the Holy of Holies (Exod 26:31–33). This room was the dwelling place of God's presence; only the high priest could enter it, and only on the Day of Atonement (Lev 16:1–19). The veil being torn **in two from top to bottom** destroys it and symbolically allows anyone to enter or leave the Holy of Holies. That **the veil of the sanctuary** is torn can mean that Jesus' death has opened up access to God to all: entering into God's presence is no longer limited to one person on one day a year. The

tearing of the sanctuary veil could also signify that God's special presence on earth is no longer restricted to one room in a Temple and could foreshadow the destruction of a Temple that is no longer needed.

Mark's first readers who were particularly alert to his use of words might have noticed that Mark uses a Greek word for **torn** only twice in his Gospel. In the first instance, Jesus sees the heavens being **torn** open for the Spirit to descend on him, marking the beginning of his public ministry as the beloved Son of God (1:10–15). Now the sanctuary veil is **torn** open as Jesus hands his breath (spirit) back to God, marking the end of his public ministry. Jesus' death on the cross is not abject failure but the fulfillment of his mission as the Son of God.

39 One person present at the cross sees through the desolation of Jesus' death to its meaning—or does he? **When the centurion who stood facing him saw how he breathed his last he said, "Truly this man was the Son of God!"** The Latin word **centurion** means someone commanding one hundred troops, and this particular commander is in charge of the soldiers who executed Jesus (see 15:44). The centurion stands **facing** Jesus on the cross, so the centurion is able to see **how he breathed his last.** The manner of Jesus' death leads the centurion to say, **Truly this man was the Son of God!** There is profound truth in the centurion's words, but why would he say this?

Son of God: See page 64

One possibility is that the centurion's words, while ironically true, are on his lips words of mockery. Jesus has repeatedly been mocked by soldiers and others for pretending to be someone exalted: the king of the Jews (15:12, 16–19, 26), the Messiah and the king of Israel (15:32), someone who could destroy the Temple and rebuild it (15:29). Is the pagan centurion continuing this stream of mockery, with **Truly this man was the Son of God!** having the sense of "His dying this horrible death certainly proves that he has a special relationship with the gods, doesn't it? So much for his pretensions!"

Another possibility is that the manner of Jesus' death has given this pagan centurion an insight that has escaped every other human in Mark's account: that **truly this man was the Son of God.** Jesus' divine sonship is revealed most clearly not through his mighty deeds but paradoxically in his dying the most horrible of deaths, abandoned by all. It would seemingly require a bolt of divine inspiration for this pagan centurion to grasp the significance of calling Jesus **the Son of God** and to realize that Jesus' divine sonship is manifested by the way he died. But all things are possible for God (10:27), whether noonday darkness, or the blind seeing, or a pagan coming to faith.

Mark clearly intends for his readers to take the centurion's words as a true statement about Jesus. Mark wrote his Gospel to proclaim Jesus as the Christ and the Son of God (1:1), and now someone in his Gospel account has finally heralded who Jesus is. It is significant that the first person to truly state Jesus' identity is a Gentile: Mark's Gospel is good news for Gentiles as well as Jews.

For reflection: What insight into the Son of God do I receive from the sight of him dying on a cross?

ORIENTATION: *Mark for the first time explicitly tells his readers that some of the followers of Jesus were women.*

The Women Who Followed Jesus

⁴⁰ There were also women looking on from a distance. Among them were Mary Magdalene, Mary the mother of the younger James and of Joses, and Salome. ⁴¹ These women had followed him when he was in Galilee and ministered to him. There were also many other women who had come up with him to Jerusalem.

Gospel parallels: Matt 27:55–56; Luke 23:49; John 19:25–27
NT: Luke 8:1–3

40 There were also women looking on from a distance. Mark will go on to tell his readers that these **women** followed and served Jesus in Galilee and accompanied him to Jerusalem (verse 41). We are left wondering whether these women took part in Jesus' last supper with his disciples and whether they accompanied him to Gethsemane. If they were among those who fled at his arrest, then apparently they, like Peter, did not completely run away but followed behind at a safe distance (14:54). Peter parted company with Jesus at the house of the high priest

(14:66–72), but these women followed Jesus to Golgotha, where they are **looking on from a distance.** They kept watch as Jesus died, not abandoning him, as his men disciples did. Yet Mark does not necessarily hold these women up as perfect examples of discipleship: following Jesus completely means taking up one's cross and accompanying him all the way to Golgotha (8:34), not observing from a distance.

Mark identifies three of these women by name because they will play a role in the events that follow. **Among them were Mary Magdalene,** that is, **Mary** who came from the town of Magdala, about four miles southwest of Capernaum on the Sea of Galilee. She is elsewhere identified as a woman Jesus delivered from seven demons (16:9; Luke 8:2). Another of the women looking on at a distance is **Mary the mother of the younger James and of Joses.** This **James** is called **the younger** (literally, the smaller) to distinguish him from other men named James. The name **Joses** is a variant of the name Joseph. Mark's mention of **James** and **Joses** by name might indicate that they were individuals whom some of his readers knew or had heard of, or it might simply be Mark's way of distinguishing their mother, **Mary,** from other women named Mary. We can note that Mark earlier listed a James and a Joses as brothers of Jesus (6:3), but these were very common names. If the Mary who was the mother of James and Joses was also the mother of Jesus, Mark surely would have identified her as the mother of Jesus rather than as the mother of James and Joses. A third woman watching from a distance is named **Salome.**

41 **These women had followed him when he was in Galilee.** Women traveling with Jesus would have run against cultural norms of the time. A woman's place was in the home; in public a woman was to be with other women or relatives, not with unrelated men. Yet following Jesus, traveling with him as he carried out his ministry, was generally a requirement for discipleship (1:17; 2:14; 10:21). Mark has not recounted Jesus calling women to follow him, nor has he explicitly mentioned women disciples up until now, but **these women** seem to qualify as Jesus' disciples because they **followed him when he was in Galilee.**

Not only did they accompany Jesus, but they also **ministered to him.** The word translated **ministered** can also be translated "served" and can mean to serve food and take care of physical needs: Mark used the word to describe Peter's mother-in-law waiting on Jesus and his disciples (1:31). But the word *minister,* or *serve,* also has broader meaning. Jesus taught that whoever wished to be first must be last of all and servant of all (9:35); he taught that "whoever wishes to be great among you will be your servant; whoever wishes to be first among you will be the slave of all" (10:43–44). Perhaps one interpretation of the fact that Mark has not mentioned these women disciples until now is that they did such a good job of serving and being last that they were hardly noticeable—and in this they fulfilled one of the ideals of discipleship.

Mark has mentioned only three women by name, but he assures his readers that **there were also many other women** who were looking on from a distance and who observed the death of Jesus. If there were **many** women who followed Jesus and served him, could this imply that Jesus may have had as many women disciples as men disciples? All of these women **had come up with him to Jerusalem,** traveling with him from Galilee as he made his journey to Jerusalem and following him to Golgotha, where they kept watch as he died.

For reflection: What lessons might I learn from the women who followed Jesus to Golgotha?

Jesus' Corpse Is Buried

⁴² When it was already evening, since it was the day of preparation, the day before the sabbath, ⁴³ Joseph of Arimathea, a distinguished member of the council, who was himself awaiting the kingdom of God, came and courageously went to Pilate and asked for the body of Jesus. ⁴⁴ Pilate was amazed that he was already dead. He summoned the centurion and asked him if Jesus had already died. ⁴⁵ And when he learned of it from the centurion, he gave the body to Joseph. ⁴⁶ Having bought a linen cloth, he took him down, wrapped him in the linen cloth and laid him in a tomb that had been hewn out of the rock. Then he rolled a stone against the entrance to the tomb. ⁴⁷ Mary Magdalene and Mary the mother of Joses watched where he was laid.

Gospel parallels: Matt 27:57–61; Luke 23:50–55; John 19:38–42
OT: Deut 21:22–23

42 Mark begins his account of the burial of Jesus' body by noting that **it was already evening,** which in context means it was before sunset. Mark also notes that **it was the day of preparation, the day before the sabbath.** By Jewish reckoning, the **sabbath** (the seventh day of the week—Saturday) began at sunset (i.e., sunset on Friday). Friday up until sunset was a **day of preparation,** when cooking and other tasks forbidden on the Sabbath were done.

Jewish burials customarily took place on the day of death. A burial could not take place on the Sabbath because it involved activities, like carrying the corpse, that were considered works forbidden on the Sabbath. Jesus died around three in the afternoon (15:34–37); his body needed to be buried before the Sabbath began at sunset.

43 Burials were normally handled by family members or friends of the deceased. John the Baptizer was buried by his disciples (6:29), but the disciples of Jesus have run away. Family or friends of Jesus could have had difficulty claiming his body: Roman authorities normally did not give the bodies of those executed for rebellion to their supporters. However, someone does step forth to claim the body of Jesus: **Joseph of Arimathea.** This **Joseph** is identified as being originally from **Arimathea,** a town whose location is uncertain (one suggestion is that it was twenty miles northwest of Jerusalem). Joseph apparently now lives in Jerusalem, where he is **a distinguished member of the council,** an elder. By **council** Mark probably means the Sanhedrin, but Mark does not indicate whether Joseph was among those who handed Jesus over to death (14:53–65; 15:1). Mark does characterize Joseph as one **who was himself awaiting the kingdom of God.** This does not necessarily mean that Joseph was a disciple of Jesus. Jesus announced that the **kingdom of God** was at hand (1:15), but Jews who had no connection with Jesus could long for God to vanquish evil and establish his reign over everyone and everything. If Mark had wanted to identify Joseph as a disciple of Jesus, he could have done so. Mark only says that Joseph was a distinguished and devout Jewish leader.

Kingdom of God: See page 96

Joseph **came and courageously went to Pilate and asked for the body of Jesus** so that he might bury it. Joseph's act could have been courageous for a variety of reasons. He might have been breaking with the rest of the Sanhedrin by providing a proper burial for someone they wanted dead and disgraced. He might have been risking being branded a sympathizer of Jesus in the eyes of the Roman governor who had ordered Jesus' execution.

Romans often left the bodies of those they crucified on display until they were eaten by scavenging animals or decayed, but in Palestine Romans may have made concessions to Jewish beliefs. The law of Moses forbade leaving the corpse of an executed criminal hanging on a tree overnight (Deut 21:22–23), and this law was applied to crucifixions. Joseph of Arimathea might have undertaken the burial of Jesus' body out of obedience to the Mosaic law. For a corpse to go unburied was abhorrent to Jews, and there was a tradition of pious Jews providing burials for those who would otherwise go unburied (see Tobit 1:16–20; 2:3–8).

> If a man guilty of a capital offense is put to death and his corpse hung on a tree, it shall not remain on the tree overnight. You shall bury it the same day; otherwise, since God's curse rests on him who hangs on a tree, you will defile the land which the LORD, your God, is giving you as an inheritance.
>
> Deut 21:22–23

44 **Pilate was amazed that he was already dead.** A person who was crucified might linger alive for several days on the cross, depending on the severity of the preliminary scourging and the manner of crucifixion. Jesus' death might have been hastened by the harsh scourging he endured (15:15). **Pilate was amazed** that Jesus is dead after only six hours and wants to verify it, lest he allow Jesus to be taken down from the cross while yet alive. **He summoned the centurion** who was in charge of the crucifixions that day (15:39) **and asked him if Jesus had already died.** The summoning of the centurion and his reporting to Pilate would not have taken long if Pilate was using Herod's palace as his headquarters (15:1, 16), for it was situated only a short distance from Golgotha.

45 **And when he learned of it from the centurion, he gave the body to Joseph.** The word translated here as **body** is the Greek word for corpse, and Mark may have used this word to underline the fact of Jesus' death. Perhaps Pilate granted Joseph's request because Joseph was a distinguished member of the council that had handed Jesus over to Pilate for execution. Pilate could then forget the whole affair: he had done all that the Sanhedrin had asked of him. What Joseph did with the corpse of Jesus was not Pilate's concern.

46 **Having bought a linen cloth, he took him down, wrapped him in the linen cloth:** normally a corpse was washed and anointed with perfumes before being wrapped in a burial shroud. Joseph may have given the body of Jesus a rather hasty burial without washing or anointing because sunset was at hand. Joseph **laid him in a tomb that had been hewn out of the rock.** Jerusalem lies in the rocky Judean highlands, and those with financial means had tombs carved into the bedrock or into a hillside. The fact that Joseph had ready access to a tomb may indicate that it was his own family tomb. **Then he rolled a stone against the entrance to the tomb.** Family tomb complexes were used by successive generations. Rolling a **stone against the entrance to the tomb** would keep out scavenging animals; the stone could later be rolled back to provide access to the tomb.

BACKGROUND: BURIAL PRACTICES Jewish burials took place as soon as possible after death. The corpse was washed and anointed with ointments and perfumes and wrapped in cloth. Burials in Jerusalem were done in cavelike tombs carved into the limestone hillsides surrounding the city. These tombs usually contained several chambers and served entire families. A Jewish burial was usually a two-step process. First the corpse lay on a shelf in the tomb for about a year. Then, after the flesh had decayed away, the bones were collected and placed in a pit containing the bones of the person's ancestors. In Jerusalem at the time of Jesus, a person's bones were often placed instead in a lidded box carved from limestone; typically such boxes were about twenty-four by eighteen by twelve inches. The box was then set in a recess in the tomb complex. Sometimes the bones of several members of a family were placed in the same box. In 1990, archaeologists excavated a tomb on the southern edge of Jerusalem and found a bone box with an Aramaic form of the name Caiaphas inscribed on it. Inside were bones identified as those of a man about sixty, an adult woman, a teenage boy, a young child, and two infants. Archaeologists believe that the bones of the man are those of the Caiaphas who was high priest from AD 18 to 36. *Related topic: Tomb of Jesus (page 449).*

---

47 **Mary Magdalene and Mary the mother of Joses watched where he was laid.** These women, along with Salome, kept watch from a distance as Jesus died (15:40). They continue to watch as Joseph removes the body of Jesus from the cross and carries it to a tomb. Although Mark does not indicate the location of Jesus' tomb, it was less than two hundred feet from Golgotha, making it easy for **Mary Magdalene and Mary the mother of Joses** to observe where the body of Jesus was entombed.

The fact that Mary Magdalene and Mary the mother of Joses only watch and do not take part in the burial of Jesus is an indication that Joseph of Arimathea was not a disciple of Jesus: had he been a disciple, it would have been natural for the two women to step forward to assist him. Jesus remains as seemingly abandoned in death as he was in dying: the men whom he called to be with him have fled, leaving only a few of the women who followed him to watch from a distance. If Mark's readers did not know otherwise, they might conclude that this is the somber end of a tragic story. Jesus is crucified like a common criminal and buried by a pious stranger.

For reflection: What is my reaction to this scene?

CHAPTER 16

The Women at the Tomb

¹ When the sabbath was over, Mary Magdalene, Mary, the mother of James, and Salome bought spices so that they might go and anoint him. ² Very early when the sun had risen, on the first day of the week, they came to the tomb. ³ They were saying to one another, "Who will roll back the stone for us from the entrance to the tomb?" ⁴ When they looked up, they saw that the stone had been rolled back; it was very large. ⁵ On entering the tomb they saw a young man sitting on the right side, clothed in a white robe, and they were utterly amazed. ⁶ He said to them, "Do not be amazed! You seek Jesus of Nazareth, the crucified. He has been raised; he is not here. Behold, the place where they laid him. ⁷ But go and tell his disciples and Peter, 'He is going before you to Galilee; there you will see him, as he told you.'" ⁸ Then they went out and fled from the tomb, seized with trembling and bewilderment. They said nothing to anyone, for they were afraid.

Gospel parallels: Matt 28:1–8; Luke 24:1–10; John 20:1
NT: Mark 14:28; 15:40–41, 47

1 **When the sabbath was over:** Jesus' corpse was buried before sunset, the beginning of **the sabbath** (15:42); Mark skips ahead to the following sunset. There is a gap of a day in Mark's account: he does not tell his readers anything about the activities of Jesus' disciples during this time, or anything about Jesus. Mark recounted the previous twenty-four hours in some detail (14:17–15:47), making his silence here all the more striking. It is as if the burial of Jesus' body created a pregnant emptiness.

When the sabbath was over, Mary Magdalene, Mary, the mother of James, and Salome bought spices so that they might go and anoint him. These women kept watch as Jesus died (15:40), and two of them observed the hasty burial of Jesus' body without the customary anointing (15:46–47). Shops were closed on the **sabbath,** but some might open for a few hours after sunset. The women go and buy **spices** (perfumed oils) **so that they might go and anoint him.** These women ministered to Jesus in Galilee (15:41), and they will perform one last act of service for him. While perfumed oils or ointments might be bought after sunset, anointing a body in darkness was another matter. The women wait for daylight before going to the tomb of Jesus.

For reflection: What acts of service do I do for Jesus?

2 **Very early when the sun had risen, on the first day of the week, they came to the tomb.** As soon as there is light, the women **came to the tomb.** It is **the first day of the week**—Sunday by our calendar. Jesus died roughly forty hours earlier. The women do not seem fazed by the prospect of anointing a corpse that has already begun to decay, but they act as if they want to perform their service as soon as possible.

3 **They were saying to one another, "Who will roll back the stone for us from the entrance to the tomb?"** The **entrance** to a tomb was normally small, perhaps a yard square, so that it could be closed with a boulder or a circular **stone,** such as the women observed Joseph rolling against the entrance of the tomb of Jesus (15:46). A couple of men could roll away such a stone, but the three women think it

---

BACKGROUND: TOMB OF JESUS At the time of Jesus, an abandoned limestone quarry lay just outside the western wall of Jerusalem. Here Golgotha rose as a hump of unquarried rock. Tombs were dug in the old quarry, just as tombs were dug into virtually all the hills surrounding biblical Jerusalem. The tomb in which Jesus' corpse was buried, located less than two hundred feet from Golgotha, was cut into the side of the quarry. This tomb had at least two chambers: a small antechamber at its entrance and a second chamber with a shelf cut into its wall where a corpse could be laid. There were likely other chambers for other corpses or for their bones after the flesh had decayed away. After Jesus' body was taken down from the cross, it was placed on the shelf in the second chamber. In the fourth century, the Roman emperor Constantine ordered a church to be built at the site of Golgotha and the tomb of Jesus. Workers cut away the hillside surrounding the tomb of Jesus in order to isolate it as a freestanding chapel. This chapel was largely destroyed in the eleventh century and has been rebuilt several times since. Today Golgotha and the tomb of Jesus are within the Church of the Holy Sepulchre in Jerusalem. *Related topics: Burial practices (page 446), Golgotha (page 427).*

is heavier than they can manage. An obvious solution would have been for the women to ask some of the men who had followed Jesus to accompany them, but apparently none were available—perhaps an indication of how thoroughly these men had deserted Jesus. The women go to the tomb anyway, hoping they can find someone to **roll back the stone** for them.

While these women's determined devotion to Jesus is obvious, it is equally obvious that they have no expectation that they will find Jesus risen from the dead. Jesus foretold his rising when he spoke of his coming death (8:31; 9:31; 10:34), but these women have apparently not grasped what he was talking about. Nor apparently have his men disciples (9:9–10): their absence is conspicuous. The women go to the tomb of Jesus expecting to anoint his corpse, and their only concern is finding someone up at that early hour to roll back the stone for them.

4 **When they looked up, they saw that the stone had been rolled back; it was very large.** Mark does not describe the reactions of the women to the sight of the **stone** already **rolled back.** We might surmise that they were surprised but also relieved, for **it was very large,** and they could not have moved it themselves. With apparently no hesitation they stoop down and go into the tomb to anoint the corpse of Jesus.

5 **On entering the tomb they saw a young man sitting on the right side, clothed in a white robe.** Jews of the time of Jesus visualized angels as having the appearance of young men (Tobit 5:4–5; 2 Macc 3:26, 33), and heavenly figures were sometimes portrayed wearing white robes (see Rev 7:9, 13–14). The women realize that the person sitting in the tomb of Jesus is an angel or a heavenly messenger, **and they were utterly amazed.** The word **amazed** has connotations of awed and agitated, terrified and distressed. The three women expected to find the corpse of Jesus in the tomb, not a heavenly being.

6 **He said to them, "Do not be amazed!"** If these women could grasp the significance of an angel being where they expected to find the corpse of Jesus, then they would be filled with joy instead of terror. The angel tells the women, **You seek Jesus of Nazareth, the crucified.** The

angel will go on to speak of Jesus being raised. The Jesus who has been raised is the **Jesus** who grew up in **Nazareth;** the Jesus who lives is **the crucified** Jesus. Even if resurrection is a radical transformation (12:25), the person raised is the person who died. This was true for Jesus in his rising and will be true for us when we are raised.

For reflection: What are the implications for me of Jesus' rising?

The angel continues: Jesus of Nazareth, the crucified, **has been raised:** the implication is has been raised *by* God. Jesus' cry from the cross (15:34) has not gone unanswered; God did not forsake his Son. The angel provides no explanation for what it means that Jesus **has been raised.** Jews who lived in hope of rising from the dead thought that it would occur at the end of this age, when the just would be rewarded and the evil punished (Dan 12:2–3). That hasn't happened yet. Nonetheless, the angel proclaims that Jesus **has been raised** and **is not here.** The angel invites the women to see for themselves that the body of Jesus is not where Joseph laid it: **Behold, the place where they laid him.** Corpses were placed on a shelf or a ledge in the tomb, where they would lie until the flesh decayed away. Jesus is clearly **not here,** not in the tomb.

There is a broader sense in which Jesus **is not here:** Jesus is no longer physically present in this world. The empty tomb is a sign not only of Jesus' resurrection but also of Jesus' bodily absence. Jesus has been raised to new life and is no longer constrained by the world of space and time.

For reflection: How do I experience the presence and absence of Jesus?

7 The three women are the first followers of Jesus to learn that he has been raised, and so they have the privilege and the obligation of telling others about it. The angel sends them on a mission: **Go and tell his disciples and Peter, "He is going before you to Galilee; there you will see him, as he told you."** In mentioning **Peter** by name the angel seems to be saying, Tell especially Peter the denier. Jesus knew that after he was arrested his followers would scatter and even deny him, but he nevertheless promised them, "After I have been raised up,

I shall go before you to Galilee" (14:28). Now Jesus has risen and will gather together again those who deserted him. Jesus is **going before his disciples to Galilee:** the angel's words are both a guarantee of Jesus' presence in Galilee and a summons to once more follow Jesus as his disciples. **You will see him:** Mark's audience would have heard of appearances of the risen Jesus, for these appearances were part of the gospel message proclaimed in the early Church (1 Cor 15:3–7). These appearances came to an end (1 Cor 15:8), but Jesus' promise to gather and lead his disciples is open-ended: **Galilee** is a symbol for wherever followers of Jesus live.

After the events of the past few days, the angel's words herald breathtaking reversals. Jesus has been raised from death and will gather his disciples to him once again. His death did not mark the end but a radical new beginning. The angel's words are a message of hope for the amazed women as well as for Jesus' scattered disciples.

For reflection: What message of hope do the angel's words have for me?

8 **Then they went out and fled from the tomb, seized with trembling and bewilderment.** The women bolt from the tomb, quaking in fear and utter astonishment, overwhelmed by the angel's presence and words. The women **fled,** just as the men who followed Jesus fled when he was arrested (14:50). **They said nothing to anyone, for they were afraid.** Their silence is a final irony at the end of Mark's Gospel. During his ministry, Jesus imposed silence about himself. "See that you tell no one anything," Jesus instructed a leper he healed (1:44). Now women who followed Jesus are commissioned to tell others about the risen Jesus awaiting his disciples in Galilee, but unlike the leper (1:45), **they said nothing to anyone.**

In the oldest and best manuscripts, Mark's Gospel ends with the words **for they were afraid.** Some speculate that Mark died before completing his Gospel, or that the ending Mark wrote was lost. The prevailing view of biblical scholars is that Mark indeed ended his Gospel on the somber note of the women being so fearful that they say nothing to anyone. We must ponder why Mark would conclude his good news this way.

For reflection: What is my reaction to Mark ending his Gospel in this manner?

The very fact that there were Christians to read the Gospel of Mark presumes that the good news of Jesus did not remain a secret but was preached and accepted. Mark knew that his readers were aware of the risen Jesus appearing to his followers, of Peter playing a leadership role in the early Church, and of the spread of the Church to Rome and other cities in the Roman Empire. But despite the success of the gospel, Mark's readers were being tested by betrayal, persecution, and suffering.

Mark addressed their needs by writing, "The beginning of the gospel of Jesus Christ" (1:1). The good news begins with Jesus healing the sick, freeing the possessed, proclaiming that the reign of God is at hand—and dying on a cross. Mark's Gospel is an invitation to follow in the footsteps of one who suffered and was crucified. The good news begins with Jesus calling disciples to follow him—men and women who will misunderstand him, desert him, and fail him even after he has been raised. Mark's Gospel is addressed to those who fail and find themselves in the company of others who fail. By ending with the women's failure to make Jesus' resurrection known, Mark conveys to his readers, "Yes, we have the hope of rising with Christ—but it can be pretty messy in the meantime."

Mark does not conclude his Gospel with a tidy, satisfying ending but leaves his account incomplete. Mark's readers must provide the conclusion: Mark has set down only the beginning of the good news. It is left to Mark's readers to live and proclaim the message entrusted to the women at the tomb.

For reflection: What is my response to Mark's proclamation of the good news of Jesus Christ?

ORIENTATION: *Some who made copies of the Gospel of Mark thought that verse 8 of chapter 16 did not provide a satisfactory conclusion, and they added new endings. One addition, commonly called the Longer Ending, was probably written early in the second century and may have circulated on its own before being added to Mark's Gospel. Although this addition was not written by Mark, it is accepted as canonical Scripture by the Catholic Church and is numbered as verses 9 through 20 of chapter 16 of Mark's Gospel.*

The Longer Ending

[⁹ **When he had risen, early on the first day of the week, he appeared first to Mary Magdalene, out of whom he had driven seven demons. ¹⁰ She went and told his companions who were mourning and weeping. ¹¹ When they heard that he was alive and had been seen by her, they did not believe.**

¹² After this he appeared in another form to two of them walking along on their way to the country. ¹³ They returned and told the others; but they did not believe them either.

¹⁴ [But] later, as the eleven were at table, he appeared to them and rebuked them for their unbelief and hardness of heart because they had not believed those who saw him after he had been raised. ¹⁵ He said to them, "Go into the whole world and proclaim the gospel to every creature. ¹⁶ Whoever believes and is baptized will be saved; whoever does not believe will be condemned. ¹⁷ These signs will accompany those who believe: in my name they will drive out demons, they will speak new languages. ¹⁸ They will pick up serpents [with their hands], and if they drink any deadly thing, it will not harm them. They will lay hands on the sick, and they will recover."

¹⁹ So then the Lord Jesus, after he spoke to them, was taken up into heaven and took his seat at the right hand of God. ²⁰ But they went forth and preached everywhere, while the Lord worked with them and confirmed the word through accompanying signs.]

Gospel parallels: Matt 28:16–20; Luke 8:2; 24:9–53; John 20:11–23

9 **When he had risen, early on the first day of the week, he appeared first to Mary Magdalene, out of whom he had driven seven demons.** The author of the Longer Ending composed a résumé of some of the appearances of the risen Jesus that are narrated in the Gospels of Matthew, Luke, and John. The Gospel of John presents **Mary Magdalene** as the **first** person to whom the risen Jesus appears (John 20:11–17). The Gospel of Luke describes her as one "from whom seven demons had gone out" (Luke 8:2). Unlike John's Gospel, the Longer Ending recounts no conversation between Jesus and Mary Magdalene: Jesus simply **appeared** to her.

10 **She went and told his companions who were mourning and weeping.** John 20:18 tells of Mary Magdalene announcing to the disciples, "I have seen the Lord." The Longer Ending contains the note that the disciples are **mourning and weeping,** presumably over the death of Jesus.

11 **When they heard that he was alive and had been seen by her, they did not believe.** The disciples do not believe that Jesus has risen and is **alive.** Luke's Gospel describes skepticism on the part of the disciples when they are told that Jesus has been raised (Luke 24:9–11).

12 **After this he appeared in another form to two of them walking along on their way to the country.** The author of the Longer Ending alludes to a tradition that Luke recounts of two disciples encountering the risen Jesus on the road to Emmaus (Luke 24:13–32). In Luke's account, the two disciples do not initially recognize Jesus (Luke 24:16); the Longer Ending explains that Jesus **appeared in another form** but does not provide further details about what Jesus looks like.

13 The Longer Ending implies that the two disciples do come to recognize the person walking with them as the risen Jesus, for **they returned and told the others; but they did not believe them either.** This is the second report of Jesus' resurrection to reach the disciples, but they remain skeptical: **they did not believe them either.** Luke reports the two disciples telling the other followers of Jesus about their encounter with him (Luke 24:33–35).

14 **[But] later, as the eleven were at table, he appeared to them.**
The Gospels of Luke and John tell of Jesus appearing to his disciples
when they are gathered together (Luke 24:36–49; John 20:19–23). Jesus
**rebuked them for their unbelief and hardness of heart because
they had not believed those who saw him after he had been
raised.** The Greek word translated **rebuked** conveys a strong reproach,
not a gentle chiding. Jesus rebukes his skeptical disciples for their **unbelief** (for their not believing that he was raised—verse 11) and for their
hardness of heart, their stubborn refusal to believe. Jesus also rebukes
the disciples for not accepting the testimony of those who bore witness
to his having been raised (verse 13): **they had not believed those who
saw him after he had been raised.**

The Longer Ending recounts appearances of the risen Jesus with
great brevity but highlights the issue of belief and disbelief. Jesus
severely rebukes those who refuse to believe in his resurrection and
who do not accept the testimony of those who bear witness to his
resurrection.

15 Even though Jesus rebukes his disciples for their disbelief and hardness of
heart, he commissions them to be his witnesses. **He said to them, "Go
into the whole world and proclaim the gospel to every creature."**
Jesus gives a similar charge to his disciples at the end of Matthew's
Gospel (Matt 28:18–20; see also Luke 24:47). The Longer Ending leaves
no doubt that the good news of Jesus Christ is intended for everyone,
Gentiles as well as Jews.

*For reflection: Has Jesus commissioned me to be his witness despite my
doubts and confusions?*

16 **Whoever believes and is baptized will be saved; whoever does
not believe will be condemned.** Belief is not enough; belief must
be expressed and completed by baptism, which incorporates the
believer into the Church. Jesus' final instructions to his disciples
in the Gospel of Matthew include a commission to baptize (Matt
28:19). The Longer Ending continues to focus on belief and disbelief,
pointing out their consequences. Those who believe and are baptized
will be saved; those who hear the gospel but refuse to believe (and

consequently are not baptized) **will be condemned.** The Gospel of John also portrays salvation and condemnation in stark, either-or terms (John 3:18, 36; 12:44–50). Our responses to Jesus and his message have eternal consequences.

17 **These signs will accompany those who believe:** the **signs** will be manifest in the lives of **those who believe** the preaching of the gospel. We might have expected the signs to be associated with the disciples as they preached, as a confirmation of their message. While this may be implied (see verse 20), the promise is for those who accept the gospel rather than those who preach it. Those who accept it, **those who believe** the gospel, will experience God's power in their lives in dramatic ways. The author of the Longer Ending will provide examples of this, drawing heavily on traditions related in Acts.

For reflection: What are the signs of God's power at work in my life?

In my name they will drive out demons: Jesus gave the Twelve authority to drive out demons (3:15; 6:7), which they exercised (6:13). Acts recounts others in the early Church expelling demons (Acts 8:5–7; 16:18; 19:11–12). **They will speak new languages:** those filled with the Holy Spirit on Pentecost began to speak in different tongues (Acts 2:4), and speaking in tongues also marked later outpourings of the Spirit (Acts 10:44–46; 19:6). Paul discusses speaking in tongues in his first letter to Corinth (1 Cor 12:10, 30; 14:1–28).

18 **They will pick up serpents [with their hands], and if they drink any deadly thing, it will not harm them.** Those who believe (verse 17) will be protected from poisons, whether in snakes or in drinks. Acts gives an account of Paul being bitten by a viper without suffering harm (Acts 28:1–6). There is no New Testament record of someone drinking a poison and being immune to it, but such stories did circulate in the early Church. Verse 18 is not an invitation to handle snakes or drink poison to prove one's faith; it is rather a promise of protection for Christians who encounter deadly perils.

For reflection: How have I experienced God's protection?

They will lay hands on the sick, and they will recover. Those who believe will be able to carry on the healing ministry of Jesus, which was entrusted to the Twelve (3:14–15; 6:13) and carried out by the early Church (Acts 3:1–10; 5:15–16; 8:7; 9:33–34; 14:8–10; 20:9–12; 28:8–9). Jesus' healing power remains with the Church, but Christians have drawn on it more in some ages and places than others.

For reflection: Do I pray that those I love will be healed?

19 **So then the Lord Jesus, after he spoke to them, was taken up into heaven and took his seat at the right hand of God.** The author of the Longer Ending speaks of **the Lord Jesus,** calling Jesus **Lord,** just as God is called **Lord.** Luke is the only Gospel author to recount Jesus being **taken up into heaven** (Luke 24:50–51; Acts 1:9–11). Jesus spoke of his being seated **at the right hand** of God (14:62), and his words are echoed in New Testament writings (Rom 8:34; Eph 1:20; Col 3:1; Heb 8:1; 10:12; 12:2; 1 Pet 3:22). The seat to the right of a ruler was a top position of power and honor, second only to that of the ruler himself. Jesus has been **taken up into heaven** and is now seated **at the right hand of God,** sharing in the lordship of God as ruler over all.

20 **But they went forth and preached everywhere, while the Lord worked with them and confirmed the word through accompanying signs.]** Jesus is now referred to simply as **the Lord.** Acts recounts how the early Church carried out Jesus' mandate to "be my witnesses in Jerusalem, throughout Judea and Samaria, and to the ends of the earth" (Acts 1:8). Just because Jesus is seated at the right hand of God in heaven does not mean that Jesus is removed from the affairs of this earth. On the contrary: from his position of power Jesus is able to empower those who witness to him. The promise that signs will accompany those who believe (verse 17) also applies to those who **preached,** for **the Lord worked with them and confirmed the word through accompanying signs**—presumably such signs as those listed in verses 17 and 18. Paul writes that "our gospel did not come to you in word alone, but also in power and in the holy Spirit and [with] much conviction" (1 Thess 1:5). In Acts, the Lord "confirmed the word about his

grace by granting signs and wonders" (Acts 14:3; see also 2:43; 4:30; 5:12; 6:8; 15:12).

If the Longer Ending circulated on its own before being appended to Mark's Gospel, then it may have served as an exhortation to believe in and bear witness to the risen Jesus, trusting in his power. While the Longer Ending mentions appearances of the risen Jesus, it highlights Jesus' charge to preach the gospel to the whole world, relying on him to provide signs that will confirm the message.

If the Longer Ending is read as the conclusion of the Gospel of Mark, then it not only narrates appearances of the risen Jesus but also subtly modifies the Gospel of Mark. While Mark's Gospel portrays the followers of Jesus being empowered to drive out demons and heal the sick (3:15; 6:7, 13), the accent in Mark's Gospel falls on following Jesus along the way of the cross. Followers of Jesus should anticipate being beaten and put to death (13:9, 12) rather than enjoying miraculous immunity from poisons. The gospel will be preached to all nations with the help of the Holy Spirit (13:10–11), but even the elect will endure tribulations (13:19–20). Mark concluded his Gospel on a note of failure: the women are too afraid to tell anyone about the risen Jesus (16:7–8). The Longer Ending concludes with Jesus working through his followers to provide signs that confirm the gospel message—a more upbeat conclusion.

For reflection: Do I find more meaning in the Gospel of Mark's concluding with verse 8 of chapter 16 or in its concluding with the Longer Ending? Why?

COMMENT: THE FEAST OF ST. MARK is celebrated on April 25, and the Gospel reading used in the liturgy for this feast is the Longer Ending (16:9–20). Some may find it ironic that a passage apparently not written by Mark has been chosen to honor Mark, particularly since this passage puts a different concluding accent on the Gospel of Mark than Mark apparently intended. But Mark was well aware that ironies and paradoxes were integral to the Christian life: the last were to be first, honors were to be avoided, and one saved one's life by losing it. I suspect that if Mark was asked his opinion about the lectionary using something he didn't write to commemorate him as an author and saint, he might respond, "Perfect! I wouldn't want it any other way."

ORIENTATION: *Some manuscripts of Mark's Gospel contain another addition, commonly called the Shorter Ending, which was probably written in the second century. Some copyists added the Shorter Ending after verse 8 in chapter 16; in all but one manuscript in which it appears it is followed by the Longer Ending. The Shorter Ending is not accepted as canonical Scripture by the Catholic Church but is printed in the New American Bible as an addendum.*

The Shorter Ending

[And they reported all the instructions briefly to Peter's companions. Afterwards Jesus himself, through them, sent forth from east to west the sacred and imperishable proclamation of eternal salvation. Amen.]

The Shorter Ending comes to the rescue of the women who fled from the tomb and told no one that Jesus had been raised (16:8). They report the message given them by the angel, presumably after their fear subsides, and the gospel begins to be proclaimed to the ends of the earth.

THE WRITING AND INTERPRETATION OF THE GOSPEL OF MARK

The Writing of the Gospels

Each of the four Gospels is a product of a three-stage process.[1]

The *first stage* is what Jesus did and taught while on earth.[2] He called disciples who saw his works and heard his teachings and could serve as his witnesses after his resurrection and ascension. In his teachings, "Jesus accommodated himself to the mentality of his listeners,"[3] speaking as a Palestinian Jew of the first third of the first century to other Palestinian Jews.

In the *second stage* the apostles and other witnesses handed on to their hearers what Jesus had said and done but "with that fuller understanding which they, instructed by the glorious events of Christ and enlightened by the Spirit of truth, now enjoyed."[4] The apostles in their preaching took into account the circumstances of their audiences and interpreted Jesus' words and deeds according to the needs of their listeners. They used modes of speaking that were suited to their purposes and to the mentality of their listeners.[5]

In the *third stage* the authors of the four Gospels "selected certain of the many elements which had been handed on, either orally or already in written form," and incorporated them in their Gospels, sometimes synthesizing these elements or explaining them in light of the situation of those for whom they wrote, "but always in such a fashion that they have told us the honest truth about Jesus."[6]

> From what they had received, the sacred writers above all selected the things which were suited to the various situations of the faithful and to the purposes which they had in mind, and adapted their narration of them to the same situations and purpose. Since the meaning of a statement also depends on the sequence, the evangelists, in passing on the words and deeds of our savior, explained these now in one context, now in another, depending on (their) usefulness to the readers. . . . For the truth of a story is not at all affected by the fact that the evangelists relate the words and deeds of the

461

Lord in a different order, and express his sayings not literally but differently, while preserving their sense.[7]

That the written Gospels are the result of a three-stage process has implications:

- The Gospel authors present incidents and teachings from Jesus' public ministry in an order suited to their purposes in writing, which is not necessarily the order in which they historically occurred. Accounts from the four Gospels cannot be synthesized to produce an actual time line of events from Jesus' baptism by John to the Last Supper. Each Gospel narration must be read for the meaning that events have in the order in which they are recounted.

- In expressing the teachings of Jesus, the Gospels do not necessarily transmit the exact words Jesus used. Jesus taught in Aramaic; the Gospels were written in Greek. Just as Jesus accommodated his teachings to his listeners, so those who passed on his teachings also formulated them in light of the needs of their audiences while preserving the sense of Jesus' words.

- Because the Gospel authors were writing for different audiences and had different purposes in writing, each of the four Gospels has its distinctive traits and emphases. The four Gospels cannot be combined or harmonized into a single document that preserves the unique riches of each. Rather, each Gospel must be read as an inspired presentation of the life and teachings of Jesus and relished for its particular perspective.

That the Gospels came to be written by a three-stage process does not mean that they are not reliable witnesses to Jesus. The Second Vatican Council stated that "Holy Mother Church has firmly and with absolute constancy maintained and continues to maintain, that the four Gospels, whose historicity she unhesitatingly affirms, faithfully hand on what Jesus, the Son of God, while he lived among men, really did and taught for their eternal salvation, until the day when he was taken up."[8]

The Gospel of Mark

Mark, like all the Gospel authors, did not sign his name to his Gospel. The heading, *According to Mark* was added to this Gospel sometime in the second century. A second-century tradition recounted by the fourth-century historian and bishop Eusebius in his *History of the Church* identifies Mark as Peter's interpreter:

> *Mark, who had been Peter's interpreter, wrote down carefully, but not in order, all that he remembered of the Lord's sayings and doings. For he had not heard the Lord or been one of his followers, but later, as I said, one of Peter's. Peter used to adapt his teaching to the occasion, without making a systematic arrangement of the Lord's sayings, so that Mark was quite justified in writing down some things just as he remembered them.*[9]

Mark was a common name; tradition eventually identified the Mark who was Peter's interpreter in Rome with a Mark mentioned in Acts and in some of the letters of the New Testament (Acts 12:12, 25; 15:37, 39; Col 4:10; 2 Tim 4:11; Phlm 24; 1 Peter 5:13). Many scholars question this identification, but most believe that the Gospel of Mark was written in Rome shortly before or after AD 70. The Gospel of Mark seems to address a Church undergoing persecution, and Christians in Rome experienced harsh persecution in the years following AD 64.

Interpreting the Gospel of Mark

Biblical scholars have developed various methods for analyzing the Gospels; some of these methods address the process by which the Gospels came to be written. Some methods try to reconstruct the first stage of Gospel tradition—what Jesus did and said. Other methods address how the gospel message was handed on during the second stage of tradition, examining the modes of speech or literary forms employed. Still other methods examine how a Gospel author edited the written and oral traditions he incorporated in his Gospel or analyze the narrative techniques he employed in telling the good news of Jesus Christ.

Each of these methods can contribute to our understanding of the Gospels, but each of them also has its limitations.[10] Reconstructions of what Jesus "really" did and said are speculative and inevitably shaped by the methods employed in making the reconstruction as well as by the data provided by the Gospels. While the modes of speaking that might have been used during the oral transmission of the gospel can be studied, it is each Gospel as a written document that is inspired Scripture, not reconstructed earlier versions of individual stories and teachings. If we know or can reconstruct the sources a Gospel writer used in writing his Gospel, then the way he edited his sources can be an indication of the message he wanted to convey in his Gospel. However, most scholars believe that the Gospel of Mark was the first Gospel to be written; reconstructing the sources Mark used has proven to be an impossible task. Fr. Raymond Brown wrote that readers being introduced to this Gospel "will understand Mark better by reading on a surface level."[11] Brown was not advising that the Gospel of Mark be read superficially; he was advocating paying attention to the text of Mark as we have it rather than to speculations about the sources Mark might have used.

The exposition of the Gospel according to Mark contained in this book focuses on the Gospel of Mark as it is found in the Bible—on the final product, not on the pieces that Mark might have assembled in producing the final product. The exposition tries to provide a reading of the Gospel of Mark as a coherent narrative. This means following Mark's account as he relates it and making sense of it against a first-century background, in order to understand the message conveyed by his words.

The Second Vatican Council spoke of the inspired meaning of Scripture in terms of the meaning expressed by the authors of the biblical books: "Since, therefore, all that the inspired authors, or sacred writers, affirm should be regarded as affirmed by the Holy Spirit, we must acknowledge that the books of Scripture, firmly, faithfully and without error, teach that truth which God, for the sake of our salvation, wished to see confided to the sacred Scriptures."[12] The council also spoke of "the meaning which the sacred writers really had in mind, that meaning which God had thought well to manifest through the medium of their words."[13] The council linked the meaning an inspired author "intended to express" with what he "did in fact express" by his words.[14] The focus of this exposition of the Gospel of Mark is on what Mark expressed by his words, since they convey the inspired meaning of his Gospel.

Understanding the meaning expressed by Mark's words involves an interaction between his words and a reader. (By analogy, music is not simply notes on a piece of paper but exists in performance and listening.) Meaning comes alive in an encounter between a reader and a text. Each reader brings his or her perspective, knowledge, experiences, questions, and interests to a text, and these influence what a reader takes away from a text. This does not mean that a biblical text is a blank slate on which we can write whatever meaning we like; it does mean that there is a richness of meaning in Scripture that no single reading or reader can fully capture.

All of us in reading the Gospel of Mark bring our knowledge of and experience of Jesus to the text: none of us is hearing about Jesus for the very first time. Our understanding of Jesus is shaped by many factors: by what we have read in the rest of the New Testament about Jesus, by centuries of theological reflection on Jesus, by Church pronouncements on Jesus, and by our own experiences of Jesus in private prayer, public worship, and the Christian community. Even if we wanted to, we would not be able to set all this aside in reading the Gospel of Mark. As we read Mark's words about Jesus we understand them in light of our previous understanding of Jesus, even as Mark's words enrich, challenge, and modify our understanding of Jesus. Mark's words have meaning for us as we integrate what they say to us with what we already know and believe, even if they lead us to rethink what we thought we knew and challenge us to greater faith.

My exposition of the Gospel of Mark represents my reading, my understanding of this Gospel. If my life experiences and education had been different, if I were part of a different culture or Church body, I would have been alert to facets of meaning in Mark that escape my notice. I hope that my reading of Mark will aid others in arriving at their own reading of Mark, and in encountering the Jesus he proclaims.

1. The Second Vatican Council in its decree on revelation summarizes the three stages that culminated in the written Gospels (Second Vatican Council, *Dogmatic Constitution on Divine Revelation [Dei Verbum]* [1965], 19; hereafter abbreviated as *Revelation*). The decree cites the Pontifical Biblical Commission's *Instruction on the Historical Truth of the Gospels* (Pontifical Biblical Commission, *Instruction on the Historical Truth of the Gospels* [1964]; hereafter abbreviated as *Truth*), which described "the three stages of tradition by which the teaching and the life of Jesus have come down to us" (*Truth*, 6).

2. *Revelation*, 19.

3. *Truth*, 7.

4. *Revelation*, 19

5. *Truth*, 8.

6. *Revelation*, 19.

7. *Truth*, 9.

8. *Revelation*, 19.

9. Eusebius, *The History of the Church from Christ to Constantine*, trans. G. A. Williamson (Baltimore: Penguin Books, 1965), 152.

10. See Pontifical Biblical Commission, *The Interpretation of the Bible in the Church* (Rome: Libreria Editrice Vaticana, 1993), chap. 1.

11. Raymond E. Brown, *An Introduction to the New Testament*, The Anchor Bible Reference Library (New York: Doubleday, 1997), 156.

12. *Revelation*, 11.

13. Ibid., 12.

14. Ibid.

SELECTED BIBLIOGRAPHY

Commentaries on the Gospel of Mark

Cranfield, C. E. B. *The Gospel according to Saint Mark: An Introduction and Commentary*. Cambridge: Cambridge University Press, 1977.

Donahue, John R., SJ, and Daniel J. Harrington, SJ. *The Gospel of Mark*. Sacra Pagina Series, vol. 2. Collegeville, MN: Liturgical Press, 2002.

Dowd, Sharyn E. *Reading Mark: A Literary and Theological Commentary on the Second Gospel*. Macon, GA: Smyth & Helwys, 2000.

Evans, Craig A. *Mark 8:27–16:20*. Word Biblical Commentary, vol. 34B. Nashville: Thomas Nelson Publishers, 2001.

Geddert, Timothy J. *Mark*. Scottdale, PA: Herald Press, 2001.

Guelich, Robert A. *Mark 1–8:26*. Word Biblical Commentary, vol. 34A. Dallas: Word Books, 1989.

Gundry, Robert H. *Mark: A Commentary on His Apology for the Cross*. Grand Rapids, MI: Eerdmans, 1993.

Harrington, Wilfrid J., OP. *Mark*. Wilmington, DE: Michael Glazier, 1979.

Hooker, Morna D. *The Gospel according to St. Mark*. London: A & C Black, 1991.

LaVerdiere, Eugene. *The Beginning of the Gospel: Introducing the Gospel according to Mark*. 2 vols. Collegeville, MN: Liturgical Press, 1999.

Marcus, Joel. *Mark 1–8: A New Translation with Introduction and Commentary*. The Anchor Bible, vol. 27. New York: Doubleday, 2000.

Moloney, Francis J., SDB. *The Gospel of Mark: A Commentary*. Peabody, MA: Hendrickson Publishers, 2002.

Montague, George T., SM. *Mark, Good News for Hard Times: A Popular Commentary on the Earliest Gospel*. Ann Arbor, MI: Servant Books, 1981.

Nineham, D. E. *Saint Mark*. Baltimore: Penguin Books, 1969.

Stock, Augustine, OSB. *The Method and Message of Mark*. Wilmington, DE: Michael Glazier, 1989.

Taylor, Vincent. *The Gospel according to St. Mark*. 2nd ed. Grand Rapids, MI: Baker Book House, 1966.

Witherington, Ben, III. *The Gospel of Mark: A Socio-Rhetorical Commentary*. Grand Rapids, MI: Eerdmans, 2001.

Studies and Resources

Binz, Stephen J. *The Passion and Resurrection Narratives of Jesus: A Commentary*. Collegeville, MN: Liturgical Press, 1989.

Brown, Raymond E., SS. *The Death of the Messiah: From Gethsemane to the Grave: A Commentary on the Passion Narratives in the Four Gospels*. 2 vols. The Anchor Bible Reference Library. New York: Doubleday, 1994.

———. *An Introduction to the New Testament*. The Anchor Bible Reference Library. New York: Doubleday, 1997.

———. *An Introduction to New Testament Christology*. New York: Paulist Press, 1994.

Brown, Raymond E., SS, Karl P. Donfried, Joseph A. Fitzmyer, SJ, and John Reumann, eds. *Mary in the New Testament: A Collaborative Assessment by Protestant and Roman Catholic Scholars*. New York: Paulist Press, 1978.

Brown, Raymond E., SS, Joseph A. Fitzmyer, SJ, and Roland E. Murphy, OCarm, eds. *The New Jerome Biblical Commentary*. Englewood Cliffs, NJ: Prentice-Hall, 1990.

Catechism of the Catholic Church, 2nd ed. Washington, DC: United States Catholic Conference, 1997.

Charlesworth, James H., ed. *The Old Testament Pseudepigrapha*. 2 vols. Garden City, NY: Doubleday, 1983–85.

Chilton, Bruce. *A Galilean Rabbi and His Bible: Jesus' Use of the Interpreted Scripture of His Time*. Wilmington, DE: Michael Glazier, 1984.

Collins, John J. *The Apocalyptic Imagination: An Introduction to the Jewish Matrix of Christianity*. New York: Crossroad, 1987.

Cunningham, Phillip J. *Mark: The Good News Preached to the Romans*. New York: Paulist Press, 1995.

Eusebius. *The History of the Church from Christ to Constantine*. Translated by G. A. Williamson. Baltimore: Penguin Books, 1965.

Evans, Craig A., and Stanley E. Porter, eds. *Dictionary of New Testament Background*. Downers Grove, IL: InterVarsity Press, 2000.

Fitzmyer, Joseph A., SJ. *The Biblical Commission's Document "The Interpretation of the Bible in the Church": Text and Commentary.* Rome: Pontificio Istituto Biblico, 1995.

———. *A Christological Catechism: New Testament Answers.* New York: Paulist Press, 1991.

———. *Responses to 101 Questions on the Dead Sea Scrolls.* New York: Paulist Press, 1992.

Flannery, Austin P., OP, ed. *Documents of Vatican II.* New York: Pillar Books, 1975.

Fredriksen, Paula. *Jesus of Nazareth, King of the Jews: A Jewish Life and the Emergence of Christianity.* New York: Vintage Books, 2000.

Freedman, David Noel, ed. *The Anchor Bible Dictionary.* 6 vols. New York: Doubleday, 1992.

Freyne, Séan. *Galilee, from Alexander the Great to Hadrian, 323 BCE to 135 CE: A Study of Second Temple Judaism.* Wilmington, DE: Michael Glazier, 1980.

———. *Galilee, Jesus, and the Gospels: Literary Approaches and Historical Investigations.* Philadelphia: Fortress Press, 1988.

———. *The World of the New Testament.* Wilmington, DE: Michael Glazier, 1980.

García Martínez, Florentino, ed. *The Dead Sea Scrolls Translated: The Qumran Texts in English.* Translated by Wilfred G. E. Watson. 2nd ed. Grand Rapids, MI: Eerdmans, 1996.

Green, Joel B., and Scot McKnight, eds. *Dictionary of Jesus and the Gospels.* Downers Grove, IL: InterVarsity Press, 1992.

Hendrickx, Herman. *Passion Narratives.* London: Geoffrey Chapman, 1984.

Hengel, Martin. *Crucifixion in the Ancient World and the Folly of the Message of the Cross.* Philadelphia: Fortress Press, 1977.

Horsley, Richard A. *Bandits, Prophets, and Messiahs: Popular Movements in the Time of Jesus.* With John S. Hanson. San Francisco: Harper & Row, 1988.

Hultgren, Arland J. *The Parables of Jesus: A Commentary.* Grand Rapids, MI: Eerdmans, 2000.

Kingsbury, Jack Dean. *The Christology of Mark's Gospel.* Philadelphia: Fortress Press, 1983.

Leaney, A. R. C. *The Jewish and Christian World 200 BC to AD 200.* Cambridge: Cambridge University Press, 1984.

Léon-Dufour, Xavier, SJ. *Sharing the Eucharistic Bread: The Witness of the New Testament.* Translated by Matthew J. O'Connell. New York: Paulist Press, 1987.

McNamara, Martin, MSC. *Intertestamental Literature.* Wilmington, DE: Michael Glazier, 1983.

———. *Palestinian Judaism and the New Testament.* Wilmington, DE: Michael Glazier, 1983.

Meier, John P. *A Marginal Jew: Rethinking the Historical Jesus.* 3 vols. New York: Doubleday, 1991–2001.

Meyers, Eric M., and James F. Strange. *Archaeology, the Rabbis, and Early Christianity.* Nashville: Abingdon, 1981.

Murphy-O'Connor, Jerome, OP. *The Holy Land: From Earliest Times to 1700.* 4th ed. Oxford Archaeological Guides. Oxford: Oxford University Press, 1998.

O'Grady, John F. *Mark, The Sorrowful Gospel: An Introduction to the Second Gospel.* New York: Paulist Press, 1981.

Pontifical Biblical Commission. *Instruction on the Historical Truth of the Gospels.* 1964. Translation and commentary in Fitzmyer, *A Christological Catechism.*

Pontifical Biblical Commission. *The Interpretation of the Bible in the Church.* Rome: Libreria Editrice Vaticana, 1993.

Reed, Jonathan L. *Archaeology and the Galilean Jesus: A Reexamination of the Evidence.* Harrisburg, PA: Trinity Press, 2000.

Rossé, Gérard. *The Cry of Jesus on the Cross: A Biblical and Theological Study.* Translated by Stephen Wentworth Arndt. New York: Paulist Press, 1987.

Rousseau, John J., and Rami Arav. *Jesus and His World: An Archaeological and Cultural Dictionary.* Minneapolis: Fortress Press, 1995.

Russell, D. S. *The Method and Message of Jewish Apocalyptic, 200 BC–AD 100.* Philadelphia: Westminster Press, 1964.

Saldarini, Anthony J. *Pharisees, Scribes and Sadducees in Palestinian Society: A Sociological Approach.* Wilmington, DE: Michael Glazier, 1988.

Sanders, E. P. *Jesus and Judaism.* Philadelphia: Fortress Press, 1985.

Schneiders, Sandra M. *The Revelatory Text: Interpreting the New Testament as Sacred Scripture.* 2nd ed. Collegeville, MN: Liturgical Press, 1999.

Senior, Donald, CP. *The Passion of Jesus in the Gospel of Mark.* Wilmington, DE: Michael Glazier, 1984.

Stanley, David M., SJ. *Jesus in Gethsemane.* New York: Paulist Press, 1980.

Tanner, Norman P., SJ, ed. *Decrees of the Ecumenical Councils.* 2 vols. Washington, DC: Georgetown University Press, 1990.

Thompson, Mary R., SSMN. *The Role of Disbelief in Mark: A New Approach to the Second Gospel.* New York: Paulist Press, 1989.

VanderKam, James C. *The Dead Sea Scrolls Today.* Grand Rapids, MI: Eerdmans, 1994.

Williamson, Peter S. *Catholic Principles for Interpreting Scripture: A Study of the Pontifical Biblical Commission's "The Interpretation of the Bible in the Church."* Rome: Pontificio Istituto Biblico, 2001.

INDEX OF BACKGROUND MATERIAL
AND COMMENTS

Note: Italics indicate comments

Palestine

at the time of Jesus

© 2005 Loyola Press

Jerusalem

at the time of Jesus

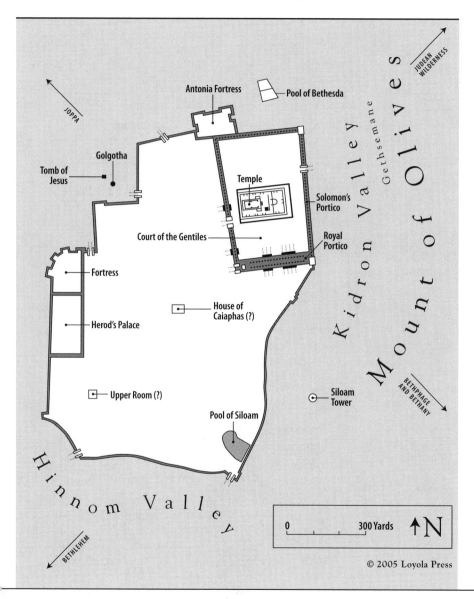

Antonia Fortress

Pool of Bethesda

JOPPA

JUDEAN WILDERNESS

Golgotha

Tomb of Jesus

Temple

Solomon's Portico

Court of the Gentiles

Royal Portico

Gethsemane

Kidron Valley

Mount of Olives

Fortress

House of Caiaphas (?)

Herod's Palace

Upper Room (?)

Siloam Tower

Pool of Siloam

BETHPHAGE AND BETHANY

Hinnom Valley

BETHLEHEM

0   300 Yards   ↑N

© 2005 Loyola Press